CORPORATE GOVERNANCE, COMPETITION, AND POLITICAL PARTIES

Corporate Governance, Competition, and Political Parties

Explaining Corporate Governance Change in Europe

ROGER M. BARKER

UNIVERSITY PRESS

OXFORD
UNIVERSITY PRESS

Great Clarendon Street, Oxford OX2 6DP

Oxford University Press is a department of the University of Oxford.
It furthers the University's objective of excellence in research, scholarship,
and education by publishing worldwide in

Oxford New York

Auckland Cape Town Dar es Salaam Hong Kong Karachi
Kuala Lumpur Madrid Melbourne Mexico City Nairobi
New Delhi Shanghai Taipei Toronto

With offices in

Argentina Austria Brazil Chile Czech Republic France Greece
Guatemala Hungary Italy Japan South Korea Poland Portugal
Singapore Switzerland Thailand Turkey Ukraine Vietnam

Oxford is a registered trade mark of Oxford University Press
in the UK and in certain other countries

Published in the United States
by Oxford University Press Inc., New York

© Roger M. Barker 2010

The moral rights of the author have been asserted

Database right Oxford University Press (maker)

Reprinted 2011

All rights reserved. No part of this publication may be reproduced,
stored in a retrieval system, or transmitted, in any form or by any means,
without the prior permission in writing of Oxford University Press,
or as expressly permitted by law, or under terms agreed with the appropriate
reprographics rights organization. Enquiries concerning reproduction
outside the scope of the above should be sent to the Rights Department,
Oxford University Press, at the address above

You must not circulate this book in any other binding or cover
And you must impose this same condition on any acquirer

ISBN 978-0-19-957681-4

Printed in the United Kingdom by
Lightning Source UK Ltd., Milton Keynes

Contents

Preface vii
List of Figures x
List of Tables xv
List of Abbreviations xix

1. Introduction: Political Partisanship and the
   Puzzle of Corporate Governance Change in Europe 1
   1.1 Why corporate governance matters? 2
   1.2 Recent developments in European corporate governance 5
   1.3 Corporate governance and partisanship 19
   1.4 Plan of the book 26
   1.5 Chapter Appendix 26
2. A Theory of Partisanship and Corporate Governance Change 33
   2.1 Change in corporate governance outcomes – between blockholder and shareholder models 34
   2.2 The nature of economic rents 42
   2.3 Corporate governance and economic rents 45
   2.4 The argument: interaction of partisanship and product market competition 51
3. Alternative Explanations of Corporate Governance: A Critique of the Literature 67
   3.1 Economic approaches to corporate governance 67
   3.2 Legal approaches to corporate governance 72
   3.3 Political approaches to corporate governance 77
   3.4 Sociological approaches to corporate governance 84
   3.5 Corporate governance and nondomestic factors 87
4. Measuring Change in Corporate Governance 91
   4.1 Measures of *de facto* corporate governance behavior 92
   4.2 Measures of corporate governance regulation 105
5. The Measurement of Product Market Competition 116
   5.1 Real price levels 117
   5.2 Concentration indices 121
   5.3 Profit margins 123
   5.4 Openness to trade 126
   5.5 Survey measures of competition 130
   5.6 OECD indices of product market competition 131

6.	A Panel Data Analysis of Corporate Governance Change	137
	6.1 The variables	138
	6.2 Methodology	148
	6.3 Findings	154
7.	Robustness and Dynamic Modeling	190
	7.1 Tests of robustness	190
	7.2 Dynamic modeling of corporate governance	206
8.	Qualitative Analysis: Introduction to the Case Studies	214
	8.1 Rationale for the case studies	214
	8.2 Choice of country cases	216
9.	The Case of Germany: From Blockholding to Hybrid Corporate Governance Regime	223
	9.1 The corporate governance of Deutschland AG	224
	9.2 Economic rents and German corporate strategy	229
	9.3 The politics of corporate governance in Germany	239
	9.4 Explaining corporate governance change in Germany	252
10.	The Case of Italy: Everything Changes, Everything Stays the Same	256
	10.1 The nature of postwar corporate governance in Italy	258
	10.2 Reform of Italian corporate governance?	262
	10.3 EMU and the empowerment of the technocrats	269
	10.4 Corporate governance reform: partisan politics or elite project?	273
	10.5 Conclusion: economic rents and Italian corporate governance	280
11.	Conclusions	283
Bibliography		292
Index		325

Preface

During much of the postwar period, the corporate governance systems of continental Europe have remained distinct from those of the liberal market economies. European company ownership has been dominated by incumbent blockholders, with a relatively minor role for minority shareholders and institutional investors. Business strategy has focused on the achievement of social stability – taking into account the interests of a broad group of stakeholders – rather than the maximization of shareholder value.

However, since the mid–1990s, European corporations have adopted many of the characteristics of the Anglo-American shareholder model. Furthermore, such an increased shareholder orientation has coincided with a significant role for the Left in European government. This is a surprising turn of events, as conventional wisdom does not conceive of the European Left as a natural ally of pro-shareholder capitalism. This book provides an analysis of this paradox by examining how economic factors have interacted with the policy preferences of political parties to cause a significant change in the European system of corporate governance.

The book's key hypothesis is that European corporate governance has shifted in a pro-shareholder direction as a result of a distinctive interaction between political partisanship and product market competition. The postwar blockholder-dominated corporate systems in Europe depended on the willingness of blockholders to share economic rents with employees, both through higher wages and greater employment stability. However, during the 1990s, product markets became more competitive in many European countries. As a result, the sharing of economic rents between social actors became increasingly difficult to sustain. In such an environment, the Left in government chose to relinquish its traditional social partnership with blockholders and embraced many aspects of the shareholder model.

Corporate governance is an inherently interdisciplinary subject area. Although originally the province of economists and legal scholars, it is now an important field of discourse for political scientists and economic sociologists. Consequently, although this work's direct contribution is to comparative political economy, it is likely to be of equal interest to readers in other areas of social science, including researchers in law and business schools.

Most chapters of the book are accessible to scholars (and advanced undergraduates) with a general interest in corporate governance. The only exceptions are Chapters 6 and 7, which present a panel data econometric analysis of corporate governance change (along with associated robustness testing and dynamic modeling). Both of these chapters require a relatively advanced knowledge of statistical techniques. Nonetheless, nonspecialists will still be able to draw the necessary conclusions from these chapters without needing to immerse themselves in the technical detail.

Chapters 4 and 5 are concerned with the measurement of two key variables: corporate governance and product market competition. As well as representing a necessary prelude to the subsequent statistical analysis, these chapters provide a guide – currently unavailable in the literature – to the operationalization of two important economic concepts. This will be of interest to researchers seeking to utilize such variables in other empirical contexts.

In writing this book, I have incurred a massive debt of gratitude to my former doctoral supervisor at Oxford University, Professor David Rueda. At every stage of this book's development, David has been an unfailing source of wisdom, insight, and intellectual rigor. Thank you for everything, David.

A special thanks is due to Desmond King (Nuffield College, Oxford), Philip Manow (Universität Konstanz), Richard Deeg (Temple University), and Pepper Culpepper (Harvard University). Each provided valuable input at various stages of the book's evolution. Mark Roe (Harvard Law School) supplied detailed comments on a related paper, many of which were also relevant for this book. I also wish to acknowledge the advice of Katrin Auel (Mansfield College, Oxford) in respect of the German case study chapter.

A number of other people have offered helpful feedback at various stages of the project. At Oxford, the Political Economy Colloquium and the Comparative Political Economy Seminar provided useful forums in which to present and debate new ideas. The inputs of Lucie Cerna, Marco Hernandez, Tim Hicks, Timo Idema, Johannes Lindvall, Zim Nwokora, and Paul Scalise at these meetings were particularly appreciated.

At the conference, *Changing Institutions in Developed Democracies: Economics, Politics and Welfare* (Paris, May 2007), I benefited from the insights of leading scholars from various disciplines, including Jean-Bernard Chatelain (Paris), Simon Deakin (Cambridge), Robert Franzese (Michigan), Peter Hall (Harvard), Torben Iversen (Harvard), Thomas Plümper (Essex), and David Soskice (Oxford).

I am obliged to Ronald Rogowski (University of California at Los Angeles) for his perceptive review of my paper at the conference of the Midwest Political Science Association (Chicago, April 2007). Peter Gourevitch (University of California at San Diego) and John Cioffi (University of California at Riverside) offered excellent advice at the biannual conference of the Council for European Studies (Chicago, March 2006). Simon Deakin and Mathias Siems generously shared data compiled at the Centre for Business Research at the University of Cambridge. At Oxford, Ngaire Woods (University College) supplied valuable early feedback. I am also grateful for input provided by David Hine (Christ Church).

Finally, I would like to thank David Musson and Matthew Derbyshire at Oxford University Press.

Needless to say, none of the above bears any responsibility for the final result, which is the sole responsibility of the author.

List of Figures

Figure 1.1	The relationship between government ideology and ownership concentration	23
Figure 1.2	Participation of Left and conservative parties in European government, 1975–2003 (mean percentage of cabinet posts)	24
Figure 2.1	Consumer and producer surplus in competitive market conditions	43
Figure 2.2	Producer and consumer surplus and deadweight loss in uncompetitive market conditions	44
Figure 2.3	Ownership concentration (early to mid–1990s) and product market competition (1998)	47
Figure 2.4	Product market competition and employment protection index (1998)	48
Figure 2.5	Economic openness versus product market competition	62
Figure 4.1	Equity share, 1975–2003: Austria, Belgium, France, and Switzerland	96
Figure 4.2	Value traded, 1975–2003: Italy, Sweden, the Netherlands, and Denmark	101
Figure 4.3	International equity issuance, 1983–2003: Germany, Norway, Spain, and Greece	103
Figure 4.4	Aggregate shareholder protection index	113
Figure 5.1	Markups in manufacturing and nonmanufacturing (average values, 1975–2002)	124
Figure 5.2	The OECD PMR index in 1998 and 2003	133
Figure 6.1	Conditional effects of Left government on corporate governance. Dependent variable: equity share. No fixed effects. Legal origin controls	171
Figure 6.2	Conditional effects of Left government on corporate governance. Dependent variable: equity share. Country and decade fixed effects	171
Figure 6.3	Conditional effects of Left government on corporate governance. Dependent variable: value traded. No fixed effects. Legal origin controls	172

List of Figures

Figure 6.4	Conditional effects of Left government on corporate governance. Dependent variable: value traded. Country and decade fixed effects	172
Figure 6.5	Conditional effects of Left government on corporate governance. Dependent variable: international equity issuance. No fixed effects. Legal origin controls	173
Figure 6.6	Conditional effects of Left government on corporate governance. Dependent variable: international equity issuance. Country and decade fixed effects	173
Figure 6.7	Conditional effects of conservative government on corporate governance. Dependent variable: equity share. No fixed effects. Legal origin controls	174
Figure 6.8	Conditional effects of conservative government on corporate governance. Dependent variable: equity share. Country and decade fixed effects	174
Figure 6.9	Conditional effects of conservative government on corporate governance. Dependent variable: value traded. No fixed effects. Legal origin controls	175
Figure 6.10	Conditional effects of conservative government on corporate governance. Dependent variable: Value traded. Country and decade fixed effects	175
Figure 6.11	Conditional effects of conservative government on corporate governance. Dependent variable: international equity issuance. No fixed effects. Legal origin controls	176
Figure 6.12	Conditional effects of conservative government on corporate governance. Dependent variable: international equity issuance. Country and decade fixed effects	176
Figure 6.13	Conditional effects of lagged Left government on corporate governance. Dependent variable: equity share. Country and decade fixed effects	179
Figure 6.14	Conditional effects of lagged Left government on corporate governance. Dependent variable: value traded. Country and decade fixed effects	180
Figure 6.15	Conditional effects of lagged Left government on corporate governance. Dependent variable: international equity issuance. Country and decade fixed effects	181

List of Figures

Figure 6.16	Conditional effects of lagged conservative government on corporate governance. Dependent variable: equity share. Country and decade fixed effects	182
Figure 6.17	Conditional effects of lagged conservative government on corporate governance. Dependent variable: value traded. Country and decade fixed effects	183
Figure 6.18	Conditional effects of lagged conservative government on corporate governance. Dependent variable: international equity issuance. Country and decade fixed effects	184
Figure 6.19	Product market competition experiences in three European countries (6 = least competitive, 0 = most competitive)	187
Figure 6.20	Equity share for a range of European countries (mean value 1975–2003)	188
Figure 6.21	Value traded for a range of European countries (mean value 1975–2003)	188
Figure 6.22	International equity issuance for a range of European countries (mean value 1983–2003)	189
Figure 7.1	Extreme bounds of Left government coefficient. Dependent variable: equity share. Country and decade fixed effects	192
Figure 7.2	Extreme bounds of Left government coefficient. Dependent variable: value traded. Country and decade fixed effects	193
Figure 7.3	Extreme bounds of Left government coefficient. Dependent variable: international equity issuance. Country and decade fixed effects	193
Figure 7.4	Extreme bounds of conservative government coefficient. Dependent variable: equity share. Country and decade fixed effects	194
Figure 7.5	Extreme bounds of conservative government coefficient. Dependent variable: value traded. Country and decade fixed effects	194
Figure 7.6	Extreme bounds of conservative government coefficient. Dependent variable: international equity issuance. Country and decade fixed effects	195

List of Figures

Figure 7.7	Jackknife analysis of Left government coefficient. Dependent variable: equity share. Country and decade fixed effects	197
Figure 7.8	Jackknife analysis of Left government coefficient. Dependent variable: value traded. Country and decade fixed effects	197
Figure 7.9	Jackknife analysis of Left government coefficient. Dependent variable: international equity issuance. Country and decade fixed effects	198
Figure 7.10	Jackknife analysis of conservative government coefficient. Dependent variable: equity share. Country and decade fixed effects	198
Figure 7.11	Jackknife analysis of conservative government coefficient. Dependent variable: value traded. Country and decade fixed effects	199
Figure 7.12	Jackknife analysis of conservative government coefficient. Dependent variable: international equity issuance. Country and decade fixed effects	199
Figure 7.13	Dynamic impact of Left government on corporate governance (first differences). Dependent variable: equity share	209
Figure 7.14	Dynamic impact of Left government on corporate governance (first differences). Dependent variable: value traded	210
Figure 7.15	Dynamic impact of Left government on corporate governance (first differences). Dependent variable: international equity issuance	210
Figure 7.16	Dynamic impact of conservative government on corporate governance (first differences). Dependent variable: equity share	211
Figure 7.17	Dynamic impact of conservative government on corporate governance (first differences). Dependent variable: value traded	211
Figure 7.18	Dynamic impact of conservative government on corporate governance (first differences). Dependent variable: international equity issuance	212

List of Figures

Figure 8.1 Conditional effects of Left government on corporate governance. Dependent variable: value traded. Country and decade fixed effects — 219

Figure 8.2 PMR index of "whole economy" product market competition, 1998 — 222

List of Tables

Table 1.1	Percentage of shares in selected French companies represented by cross-shareholdings	11
Table 1.2	Corporate governance ratings (median values) of large European companies (by country) – 2004 versus 2000	13
Table 1.3	Shareholder orientation of firm-level corporate governance, 2005 (aggregate country scores)	17
Table 1.4	Country scores in relation to specific corporate governance attributes (in %), 2005	18
Table 1.5	Median compensation of the CEO of a medium-sized company, 1996	21
Table 1.6	Summary of regulatory reforms favoring minority shareholders in France, Germany, and Italy (since 1990)	27
Table 1.7	Partisan composition of governments in continental Europe, 1990–2005	31
Table 2.1	Shareholder and blockholder models of corporate governance	35
Table 2.2	Employment stability in liberal and nonliberal market economies (1990)	49
Table 2.3	OECD employment protection index, change over time	56
Table 2.4	IMF econometric analysis of determinants of product market liberalization	60
Table 2.5	Summary of theoretical claims	65
Table 3.1	Assets and equity investment of private pension funds, and public pension expenditure	80
Table 3.2	Main EU directives and regulations concerning company law and corporate governance since 1990	89
Table 4.1	Ownership concentration (%), early 1990s	93
Table 4.2	European private equity investment as a percentage of GDP, 2005	98

xvi   List of Tables

Table 4.3	Descriptive statistics for equity share (equity market capitalization of listed companies divided by GDP), 1975–2003	99
Table 4.4	Descriptive statistics for value traded (value of listed companies traded, divided by GDP), 1975–2003	102
Table 4.5	Descriptive statistics for International equity issuance, 1983–2003 (value of equity issuance to international investors as percentage of GDP)	104
Table 4.6	Correlation matrix of chosen corporate governance proxies (and ownership concentration)	105
Table 4.7	Antidirector rights index – original assessment of legal protections of minority shareholder protections relating to the early 1990s by LLSV	109
Table 4.8	Antidirector rights index – revised assessment of shareholder protections (as of 2003)	111
Table 5.1	Real prices levels, private consumption (United States = 100)	119
Table 5.2	Indirect taxation, average 2000–5 (as % GDP)	120
Table 5.3	HHIs of industry concentration in miscellaneous industries, late 1990s	122
Table 5.4	Hiscox and Kastner's measure of trade policy orientation versus import penetration	127
Table 5.5	Intensity of local competition 2006, GCR survey results (scale from 1 [least] to 7 [most])	130
Table 5.6	Subindices of the OECD product market regulation indicator (the PMR index)	132
Table 5.7	The NMR index of product market competition, 1975–2003 (6 = least competitive, 0 = most competitive)	135
Table 5.8	Descriptive statistics for the OECD's NMR index of product market competition, 1975–2003 (6 = least competitive, 0 = most competitive)	135
Table 6.1	Data sources and coverage of proxies used for the dependent variable (corporate governance)	139
Table 6.2	Descriptive statistics of proxies used for the dependent variable (corporate governance)	139
Table 6.3	Description of explanatory and control variables	140

List of Tables xvii

Table 6.4	Descriptive statistics for explanatory and control variables	142
Table 6.5	Left-conservative positioning of governing political parties in fifteen nonliberal market economies	145
Table 6.6	Levin-Lin-Chu panel unit root test	150
Table 6.7	Im-Pesaran-Shin panel unit root test	150
Table 6.8	Direct relationship between Left government and corporate governance	156
Table 6.9	Direct relationship between conservative government and corporate governance	158
Table 6.10	Direct relationship between lag of Left government and corporate governance	161
Table 6.11	Direct relationship between lag of conservative government and corporate governance	163
Table 6.12	Relationship of interaction of Left government/product market competition, and corporate governance	167
Table 6.13	Relationship of interaction of conservative government/product market competition, and corporate governance	169
Table 6.14	Substantive implications of Left government on corporate governance. Impact on the sample mean of equity share (sample mean = 0.39)	184
Table 6.15	Substantive implications of conservative government on corporate governance. Impact on the sample mean of equity share (sample mean = 0.39)	185
Table 6.16	Substantive implications of Left government on corporate governance. Impact on the sample mean of value traded (sample mean: 0.25)	185
Table 6.17	Substantive implications of conservative government on corporate governance. Impact on the sample mean of value traded (sample mean: 0.25)	185
Table 6.18	Substantive implications of Left government on corporate governance. Impact on the sample mean of international equity issuance (mean value: 0.50)	186

List of Tables

Table 6.19	Substantive implications of conservative government on corporate governance. Impact on the sample mean of international equity issuance (mean value: 0.50)	186
Table 7.1	Control variables with greatest impact on estimated coefficients	196
Table 7.2	Countries with greatest impact on estimated coefficients	201
Table 7.3	Most influential observations (top 1%). Dependent variable: equity share	202
Table 7.4	Most influential observations (top 1%). Dependent variable: value traded	203
Table 7.5	Most influential observations (top 1%). Dependent variable: international equity issuance	204
Table 8.1	Levels of product market competition (NMR index, 0 = highest, 6 = lowest)	218
Table 8.2	The Left in European government: before and after achievement of "threshold" product market competition	220
Table 9.1	Number of mergers and acquisitions in Germany	231
Table 9.2	Rates of employment reduction for selected countries, 1999–2001	232
Table 9.3	Flows into financial assets by German households	234
Table 9.4	Development of balance sheets of German universal banks, 1990–2001	237
Table 10.1	Average ownership concentration of thirty largest Italian companies, 1996–2005	265
Table 10.2	Political parties supporting the Olive Tree coalition government of 1996	277

List of Abbreviations

BIS	Bank for International Settlements
CDU	Christian Democratic Union
CME	Coordinated Market Economy
CSU	Christian Social Union
EMU	Economic and Monetary Union
EU	European Union
FDP	Free Democratic Party
GBA	German Banking Association
GCR	Global Competitiveness Report
GDP	Gross Domestic Product
GMM	Generalized Method of Moments
HHI	Hirschman – Herfindahl Index
IAS	International Accounting Standards
IFRS	International Financial Reporting Standards
ISS	Institutional Shareholder Services
IV	Instrumental Variable
KonTraG	Control and Transparency Law
LAD	Least Absolute Deviations
LDV	Lagged Dependent Variable
LLSV	La Porta, Lopez-de-Silanes, Shleifer and Vishny
LME	Liberal Market Economy
MA	Moving Average
ND	New Democracy
NMR	Non-Manufacturing Regulation
OECD	Organisation for Economic Co-operation and Development
OLS	Ordinary Least Squares
PCSE	Panel-Corrected Standard Error
PDS	Party of Democratic Socialism
PMR	Product Market Regulation

PPP	Purchasing Power Parity
PR	Proportional Representation
SEC	Securities and Exchange Commission
SME	Small-and-Medium-Sized Enterprise
SWF	Sovereign Wealth Fund

1

Introduction: Political Partisanship and the Puzzle of Corporate Governance Change in Europe

> Much of the institutional scenery of two decades ago – distinct national business elites, stable managerial control over companies and long-term relationships with financial institutions – is disappearing into economic history. We have, instead the triumph of the global over the local, of the speculator over the manager and of the financier over the producer. We are witnessing the transformation of mid-20th century managerial capitalism into global financial capitalism.
>
> Martin Wolf, *Financial Times*, June 19, 2007.

Since the early 1990s, evidence has been accumulating of significant change in the regulation and practice of corporate governance in the nonliberal economies of continental Europe. Corporate enterprises in these countries have increasingly eschewed their traditional stakeholder-orientation in favor of a strategy centered on the maximization of "shareholder value." This has occurred during a period in which social democratic or labor-oriented political parties have played a significant role in European government. Such a concurrence of events is puzzling, as the pro-shareholder stance of business would appear to be alien to many of the traditional goals of the Left, such as high wage levels, employment security, and income equality. What is even more surprising is that Left government has not only acquiesced in these changes, but – in many cases – actively encouraged them (Höpner 2003; Cioffi and Höpner 2006).

The purpose of this book is to present a hypothesis of corporate governance change in nonliberal market economies that explains this paradoxical outcome. In the coming chapters, I will argue that the prevalence or absence of economic rents in such economies plays a key role in the politicization of corporate governance. When economic rents are abundant (due to a lack of competition in product markets), the main political parties on both the

Left and Right of the political spectrum – along with their respective core constituents – perceive little benefit in pushing for a transition to a shareholder-oriented corporate governance regime. In such circumstances, the political complexion of government does not matter for corporate governance. However, if these rents diminish (due to greater competition), corporate governance becomes a more polarized area of policy. The Left increasingly favors a shift to a shareholder orientation, while conservative political parties retain a preference for the status quo. Consequently, a shift toward more shareholder-orientated corporate governance in nonliberal market economies will be associated with the interaction of Left government partisanship and product market competition.

A detailed exposition of these theoretical claims is reserved for Chapter 2. In the first half of this chapter, a range of evidence on recent corporate governance developments in continental Europe is presented in order to substantiate the assertion that European economies have experienced significant pro-shareholder change during the last ten to fifteen years. This is followed by a discussion of the likely relationship between partisanship and corporate governance. An assessment is made of the extent to which the actual experience of European corporate governance change since the early 1990s has been consistent with such expectations. However, before proceeding further, it is worthwhile considering why corporate governance is such an integral component of the institutional framework of a modern political economy. In other words, why does corporate governance matter?

1.1 WHY CORPORATE GOVERNANCE MATTERS?

The corporation is one of the most successful socioeconomic institutions of modern society.[1] Since the end of the nineteenth century, it has firmly established itself as the preeminent economic unit of capitalism, having overcome inauspicious beginnings in the seventeenth and eighteenth centuries.[2] Along with markets, firms serve to mobilize and coordinate the

---

[1] In the opinion of Bakan (2004) and Micklethwait and Wooldridge (2003), the firm is the most successful of all modern institutions, having outpaced rivals such as the political party, the commune, the parish church, the feudal manor, the monarchy, and even the state (Micklethwait and Wooldridge 2003: 2).

[2] The first joint stock company – The United East India Company – was chartered by the Dutch Republic in 1602 (Frentrop 2002). However, joint stock companies were banned in Britain in 1720, following the collapse of the South Sea Company. In the same year, the collapse of John Law's Mississippi Company almost destroyed the French economy. Limited liability

use of capital in the generation of economic growth (Roberts 2004: 74). However, unlike markets, firms organize production in terms of hierarchical authority relations between economic agents (Coase 1937). Their pervasiveness in modern economic life is arguably even greater than that of markets. According to McMillan (2002: 168), 70 percent of transactions in the US economy occur within firms, as compared to only 30 percent in markets.

Although the key features of the corporate institutional form – such as separate legal personality, limited liability, shared ownership by investors, a board structure, and transferable shares – are salient in firms around the world, the authority and power structure (i.e., the governance) of a firm can be organized in a variety of ways. The wide range of possibilities is reflected in the postwar diversity of national corporate governance practices, which appear to have defied the harmonizing impulses of economic globalization (Nenova 2003; Dyck and Zingales 2004b; Stulz 2005). Recent empirical research suggests that the choice among governance alternatives is important for a number of reasons. First, corporate governance affects the organizational structure of firms, which in turn differentiates their response to common external challenges (Knetter 1989; Hall and Soskice 2001; Roe 2003; Morck and Steier 2005). This leads corporate governance to play a key role in the prevailing style of capitalism (Aoki 1988; Hollingsworth and Boyer 1997; Hall and Soskice 2001). Second, corporate governance has been implicated as a key factor in the determination of a number of economic and political outcomes, including levels of economic growth and efficiency (Carlin and Mayer 2003; Mueller 2005); innovation capability (Allen and Gale 2000; Huang and Xu 1999); levels of competition (Fulghieri and Suominen 2005); financial openness (Stulz 2005); relative prevalence of public and private companies; levels of control premia (Dyck and Zingales 2004a); and the emergence of social democracy (Belloc and Pagano 2005).

A particularly distinctive approach to corporate governance has underpinned the nonliberal economic models of continental Europe.[3] Unlike firms operating according to the Anglo-American business model, European corporations have existed within a framework of incentives that have shielded them from engagement in short-term earnings and share-price maximization. This has facilitated their cooperation with other social actors in fulfillment of

---

companies only became legalized in Britain in 1856, and were introduced in the United States and elsewhere at the end of the nineteenth century (Bakan 2004: 6).

[3] The term "nonliberal market economy" is used here rather than Hall and Soskice's "coordinated market economy" terminology, in order to encompass a number of "Mediterranean" capitalist economies – such as France, Italy, Spain, Portugal, and Greece – whose relatively liberal arrangements in labor markets do not qualify them as coordinated market economies (Rhodes 1997; Hall and Soskice 2001: 19; Streeck and Yamamura 2003: 3).

the postwar "corporatist compromise" (Goldthorpe 1984). More stable corporate behavior has also given rise to an environment in which economic actors are more willing to engage in long-term commitments and nonmarket forms of cooperation (e.g., training, R&D, industrial relations, etc.). This proved to be a particularly efficient form of economic organization in the early postwar era of "diversified quality production" (Porter 1992; Streeck 1992; Hall and Soskice 2001).

There is, however, evidence of significant change underway in European corporate governance, particularly since the mid-1990s. The postwar framework gave a privileged position to controlling shareholders (or blockholders), who were willing to restrain their profit-maximizing impulses in order to be viewed as reliable social partners by other social actors, for example, employees and social democratic parties.[4] However, a key development over the last decade has been a rebalancing of corporate governance in favor of minority shareholders. This has significant implications for the operation of the corporate sector, as minority shareholders are more likely than blockholders to impose a strategy of shareholder value maximization on company management.

According to Frank Dobbin and Dirk Zorn, a shareholder value system gives rise to a distinctive pattern of corporate behavior. First, corporate management focuses attention on maximizing the firm's stock price. Other possible objectives, such as the pursuit of growth, sales, employment stability, or broader social goals, are subservient to this goal. Second, firms are incentivized through the stock price to focus on activities that reflect their "core competencies." The adoption of diversified conglomerate structures is viewed as inefficient and inappropriate; risk diversification is the job of company owners within their investment portfolios, not corporate managers. Third, a high stock price is sustained by fulfilling the short-term corporate earnings expectations of capital market participants, particularly securities analysts and institutional fund managers. A key task for corporate managers, therefore, is to generate earnings growth that "make the quarter" (Dobbin and Zorn 2005: 195).

Adoption of this kind of business model has significant implications for the nature of European capitalism, and ultimately represents a shift in the direction of the Anglo-American business model, which has based its activities on a shareholder value philosophy since the early 1980s (Fligstein 2005: 225).[5]

---

[4] Such actors are described by Hall and Soskice (2001) as "patient capital."

[5] Although the corporate governance scandals of recent years in the United States (Enron, Worldcom, Tyco International, Hollinger International, etc.), and the rise of shareholder activism, suggest that – even in liberal market economies – the ideal of a shareholder-aligned public corporation is often only imperfectly realized (Fligstein 2005: 226).

The next section considers evidence that suggests the balance of power in continental European corporate governance is indeed shifting toward minority shareholders, along with their favored strategy of shareholder value maximization.

1.2 RECENT DEVELOPMENTS IN EUROPEAN CORPORATE GOVERNANCE

The rebalancing of European corporate governance in favor of minority shareholders – the class of shareholder holding relatively small, noncontrolling ownership stakes (i.e., typically less than 3%) in individual companies – is evident from a variety of perspectives. First, the regulatory landscape has shifted in their favor, as national governments have attempted to redefine the "rules of the game" in which firms operate. The European Union (EU) and other international organizations have also sought to influence corporate behavior, both through European legislation and the promotion of "best practice" codes of conduct. Second, and most importantly, the actual behavior of European companies has exhibited a growing tendency to emphasize the interests of minority shareholders vis-à-vis other corporate stakeholders. Sections 1.2.1 and 1.2.2 present evidence of change from both of these perspectives in turn.

1.2.1 Changes in the regulatory environment

Regulatory reform in Europe has sought to improve the position of minority shareholders in a variety of ways (Enriques and Volpin 2007: 125). First, internal governance mechanisms, such as boards and audit committees, have been strengthened in many countries. A function of the board of a company in a pro-shareholder system is to counter the influence of company insiders – such as management or blockholders – on behalf of company stakeholders as a whole. However, in Europe, boards have traditionally done little to favor minority shareholders, although codetermination (i.e., the participation of employee representatives on company boards) has played a role in safeguarding the interests of employees (most notably in Germany). Recent reforms in Europe have sought to empower the ability of boards to monitor and oversee business processes that are of concern to minority shareholders, such as auditing, the setting of executive compensation, approval of related-party transactions (i.e., company transactions giving rise to a conflict of interest), and disclosure of company information to outsiders.

Second, the legal rights of minority shareholders across Europe have been upgraded. It is now more feasible for shareholders to sue company management when their interests have been ignored or overridden. Furthermore, they have acquired more power to determine the outcome of deliberations at company general meetings. Measures have been taken to reduce the cost of voting at these meetings – which are often impracticable for minority shareholders to attend in person – and to mandate improved representation of minority shareholders on company boards. Progress has been made, albeit unevenly, toward the objective of a "one-share, one-vote" ownership structure through the abolition of multiple voting rights on particular classes of share. Such shares have traditionally been used by blockholders to exert disproportionate influence over the operation of the firm.

Third, traditionally opaque European companies have been mandated to improve financial disclosure to outsiders. International accounting standards were adopted in all EU member states in 2006, and legislation has been introduced in many countries regarding the public disclosure of executive compensation, related-party transactions, and price-sensitive information (which could potentially be used for insider trading). Measures have been taken by governments to improve the enforcement of corporate governance regulation, and increase the sanctions for corporate malfeasance (see Table 1.6).

In the specific case of France, the interests of the state have traditionally overshadowed the interests of other stakeholders, such as minority shareholders (Enriques 2004). Until the early 1980s, state involvement in the corporate sector was reflected in state blockholdings, state involvement in the allocation of credit, and a high level of interlinkage between French corporate and governmental elites (Schmidt 1996). At that time, the state was the sole owner of thirteen of the twenty largest industrial firms and all of the leading banks, and had ownership stakes of various sizes in many other enterprises (Zysman 1983; O'Sullivan 2001).

However, the state withdrew from the allocation and rationing of credit in the mid-1980s, and commenced a substantial program of privatization (Loriaux 1997). The first major steps to improve the situation of minority shareholders occurred in the late 1980s/early 1990s through attempts to promote the development of capital markets. New rules on disclosure, insider trading, and market manipulation were introduced, and a mandatory bid rule was instituted (to ensure equal treatment of minority shareholders during takeover transactions).

The most significant reforms have occurred since 1995. The New Economic Regulations of 2001 improved disclosure of company finances and executive compensation, and facilitated the ability of shareholders to sue company management. In 2002, the rights of shareholders were improved in terms of facilitating their ability to call shareholder meetings and appoint experts to review management decisions. Since 2003, public companies have been required to publish a dedicated report on their corporate governance arrangements, and justify any deviations from a newly introduced national corporate governance code.

In Germany, the key source of external influence over corporations has traditionally been private universal banks rather than the state, with the big three universal banks (Deutsche Bank, Dresdner Bank, and Commerzbank) acting as the main conduits of influence between the private and public spheres (Dyson 1986). Unlike in France, German companies have traditionally enjoyed a dual board structure, consisting of a management board (*Vorstand*) and a supervisory board (*Aufsichtsrat*). Bank representatives have played a major role on supervisory boards due to both their extensive blockholdings in individual companies and voting power derived from acting as proxy shareholders for small shareholders (whose shares are held in their custody accounts) (Prowse 1994; Fohlin 2005).[6] German supervisory boards have also been characterized by the strong representation of employees. The *Mitbestimmungsgesetz* (codetermination law) of 1976 mandated companies with more than 2,000 employees to allocate half of the seats on their supervisory boards to employee representatives. Such a board structure – dominated by representatives of management, banks, other blockholders, and employees – was, therefore, not structured in a manner that was likely to give much of a voice to minority shareholders (Theisen 1998).

Some limited pro-shareholder measures were implemented in Germany in the early 1990s to encourage the development of *Finanzplatz Deutschland* (i.e., Frankfurt as a leading financial center), including the creation of a securities market regulator (*Die Bundesaufsichtamt für den Wertpapierhandel*),[7] and the outlawing of insider trading. However, the first major policy shift in favor of minority shareholders came in 1998 with the so-called KonTraG law,[8] which, *inter alia*, authorized share buybacks and stock option plans, restricted deviations from the principle of "one-share, one-vote," and weakened the voting power and supervisory board representation of blockholders and universal banks. A symbolic aspect of the law was that it recognized shareholder value as a valid corporate objective for the first time in German corporate history.[9] Another major action to counter the extent of

---

[6] It should be noted, however, that the largest cross-shareholdings in the German system have been held by corporations rather than banks (Franks and Mayer 1997: 283).

[7] This was superseded by *Die Bundesanstalt für Finanzdienstleistungsaufsicht* (BaFin) in May 2002.

[8] *Gesetz zur Kontrolle und Transparenz im Unternehmensbereich* – Law for Control and Transparency in the Corporate Sector (1998).

[9] This measure was praised by Espen Eckbo of the Tuck School of Business as a "giant step forward for German corporate governance. Adam Smith would have approved" (Eckbo 2005: 3).

blockholding was the abolition of capital gains tax on blockholdings in 2002, which removed a potential disincentive to the unwinding of cross-shareholdings. Subsequent reforms have improved corporate disclosure, enhanced the litigation options of shareholders, and introduced a mandatory bid rule. As in France, it has also become necessary (since 2002) for German companies to explain any deviation from a national code of corporate governance.

Like in France, the postwar corporate sector in Italy has been characterized by a strong relationship between corporate elites and the state. Even as late as the mid-1990s, eight out of the largest twenty corporations were state-owned (La Porta et al. 1998). However, unlike in France, a major role has also been played by a small group of elite families – the so-called *salotto buono* – which hold blockholdings in many large corporations. This has led to the description of the Italian corporate sector as "family capitalism" (Pagano and Trento 2002). Such a regime has traditionally placed a low priority on securing the rights of minority shareholders.

Although insider trading was made illegal in the early 1990s, the first major reform of corporate governance in favor of minority shareholders was the so-called Draghi law of 1998.[10] This introduced a range of measures to improve the rights of minority shareholders, improve disclosure, and improve the board accountability of audit committees. In the same year, a mandatory bid rule was introduced. In 2003, Italy followed Germany in abolishing the payment of capital gains tax on the sale of cross-shareholdings. As in France and Germany, a national corporate governance code was introduced in 2005, with which companies must either comply or explain their divergence.

Most substantive reform in European corporate governance regulation has been driven by regulators at the national level (Enriques 2006). However, a number of transnational organizations – most notably the Organisation for Economic Co-operation and Development (OECD) – have also played a role in recent years in promoting the interests of minority shareholders.[11] The OECD published its Principles of Corporate Governance in 1999 (although they were revised and reissued in 2004). Although the Principles have no legal enforceability, they have become an influential benchmark in the design of national level corporate governance codes and regulation. The primary objective of the OECD code is to outline the key components of a corporate governance regime that protects the interests of non-insiders in general,

---

[10] This was named after Mario Draghi, the Director General of the Italian Treasury, and Chairman of a commission on corporate governance reform. See Chapter 10.

[11] Other international organizations that have sought to promote "good," that is, pro-shareholder, corporate governance include the World Bank, the International Corporate Governance Network, the International Accounting Standards Board (formerly the International Accounting Standards Committee), and the International Organization of Securities Commissions.

although the overwhelming focus is on minority shareholders. Key sections of the Principles cover the rights of shareholders, the equitable treatment of shareholders, disclosure and transparency, and the responsibilities of the board – all key areas of concern for minority shareholders.

The EU has signaled support for minority shareholder interests through a number of recent directives (although enacted measures have often served to systematize protections that were already embodied in national level legislation). An EU law passed in 2002, for example, required that all listed corporations in the EU prepare their accounts according to international financial reporting standards (IFRS) from 2006 onward. International accounting standards – as well as establishing a level playing field for the comparison of companies on a transnational basis – often require greater disclosure than many national accounting codes in respect of items such as hidden reserves, which have historically been used by European corporate insiders to retain resources within the company for strategic rather than profitability reasons.[12] The market abuse directive of 2003 defined the type of price-sensitive information to be disclosed by companies in order to prevent insider trading, and required directors and related persons to disclose trading activities.[13] These requirements were incorporated into national law between 2003 and 2005. In June 2007, a shareholder rights directive[14] was adopted, which outlined measures to reduce the cost of voting for minority shareholders, eliminate share blocking, allow shareholders to question management, and receive relevant information regarding shareholder meetings. EU law requires that these protections be adopted into national laws by 2009.

However, the EU has also experienced setbacks when it has attempted to move too fast in the direction of pro-shareholder corporate governance reform. For example, in July 2001, a draft directive to promote the development of a European market for corporate control was blocked by the European Parliament and several European governments (see Section 1.2.2). More recently, the European Commission announced, in October 2007, its abandonment of previously announced plans to enforce the principle of "one-share, one-vote" across the EU, following opposition from the French, Spanish, and Swedish governments (Bounds and Burgess 2007). Reflecting these nationally located political constraints, the Commissioner for the Internal

---

[12] Regulation (EC) No 1606/2002 of the European Parliament and of the Council of July 19, 2002 on the application of international accounting standards.

[13] Directive 2003/58/EC of the European Parliament and of the Council of July 15, 2003 amending Council Directive 68/151/EEC, as regards disclosure requirements in respect of certain types of companies.

[14] Directive 2007/36/EC of the European Parliament and of the Council of July 11, 2007 on the exercise of certain rights of shareholders in listed companies.

Market, Charlie McCreevy, has conceded the impracticability of imposing a "one-size-fits-all" corporate governance model on member states through EU legislation (McCreevy 2007).

1.2.2 Changes in "firm-level" corporate governance

Although the reform of corporate governance regulation may change the formal "rules of the game" in which firms operate, it does not necessarily imply a corresponding change in the actual corporate governance behavior of companies (Culpepper 2005: 176; Khanna et al. 2006). Nevertheless, a substantial body of evidence suggests that firm-level governance has also shifted in a pro-shareholder direction in many European countries since the early to mid-1990s.

In the case of Germany, Beyer and Höpner (2003) contend that corporate governance change has actually been led from the "bottom-up," that is, by the changed behavior of companies, rather than by top-down reforms in corporate governance regulation (which have been reflective rather than causative of changed *de facto* outcomes). During the second half of the 1990s, devices such as profitability goals, measures to increase financial transparency, investor relations activities, and stock options as a method of executive remuneration, were introduced by major German companies such as Bayer, Hoechst, DaimlerChrysler, and VEBA. Furthermore, between 1996 and 2000, the number of cross-shareholding networks between the 100 largest German companies declined significantly (from 169 to 80). The hostile takeover of Mannesmann in 2000 by the British firm Vodafone was the first ever acquisition of a large German corporation by a foreign bidder.[15]

As will be described in Chapter 9, a fundamental change also occurred in the role of the major German banks. These former guardians of "patient capital" increasingly found themselves promoting shareholder rights and capital markets through their activities in investment banking. A landmark event reflecting their changing role related to the 1997 takeover battle between Krupp and Thyssen. Both Deutsche Bank and Dresdner Bank supported (and provided M&A advice) for Krupp's hostile bid for Thyssen, despite also having seats on Thyssen's supervisory board. A further indication of the banks' increasing rejection of its network guardian role came to light in 2001, when Deutsche Bank announced that it would entirely withdraw from

---

[15] According to Franks and Mayer, between 1945 and the early 1990s, there were only four hostile takeovers in Germany (Franks and Mayer 1997: 41).

supervisory board chairmanships in other companies. All of these developments occurred largely independently of state-driven regulatory change (Beyer and Höpner 2003: 180).

Gregory Vincent (2004) documents an insightful case study of bottom-up change in French corporate governance practices in the late 1990s. In 1997, the AXA insurance group merged with another French insurer – UAP – which stood at the center of a network of cross-shareholdings coordinated by the Banque Nationale de Paris (BNP). In defiance of the French government's desire to establish a *keiretsu*-style network of cross-shareholding (*noyaux durs*) centered on BNP – the new management of the combined AXA–UAP group pledged to manage its financial assets according to "Anglo-Saxon norms of profitability" (Morin 2000; Vincent 2004). This undermined the viability of the proposed BNP-coordinated cross-shareholding network, and catalyzed other major companies to reconsider their attitude to strategic ownership. As can be seen in Table 1.1, the result was an unwinding of a number of major cross-shareholdings in the French corporate sector in subsequent years (Culpepper 2005).

A newly available means by which corporate governance practices can be measured at the level of the firm is through corporate governance ratings (Tucker 2004). Ratings agencies – such as Standard & Poor's and Moody's – have long provided assessments of the credit ratings of individual companies for their institutional clients. However, during the last few years, a number of companies – such as Institutional Shareholder Services (ISS) and GovernanceMetrics International – have begun rating companies in terms of corporate governance. The proprietary criteria with which companies are assessed vary by rating agency. However, the ratings embody a common

Table 1.1 Percentage of shares in selected French Companies represented by cross-shareholdings

Company	1995	1996	1997	1998	1999	2000
BNP	16.9	16.8	16.1	11.0	8.2	8.6
St. Gobain	22.7	22.6	22.3	22.3	13.5	7.6
Suez/Lyonnaise des Eaux	9.0	8.4	8.4	8.4	1.7	1.4
UAP/AXA	9.0	9.0	9.0	6.9	6.9	6.9
Vivendi	17.9	16.5	15.1	14.1	8.7	4.9
AGF	2.8	4.5	5.6	6.0	2.5	2.5
Alcatel	8.0	7.0	6.7	8.4	5.0	4.4
Aventis	10.8	11.5	12.3	14.4	7.5	6.9
Société Générale	21.5	23.0	24.7	28.8	15.0	13.7

Source: Culpepper (2005: 191).

commitment toward minority-shareholder orientation, and ratings are frequently structured in a similar manner to the OECD Principles of Corporate Governance (Balling et al. 2005).

Most of the newly created indices of corporate governance have not been around long enough to permit an assessment of temporal change over a significant period of time. However, Deminor – a Brussels-based rating agency – has produced ratings since 2000.[16] Their figures evaluate companies on a scale of 1 to 10 in four categories of corporate governance behavior: shareholders' rights and duties, disclosure, board structure, and functioning and takeover defenses, and relate to the 300 constituents of the FTSE Eurotop index of large European companies. A higher score represents a more pro-shareholder orientation. Dariusz Wójcik (2006) has compared the Deminor country ratings in 2000 and 2004 for evidence of change in European corporate governance. A country breakdown of his results is shown in Table 1.2.

The conclusions of Wójcik's study need to be treated with some caution, given the small number of companies involved in calculating the median country ratings of certain countries. For example, the country score relating to Austria is based on only two companies, as Austria contributes only two companies to the FTSE Eurotop index. Furthermore, the comparison between the 2000 and 2004 ratings can only be undertaken with 190 companies, as the composition of the FTSE Eurotop index changes over time,[17] and a ratings comparison is only made with companies that appear in the index in both years (i.e., on a like-for-like basis). Taking account of these data limitations, a nonparametric test of statistical significance is presented alongside each item of data.

Notwithstanding these caveats, and despite the relatively short time frame of comparison (i.e., four years), the data suggests that companies in most continental European countries have undergone a major process of change in respect of minority-shareholder orientation in recent years. For example, the Deminor rating of shareholder rights and duties improved substantially over the four-year period in the Netherlands, Norway, Spain, and Switzerland. Even more significant was the substantial improvement of disclosure practices in Germany, the Netherlands, Portugal, Spain, Sweden, and Switzerland. Board structure and functioning made major progress in Finland, the Netherlands, and Switzerland.

---

[16] Deminor's corporate governance rating unit was merged into ISS in 2005.
[17] The composition of the FTSE Eurotop index is periodically adjusted to take account of changes in the relative value of companies. This results in new companies entering the index, while others drop out. In addition, companies may disappear from the index due to delisting (i.e., going private), takeover, or bankruptcy.

Table 1.2 Corporate governance ratings (median values) of large European companies (by country) – 2004 versus 2000

Country	Number of firms in 2004 sample	Shareholder rights and duties 2004 rating	Shareholder rights and duties Change since 2000	Disclosure 2004 rating	Disclosure Change since 2000	Board structure and functioning 2004 rating	Board structure and functioning Change since 2000	Takeover defenses 2004 rating	Takeover defenses Change since 2000
Austria	2	6.7		6.0		3.8		2.6	
Belgium	9	6.1**	−0.2***	5.8***	1.7***	5.0	0.5	1.0**	0.5
Denmark	5	6.7	0.4	6.2	2.9**	3.6	1.8	1.0**	0.0
Finland	5	7.5	−0.2	7.0	1.6	6.7**	2.9*	1.0	−3.2
France	42	6.5***	0.1***	6.9**	2.3	6.0	1.4	1.0	1.0
Germany	32	6.9	−0.2***	6.7**	3.1***	4.5*	1.7	1.0***	−1.6**
Greece	6	6.7	−0.3	5.3**	0.8	3.7**	−0.1	1.0**	−9.0
Ireland	7	7.8	0.7	7.6	1.5*	7.0*	1.0*	9.0***	−1.0
Italy	25	5.7***	−0.6***	6.6	1.9	5.1***	1.5	1.0***	1.0
Netherlands	21	5.5**	1.8**	8.1	3.2***	6.6**	3.3***	3.8	1.0***
Norway	5	7.7**	1.9	5.9**	2.6	5.2	2.7	1.0	−0.8
Portugal	4	4.9	0.7	6.6	4.3*	4.6**	2.5*	1.0**	1.0
Spain	17	6.8	1.2	6.5**	3.4**	5.1	1.1	1.0***	1.0
Sweden	16	6.2	0.8	6.8**	3.3**	5.2**	1.8	5.1	−1.4
Switzerland	17	7.0	1.1*	5.9**	3.5***	5.7	3.4**	1.0	0.0
United Kingdom	81	8.0***	1.1***	8.1***	1.5***	7.3***	1.1***	9.0***	1.0***
Total	296	7.0	0.6	7.2	2.3	5.8	1.5	2.7	1.0

Note: The significance tests are based on a nonparametric means of testing the null hypothesis that a country rating has the same median rating as the sample as a whole. Asymptotic significance based on calculated Chi-square values: *p < .1, **p < .05, and ***p < .01.

Source: Data presented in Wójcik (2006).

However, an area where negligible progress was made relates to takeover defenses. It is argued in the finance literature that the threat of hostile takeover represents an important mechanism whereby minority shareholders can align management behavior with shareholder interests (Manne 1965). According to this perspective, a corporate manager who does not maximize shareholder value runs the risk that his or her company's share price falls low enough to attract an external bidder. If the bidder is able to gain control of the company from existing shareholders (e.g., by offering a significant premium to the existing market price), the existing management regime is likely to be dismissed. The possibility of hostile takeover, therefore, provides incumbent management with an incentive to vigorously generate shareholder value, a strategy which is consistent with the interests of minority shareholders. However, if management perceives the risk of takeover to be remote – regardless of the level of the share price – management may feel less pressure to pursue a pro-shareholder approach. The threat of takeover may be reduced by the ability of the firm to implement takeover defenses,[18] or by the behavior of national governments, which may seek to deter or block advances from "undesirable" potential corporate suitors.[19]

An EU directive in 2001 aimed to curb a number of the main mechanisms – such as poison-pill defenses – used by European firms to deter hostile takeovers. However, the directive was opposed by the German government, and finally blocked by an exceptionally close vote of the European Parliament in July 2001 (Höpner 2003: 10). A compromise version of the directive was adopted in 2004, allowing member states to opt out of provisions requiring companies to seek shareholder approval for poison-pill defenses after a bid had been announced (the board neutrality rule), and preventing voting restrictions, share transfers or multiple voting rights being used at

---

[18] According to the European Commission, there are two main categories of defensive mechanism in common use in Europe. "Post-bid defenses" are put in place once a company has become subject to a takeover bid. Such defenses include share buybacks aimed at reducing the number of shares the bidder can acquire or the issue of share capital – so as to increase the cost of the bid. "Pre-bid defenses" may constitute barriers to the acquisition of shares in the company (e.g., share transfer restrictions contained in the company's articles) or to the exercise of control in the general meeting (e.g., voting restrictions or shares with multiple voting rights) (European Commission 2007).

[19] Two recent European examples of this phenomenon are particularly noteworthy. At the end of 2005, the Governor of the Bank of Italy – Antonio Fazio – was forced to resign due to allegations that he had attempted to thwart the foreign takeover of an Italian bank – Banca Antonveneta – by a Dutch bank (ABN AMRO). In August 2005, the French government announced that it planned to protect ten industry sectors from takeover by non-EU firms, following market rumors that PepsiCo of the United States was considering a bid for Danone. This provoked concern from the European Commission that France might overstep EU legal provisions relating to the protection of "strategic sectors" (*Financial Times*, August 29, 2005).

the shareholder meeting authorizing such defensive measures (the breakthrough rule). Despite the voluntary nature of these two opt-out provisions, it was hoped that they would not be exploited by most countries. However, a report by the European Commission in February 2007 observed that almost all member states had taken advantage of the opt-outs (except those countries where the protections already existed), and concluded that the success of the directive in promoting an open European market for corporate control had been limited.[20]

The low level of the indices presented in Table 1.2 confirms that continental European companies have retained their ability to resist hostile takeovers (Wójcik 2006: 651). Although mergers and acquisitions are increasingly common among European companies, the vast majority of these transactions are of a "friendly" or mutually agreed nature. Hostile takeovers remain extremely rare.[21]

1.2.3 Convergence in European corporate governance?

The changes that have occurred in European corporate governance have provoked a vigorous debate as to whether they are indicative of a process of convergence on the corporate governance systems of the liberal market economies (O'Sullivan 2003). A number of researchers have argued that the changes – although significant – do not fundamentally alter the European corporate governance landscape, and the role it plays in underpinning national varieties of capitalism (Deeg and Perez 2000; Vitols 2001; Aguilera and Jackson 2003). Blockholding remains a more prevalent form of company ownership in Europe than in liberal market economies, and the market for corporate control has yet to function properly. Both Vitols and Jackson suggest that the changes in Germany represent a hybridization of old and new approaches rather than convergence on a liberal market economy (LME) approach, with measures favoring minority shareholders coexisting with more traditional features of German corporate governance, for example, codetermination and powerful works councils (Jackson 2003; Thelen and Kume 2003; Vitols 2003). In a cross-country study of both developed and developing economies, Khanna et al. (2006) conclude that significant convergence in *de jure* corporate governance has occurred between economically

---

[20] Report on the implementation of the Directive on Takeover Bids (European Commission, February 21, 2007).
[21] Even in the United Kingdom and the United States – whose markets for corporate control are more open than those of continental Europe – less than 1 percent of merger and acquisition activity is of a hostile nature (Armour and Skeel 2006: 13).

interdependent countries, but convergence on US standards has yet to take place. Furthermore, firm-level corporate governance practices have converged much less than corporate governance law and regulation (Khanna et al. 2006: 84).

An alternative perspective on convergence is provided – in respect of Germany – by Beyer and Höpner (2003), who claim that the changes of the late 1990s represented a fundamental break from the previous system (Beyer and Höpner 2003: 180). Christel Lane (2003: 16) goes further, arguing that "the German financial system of corporate governance has converged on the Anglo-American model." Chris Mallin (2004: 207) concludes that beyond Germany "there does seem to be convergence on certain core principles based usually around the OECD Principles of Corporate Governance." Perhaps the most outspoken statement of the convergence thesis has been made by Yale law professors Henry Hansmann and Reinier Kraakman in their paper, *The End of History for Corporate Law*:

> Despite the apparent divergence in institutions of governance, share ownership, capital markets, and business culture across developed economies, the basic law of the corporate form has already achieved a high degree of uniformity, and continued convergence is likely. A principal reason for convergence is a widespread normative consensus that corporate managers should act exclusively in the economic interests of shareholders. [...] Since the dominant corporate ideology of shareholder primacy is unlikely to be undone, its success represents the 'end of history' for corporate law (Hansmann and Kraakman 2001: 89).

Resolution of the convergence debate is beyond the scope of this book, particularly as it is difficult to define what convergence really means or to pinpoint when it has finally occurred (Gourevitch 2003: 328; Yamamura and Streeck 2003: 41). For example, should convergence be defined as occurring when systems achieve equivalence in their functioning, or is equality of institutional form also a necessary precondition (Gilson 2001)? Putting aside the convergence debate, a snapshot of current firm-level corporate governance practices in Europe is provided by Aggarwal et al. (2007).[22] They report details of a sample of 2,234 non-US and 4,070 US companies in terms of forty-four corporate governance attributes derived from the ISS corporate governance rating methodology. These attributes relate to board function and structure, audit approach, antitakeover defenses, and compensation and ownership (for a list of the forty-four attributes, see Aggarwal [2007: 41]). The scores for individual companies are aggregated by country to create a country GOV score (see Table 1.3).

[22] Unfortunately, this assessment is made for one year only – 2005 – so it does not allow an evaluation of change over time.

The message conveyed by the GOV scores is largely consistent with the firm-level Deminor ratings shown in Section 1.2.2 (although the latter relate to the year 2004, and are calculated from a smaller sample of companies, i.e., FTSE Eurotop 300 constituents). The GOV scores suggest that, by 2005, minority shareholder orientation in two continental European economies – Finland and Switzerland – was comparable with that of corporations in most LMEs. The gap between firm-level corporate governance in the Netherlands and Germany and the LMEs was also relatively small. In contrast, firm-level corporate governance in Belgium, Portugal, Italy, Norway, and Sweden continued to exhibit significant divergence from that of LMEs.

These conclusions are underscored by disaggregated data provided by Aggarwal et al. (2007), which summarizes how companies perform in terms of several specific corporate governance attributes, such as board independence, the role and independence of audit committees, and the prevalence of different classes of stock (see Table 1.4). A higher percentage score represents a greater shareholder orientation in respect of each particular attribute. With

Table 1.3 Shareholder orientation of firm-level corporate governance, 2005 (aggregate country scores)

Country	GOV score (%)	Number of firms in sample	Sample as % of total market capitalization
Austria	46	19	81
Belgium	39	25	80
Denmark	45	22	80
Finland	56	31	87
France	48	83	84
Germany	50	85	74
Greece	45	44	79
Italy	41	71	82
Japan	43	589	81
Netherlands	51	47	52
Norway	41	21	77
Portugal	39	14	86
Spain	46	54	88
Sweden	43	43	85
Switzerland	55	58	89
United Kingdom	55	530	88
United States	59	4,070	–

Note: The governance score for each firm is calculated as the percentage of governance attributes for which the firm meets or exceeds a minimum satisfactory standard. The scores relate to the year 2005. Sample as percentage (%) of total market capitalization is calculated by dividing the market capitalization of the sample firms by the total market capitalization of all firms in Worldscope for a particular country.

Source: The forty-four attributes evaluated in this process are listed in Aggarwal et al. (2007: 41).

Table 1.4 Country scores in relation to specific corporate governance attributes (in %), 2005

Country	Board independence	Board size	Chairman/CEO separation	Board structure	Audit committee independence	Auditor ratification	Stock classes
Austria	0	67	100	0	0	100	100
Belgium	25	85	60	0	20	5	95
Denmark	71	79	100	64	7	100	57
Finland	64	80	100	84	40	100	68
France	28	78	49	2	22	35	38
Germany	40	82	100	0	3	100	100
Greece	3	90	90	3	7	97	100
Italy	0	87	77	0	3	33	100
Japan	1	80	0	42	2	2	100
Netherlands	83	73	98	7	54	51	68
Norway	69	46	100	23	15	0	100
Portugal	43	100	43	0	0	14	86
Spain	6	80	60	3	6	89	100
Sweden	60	97	100	100	17	14	66
Switzerland	75	81	98	19	58	98	98
United Kingdom	32	90	96	8	68	99	99
United States	89	81	41	52	88	68	94

Note: The percentage of firms in each country that meets or exceeds a minimum threshold for each governance attribute. The seven attributes are: *Board Independence*: board is controlled by more than 50% independent outside directors; *Board Size*: board size is greater than five but less than 16; *Chairman/CEO Separation*: chairman and CEO are separated or there is a lead director; *Board Structure*: annually elected board (no staggered board); *Audit Committee Independence*: audit committee comprised solely of independent outsiders; *Auditor Ratification*: auditors ratified at most recent annual meeting; *Stock Classes*: only single share class, common stock (no dual class).

Source: Aggarwal et al. (2007: 46).

respect to these criteria, Finnish, Swiss, and Dutch companies perform in a manner comparable to their British and American peers, in contrast to firms in Belgium and France.

To conclude, it appears that corporate governance diversity persists in Europe, particularly in relation to the market for corporate control. However, it is also apparent that in areas such as shareholder rights, the role and functioning of boards, and corporate disclosure, European companies are much closer to their Anglo-American counterparts than in 1990, and in some cases the gap has entirely disappeared. Although "convergence" may be an inappropriate description, European corporate governance has come a long way in the last ten to fifteen years.

1.3 CORPORATE GOVERNANCE AND PARTISANSHIP

In a recent survey of comparative political economy, James Alt (2002: 159) points to the growing use of partisanship as an explanatory variable in studies of economic outcomes. Since the pioneering work of Douglas Hibbs (1977, 1987), the role of partisanship has been examined with respect to areas such as monetary policy (Alesina et al. 1997; Way 2000), size of government (Hicks and Swank 1992; Blais et al. 1993, 1996; Alt and Lowry 2000; Garrett 2001), fiscal balance (Alesina et al. 1997; Franzese 2002), wage inequality (Pontusson et al. 2002), labor market institutions (Lange and Garrett 1985), the welfare state (Huber and Stephens 2001; Allan and Scruggs 2004), trade policy (Milner and Judkins 2004), and taxation (Cusack and Beramendi 2006).

The likely stance of political parties with respect to many policy areas may be inferred (albeit somewhat simplistically) from widely held conceptions regarding the ideological preferences of Left and Right. For example, it is often assumed that Left parties will be more enthusiastic than conservative parties about policies that promote the interests of low-income and disadvantaged groups. In contrast, the Right might be expected to prioritize measures that favor more affluent parts of the income distribution. Left parties are often viewed as more sympathetic toward an interventionist role for the state, including greater government spending, more generous welfare provision, and a highly progressive structure of taxation. Conversely, parties of the Right are frequently conceptualized as favoring smaller government, lower taxation, and a central role for markets in the allocation of societal resources (Hibbs and Dennis 1988; Bobbio 1997; Freeden 1999: 49; Klingemann et al. 2006: 5).

The application of this type of intuitive logic to corporate governance can be used to rationalize a positive (i.e., same-direction) relationship between conservative government and the adoption of greater minority-shareholder orientation. This presumption arises from a number of plausible expectations about the likely socioeconomic implications of a corporate sector focused on the maximization of shareholder value. In contrast, corporate governance arrangements that encourage patient or dedicated owners of capital appear more consistent with Left government. The reasons for these expectations concerning partisanship and corporate governance are considered in turn.

A first consideration relates to the job security and employment conditions of employees. According to Shleifer and Summers, the short-term pressures operating on firms within the shareholder model force managers to break implicit contracts with workers relating to job security and long-term career progression (Shleifer and Summers 1988: 41). A firm that is oriented toward fulfilling the short-term earnings growth expectations of capital markets and sustaining a high share price is incentivized to adopt a "hire and fire" approach to its workforce. Labor costs form a significant proportion of the total costs of many enterprises, and the ability to manage these in a flexible way – both through reductions in headcount and wage restraint – helps firms to reduce operational gearing, and thereby protects levels of profitability during economic downturns. However, this greater flexibility comes at the expense of the employment security and wage levels of employees.

These fears about shareholder-oriented systems are underpinned by empirical data relating to labor markets. According to Jackson (2001: 124), the elasticity of employment in response to output changes in Germany and Japan has typically been around one-quarter of that of the United States. Frick (1997: 215) and Aoki (1988) note the substantial difference in job tenure and labor market turnover between these two groups of countries. Such differences between liberal and nonliberal market economies serve to substantially increase levels of insecurity among workers (Cappelli et al. 1997: 37; Lazonick and O'Sullivan 2000: 18; Barker and Rueda 2007). For these reasons, a Left government might not be expected to favor a form of corporate governance that pushes firms toward a more ruthless and cost-oriented attitude *vis-à-vis* employees.

A second consideration concerns income inequality. Firms in liberal market economies – particularly those in the United States – have traditionally exhibited much higher levels of pay disparity between senior executives and the median worker than those of continental Europe (see Table 1.5).[23] One of the causes of the more unequal remuneration environment in LMEs arises

---

[23] Between 1945 and the mid-1980s, the ratio of median executive pay (including bonuses and stock options grants) to average wages in the United States remained relatively stable. However, this ratio broke down between 1985 and 2000, increasing from around 40 times to almost 120 times average wages (*The Economist* 2007: 6).

Introduction

Table 1.5 Median compensation of the CEO of a medium-sized company, 1996

Country	Base salary and bonus (US$ in thousands)	All benefits and perquisites (US$ in thousands)	Long-term compensation (US$ in thousands)	Total CEO compensation (US$ in thousands)	Ratio of CEO compensation to average manufacturing wage
Belgium	285	161	0	447	11.8
Canada	347	76	88	511	13.9
France	274	122	68	464	16.1
Germany	294	74	0	368	8.0
Italy	328	139	19	486	17.0
Japan	202	91	0	292	11.4
Netherlands	295	76	0	371	9.6
Spain	314	89	0	403	15.6
Sweden	147	94	0	241	7.4
Switzerland	264	69	12	345	11.8
United Kingdom	297	123	74	494	17.0
United States	548	97	260	905	24.3

Note: The data relates to a sample of companies with annual revenue of $200–500 million in 1990 US dollars. Benefits include pension contributions, health care costs, and other services, evaluated on an annualized basis. Long-term compensation includes stock options (the right to purchase company stock at a given price), restricted stock (stock that cannot be sold for some specified period of time), and performance share plans (formula-based stock compensation).

Source: Abowd and Kaplan (1999).

from the difficulties faced by a minority-shareholder-oriented governance system in controlling the remuneration decisions of top management. This contrasts with a blockholder system, where owners retain direct control over management remuneration (Bebchuk and Fried 2004). However, in addition, shareholder-oriented corporate governance offers greater scope for senior managers to negotiate the granting of stock options and performance bonuses. Stock options offer management the chance of achieving significant levels of personal wealth if they succeed in boosting the share price over a reasonably short time frame. Minority shareholders may encourage such techniques of remuneration, as they can be viewed as increasing the alignment of managers with the interests of shareholders. However, such a remuneration policy will clearly be detrimental to the income equality and redistributional objectives of left-of-center political actors and their core constituents.

A third reason why Left government may not be associated with minority-shareholder-oriented corporate governance is identified by Mark Roe (2003). According to Roe's argument, owners prefer a system of corporate governance based on blockholding in economies which are dominated by strong labor movements and left-wing political parties. Owners fear that the strength of the Left will translate into policy measures that favor the interests of employees in the authority structure of the firm (e.g., employment protection, codetermination rights, centralized collective bargaining, etc.). They determine that the best way to counter these potential agency costs is to take large blockholdings in individual firms. These provide owners with more direct and reliable control over the management of firms, and give them the power to ensure that management administers the firm in their interests. However, after taking controlling ownership stakes, blockholders will have little incentive to promote the interests of minority shareholders, and will anyway view a value-maximizing approach as unrealistic in a labor-dominated environment (i.e., due to political constraints). In short, the strength of the Left will give rise to a corporate governance environment that is unfavorable to the interests of minority shareholders (Roe 2003).

A final link between corporate governance and partisanship concerns the role of patient capital in an economic system oriented toward nonmarket mechanisms of economic coordination. As Hall and Soskice (2001) have argued, it is necessary for capital to exhibit a long-term behavioral profile in order to persuade workers and other social actors to invest in "specific," that is, nontransferable, skills. However, Carr and Tomkins (1998: 223) report that the average time horizon for corporate investment among UK firms (i.e., firms operating in a pro-shareholder system) is 3.3 years, almost half that of their German peers. A more ruthless, short-termist ownership approach affects the willingness of employees to commit themselves to firm-specific types of role. Furthermore, patient or dedicated capital is complementary with a range of other institutional features in so-called coordinated market economies (CMEs), such as the nature of vocational training and education, industrial relations, and interfirm relations (Aoki 1988; Porter 1992; Hall and Soskice 2001: 6). It seems unlikely that Left government would promote the dismemberment of such a variety of capitalism – given the favorable position that labor has occupied within it – in favor of economic coordination based on more market-determined outcomes.

These expectations regarding the likely relationship between partisanship and corporate governance find support in cross-sectional data relating to the early 1990s. Figure 1.1 shows a scatter diagram of the Left–Right ideology of governments in individual countries and the extent of ownership concentration. The former is measured by Thomas Cusack's index of the ideological center of gravity of the cabinet,[24] which in turn is based on an expert

---

[24] For further details, see Cusack and Fuchs (2002).

classification of the ideological Left–Right stance of governing parties undertaken by Castles and Mair (1984), Laver and Hunt (1992), and Huber and Inglehart (1995). The partisanship values presented in Figure 1.1 are mean values across the period 1970–92. The ownership concentration data is based on data compiled by Gourevitch and Shinn (2005: 299), and relates to the early 1990s. It shows the percentage of national equity markets that are closely held, that is, the proportion of firms with individual owners holding stakes in excess of 20 percent of their total market capitalization. A high value is therefore indicative of blockholding. Roe (2003) argues that this type of data is suggestive of an empirical association between the power of the Left and an unfavorable environment for minority shareholders. Conversely, a more Right-oriented political environment – such as in the United States and United Kingdom – appears more conducive to shareholders with a more diffuse equity ownership, that is, less blockholding, and hence with a greater affinity for minority shareholder-oriented corporate governance.

The arguments in favor of a positive correlation between Right partisanship and shareholder-oriented corporate governance appear plausible enough. However, they sit uncomfortably with the observation that pro-shareholder

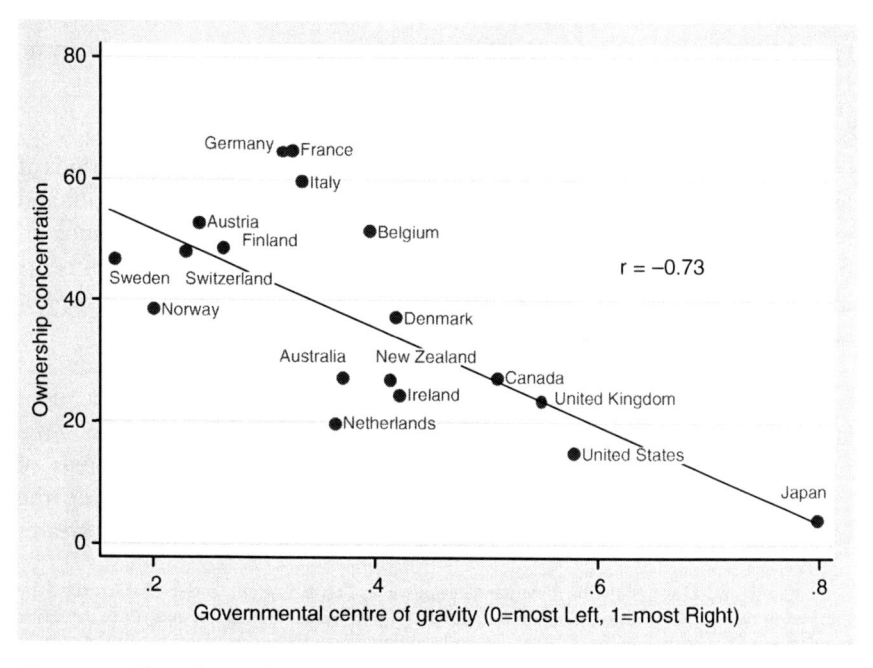

Figure 1.1 The relationship between government ideology and ownership concentration

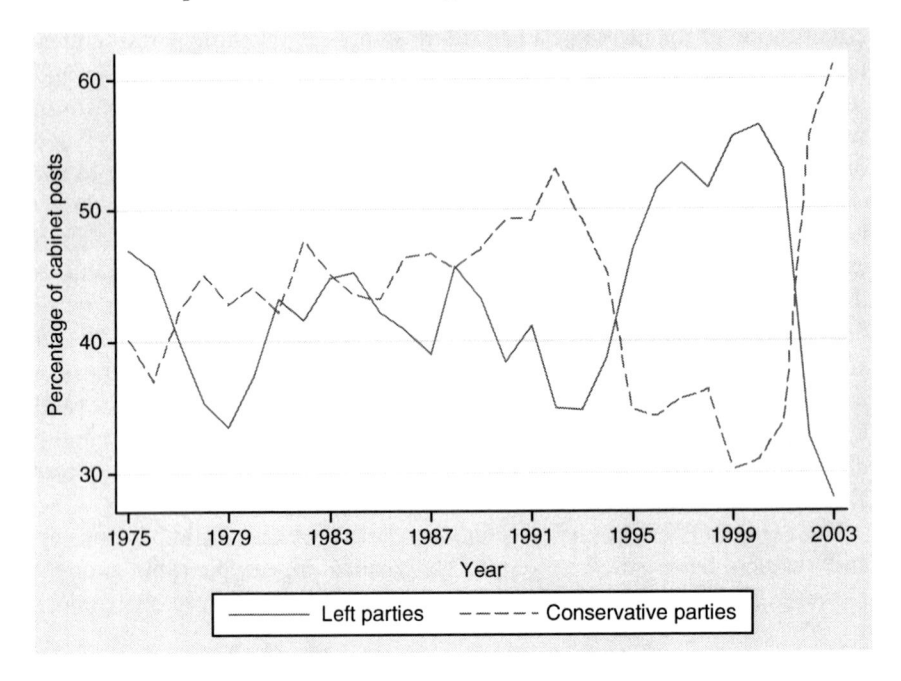

Figure 1.2 Participation of Left and conservative parties in European government, 1975–2003 (mean percentage of cabinet posts)

reform in Europe since the mid-1990s has coincided with significant periods of Left or Center-Left government in many European countries. John Cioffi and Martin Höpner have termed this phenomenon "the political paradox of finance capitalism,"[25] and have examined the role of Center-Left governments in pro-shareholder reform through case studies relating to three European countries: Germany, France, and Italy (Cioffi and Höpner 2006).[26]

Support for Cioffi and Höpner's contention that the last decade has witnessed a "greater than usual" role for the Left in European government is provided by the data presented in Figure 1.2. The graph summarizes the involvement of both the Left and conservative parties in the cabinets of fourteen European nonliberal market economies since 1975. During the second half of the 1990s, the Left participated in government to a greater

---

[25] Cioffi and Höpner define Finance Capitalism as "an economic order characterized by increasing competition, the expansion and deepening of financial markets, and more extensive regulation of the corporate firm's financial and governance practices consistent with the growth of market-driven finance" (Cioffi and Höpner 2006: 31).

[26] Cioffi and Höpner's article also considers the relationship between corporate governance reform and partisanship in the United States.

extent than at any time over the previous two decades.[27] Left-oriented governments were notable features of the political landscape in Belgium, Denmark, Finland, France, Germany, Greece, Italy, Portugal, and Sweden (although Austria and Spain provided counterexamples to this trend). In contrast, the influence of conservative parties in many countries reached a low ebb in the mid- to late 1990s, and only rebounded in the final two years of the time series.

Cioffi and Höpner's case studies (2006) – and the relative prevalence of Left government over the last decade – give rise to a number of questions concerning the relationship between partisanship and corporate governance. First, has the association between Left government and pro-shareholder reform – which Cioffi and Höpner observe in the cases of Germany, France, and Italy – been a general feature of the experience of other European economies? In other words, is such an unexpected pattern of partisanship a widely observed phenomenon in a large number of European economies, or specific to a relatively small number of special cases? Second, what explains this apparently puzzling association of Left government and pro-shareholder reform over the last ten years? Finally, does the apparent association between Left partisanship and changes in corporate governance policy (*de jure* corporate governance) – which is the focus of Cioffi and Höpner's case studies – also hold with respect to changes in firm-level corporate governance behavior (*de facto* corporate governance), which is the ultimate concern of this book?

The approach of this book is to seek a resolution of these issues through a detailed empirical analysis of the relationship between partisanship and firm-level corporate governance change in nonliberal market economies. This is undertaken in the context of testing a new hypothesis of *de facto* corporate governance change, which argues that the effect of partisanship on corporate governance change is conditional on the level of a specific economic variable: product market competition (which determines the level of economic rents in a political economy). The ultimate conclusion of the analysis is that, although Cioffi and Höpner have usefully highlighted the role played by Left government in several recent cases of pro-shareholder regulatory reform, they have crucially omitted the essential role played by economic rents in determining the corporate governance preferences of political actors and their core constituents. The relationship between partisanship and corporate governance change on a cross-country basis is more generally explained – and with greater empirical significance – in the context of partisanship's interaction with product market competition. This interaction forms the basis of the hypothesis of corporate governance change proposed by this book (which is described in Chapter 2).

---

[27] Table 1.7 in the appendix of this chapter provides a detailed summary of the party composition of European governments during the period 1990–2005.

1.4 PLAN OF THE BOOK

Given the cross-country nature of its theoretical claims, this book emphasizes a top-down macro-comparative approach in its analysis of European corporate governance change, although case study evidence is also examined. The hypothesis of the book – linking corporate governance change to the interaction of partisanship and product market competition – is outlined in Chapter 2. The relationship of this hypothesis to existing explanations of corporate governance – which derive from a number of academic literatures, including those of economics, finance, legal studies, economic sociology, and political science – is described in Chapter 3.

The subsequent methodological strategy involves establishing the validity of the theoretical claims by means of panel data econometric analysis. These techniques are applied to a pooled data set containing data relating to fifteen nonliberal industrialized democracies over the period 1975–2003. The choice of empirical proxies for two of the key variables in the data set – corporate governance and product market competition – is justified in Chapters 4 and 5. Chapter 6 presents the results emerging from the quantitative analysis. Chapter 7 examines the robustness of these results through sensitivity analysis and dynamic modeling. In the final part of the book, the relevance of the hypothesis in the European context is qualitatively investigated by means of two country case studies. The rationale for the choice of cases is outlined in Chapter 8. Chapters 9 and 10 present case study evidence for the chosen countries: Germany and Italy. The conclusions of the book are summarized in Chapter 11. The final chapter also offers some reflections on the book's broader implications for policy makers and the future of corporate governance.

1.5 CHAPTER APPENDIX

Table 1.6 provides a detailed listing of the most important changes in corporate governance regulation in the three largest nonliberal European economies – France, Germany, and Italy – since the early 1990s.[28] Table 1.7 provides the partisan composition of governments in continental Europe from 1990 to 2005.

---

[28] Corporate governance changes in Germany and Italy are examined in more detail in the case study chapters of this book (Chapters 9 and 10).

Table 1.6 Summary of regulatory reforms favoring minority shareholders in France, Germany, and Italy (since 1990)

Type of reform measure	France	Germany	Italy
Improving board effectiveness	Separation of CEO and Chairman allowed (2001). New rules on information to be provided to boards (2001 and 2003). Board approval required for nonroutine transactions involving blockholders, and some forms of executive compensation. Requirement to disclose to board significant self-dealing transactions (2001, 2003, and 2005).	Greater role for supervisory board (1998).	New rules on information to be provided to boards (1998 and 2003). Minorities represented on board (2005) and audit committee (1998). Greater power and independence of audit committee (1998 and 2005). Requirements for increased disclosure to boards, and new procedural requirements for related-party transactions (2003). Shareholder approval of stock-based compensation (2005).
Enhancing shareholder rights	Approval required at annual shareholder meeting of nonroutine transactions involving blockholders, and some forms of executive compensation (2001, 2003, and 2005). Easier exercise of shareholder voting rights (2001). Lower thresholds for minority shareholder rights (2002).	Easier exercise of shareholder voting rights (2001). Communication among smaller shareholders facilitated (2005).	Easier exercise of shareholder voting rights (2003). Qualified majority required for major resolutions at shareholder meetings (1998). Lower thresholds for minority shareholder rights (1998 and 2005).

(*Continued*)

Table 1.6 Continued

Type of reform measure	France	Germany	Italy
Promoting shareholder democracy		Multiple voting shares banned, and banks' influence over shareholder meetings curbed (1998).	Voting caps banned (2003). Limits on validity of blockholder-shareholder agreements (1998).
Encouraging unwinding of cross-shareholdings		Sale of corporate shareholdings made tax exempt (2002).	Sale of corporate shareholdings made tax exempt (2003).
Improving private legal enforcement options	Ability of individual shareholders to bring derivative suits against company already in place.	Derivative suits made easier for shareholders (2005). Civil actions by shareholders for securities fraud made easier (2003).	Derivative suits for minorities owning at least 2.5% of shares allowed (1998 and 2005). Contingency fees allowed (2006). Direct shareholder suit for damages stemming from abuse of corporate control introduced (2003).
Equalizing treatment of shareholders during control transactions	Mandatory bid rule (1992).	Mandatory bid rule (2002).	Mandatory bid rule (1998).
Improving corporate disclosure	Corporate governance report required by each company (2003). Implementation of national corporate governance code on a comply-or-explain basis (2003).	Implementation of national corporate governance code on a comply-or-explain basis (2002).	Implementation of national corporate governance code on a comply-or-explain basis (2005).

	Financial reporting according to international accounting standards — IAS/IFRS 24 (agreed 2002, effective 2006).	Financial reporting according to international accounting standards — IAS/IFRS 24 (agreed 2002, effective 2006).	Financial reporting according to international accounting standards — IAS/IFRS 24 (agreed 2002, effective 2006).
	Disclosure of nonroutine transactions with blockholders, and some forms of executive compensation (2001, 2003, and 2005).	New rules concerning disclosure of price-sensitive information (1994 and 2004).	New rules concerning disclosure of price-sensitive information (1991 and 2005).
	New rules concerning disclosure of price-sensitive information (2005).	Disclosure of directors' and company officers' trading activities (2002 and 2004).	Disclosure of directors' and company officers' trading activities (2005).
	Disclosure of directors' and company officers' trading activities (2005).	Disclosure of individual compensation of top managers (2006).	Disclosure of individual compensation of top managers (1999).
	Disclosure of individual compensation of top managers (2001).		Disclosure of major shareholders' trades (2005).
	New rules concerning appointment and activities of auditors (2003).	New rules concerning appointment and activities of auditors (1998 and 2004).	New rules concerning appointment and activities of auditors (1998 and 2005).
Supervisory and enforcement reform	Merger of securities and banking authorities (2003).	Creation of securities regulator (1994).	Increased investigative and sanctioning powers for regulator (1998 and 2005).
		Merger of securities and banking authorities (2002).	

(*Continued*)

Table 1.6 Continued

Type of reform measure	France	Germany	Italy
	Market abuse regime tightened (2005).	Increased investigative and sanctioning powers for regulator (various years). Criminal sanctions for insider trading (1994) and market manipulation (2002). Market abuse regime tightened (2002 and 2004).	Criminal sanctions for insider trading (1991) and market manipulation (1998). Market abuse regime tightened (2005).
	Creation of public company accounting oversight board (2003).	Securities agency review of financial reports of public companies (2004). Creation of public company accounting oversight board (2004).	Securities agency review of financial reports of public companies (2005). Securities regulator's power over audit firms strengthened (2005).

Source: Enriques and Volpin (2007) and author's own research.

Table 1.7 Partisan composition of governments in continental Europe, 1990–2005

Austria	*Prior to 1999*: Coalition of the Social Democratic Party of Austria (SPÖ) and Austrian People's Party (ÖVP). Chancellors: Franz Vranitzky (SPÖ, 1986–97); Viktor Klima (SPÖ, 1997–9). *2000–6*: Coalition of the Austrian People's Party (ÖVP) and the Freedom Party of Austria (FPÖ). Chancellor: Wolfgang Schüssel (ÖVP).
Belgium	*Prior to 1999*: Christian Democrat (CVP)-led coalition. Prime Minister (from 1992): Jean-Luc Dehaene (CVP). *1999–2008*: "Rainbow Coalition" of Flemish and French-speaking Liberals, Social Democrats, and (until 2003) Greens. Prime Minister: Guy Verhofstadt (VLD).
Denmark	*Prior to 1993*: Conservative People's Party (CON)-led coalition. Prime Minister (from 1982): Poul Schlüter (CON). *1993–2009*: Social Democrat (SD)-led coalition. Prime Minister: Poul Nyrup Rasmussen (SD). *2001–2009*: Liberal Party (Venstre)-led coalition. Prime Minister: Anders Fogh Rasmussen (Venstre).
Finland	*Prior to 1991*: National Coalition Party (KOK) coalition. Prime Minister (from 1987): Harri Holkeri (KOK). *1991–5*: Center Party (KESK)-led coalition. Prime Minister: Esko Aho (KESK). *1995–2003*: Social Democrat (SDP)-led coalition. Prime Minister: Paavo Lipponen (SDP). *2003–present*: Center Party-led coalition. Prime Minister: Matti Vanhanen (KESK).[29]
France	*Prior to 1993*: Socialist (PSF)-led government. Prime Ministers: Michel Rocard (1988–91); Édith Cresson (1991–2); Pierre Bérégovoy (1992–3). *1993–7*: Rally for the Republic (RPR) government. Prime Ministers: Édouard Balladur (1993–5); Alain Juppé (1995–7). *1997–2002*: Socialist (PSF)-led government. Prime Minister: Lionel Jospin (1997–2002). *2002–7*: Union for a Popular Movement (UMP)-led government. Prime Ministers: Jean-Pierre Raffarin (2002–5); Dominique de Villepin (2005–7).
Germany	*Prior to 1990*: Christian Democrat-led coalition. Chancellor (from 1982): Helmut Kohl (CDU). *1998–2005*: Social Democratic Party (SPD) and Green Party coalition. Chancellor: Gerhard Schröder (SPD).
Greece	*1990–3*: New Democracy (ND) government. Prime Minister: Constantine Mitsotakis. *1993–2004*: PASOK government. Prime Ministers: Andreas Papandreou (until 1996); Costas Simitis. *2004–present*: New Democracy government. Prime Minister: Kostas Karamanlis.
Italy	*Prior to 1992*: Christian Democrat-led coalition. Prime Minister (from 1989): Giulio Andreotti. *1992–1993*: Socialist-led coalition. Prime Minister: Giuliano Amato. *1993–4*: Independent government. Prime Minister: Carlo Azeglio Ciampi.

[29] Anneli Jäätteenmäki became the first female Prime Minister of Finland in April 2003, but left office after only two months.

	1994–5: Forza Italia (FI) government. Prime Minister: Silvio Berlusconi. *1995–6*: Independent government. Prime Minister: Lamberto Dini. *1996–2001*: Center-left coalitions: Prime Ministers: Romano Prodi (1996–8); Massimo D'Alema (1998–2000); Giuliano Amato (2000–1). *2001–6*: Forza Italia (FI) government. Prime Minister: Silvio Berlusconi.
Netherlands	*Prior to 1994*: Christian Democrat (CDA)-led coalition. Prime Minister (from 1982): Ruud Lubbers (CDA). *1994–2002*: Labour Party (PvdA)-led coalition. Prime Minister: Wim Kok (PvdA). *2002–present*: Christian Democrat (CDA)-led coalition. Prime Minister: Jan Peter Balkenende (CDA).
Norway	*1990–7*: Labour Party (AP) government. Prime Ministers: Gro Harlem Brundtland (1990–96); Thorbjørn Jagland (1996–97). *1997–2000*: Christian Democrat-led coalition. Prime Minister: Kjell Magne Bondevik (CPP). *2000–1*: Labour Party (AP) government. Prime Minister: Jens Stoltenberg *2001–5*: Christian Democrat-led coalition. Prime Minister: Kjell Magne Bondevik (CPP).
Portugal	*Prior to 1995*: Social Democratic Party (PSD) government.[30] Prime Minister (from 1985): Aníbal Cavaco Silva. *1995–2002*: Socialist Party (PSP) government. Prime Minister: António Guterres. *2002–5*: Social Democratic-led coalition. Prime Ministers: José Manuel Barroso (PSD, 2002–4); Pedro Santana Lopes (PSD, 2004–5). *2005–present*: Socialist (PS) government. Prime Minister: José Sócrates.
Spain	*Prior to 1996*: Spanish Socialist Workers' Party (PSOE) government. Prime Minister (from 1982): Felipe González. *1996–2004*: Peoples' Party (PP) government. Prime Minister: José María Aznar. *2004–present*: Spanish Socialist Workers' Party (PSOE) government. Prime Minister: José Luis Rodríguez Zapatero.
Sweden	*Prior to 1991*: Social Democratic Party (SDA)-led coalition. Prime Minister (from 1986): Ingvar Carlsson (SDA). *1991–4*: Moderate Party (MUP)-led coalition. Prime Minister: Carl Bildt (MUP). *1996–2006*: Social Democratic Party (SDA)-led coalition. Prime Minister: Göran Persson (SDA).
Switzerland	Permanent grand coalition. *Prior to 2003*: Federal Council formed according to the "magic formula" as follows: Free Democratic Party (FDP): 2 members; Christian Democratic People's Party (CVP): 2 members; Social Democratic Party (SPS): 2 members; Swiss People's Party (SVP): 1 member. *Since 2003*: 1 seat reallocated from CVP to SVP.

Source: Constructed by the author.

---

[30] Contrary to the impression given by its name, the Portuguese Social Democratic Party (Partido Social Democrata, PSD) is a party of the center-right.

2

A Theory of Partisanship and Corporate Governance Change

This book offers an explanation of firm-level corporate governance change in nonliberal market economies in terms of the interaction between party politics and domestic product market competition. The specific theoretical claims may be stated as follows:

Proposition one: In economies in which incumbent producer interests benefit from significant economic rents, there will be no discernible relationship between partisanship and corporate governance outcomes. Both Left and conservative government will be associated with a blockholder model of corporate governance.

Proposition two: In economies in which economic rents have been eroded due to high levels of product market competition, changes in corporate governance outcomes will be associated with partisanship. Specifically, Left government will be associated with shifts from a blockholder to a shareholder model of corporate governance. Conservative government will continue to be more associated with the blockholder model.

In other words, party politics matters in competitive market conditions, but not otherwise. The second half of this chapter provides a detailed justification of these theoretical claims. However, this is preceded by a discussion of the manner in which two key terms – "corporate governance change" and "economic rents" – are conceptualized by the analysis. It is important to clarify these terms, as European corporate governance change represents the dependent variable under examination in this book, whilst economic rents – via their interaction with partisanship – are the key explanatory variable.

2.1 CHANGE IN CORPORATE GOVERNANCE OUTCOMES – BETWEEN BLOCKHOLDER AND SHAREHOLDER MODELS

One of the most frequently cited definitions of corporate governance in the economics literature is that of Andrei Shleifer and Robert Vishny (1997: 737): "Corporate governance deals with the ways in which suppliers of finance to corporations assure themselves of getting a return on their investment." Such a definition locates the origin of the corporate governance problem in the separation of ownership and control of the joint stock company. This problem was given succinct expression by Adam Smith in *The Wealth of Nations* (1776).

Being the managers rather of other people's money than of their own, it cannot well be expected that they should watch over it with the same anxious vigilance with which the partners in a private copartnery frequently watch over their own. Like the stewards of a rich man, they are apt to consider attention to small matters as not for their master's honour, and very easily give themselves a dispensation from having it. Negligence and profusion, therefore, must always prevail, more or less, in the management of the affairs of such a company.[1]

Two-and-a-half centuries later, the underlying dilemma remains the same: Corporate owners who are no longer directly involved in the direction of the corporation must delegate discretionary power over company resources to designated agents (company management). However, how can the owners be sure that this power is not being used to further the interests of the managers themselves – or other social actors that can exert power over managers? *Quis custodiet ipsos custodes.*[2]

The issue of agency costs arising from the principal–agent relationship within a firm has been central to the modern theories of corporate governance and corporate finance since the 1980s, following a series of pathbreaking papers by Jensen and Meckling (1976), Myers (1977), and Ross (1977). Economists had previously conceived of economic agents operating within an equilibrium world of perfectly competitive frictionless markets, unhampered by taxes, transactions costs, and information asymmetries (Arrow and Debreu 1954). In such a world, it was assumed that relationships between managers and owners were perfectly contractable, and therefore agency

---

[1] Adam Smith (1776), *An Inquiry into the Nature and Causes of the Wealth of Nations*, book V, chapter 1.

[2] "Who watches the watchmen?" (Juvenal, *Sixth Satire*), an issue notably discussed in Plato's *Republic* in relation to the Guardians of the state.

A Theory of Partisanship and Corporate Governance Change 35

problems would not arise. However, in the real world, there exist significant asymmetries of information between managers and external owners, for example, concerning the firm's technology, business environment, and earning's prospects. Recognition of the importance of agency costs to real-world institutional structures and behavior has allowed economists to incorporate corporate governance as a central component in the modern theory of finance (Tirole 2006: 1).

According to finance theory, two distinct models of corporate governance are available to overcome the problem of managerial agency costs: the blockholder model and the shareholder model (Gourevitch and Shinn 2005: 4). Some of the key characteristics of the two models are summarized in Table 2.1.

According to the blockholder model, the owners of capital seek to obviate agency costs by establishing a significant degree of direct control over the management of individual public companies, normally through ownership of a large proportion of the company's equity capital (Stiglitz 1985; Allen and Gale 2000). Unlike in a company with a diversified ownership base, such an ownership strategy minimizes the separation of ownership and control between managers and owners. In such circumstances, both management and the dominant blockholder can be viewed as company "insiders" in the sense that they are able to exert direct control over the company's assets and activities.

Table 2.1 Shareholder and blockholder models of corporate governance

	Shareholder model	Blockholder model
Ownership and control	Diversified ownership.	Controlling owner.
Types of owner	Professional money managers.	Families, nonfinancial corporations, banks, the state.
Minority shareholder protection	Strong.	Weak.
Board	Often close to management.	Close to controlling owner.
Management power	Strong, autonomous.	Weak, close to controlling owner.
Management incentives	Determined by market signals in capital markets.	Directly supervised by controlling owner.
Management behavior	Shareholder value maximization.	Dependent on preferences of controlling owner.
Bank relations	Arm's length, diversified, no ownership.	Close, concentrated, possible ownership.
Capital structure	Lower ratio of debt-to-equity.	Higher ratio of debt-to-equity.
Market for corporate control	Hostile bids important.	Hostile bids rare.
Political power of owners	Weak, indirect.	Strong, direct.

A public company whose ownership is dominated by blockholders occupies, in effect, an intermediate position between a private company on the one hand, and a public company with diffuse ownership on the other. In the former case, the owner (e.g., the founding entrepreneur) normally enjoys full control over the company through ownership of a sizeable proportion of the company's equity. However, the lack of a public listing restricts access to external capital. In the case of a public company with diffuse ownership, a stock market listing facilitates access to external equity financing from capital markets, however there are no longer control rights enjoyed by any single investor (Hellwig 2000). By securing control rights over a public company, therefore, blockholders seek to achieve the best of both the private and public corporate worlds that is by gaining access to the increased financing opportunities associated with a public listing, and retention of the control rights typically enjoyed by the owners of private companies (Hellwig 2000: 101). Such an ownership structure has been characteristic of many public companies in the postwar corporate sectors of nonliberal market economies, particularly in continental Europe (Becht and Mayer 2001).

In contrast, the shareholder model is preferred by investors unwilling to assume the role of blockholder, and with relatively small equity participations in individual companies. Mizruchi and Bey (2005) describe such a system as "capitalism without capitalists." Minority shareholders tend to be passive holders of a company's stock, and are not generally able to influence company performance directly, for example, by exerting pressure on company management.[3] Unless explicit legal or regulatory safeguards exist to safeguard their interests (described in the legal studies literature as Quality Corporate Law or minority shareholder protection), minority shareholders' main channel of influence over company management is through the effect of aggregate buying and selling decisions on company share prices, which play a role in determining the vulnerability of firms to hostile takeover bids (Alchian and Kessel 1962; Manne 1965; Gordon 2007), and their access to external financing from capital markets. The main sanction of minority shareholders *vis-à-vis* management is, therefore, to exercise a policy of "exit" rather than "voice" (Hirschman 1970). Alfred Chandler (1977) depicts the shift in approach from a blockholder to a shareholder model of corporate governance

---

[3] Activist fund management – in which fund managers use their ownership stakes to exert direct pressure on management – is only a niche (albeit growing) ownership style amongst professional money managers in liberal market economies. The main exponents of such an approach have traditionally been the managers of public sector workers' pension funds, such as CalPERS and TIAA-CREF in the United States, and Hermes in the United Kingdom (Gourevitch and Shinn 2005: 240). However, in recent years, activist strategies have also been pursued by hedge funds (Schurr 2006; Cheffins 2007).

– which occurred in the United States in the early twentieth century, and is now typical of corporate governance in liberal market economies – as the transfer of control from the "visible hand" of company insiders (blockholders), to the "invisible hand" of company outsiders, that is, minority shareholders and capital market.

In order to pursue a blockholder strategy, it is necessary for investors to take substantial positions in the stock of individual companies. Although equity participation in excess of 50 percent of the votable stock guarantees control, it is often possible to achieve effective control with significantly smaller blockholdings (e.g., 15–20% or less). This is possible, for example, if the blockholder is able to coordinate the voting activities of smaller shareholders. Alternatively, the firm may permit issuance of different classes of share, some of which may provide multiple votes at company general meetings. Owners of the latter category of share are hence able to attain control whist owning only a relatively small proportion of the total equity capital. Smaller blockholdings may also be sufficient for effective control due to the collective action problem faced by minority shareholders, who are often unable to mobilize and coordinate the support of their fellow minority shareholders against the wishes of a large blockholder. This problem is particularly salient if the ownership stakes of individual minority shareholders are low (e.g., below 3% of a firm's total market capitalization), as is typical of an institutional investor in a liberal market economy.

The portfolio diversification strategy of a minority shareholder is fundamentally different to that of a blockholder. The former seeks to avoid high levels of concentration risk arising from taking large positions in individual firms. By investing in the equity of a large number of companies, minority shareholders seek to benefit from the diversification benefits identified by modern portfolio theory (Markowitz 1952). However, the price that is paid for such a diffuse ownership strategy is an inability to exert direct control over the management of individual companies. It is necessary for small shareholders to rely on the indirect mechanism of capital market signals and incentives in order to ensure that managers administer the firm in their interests (Davis and Steil 2001). The risks inherent in this approach were first discussed by Adolph Berle and Gardiner Means in their 1932 classic, *The Modern Corporation and Private Property*. Berle and Means (1932) describe how diffuse ownership can create potential agency problems due to the removal of management from the hierarchical control of blockholders.

The distinction between blockholder and shareholder models of corporate governance has been defined so far in terms of ownership strategy rather than institutional form. However, within the major industrialized democracies, it is possible to identify categories of organization that are frequently associated with blockholder or minority shareholder investment strategies. For example, blockholding is generally employed by pyramidal business groups, which are ubiquitous players in the corporate sectors of many continental European economies (La Porta et al. 1999; Morck and Steier 2005). In such a structure, an apex shareholder (often a wealthy family) directly controls a single company (which may or may not be publicly listed), which in turn controls large blockholdings in other companies. A complex web of cross-shareholdings may exist across the corporate sector, although control may ultimately reside with an opaque group of elite actors. Blockholding has also been pursued in many postwar nonliberal market economies by industrial corporations (through cross-shareholdings in other corporations), universal banks (particularly in Germany and Japan), family networks (e.g., the Wallenberg family empire in Sweden, or the Agnelli family in Italy), and the state (e.g., via nationalization or public investment in "strategic" industries). In contrast, the shareholder model is characteristic of institutional investors, such as pension funds, insurance companies, mutual funds, and hedge funds, which dominate the ownership structure of liberal market economies (Useem 1996).

The institutional and regulatory frameworks of blockholder and shareholder models of corporate governance tend to be very different. Once blockholders have acquired control of major companies, there exists little incentive for them to support the introduction of corporate governance safeguards for minority shareholders, for example, independent nonexecutive boards, financial reporting requirements, laws to secure the voting rights of minorities, etc.[4] The potential agency costs generated by a weak financial contracting framework are no longer something to which they are exposed, as they have obviated agency costs by securing direct control over management (Rajan and Zingales 2003).

Indeed, in the absence of regulatory safeguards, blockholders may seek to exploit their position of control to expropriate resources from minority shareholders via a variety of mechanisms. These could take the form of directing management to favor chosen suppliers, choosing management based on non-meritocratic or dynastic considerations, or requiring management to pursue a business strategy based on personal objectives such as growth, empire-building, or philanthropy, rather than profit or value maximization. They may involve instructing management to retain profits within the company – despite a dearth of attractive investment opportunities – rather than returning cash to shareholders through higher dividend payments or share buybacks. At worst, control rights may facilitate the blockholder's

---

[4] This assumes that they are not particularly dependent on external finance. See Section 2.4 for further discussion of this issue.

ability to undertake outright theft of the company's assets, or to indulge in insider trading.[5] Each of these (and many other) forms of self-dealing are harmful to the interests of minority shareholders, and will result in blockholders benefiting disproportionately from their investment in a firm – either in financial or nonfinancial terms – in relation to minority shareholders. They are termed "the private benefits of control" by the corporate governance literature (Aggarwal et al. 2007: 7).

Blockholders often represent the incumbent or dominant domestic players in many sectors of European economies. A major concern of any incumbent is its ability to sustain that position of incumbency against potential competition (Morck and Steier 2005: 40). Incumbents are unlikely to favor policies – such as law and regulation safeguarding the rights of minority shareholders – that reduce the barriers to entry faced by nonincumbents, and thereby increase the competitive pressure on their enterprises. Such an anticompetitive perspective is also likely to color their attitude toward the development of capital markets. Whereas blockholders have already sunk the capital to finance their existing operations, and may be able to finance additional investment from retained earnings or insider networks, capital markets offer the potential for nonincumbents to raise funds for investment, and subsequently threaten the position of existing players. In short, blockholders may not only view pro-minority corporate governance reform and the encouragement of capital markets as unnecessary for their own strategy, but also a threat to their position of incumbency in the domestic corporate sector (Rajan and Zingales 2003).

The capacity of blockholders to retain an institutional environment favorable to their interests is likely to benefit from their superior ability to act as political actors. As Mancur Olson has argued, interest groups composed of small numbers of relatively homogeneous actors can more easily overcome collective action problems than those containing large numbers of diverse enterprises. Such groups will then bargain with other organized interest groups at the expense of those interests that are not able to organize themselves (Olson 1982: 37). As a small and cohesive group of elite actors, blockholders are potentially able to acquire political leverage that can be used to block the

---

[5] The most egregious example of this sort of expropriation in recent years relates to Parmalat — an Italian food and dairy products enterprise — which collapsed in December 2003. The firm was listed on the Milan stock exchange, and controlled by the Tanzi family through a pyramidal ownership structure. During the thirteen years leading up to the collapse, the Tanzis illegally extracted an estimated (13 billion from Parmalat. The methods used to undertake this fraud were relatively straightforward, and included hiding losses, overstating assets, recording nonexistent assets, understating debt, and forging bank documents (Ferrarini and Giudici 2005).

lobbying demands of minority shareholders for law and regulation to promote their interests relative to blockholders (Perotti and Volpin 2007).

In contrast, individual minority shareholders may find it more difficult to achieve a similar level of direct political influence. The low level of their investment positions in individual companies will not accord them the status of major strategic players in a domestic political economy. Furthermore, their lack of long-term commitment to individual companies and, more generally, to national economies is not conducive to a high level of domestic political legitimacy. Within individual political economies, minority shareholders tend to be composed of a large number of individual investors, with a wide diversity of styles and strategies. Just as they face a collective action problem in exerting control over individual companies, minority shareholders face similar difficulties in unifying their interests for the purpose of political lobbying. As Robert Dahl (1958) has argued, for a group to exert influence over the political process, it is not enough that they are collectively powerful; they also need unity. This is less likely to be apparent amongst minority shareholders than amongst an elite group of incumbent controlling shareholders.

The main influence of minority shareholders over the political process arises from their aggregate investment decisions – transmitted through the price-signaling mechanisms of capital markets. In other words, the mechanism used to influence the political system is the same as that used to discipline company management. The ultimate impact of such market signals on political outcomes may well be significant. However, market signals reflect the aggregate preferences of all market participants, and individual actors play a highly decentralized role within this mechanism (Mizruchi and Bey 2005: 330). It is, therefore, difficult for minority shareholders to operate as a cohesive political actor capable of determining corporate governance outcomes, either individually or through participation in domestic distributional coalitions with other organized social actors.[6]

The distinction between the blockholder and shareholder models of corporate governance is not the only taxonomy of corporate governance to have emerged from the academic and nonacademic literature. Recent surveys of

---

[6] In the view of early economic sociologists such as Daniel Bell (1960) and Talcott Parsons (1969), the decline of blockholding in early-twentieth-century America was a positive development for American democracy. The "elite pluralism" described by Schumpeter (1943), Galbraith (1952), and Lipset (1962) was only compatible with democracy if elite groups — such as the owners of capital — were fundamentally divided amongst themselves. The decomposition of blockholdings in America reduced the ability of the captains of industry to run politics, and was hence a substantial improvement on the concentrated industrial structure of American capitalism between 1890 and 1920, when individuals such as J. P. Morgan, John D. Rockefeller, George F. Baker, and James Stillman exerted significant influence (Mizruchi 1981).

the field by Hawley and Williams (2000), Shleifer and Vishny (1997), Turnbull (1997), Keasey et al. (1997), and Letza et al. (2004) document a range of possibilities.[7] However, the most common alternative categorization (the stakeholder – shareholder distinction) demarcates between corporate governances systems on the basis of corporate behavior rather than agency cost considerations (Kakabadse and Kakabadse 2001; Friedman and Miles 2002; O'Sullivan 2003). Firms within a shareholder system maximize profits in the interests of private shareholders (Hayek and Streissler 1969; Friedman 1970).[8] In contrast, the firm in a "stakeholder" system is motivated by broader obligations to a wider range of stakeholders (e.g., employees, suppliers, customers, creditors, the state, and local community), and may be conceptualized as a social entity rather than a "nexus of contracts" for the optimization of private interests (Freeman 1984; Hutton 1995).

The shareholder–stakeholder distinction is insightful from a descriptive and normative perspective. It reflects the idea that the importance of corporate governance lies in its implications for corporate behavior and the role played by the corporation in modern society. However, it is not the main typology utilized in empirical studies in the law and financial economics literature, which favor the shareholder–blockholder distinction. The neglect of the shareholder–stakeholding conception arises from the difficulty in operationalizing a concept such as stakeholding in a positivist analysis of corporate governance. There is no agreement, for example, regarding which actors are the legitimate stakeholders of a firm in each social context, and how the differing interests of these actors should be measured, aggregated, and compared across countries (Donaldson 1989).

Furthermore, there is a sense in which blockholding and stakeholding are related concepts. In order to pursue a stakeholder approach to corporate governance, blockholding is a necessary prerequisite. A controlling shareholder is at liberty to operate the firm in a manner that involves the fulfillment of broader social responsibilities rather than profit maximization. Such a preference may arise due to altruism, political pressure from other social actors, or culturally generated norms of behavior. The result is a shielding of management from the imperatives of capital markets (e.g., regarding fulfillment of short-term earnings forecasts). In contrast, managers of firms

---

[7] Hawley and Williams (1996), for example, distinguish between the finance model, the stewardship model, the stakeholder model, and the political model. Keasey et al. (1997: 244) identify the principal–agent model, the myopic market model, the abuse of executive power model, and the shareholder model.

[8] Such corporations follow the well-known advice of Milton Friedman (1970): "There is one and only one social responsibility of business — to use its resources and engage in activities designed to increase its profits."

operating within the shareholder model have less scope for behavioral flexibility. A policy of "corporate social responsibility" that is genuinely deleterious to the interests of shareholders, and not just a self-serving public relations exercise, will be punished through the disapproval of capital markets, for example, a lower share price, increased risk of takeover, higher cost of capital, etc. Stakeholding, therefore, is dependent on a blockholder model of corporate governance, and a commitment to benevolent ownership amongst blockholders.

In summary, the theoretical propositions advanced by this book conceive of "corporate governance change" as representing a process of adjustment from a blockholder to a shareholder model of corporate governance by the firms of a national political economy.

2.2 THE NATURE OF ECONOMIC RENTS

Continental European economies are frequently depicted as sustaining high levels of economic rents relative to the liberal market economies. For example, Alberto Alesina and Francesco Giavazzi (2006: 6) assert in a recent book: "In Europe incumbent firms enjoy large rents. They rarely close down, and potential entrants face high barriers.... The result is that there is insufficient innovation and no 'creative destruction' by which the natural disappearance of less efficient firms leaves room for more efficient ones."

The notion of economic rent was first introduced by David Ricardo in the early nineteenth century in the context of his Law of Rent on land.[9] It is typically defined as a payment for the services of an economic resource which is not necessary as an incentive for its production (Black 2002: 135). From an efficiency perspective, therefore, such a payment may be regarded as a superfluous or "unnecessary" transfer to a producer, given that the good or service would anyway have been produced at a lower price or level of payment (Kay 2003: 283).

Economic rents occur in uncompetitive product markets, and arise due to the market power of producers vis-à-vis consumers. Such power allows producers to charge a price for their products in excess of the price that would pertain in competitive market conditions. However, market power erodes if new producers enter the market, and the business environment

[9] Ricardo defined land rent as the economic return accruing to land purely on account of its natural features or location, that is in excess of the return available on marginal land that could fulfill the same function with similar investment of labor and capital (Blaug 1997).

A Theory of Partisanship and Corporate Governance Change

becomes more competitive. In such conditions, producers are incentivized to cut their prices, and thereby reduce their capacity to generate economic rents. The magnitude of economic rent, therefore, is a negative function of the intensity of product market competition.

Measurement of economic rent requires a counterfactual comparison of existing market prices or rates of return with those that would have prevailed in the same market under competitive market conditions. However, this begs the question of what constitutes "competitive market conditions." According to traditional neoclassical economic theory, the appropriate benchmark for comparison is the level of prices pertaining in a perfectly competitive market situation. In such conditions, all firms are price-takers, and the equilibrium price level equates to marginal costs. Economic rents are, therefore, a consequence of market prices exceeding marginal costs.

Figure 2.1 reproduces the static welfare analysis of perfect competition found in introductory economics textbooks. When prices are equated to marginal costs, the magnitude of the consumer surplus – the aggregate benefit obtained by consumers for goods and service in excess of the amount paid for them – is maximized. Increasing the price to a higher level (i.e., above marginal cost) serves to increase the size of the producer surplus – the aggregate benefit received by producers from selling goods and services in excess of marginal cost (see Figure 2.2). This additional benefit to producers can be regarded as economic rent. However, it arises at the cost of a reduced consumer surplus.

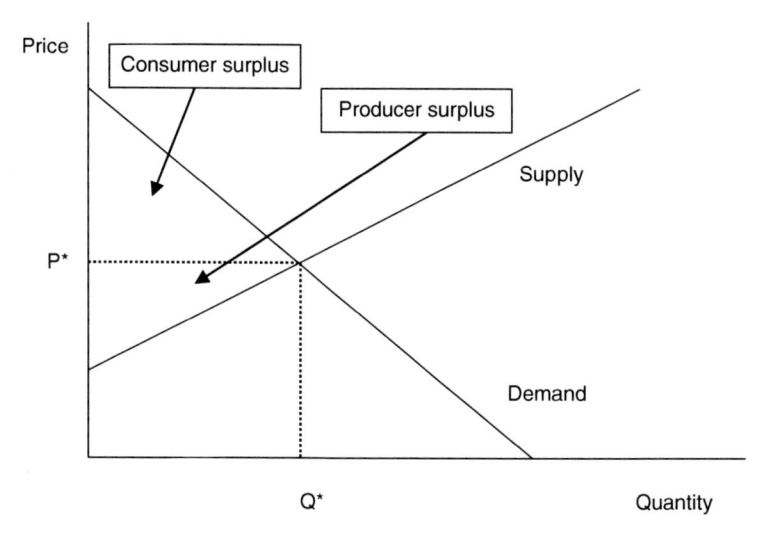

Figure 2.1 Consumer and producer surplus in competitive market conditions

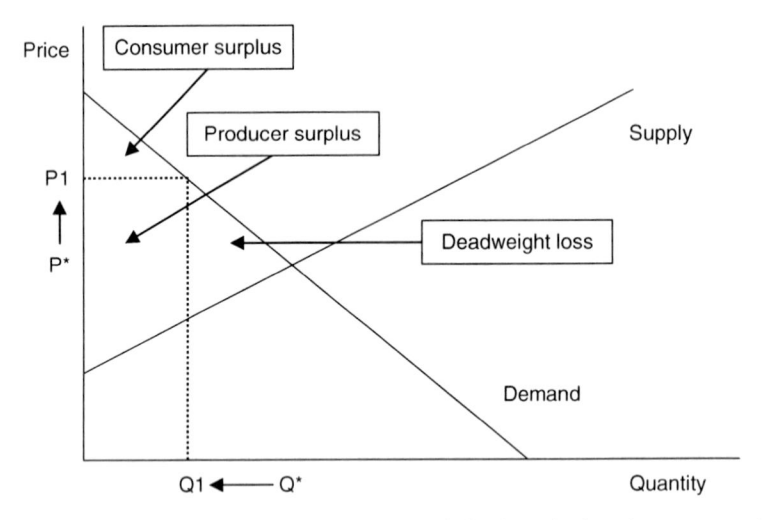

Figure 2.2 Producer and consumer surplus and deadweight loss in uncompetitive market conditions

Furthermore, the magnitude of the reduction in the consumer surplus is greater than the increase in the size of the producer surplus, resulting in a "deadweight loss" to society. Although this is not a reduction in welfare in a Paretian sense (i.e., it has not been an unambiguous loss in welfare for all social actors), consumers have lost more than what producers have gained. In addition, the public choice literature has argued that the process of rent-seeking – whereby producers spend time and money trying to persuade government and regulators to favor their interests – serves to reduce welfare even further through the dissipation of the producer surplus (Posner 1975).

The implication of this type of static neoclassical economic analysis – and the thrust of antitrust policy in many economies – is that economic rents are a "bad thing," and should be reduced as much as possible through the application of policies to enhance product market competition. However, this is not the only interpretation of the welfare implications of economic rents. The static analysis in Figure 2.1 is based on the assumption that the existing distribution of resources in society is regarded as appropriate. One purpose served by economic rent generation is to redistribute resources from one group of social actors to another. If such a redistribution is regarded as legitimate transfer of resources by society at large, then the positive impact of economic rents in terms of social equity may outweigh the negative impact in terms of efficiency considerations (Carlton and Perloff 2005: 84). It cannot, therefore, be assumed that economic rents are unambiguously detrimental to social welfare.

Perfect competition may be too stringent a benchmark for the calculation of economic rents. First, it is achievable only under the most unrealistic of assumptions. These include the existence of a large number of price-taking firms, selling identical products based on perfect information, and with no transaction costs or externalities. In the real world, such assumptions are an unattainable ideal for most types of product market. Second, it may be reasonable for firms to set prices above marginal costs – and thereby generate profits – in order to provide them with incentives to innovate and invest. The existence of profits, that is, revenues in excess of costs, therefore, may not be synonymous with the existence of economic rents (Motta 2004).

Regardless of whether perfect competition or a less stringent definition of competition is utilized as a benchmark for economic rent generation, it is often difficult to determine the level of prices that would have prevailed in the counterfactual situation of "competitive market conditions." Consequently, it is difficult to make a direct calculation of the value of economic rents. The normal procedure in empirical work is to estimate their relative (not absolute) magnitude in terms of proxy variables that are indicative of the extent of product market competition in various markets or political economies. Such proxies include, *inter alia*, price levels, measures of profitability, the number and concentration of producers, and the ease of entry and exit for market participants. Potential empirical proxies for product market competition are discussed in detail in Chapter 5.

2.3 CORPORATE GOVERNANCE AND ECONOMIC RENTS

Economic rents are viewed in the corporate governance literature as a source of potential agency costs for shareholders. In cases where firms have access to significant rents (due to low levels of competition), there is a greater risk of expropriation, wastage, or inefficient use of resources by managers. At the very least, high levels of economic rents provide a cushion of revenues that facilitate managerial shirking (Nickell 1999: 12). As Nobel laureate economist John Hicks (1935) puts it, "the best of all monopoly profits is a quiet life." Economic rents allow managers to administer the firm in a relatively inefficient manner without significant consequences. For example, even if the firm operates below potential, there are still surplus funds available for business investment. However, in a firm without access to economic rents, managers either have to generate investment funds through high levels of efficiency or rely on capital markets for funds, thereby increasing their accountability to external investors. In both cases, the pressure on managers to operate the firm in an efficient manner is increased, and this serves to increase the alignment of their interests with those of shareholders (i.e., reduce agency costs). The competitiveness of product markets, in effect, exerts a form of corporate governance discipline over managers similar to that provided by a falling share price or the threat of takeover (Rey and Tirole 1986; Scharfstein 1988; Hermalin 1992; Jagannathan and Srinivasan 2000).

Mark Roe (2003) suggests an additional concern for an economy with high levels of economic rents. In such an economy, other corporate stakeholders – particularly employees – will wish to benefit from these rents. If these actors are politically powerful, they will attempt to exert influence over management – for example, via legislation, the regulatory system or through the advocacy of particular norms of behavior – as a means of incentivizing management to operate the firm in a manner that favors their interests. In short, the desire of other stakeholders to obtain a share of economic rents will increase the number of social actors seeking to assert themselves in the authority structure of the firm, and thereby increase managerial agency costs for minority shareholders (Roe 2003: 131).

According to Roe's argument, the agency costs arising from economic rents make the shareholder model an impracticable model of corporate governance for company owners in an environment of uncompetitive product markets. Owners doubt that the arm's-length discipline of capital markets over management will be sufficient in such circumstances to safeguard their interests relative to other stakeholders (Stiglitz 1985). Although ownership of large stakes in an individual company creates significant concentration risk for investors, they nonetheless prefer to take such stakes in order to exert direct control over management, and ensure that economic rents are not dissipated by managers or other social actors. According to this logic, the blockholder model represents the most effective way for owners to benefit from economic rents, based on a realistic assessment of the ability of differing corporate governance systems to reduce agency costs (Roe 2003: 132). Such an analysis suggests an inverse relationship between blockholding and product market competition. A similar relationship has also been suggested by Rajan and Zingales (2003) and Stulz (2005), who predict a positive correlation between trade and the development of stock markets, based on Olson's argument (1982) that greater trade openness gives rise to greater domestic competition. These predictions appear supported by Figure 2.3, which plots a measure of

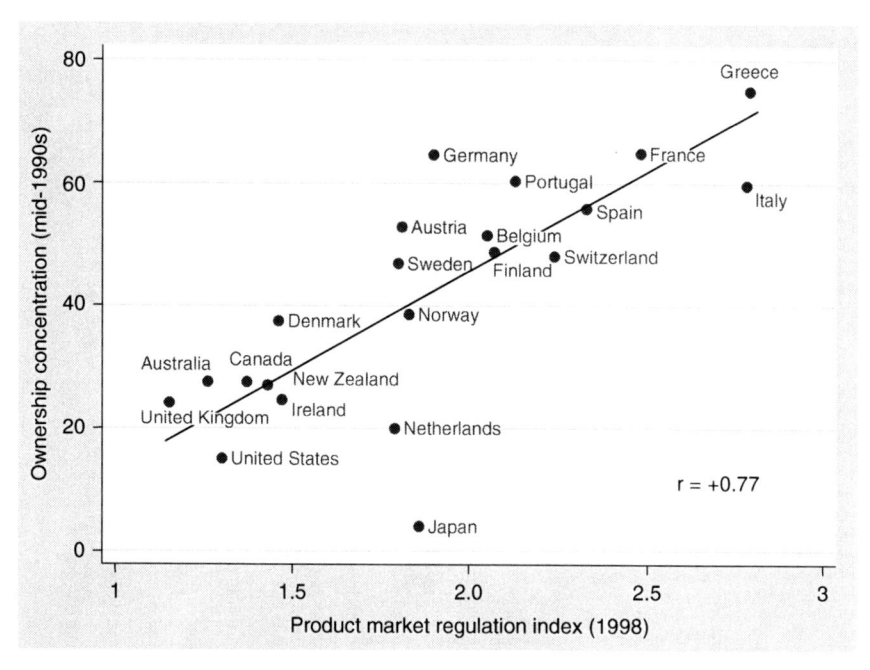

Figure 2.3 Ownership concentration (early to mid-1990s) and product market competition (1998)

product market competition (lower values of which imply greater competition)[10] against a cross-sectional measure of the extent of blockholding.

However, blockholders are not necessarily the only corporate stakeholders that benefit from economic rents. A political constraint that has shaped blockholder behavior during much of the postwar period is succinctly expressed by Mark Roe (2003: 1): "Before a nation can produce, it must achieve social peace." In a democracy, such peace is unlikely to be attained if blockholders retain all the benefit of economic rents for themselves, particularly as workers have to pay the price of uncompetitive product markets in their role as consumers. One way of appeasing potentially adversarial social actors is through the sharing of economic rents via some kind of cross-class distributional coalition. In particular, blockholder employers can share rents with employees through higher wages, improved job security, or a willingness to accept lower rates of labor productivity (Kwoka 1983; Freeman and Medoff 1984; Karier 1985). The practice of such

---

[10] Various means of operationalizing product market competition — including the PMR index presented earlier — are discussed in detail in Chapter 5. Note that a lower value of the PMR index in Figure 2.3 is indicative of a higher level of actual product market competition.

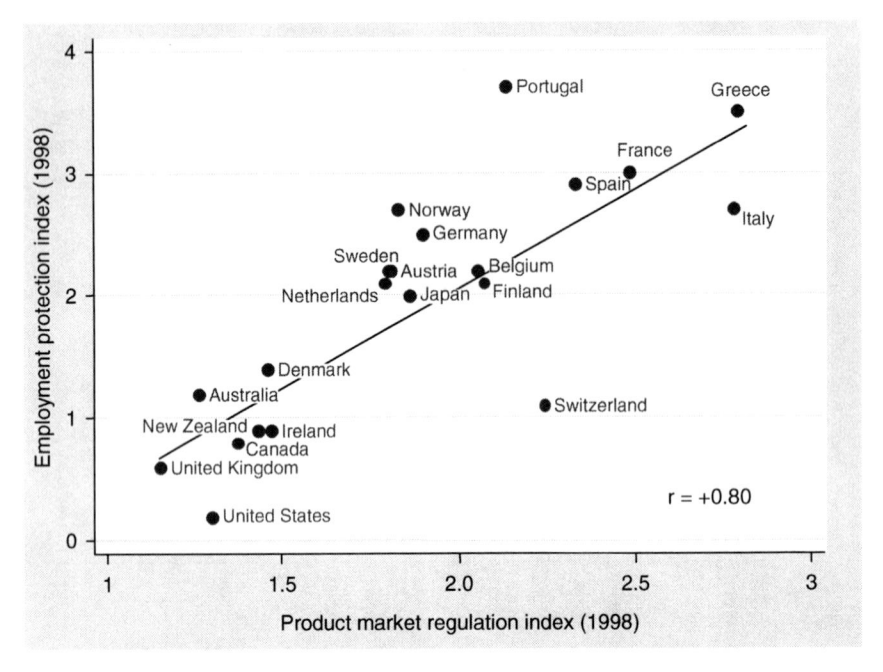

48 Corporate Governance, Competition, and Political Parties

Figure 2.4 Product market competition and employment protection index (1998)

"enlightened" capitalism is tolerable to blockholders, as it serves to "buy off" a potential source of political opposition regarding the social undesirability of uncompetitive product markets or inadequate corporate governance protections for minority shareholders. The result is that both blockholders and employees share a common interest in sustaining the status quo of high rents and blockholder self-regulation in the domestic corporate sector.

A link between the competitiveness of product markets and the employment conditions of employees is strongly supported by the labor economics literature. For example, a well-established empirical finding is that employees in economies or sectors with relatively low levels of competition enjoy higher wages than those employed in companies operating in more competitive markets. Jean and Nicoletti's conclusion (2002: 4) from their survey of the literature and their own empirical analysis is that "there is abundant evidence of a positive relationship between product market rents (or measures of market power) and wage premia."[11] Figure 2.4 shows that there also exists a

---

[11] Economic studies highlighting the significant empirical link between economic rents and wage premia include: Katz and Summers (1989), Nickell et al. (1994), Blanchflower et al. (1996), Nickell (1999), and Jean and Nicoletti (2002).

A Theory of Partisanship and Corporate Governance Change

Table 2.2 Employment stability in liberal and nonliberal market economies (1990)

	Median tenure in present job (years)	Average tenure in present job (years)
Germany	7.5	10.4
United Kingdom	4.4	7.9
Japan	8.2	10.9
United States	3.0	6.7

Note: German figures exclude apprentices. Figures relate to 1990.
Source: OECD Employment Outlook, July 1993.

strong cross-country association between levels of product market competition and levels of employment protection (Conway et al. 2005: 31). This is further reflected in Table 2.2, which shows that employees in nonliberal economies enjoy a greater degree of employment stability compared to their peers in liberal market economies (which have more competitive product markets). All of these findings strongly suggest that incumbent blockholders are not the only beneficiaries of economic rents derived from uncompetitive product markets. Rents are shared – to some degree at least – with labor market actors (Barker and Rueda 2007).

Although a distributional coalition between blockholders and employees may facilitate the preservation of social stability, it would be a mistake to assume that it distributes economic rents in a distributionally neutral manner. As Jack Knight (1992) has argued, even if political institutions appear to fulfill a public-good role in a relatively benevolent fashion, they may still favor certain social actors rather than others. In fact, neoclassical economic theory suggests that the welfare of the average employee would be greatest with completely competitive product markets (i.e., zero economic rents), as this would maximize the real wages of workers (due to the lower product prices they would encounter as consumers), and minimize levels of unemployment (due to the setting of wages at levels that would clear labor markets) (Blanchard and Giavazzi 2003). The presence of economic rents causes a deviation from this optimal state, and creates a political economy of winners and losers.

Amongst owners of capital, the winners will be incumbent blockholders (insider capital), who are able to secure a significant share of economic rents through the higher revenues or profits of their enterprises. The losers will be minority shareholders (outsider capital), who – despite owning stakes in corporations earning high levels of economic rents – are vulnerable to expropriation by blockholders through the mechanisms described in Section

2.1 unless they are explicitly protected by minority shareholder legislation. Such expropriation may result in minority shareholders earning financial returns that are disproportionately smaller than those of blockholders, and are unable to secure a significant share of any economic rents that are flowing into the firm (Pagano and Volpin 2005).

What is less explicitly discussed in the political economy literature is the precise identity of winners and losers amongst labor actors. The argument of this book is that the winners are likely to be so-called insider labor, a cleavage of labor identified and discussed in the recent work of David Rueda (2005, 2006, 2007) and Barker and Rueda (2007). This group consists of labor market participants enjoying secure or protected employment, arising from such factors as employment protection legislation, the high cost to a company of hiring and firing such workers, the valued nature of their human capital, and the strength of their union representation.[12] Employees with such established jobs-in-place are in a position to negotiate and organize within established collective bargaining frameworks and wider political institutions to secure a share of economic rents through the various types of improved employment conditions discussed earlier.

The position of insider labor contrasts with workers in a number of increasingly significant labor market groups. One such group consists of workers that are holding jobs that are relatively precarious due to low levels of employment security, a lack of labor market representation, or who are unemployed or have withdrawn from the labor market altogether. However, perhaps more importantly from the perspective of political influence and mobilization, insider labor also excludes growing numbers of nonunionized middle-class or white-collar workers, employed in professional, managerial or high value-added service-sector roles. Many of these noninsider labor market groups will be losers from the distributional coalition between insider capital and insider labor, as they are often not significant actors in the collective mediation frameworks that structure negotiations with blockholders for a share of economic rents. Furthermore, in their role as consumers, they suffer the negative implications of a lack of competition in product markets due to the necessity of paying higher domestic prices for goods and services.[13]

In terms of the static welfare analysis of Figures 2.1 and 2.2, a distributional coalition between insider labor and controlling shareholders – and its

---

[12] See Rueda (2007: chapter 2) for a more detailed description of the characteristics of insider labor.
[13] They are losers in an economy which Rogowski and Kayser (2002) describe as exhibiting a producer (as opposed to a consumer) orientation.

associated self-regulatory blockholder model of corporate governance — distributes the producer surplus extracted from consumers (via a lower consumer surplus) amongst blockholder and insider labor actors, to the detriment of minority shareholders and noninsider labor. Consequently, although such an insider-oriented political economy may facilitate the desirable public goods of social stability and cross-class cooperation, it may also be viewed as an institutionalized means of extracting rents from noninsider actors, and passing the benefit of these rents to insiders. This is the context in which the relationship between partisanship and change in corporate governance is now examined.

2.4 THE ARGUMENT: INTERACTION OF PARTISANSHIP AND PRODUCT MARKET COMPETITION

The relationship between corporate governance change and partisanship in this chapter is conceived in terms of the interaction between three social actors or corporate stakeholders: insider labor, blockholders, and outsiders. Each of these stakeholder groups is assumed to have a distinct preference regarding the nature of corporate governance outcomes in a political economy.[14]

The first two groups of stakeholders have already been defined. Insider labor's main concern as a corporate stakeholder is likely to relate to the labor market rights and protections of its insider labor constituents. Consequently, it is likely to support the introduction of codetermination or employment protection legislation. Blockholders are already in a strong position to wield significant influence in company affairs due to their controlling ownership stakes in individual corporations. Their main concern with respect to corporate governance is retention of the status quo of blockholder self-regulation. Blockholders wish to ensure that their position of direct power over

---

[14] The taxonomy of social agents presented in this section is an adaptation of the schema utilized by Pagano and Volpin (2005). Pagano and Volpin outline a formal model in terms of three social agents: rentiers, entrepreneurs, and workers. Entrepreneurs are identical to blockholders. However, no distinction is made in Pagano and Volpin's schema between insider labor and other types of workers. Furthermore, the rentiers group only relates to outsider shareholders, and does not include noncapital actors, for example, employees, that might also favor pro-shareholder corporate governance (Pagano and Volpin 2005: 1006). In contrast to the analytical framework described by Gourevitch and Shinn (2005), management is not defined as a separate social agent. In a blockholder-oriented system of corporate governance (the starting point of this analysis) management has limited autonomy to pursue its own corporate governance agenda — due to the direct control of blockholders — and is therefore not treated as an independent social actor.

corporations is not compromised by the granting of excessive protections or veto powers to other social actors or stakeholders.

The final stakeholder group (outsiders) is defined as a residual category of social actors favoring a shareholder model of corporate governance. Such a nonhomogeneous group consists of both capital and labor actors. Outsider capital includes all actual and potential owners of firms that are not blockholders, such as institutional investors, foreign investors, small private investors, and potential new entrepreneurs seeking capital. Such shareholders represent unambiguous beneficiaries of more shareholder-oriented corporate governance, both due to the greater financial returns arising from improved minority protections and greater access to capital market sources of funds. Labor actors classed as outsiders include all consumers that are not employed as insider labor. Such actors must pay higher prices (or suffer from inferior consumer choice) due to lack of competition in product markets. However, as employees, they receive no benefit in terms of higher wages or job security from the resulting economic rents. They are likely to view blockholder self-regulation of corporate governance as protective of incumbent's market power over product markets, and favor pro-shareholder corporate governance reform as a means of improving consumer welfare.

It is assumed that political parties act as political representatives of particular corporate stakeholders in negotiations over the distribution of economic rents (Roe 2003, ch.18). It is thus consistent with an approach to political science known as "partisan theory," which views democratic politics as a market in which parties and governments deliver policy outcomes in exchange for the support of social constituencies (Parsons 1959; Hibbs 1992: 316).

The main political parties of the Left (i.e., social democratic or labor parties, but not Green parties or parties of the extreme Left) are assumed to represent the interests of insider labor, for example, by promoting the introduction of employment protection legislation or codetermination rights (Rueda 2007: 16). The main conservative parties (including many Christian Democratic parties, but not parties of the extreme Right) are assumed to be representative of incumbent blockholders, for example, by supporting the activities of employer associations in collective bargaining arrangements.

It is important to stress that the assumption that blockholders are the core constituents of conservative political parties is specific to nonliberal market economies. Given the traditional domination of the corporate sector of such economies by blockholders – and the minor role played by outsider capital – this appears to be a reasonable assumption to make. However, as Helen Callaghan emphasizes in a recent paper, in a liberal market economy (e.g., the United Kingdom or the United States) – where outsider capital dominates corporate ownership – it would be a less realistic assumption (Callaghan

A Theory of Partisanship and Corporate Governance Change 53

2007: 9). The hypothesis of this book is, therefore, specifically applicable to nonliberal market economies; it assumes that blockholders are key social actors, and therefore represent a significant political constituency.

The third stakeholder group (outsiders) is assumed to differ from insider labor and blockholders in not forming the core constituency of a political party due to its lack of social homogeneity (Pagano and Volpin 2005: 1007). Although new political parties seeking the support of emerging social cleavages have become more prominent in European political systems during the last few decades – most notably Green parties and parties of the Far Right – European politics continues to be dominated by parties that arose during an earlier political era to represent the interests of the main postwar social actors, such as insider labor and insider capital (Lipset and Rokkan 1967; Mair 2001). It is beyond the scope of this book to explain why established parties have proved resilient to the challenge of newcomers (see Webb et al. [2002]). All that is assumed here is that it is invariably necessary for outsiders to express their political preferences by voting for established political parties of which they are not the traditional core constituents.

There are two reasons why – in an environment of significant economic rents – the blockholder model is unlikely to be replaced by a shareholder model of corporate governance. First, it is unlikely that either the Left or conservative parties will support such a change. Company owners regard the blockholder model as an effective means of reducing agency costs and safeguarding their claim over economic rents. Consequently, conservative parties in government are likely to support the retention of the blockholding model. However, Left parties are also likely to support the blockholder model due to the willingness of blockholders to share the benefits of economic rents with insider labor. Left parties in government will not wish to undermine this mutually beneficial distributional coalition. Consequently, they will also favor retention of the status quo model of blockholder corporate governance. In short, although conservative parties and the Left may have differing priorities in terms of the distribution of economic rents between blockholder and insider labor, corporate governance change will not be a major issue of party politics.

Second, economic rents increase the value of the private benefits of control to blockholders. Consequently, blockholders will be reluctant to give up the self-regulatory blockholder model, even when legislation and regulation favoring minority shareholders are introduced to motivate such a change. Blockholders will have an incentive to continue as before until the private benefits of control are exceeded by the costs of defying shareholder protection law. The implication of such blockholder cost–benefit analysis is that the magnitude of legislative and regulatory reform necessary to achieve a given amount of firm-level corporate governance change (particularly in terms of the resources required for law enforcement) will be greater in an environment of high economic rents.

For both of these reasons – relating to the policy preferences of partisan actors and factors affecting the ease with which *de jure* corporate governance reform can be translated into actual firm-level corporate governance change – a significant association between partisanship and *de facto* corporate governance change is not predicted in an environment of uncompetitive product markets.

Consider now the effect of an exogenously driven increase in product market competition. This implies that economic rents decline to much lower levels. This is a negative development for incumbent company owners. They are no longer able to benefit from the cushioning effects of rents. Furthermore, the erosion of rents makes it increasingly difficult to sustain a social compromise with insider labor, as there is no longer a surplus which can be shared. This point is expressed by the International Monetary Fund (IMF) in a recent report on structural reform: "The weaker pricing power by firms in competitive product markets reduces the rents to be shared between producers and workers" (Helbling et al. 2004: 123).

The overriding concern of company owners – in such increasingly challenging economic conditions – is to find ways to sustain a decent return from their investments. To that end, they will instruct their managers to operate firms in a more commercial and less socially "enlightened" manner. Firms will become more aggressive about managing their cost base, and less willing to cushion employees from employment insecurity during downturns in the business cycle. Furthermore, they will be reluctant to offer wage premia that do not reflect localized productivity conditions. In short, mutual expectations regarding employment conditions – that previously reflected the sharing of economic rents between blockholders and employees – become disregarded by company management. Companies operate in a fashion that is increasingly akin to the management style of corporations in liberal market economies.

However, this does not mean that owners will favor a reform of corporate governance toward the shareholder model. Although some will be forced to adopt a greater shareholder-orientation due to the need to access capital markets (particularly in capital-intensive sectors), most will still be able to draw on retained earnings and the resources of insider networks to fund marginal investment.[15] Such company owners will wish to retain the private

---

[15] Retained earnings, that is earnings that are not distributed to shareholders in the form of dividend payments, represent the most significant source of funds for ongoing corporate investment once firms have established themselves, both in liberal and nonliberal market economies (Mayer 1997: 164).

A Theory of Partisanship and Corporate Governance Change 55

benefits of control, that is, to benefit disproportionately from company cash flows through the expropriation of minority shareholders (Aggarwal et al. 2007: 7). Furthermore, they are likely to retain a preference for operating their firms in an independent manner, with minimal levels of accountability to minority shareholders and external capital market participants. The shareholder model would involve granting power to other actors, which would erode the position of blockholders in the authority structure of the firm.

Nonetheless, such a hardening in firm-level behavior is likely to impact on the politics of corporate governance. Left parties will observe that firms are no longer willing or able to operate in a socially restrained and benevolent manner *vis-à-vis* employees, as in the "golden age of social democracy." Consequently, they are likely to question their support for a corporate system in which incumbent owners retain a privileged position in corporate governance, that is, continuing to benefit from the private benefits of control and sustaining unaccountable dominance over the key institutions of the production structure. In the absence of a social *quid pro quo*, it becomes increasingly politically unacceptable for the corporation to be a vehicle of a privileged elite. In addition blockholders represent concentrations of economic and political power, with a much greater ability to influence the political process than diffuse shareholders. Consequently, the new low rent situation serves to reopen class antagonism between the Left and established capitalist interests which was previously contained by the sharing of economic rents.

Along with the changing behavior of corporations, an additional factor relevant to the political debate on corporate governance is the growing political importance of outsiders. Definitive data on the relative magnitude of outsider actors within European electorates is not available. However, some indication is provided by a Eurobarometer survey undertaken in fifteen European Union (EU) countries in 1996. The survey focuses on employment issues, and is based on the responses of almost 19,000 respondents, aged 15 and above. Around 22 percent of the sample fall into the insider labor category, and 8.5 percent are defined as belonging to "upscale" social groups[16] (Rueda 2007: 39). This leaves a large proportion of respondents (almost 70%) remaining as potential members of the residual category of "outsiders."

The ability of such a survey to measure the political importance of outsiders should not be exaggerated. For example, the value of the survey is reduced by its inclusion of respondents below voting age. Furthermore, social groups differ in their relative ability to influence electoral outcomes; their

---

[16] Insider labor actors were defined in the survey as respondents employed in full-time permanent jobs. The upscale group was defined as those not employed by someone else, or describing themselves as managers (Rueda 2007: 39).

Table 2.3 OECD employment protection index, change over time

	Late 1980s	2003
Austria	2.2	1.9
Belgium	3.2	2.2
Denmark	2.3	1.4
Finland	2.3	2.0
France	2.7	3.0
Germany	3.2	2.2
Greece	3.6	2.8
Italy	3.6	1.9
Japan	2.1	1.8
Netherlands	2.7	2.1
Norway	2.9	2.6
Portugal	4.1	3.5
Spain	3.8	3.1
Sweden	3.5	2.2
Switzerland	1.1	1.1

Note: Data refers to overall EPL index (version 1).
Source: OECD Employment Report (2004: 117).

numerical magnitude does not translate proportionately into political power.[17] However, the large potential size of outsider groups implied by the survey is reflective of important trends in European labor markets over recent decades, such as the decline of manufacturing employment, the rise of the service sector, greater female and immigrant participation in labor markets, and more part-time working. These changes have eroded the traditional labor market dominance of insider labor, and have promoted the role of noninsider labor market participants. The existence of such a trend is supported by developments in employment protection. As can be seen from Table 2.3, employment protections have weakened in most European countries since the 1980s.

The weakening of insider labor – and the commensurate growth in the number of outsiders – suggests that, by the 1990s at least, an outsider perspective on corporate governance represented an interesting political opportunity for political parties. By appealing to outsiders, parties were in a position to win votes that could supplement the support provided by tradi-

---

[17] For example, upscale groups may exert a disproportionately high impact due to their greater control over resources. Conversely, young and poorly educated voters may be less influential, due to their lower levels of electoral turnout and political participation (Rueda 2007: 40).

tional core constituents, and thereby increase the chances of winning governmental office.

There are a number of approaches in the comparative politics literature that purport to explain the behavior of political parties with respect to individual policy issues. The classic statement of the office-seeking approach is provided by Downs (1957: 25): "Parties formulate policies in order to win elections, rather than win elections in order to formulate policies." Based on this approach, parties of either the Left or Right should adopt pro-shareholder corporate governance policies to an extent corresponding to the power of outsiders in the electorate. An alternative approach to party behavior is provided by Hibbs (1977). This suggests that political parties retain a strong level of underlying loyalty to their core clientele. Based on this logic, conservative parties should focus only on the corporate governance preferences of blockholders. The Left should be entirely influenced by the interests of insider labor. Neither conservative parties nor the Left should pay much attention to the political opportunity offered by outsiders.

This book takes a middle path between these two approaches. It adopts the approach to party behavior expressed by James Alt (1985: 1037): "Parties are organizations of political entrepreneurs who make strategic calculations even while implementing policies that are in the interests of their supporters." In other words, policy entrepreneurs within parties are interested in reaching out to new sources of political support, as a means of increasing their chance of attaining governmental office. However, they are also constrained in this activity by party loyalties and historic ties to core political constituencies (Frey and Schneider 1982; Strøm 1990). Success in repositioning political parties in particular policy areas will depend on the ease with which policy entrepreneurs can persuade core constituents to accept the changes. If a policy innovation is consistent with the broad agenda of core constituents (albeit not necessarily one of their traditional policy priorities), it will be more readily accepted as a means of winning additional votes from new groups of supporters. However, policy innovations that run contrary to the interests of core constituents will be much harder to sell within a party, even if they promise to deliver large numbers of votes from new groups of supporters. Consequently, it is assumed that a key factor determining the relative response of political parties to policy innovations is the compatibility of such innovations with the interests of core constituents (Callaghan 2007: 7).

The argument of this book is that the erosion of economic rents offers policy entrepreneurs of the Left – in contrast to those of conservative parties – a "critical juncture" in which to acquire the votes of outsiders through pro-shareholder reform while still retaining the support of core constituents. Following the breakdown of rent sharing between blockholders and insider labor, the core clientele of the Left will view the changing behavioral profile of blockholders in a negative light. Blockholders will be perceived as representing concentrated and unaccountable centers of economic and political power. Subject to the proviso that policy initiatives do not involve any compromise of insider labor's existing codetermination and/or employment protection rights, policy entrepreneurs will be increasingly able to persuade the Left's core constituents that pro-shareholder reform will both deliver large numbers of new votes and fulfill their agenda of countering blockholder power. In addition, it will also appeal to the Left's core constituents by passing regulatory power over corporate governance to public actors with accountability to the political process, at the expense of the self-regulating blockholders (Deeg 2005).[18]

In contrast to the Left, conservative parties will be constrained by their traditional association with blockholder interests. The material interests of blockholders will continue to require opposition to pro-shareholder reform, even in an environment of falling economic rents. Consequently, policy entrepreneurs in conservative parties – although also wishing to win the votes of outsiders – will have a smaller chance than their equivalents on the Left to persuade core constituents to embrace pro-shareholder corporate governance change (Cioffi and Höpner 2006: 28). At most, conservative parties in government will be insignificantly associated with corporate governance change. Equally, conservative governments may exhibit a negative association with pro-shareholder change, as they seek to retain the blockholder model. But they will not seek to promote pro-shareholder reform. The differing response of conservative and Left political parties to economic rents will, therefore, mean that partisanship becomes associated with corporate governance outcomes.

A possible objection to the partisanship framework presented in this chapter is the view that many European conservative parties (e.g., Christian Democratic parties) are "catchall" parties that are as equally representative of insider labor as of blockholders. Such a perspective would imply that – in an environment of falling economic rents – conservative parties would be just as likely as Left parties to seek the votes of outsiders through pro-shareholder corporate governance reform.

However, the assumption made in this analytical framework is that, although political parties may seek support from a wide range of social groups

---

[18] This is consistent with the argument made by Steven Vogel in *Freer Markets, More Rules* (1996). According to Vogel, economic "liberalization" is often associated with greater state regulation — and hence a wider role for politically accountable government — not with deregulation (Vogel 1996: 5). Corporate governance is an example of a policy area where structural reform involves introducing more, not less, regulation (Helbling et al. 2004: 105).

A Theory of Partisanship and Corporate Governance Change

for electoral purposes, they retain an underlying loyalty to distinct social constituencies. Consequently, when the interests of blockholders and insider labor diverge in relation to specific policy areas, conservative parties in nonliberal market economies will favor the policy preferences of blockholders. Their ties to blockholders constrain the extent to which they can function as genuine "catchall" parties.

As well as driving change in the corporate governance preferences of Left political parties, lower economic rents will also facilitate the translation of *de jure* corporate governance reform into changes in firm-level corporate governance outcomes. The private benefits of control will be worth less to blockholders than in an environment of significant rents. Consequently, the extent of legislative and regulatory reform needed to achieve a given level of *de facto* corporate governance change – and the resources required to enforce that regulation – will be less than in a high rent environment. This will further enhance the association between Left partisanship and corporate governance change in the context of competitive markets.

An issue that arises in relation to the argument presented so far concerns the relationship between the two interacting explanatory factors: partisanship and product market competition. It is plausible to imagine that there might exist a direct line of causation from partisanship to product market liberalization. This would conflict with the assumption that has been made concerning the exogeneity of a change in product market competition. Such association would be particularly problematic for the hypothesis if Left government was systematically responsible for liberalizing product markets. In such circumstances, it would be Left partisanship alone – rather than the interaction of Left partisanship and competition – that would ultimately be driving corporate governance change. It is important, therefore, to test the validity of the assumption that product market competition is exogenous with respect to partisanship.

In recent years, both the IMF (Helbling et al. 2004) and the OECD (Høj et al. 2006) have undertaken major empirical studies of the determinants of structural reform in the major industrialized democracies. Both studies point to significant differences in the speed and extent of liberalization across countries and differing areas of policy. In the specific area of product markets, liberalization has been gradual and often sequential across industries. Product markets were highly regulated in all major economies until the mid-1970s. However, the United States began liberalizing in the 1975–85 period, in part as a response to the high and persistent inflation following the first oil crisis. This was then followed by similar changes in the United Kingdom, New Zealand, and – to a lesser extent – Canada in the early and mid-1980s. Under the influence of the EU's single market program, product market

Table 2.4 IMF econometric analysis of determinants of product market liberalization

Possible explanatory variables	Nature and significance of empirical relationship
Domestic and international attitude toward reform	
Initial structural conditions	Positive
Demographics (share of 65 year olds or older in the population)	No
Cross-border spillovers	Positive
Openness to trade	No
Macroeconomic conditions	
"Bad" year (real GDP growth at or below 1%)	Positive
Number of bad years over the past three years	Positive
Primary surplus (cyclically adjusted)	Positive
Fiscal adjustment (increase in cyclically adjusted primary surplus)	No
Policy-making process and politics	
Majoritarian electoral rule	No
Conservative-leaning government	No
Size of government majority	No
Election year (executive)	No
First year in office (executive)	No
Country and regional effects	
EU member	Positive

Note: Table summarizes the results obtained from various econometric estimations of the determinants of structural reform. Detailed statistical results and specifications are described in Helbling et al. (2004: 137). An effect is deemed "positive" or "negative" only if the corresponding coefficient is statistically significant in at least one of the estimated equations. "No" means that no statistically significant effect was found in any of the equations. Results relate to 20 OECD countries, 1975–98. Variable operationalizations are described in Helbling et al. (2004: 132–6).

Source: Helbling et al. (2004: 110).

liberalization spread more widely in continental Europe during the 1990s (Helbling et al. 2004: 106; Conway and Nicoletti 2006; Høj et al. 2006: 89).

Table 2.4 summarizes the results of the IMF's econometric analysis. Reform in product markets is measured utilizing the Organisation for Economic Cooperation and Development's (OECD) index of product market competition in nonmanufacturing industries (the NMR index), which is the proxy for competition utilized in the subsequent empirical chapters of this book (Conway and Nicoletti 2006). Government conservatism is measured by a variable from the World Bank Database of Political Institutions, which calculates a score of the average of the chief executive's ideology and the average ideology of the two main parties in the coalition (where 2 = conservative, 1 = centrist, and 0 = left-wing). Consequently, a higher score broadly indicates more conservative-oriented government (Beck et al. 2001). A comprehensive description of the operationalization of the other explanatory and dependent variables listed in the table is available from Helbling et al. (2004: 132–6).

The results do not highlight government partisanship as a significant determinant of product market liberalization. Interestingly, none of the other political variables play a significant role in relation to the liberalization of product markets. Of more significance are initial conditions in product markets, macroeconomic and fiscal conditions (in particular, the presence of low growth and budget surpluses), and whether similar reforms are being undertaken in trading partners (spillover effects). Membership of the EU is also a significant factor, suggesting the importance of the EU Single Market Programme in fostering competition (Helbling et al. 2004: 113).[19]

The OECD study produces results which are broadly consistent with those of the IMF (Høj et al. 2006: 117). A slightly larger data set is utilized (twenty-one OECD countries, over the period 1975–2003); however the OECD also uses the NMR index as a proxy for product market competition. There is agreement with the IMF regarding the significance of initial structural conditions, low economic growth, the liberalizing activities of trading partners, and participation in the EU Single Market Programme as explanatory variables.[20] A slight difference from the IMF study is that demographic factors and the maturity of the government are found to be significant. However, once again, the partisan nature of government is not indicated as a significant determinant of structural change in product markets (Høj et al. 2006: 117).

In short, there is little empirical evidence to suggest that there exists a systematic relationship between partisanship and the liberalization of product markets. It would appear, therefore, that the assumption made by this book – that changes in competition occur in manner that is exogenous with regard to partisanship (and other political factors) – is supported by the historical experience of the last three decades.

Central to the argument of this chapter is the assumption that competition in domestic product markets plays a pivotal role in driving corporate governance change. A possible counterargument to this claim is that many small

---

[19] The Single European Act introduced a variety of measures designed to reduce the barriers to the free movement of capital, labour, goods, and services amongst member countries. The Act was signed in 1986, and came into effect in 1992.

[20] The OECD study distinguishes the effect of participation in the Single Market — which is statistically significant — from general EU membership (which is not significant) (Høj et al. 2006: 117). In addition, a recent study by Duval and Elmeskov (2005) finds that membership of EMU has not, so far, exerted a liberalizing effect on product markets beyond that explained by participation in the Single Market Programme.

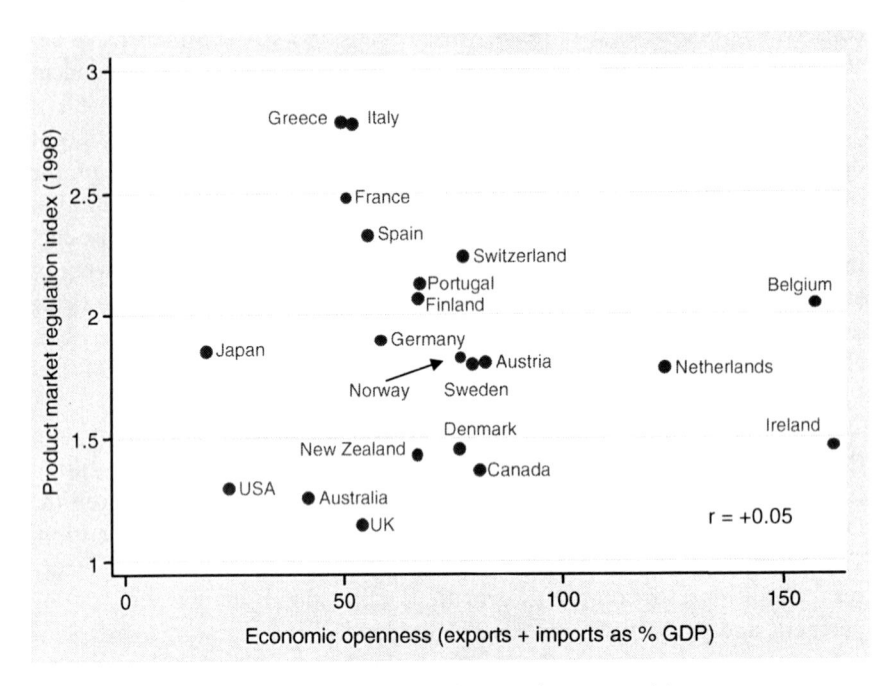

62   *Corporate Governance, Competition, and Political Parties*

Figure 2.5 Economic openness versus product market competition

European economies have pursued a postwar economic model with a highly external orientation (e.g., with significant levels of exports and imports). According to this perspective, such openness discourages the creation of economic rents that might otherwise impact on corporate governance arrangements. This reflects Mancur Olson's argument (1982: 141) that free trade and economic openness undermine distributional coalitions within national economies. Domestic product markets are not, therefore, likely to be particularly relevant in determining national models of corporate governance in small and open European economies.

However, such a postulated relationship between economic openness and the availability of economic rents does not appear to be observed in practice. Figure 2.5 plots a measure of economic openness against the OECD's most comprehensive index of product market competition (the PMR index).[21] A higher level of the PMR index is indicative of lower levels of product market competition. The scatter diagram – which is based on data relating to the late

---

[21] The PMR index is discussed in detail in Chapter 5.

A Theory of Partisanship and Corporate Governance Change 63

1990s – provides very little evidence of any association between openness and levels of competition in domestic markets. At one extreme are countries such as Canada, the United Kingdom, and Ireland, which are relatively open, and also have highly competitive domestic product markets. In contrast, a number of small continental European economies are relatively open, but lacking in terms of domestic competition (e.g., Switzerland or Belgium). Economic rents and economic openness do not, therefore, necessarily go hand in hand, a conclusion that is also borne out by the results of the IMF's econometric analysis in Table 2.4. The dichotomy between the competitiveness of internal and external sectors is further illustrated by the data on markups in the tradable manufacturing and nontradable service sectors in Chapter 5 (see Figure 5.1).

An insight into why small European countries with a significant involvement in world markets might also restrict the competitiveness of domestic markets is offered by Peter Katzenstein (1985: 47):

> The small European states complement their pursuit of liberalism in the international economy with a strategy of domestic compensation. Since their leverage over developments in international markets is insignificant, the small European states seek to exert some degree of control over their destiny through a variety of domestic policies. These policies are carried by the conviction that it is important to counter some of the harmful effects of international liberalization. Political laissez-faire is a luxury of large industrial countries, a luxury in which the small European states cannot indulge.

Consequently, product market competition may be restricted in small European economies for reasons relating to the mitigation of the domestic effects of high levels of economic openness (Rodrik 1998). Alternatively, competitive conditions may reflect the effect of another Olsonian argument – that it is easier for social actors to collude in the generation of economic rents in smaller countries. The small size of many European economies may make it easier – despite high levels of economic openness – to develop distributional coalitions amongst relevant social actors (Olson 1982: 26). Resolution of this issue is beyond the scope of this book. The key point from the perspective of the analysis is that there is nothing intrinsic to small open economies that suggests economic rents are likely to be absent from their domestic markets. Economic rents can, therefore, still play a significant role in determining corporate governance outcomes in such economies.

Chapter 3 contains a literature review of alternative approaches to corporate governance, drawing on relevant work in legal studies, economics, sociology, and political science. However, prior to concluding this chapter, it is useful to compare the argument of this book with two existing works that attempt to relate partisanship to corporate governance change: Mark

Roe's *Political Determinants of Corporate Governance* (2003), and *The Political Paradox of Finance Capitalism* by John Cioffi and Martin Höpner (2006).

Roe's argument concerning partisanship and corporate governance is that Right government is associated with the shareholder model and Left government with blockholding. This is based on the assumption that Left government is reflective of the strength of labor, which in turn gives rise to high agency costs for company owners. Right government is associated with weaker labor, and therefore lower agency costs. Consequently, company owners tend to prefer the blockholding model in circumstances of Left government, and the shareholding model with Right government (Roe 2003: 51). Such a potential relationship between partisanship and corporate governance is different from the prediction of this chapter – that Left government will be associated with corporate governance change in a shareholder direction in circumstances of competitive product markets.

The problem with Roe's assumptions regarding partisan behavior is their lack of applicability in the continental European context. The objective of confronting and overcoming the power of insider labor has not been a realistic objective for conservative government in postwar Europe (unlike in liberal market economies). For much of the period, the power of labor has been institutionally embedded, and it has been necessary for conservative parties to accept the resulting agency costs as exogenously given. Within such a context, the political role of conservative parties in European government has been to safeguard the interests of a particular social actor – incumbent company owners – and engage in some form of social partnership with insider labor, rather than to pursue policies of radical free market reform in labor and product markets. This has shaped the preferences of conservative governments to corporate governance, and has caused them to reject a major shift to a shareholder model.

An account of European corporate governance change with greater similarities to the argument of this chapter is provided by Cioffi and Höpner (2006). They emphasize the role of Left government in recent years in driving a shift toward the shareholder model. According to their explanatory framework, this occurs for three main reasons. First, it provides the Left with a means of addressing a number of emerging economic problems, including an inefficient economic structure (which empowered minority shareholders will be incentivized to restructure), and the need to finance the pensions of an ageing population (through the development of pension funds). Second, it undermines the position of incumbent economic interests, which represent a key constituency of its political opponents on the Right. Finally, it allows the Left to reach out to new sources of political support, particularly the growing number of private shareholders and the middle class.

However, the fact that a shareholder model of corporate governance would improve the efficiency of the economy in various ways is not a compelling reason for its support by the Left. A more persuasive account would demonstrate how such a policy change would fulfill the material interests of the Left's constituents, and this does not emerge from the paper. Indeed, as has been described, the intuitive expectation of such a policy change is that it will be detrimental for many of the Left's traditional political constituents. The second and third arguments of Cioffi and Höpner offer little insight into the timing of the changing policy stance of the Left. The links of the Right with incumbent economic actors have been a feature of the entire postwar period; a desire to attack the Right through adoption of the shareholder model does not explain why this policy shift occurred in the 1990s, rather than in the 1980s or 1970s. Furthermore, it is always possible (in theory) for political parties to reach out to new types of supporter through a change in policy stance. However, this is normally constrained both by ideology and the need to retain existing support. Cioffi and Höpner do not provide an explanation of why such a change was specifically feasible or desirable in the 1990s rather than at any other time. The key contribution of the argument of this chapter is to describe the crucial role that economic rents play (via their effect on insider labor and insider capital) in determining the nature of the relationship between partisanship and corporate governance change.

The claims of this book concerning the interaction of product market competition and partisanship in determining firm-level corporate governance change are summarized in Table 2.5. The interaction of Left government and high levels of product market competition is associated with corporate

Table 2.5 Summary of theoretical claims

	No change in corporate governance (blockholder model)	Corporate governance change (toward shareholder model)
Low levels of product market competition	Either conservative or Left government (partisanship insignificant).	Neither conservative nor Left government (partisanship insignificant).
High levels of product market competition	Conservative government (conservative partisanship either negatively or insignificantly associated with corporate governance change).	Left government (Left partisanship positively associated with corporate governance change).

governance change. In contrast, conservative government is not associated with a shift to a shareholder model, regardless of product market conditions. The relationship between conservative partisanship and corporate governance change is either negative or insignificant. Partisanship matters for corporate governance, therefore, when product markets are competitive, but not when economy-wide competition is insufficient to dissipate economic rents.

3

Alternative Explanations of Corporate Governance: A Critique of the Literature

> An outsider to the field of economics would probably take it for granted that economists have a highly developed theory of the firm. After all, firms are the engines of growth of modern capitalistic economies, and so economists must surely have fairly sophisticated views of how they behave. In fact, little could be further from the truth. Most formal models of the firm are extremely rudimentary, capable only of portraying hypothetical firms that bear little relation to the complex organizations we see in the world.
>
> Oliver Hart (1989: 1757)

A range of theoretical approaches have arisen to explain comparative patterns of corporate governance, and why they may be subject to change. Most of the explicit theorizing in this area has taken place since the mid-1990s, following the publication of several empirical studies highlighting the extent of variation in corporate ownership and governance practices across a range of developed and emerging economies (Franks and Mayer 1990, 1997; La Porta et al. 1999; Claessens et al. 2000; Barca and Becht 2001; Faccio and Lang 2002). In this chapter, the main competing perspectives – from the academic discourses of economics, legal studies, political science, and economic sociology – are reviewed and critiqued, and contrasted with the theoretical claims advanced by this book in Chapter 2. The starting point is the neoclassical economic theory of the firm.

3.1 ECONOMIC APPROACHES TO CORPORATE GOVERNANCE

Economic approaches to corporate governance are characterized by a focus on the role of market-determined incentives in driving corporate governance outcomes. Such explanations relate primarily to firm-level corporate governance behavior and tend to see the changing preferences of rational, optimizing, and decentralized market participants as more important for outcomes than politically driven changes in laws or institutions, or societal pressure from norms or social networks.

An early, albeit subsequently neglected, insight into corporate governance from an economic perspective was provided by the "Grand Old Man" of the Chicago school of economics, Frank Knight, in *Risk, Uncertainty and Profit* (1921). Knight argued that owners, rather than other stakeholders, should fulfill the central role in the governance of the firm in a capitalist economy. The other participants in the firm – such as employees, managers, creditors, and suppliers – are guaranteed a financial return through their complete contractual arrangements with the enterprise. The equity investor, however, lacks contractual safeguards and must ultimately bear the risk of corporate failure or inefficiency. To use the terminology of Grossman and Hart (1980), owners are confronted with a problem of incomplete contracts in their relationship with the firm, in contrast to other stakeholders. In such circumstances, investors will only provide capital, and shoulder the associated risk, if they are able to assume control over the firm's assets and personnel.[1] Furthermore, as the owner is the only stakeholder whose return is dependent on corporate efficiency, their control of the firm is the most socially desirable corporate governance outcome. Control of the firm by other actors would be subject to significant issues of moral hazard.

The implication of this argument is that, although other social actors may be important participants in the corporate governance debate, the central decision-making role will (and should) be played by company owners. If this were not the case, a capitalist economy would not deliver sufficient capital for the generation of wealth, as the potential suppliers of capital would not be prepared to shoulder the associated risk. Other social actors – such as labor or the state – are only important to the extent that they constrain or influence the preferences of the suppliers of capital.

Aside from Knight's contribution, the mainstream neoclassical theory of the firm – prior to the introduction of principal–agent theory in the late 1970s – did not focus directly on issues of corporate governance. The firm was caricatured as a "black-box" production entity, operated by indivisible

---

[1] "With human nature as we know it it would be impracticable or very unusual for one man to guarantee to another a definite result of the latter's actions without being given power to direct his work. And on the other hand the second party would not place himself under the direction of the first without such a guarantee.... The result of this manifold specialization of function is the enterprise and wage system of industry" (Knight 1921: 267).

owner-managers, which converted inputs into outputs for the purpose of profit or value maximization. From a corporate governance perspective, such a theoretical approach was relatively empty. It did not offer any insight into how conflicts of interest between the firm's various constituencies – its owners, managers, workers, and other stakeholders – were resolved, or how and why the goal of profit maximization was adopted. Nor did it attempt to examine the implications of the divorce of ownership and control, which had characterized US corporations since the early twentieth century.

According to Hart (1989), such a simplified conception of the firm was influential for three reasons. First, it lent itself to mathematical formalization. Second, it was useful for analyzing how a firm's production choices responded to exogenous change in the economic environment, such as an increase in wages or taxation. Finally, the theory was also tractable in analyzing the consequences of strategic interaction between firms in differing competitive conditions (Hart 1989: 1757). Harold Demsetz (1983: 377) summarized the approach as follows: "The chief mission of neoclassical economics is to understand how the price system coordinates the use of resources, not to understand the inner workings of real firms."

An alternative, albeit initially less mainstream approach to the theory of the firm developed in parallel under the banner of "transaction cost economics." In a seminal paper in 1937, Ronald Coase argued that a significant amount of economic activity was undertaken within firms – rather than outside firms in the form of market exchange between independent economic agents – in order to avoid the transaction costs of continually engaging in price discovery and transaction renegotiation. Building on this perspective, Alchian and Demsetz (1972) argued that an alternative source of transaction costs arose from the difficulty of observing the contribution of individual workers in a team production process. Without direct monitoring within a hierarchical authority structure, there was a temptation for workers to free ride without the fear of detection. In another major contribution, Oliver Williamson emphasized the role of specific assets in justifying the firm. If firms devote resources to assets that are subject to lower returns outside of the activities to which they are originally dedicated, then owners are vulnerable to "hold up" by other factors of production, that is, other actors can opportunistically threaten to withdraw their services as a means of renegotiating terms of cooperation. The firm provides a vertically integrated organizational structure – based on longer-term relationships between factors of production – to protect against this possibility (Williamson 1975; 1985; Klein et al. 1978).

Notwithstanding these differing ideas about the main source of transaction costs, the common insight of transaction cost economics is that the *raison d'être* of the firm as an organizational entity is the reduction of transaction costs. Efficiency considerations, therefore, underpin all aspects of a firm's behavior and organizational structure. Furthermore, the operation of competition is likely to ensure that firms experience significant pressure to adopt the most efficient forms. Those firms that reject or fail to recognize the configuration of the firm delivering greatest efficiency will either disappear or be taken over by more efficient competitors (Alchian 1950; Stigler 1958; Manne 1965; Hayek 1967).

What was missing prior to the introduction of the principal–agent approach by Michael Jensen and William Meckling in 1976 was a pinpointing of what efficiency meant in the context of corporate governance. The achievement of Jensen and Meckling was to demonstrate that the managerial agency costs faced by corporate owners are the most significant form of transaction costs resulting from a firm's corporate governance decision. The job of rational economic agents, therefore, is to identify the system of corporate governance that minimizes these agency costs (Jensen and Meckling 1976).

However, the subsequent economic literature has been less definitive about specifying the system of corporate governance that best serves to fulfill this objective (Goergen 2007). Advocates of the shareholder model argue that an outsider capital-oriented system offers firms a competitive edge, as it provides access to cheaper and more extensive funding opportunities in global capital markets. This is supported by various empirical studies that suggest that capital markets reward firms that adopt minority shareholder-friendly governance, for example, through a lower cost of capital and higher valuations (Gompers and Metrick 2001; Gourevitch and Shinn 2005: 105; Chhaochharia and Laeven 2007). In addition, it is often contended that the shareholder model – based on capital market financing – is more conducive to risk-taking and radical innovation. This will also convey competitive advantage at times of significant technological change (Huang and Xu 1999; Allen and Gale 2000; Hall and Soskice 2001).

In contrast, blockholder firms must rely on retained earnings or funds from within insider networks for the funding of investment (Jürgens et al. 2000; Lazonick and O'Sullivan 2000). Their reduced ability to tap global capital markets at low cost will severely hamper their ability to compete with shareholder-oriented firms. In the long run, their corporate governance decision will be unsustainable due to the superior performance of competitors with more efficient corporate governance.

Similar conclusions regarding the greater efficiency of the shareholder model are reached by Alfred Chandler (Chandler and Hikino 1990). According to his approach, the firm is engaged in an evolutionary process that mirrors the increasing complexity of the overall economic environment. The culmination of this development is a situation in which professional managers, selected on the basis of merit, achieve effective control over the largest public companies at the expense of family or elite capitalist interests, who lack the management skills to effectively operate a modern corporation. The model of corporate governance that promotes this handover is the outsider system of corporate governance, which frees managers from the direct hierarchical control of owners. Once again, if firms do not conform to this pattern, they are likely to become inefficient and ultimately disappear (Chandler and Hikino 1990).

However, other parts of the economics literature have highlighted some major disadvantages with the shareholder model from an efficiency perspective (Blair 1995; Rebérioux 2007). In particular, the seminal contribution of Adolph Berle and Gardiner Means in The *Modern Corporation and Private Property* (1932) was to observe that the separation of ownership and control encouraged by the shareholder model potentially gives rise to significant agency costs. As they state: "The separation of ownership from control produces a condition where the interests of owner and ultimate manager may, and often do, diverge, and where many of the checks which formerly operated to limit the use of power disappear" (Berle and Means 1932).

Jensen and Meckling's rediscovery (1976) and formalization of the principal–agent problem also reached the conclusion that less value will be created for shareholders in a diffusely owned corporation, due to problems of unobservability and asymmetries of information between owners and managers. In a later article, however, Fama and Jensen (1985) contended that the relinquishment of control might nonetheless be a rational strategy for owners to pursue if they wish to diversify their wealth, or if they lack sufficient capital, management talent, or risk tolerance for particularly rewarding projects. Eugene Fama (1980) has been more optimistic than Jensen and Meckling about the size of agency costs in the shareholder model, based on a belief that competition between managers will cause them to monitor each other in the interests of shareholder value, even in a diffusely owned corporation.

The argument advanced by this book is consistent with these economic approaches in assuming that agency cost considerations play the central role in determining firm-level corporate governance outcomes. However, a focus on agency costs does not necessarily require acceptance of the idea that a particular model of corporate governance is inherently better at minimizing agency costs in all contexts. Such an argument faces difficulties in accounting for the resilience of diversity in corporate governance practices during the postwar period (La Porta et al. 1999). Furthermore, empirical studies of economic development also suggest only a loose relationship between the type of corporate governance and levels of national wealth (Rajan and Zingales 2003; Roe 2003; Morck and Steier 2005). Economic success has been achieved by firms and national economies employing significantly different systems of corporate governance. It is noticeable that arguments about the relative efficiency of different models of corporate governance tend to move in cycles, depending on the recent economic performance of the countries employing such systems.[2] However, a knockout blow regarding the identity of the most efficient system has proved hard to achieve, due to the inability of any single system to demonstrate an unambiguous long-term record of superior performance over competing systems.

The perspective of this book is that company owners will rationally adopt the shareholder model if the perceived agency costs of such a strategy are minimized in prevailing socioeconomic and political conditions. However, support of a blockholder model of corporate governance is equally rational if levels of economic rents – which impact on perceived agency costs – make it a more efficient option. In such circumstances, these nationally determined sources of agency costs will override the incentive of lower external funding costs arising from adoption of the shareholder model. In short, different perceptions of agency costs in differing economic and political conditions will drive variation in comparative corporate governance outcomes.

3.2 LEGAL APPROACHES TO CORPORATE GOVERNANCE

It is possibly surprising that there exists a distinctly "legal" approach to corporate governance. Laws are ultimately the outcomes of political processes and could, therefore, be regarded as politically derived explanatory factors. However, several seminal articles by La Porta et al. (1997, 1998)[3] have proposed ways in which the intrinsic nature of law, independently of its political determinants, may impact corporate governance. Three propositions emerge from this literature, each of which may be evaluated separately.

The first is that the legal and regulatory environment is an essential determinant of corporate governance outcomes. This contrasts with the

---

[2] For example, vocal support for the shareholder model in the 1990s has coincided with a period of strong US economic performance relative to other countries. This represented a reversal of the earlier admiration for the Japanese and German models of "patient" capital (e.g. Porter [1992], Albert [1993]), which coincided with a period of underperformance in the liberal market economies in the 1980s.

[3] La Porta et al. are commonly referred to in the corporate governance literature as LLSV, an acronym of the names of Rafael La Porta, Florencio Lopez-de-Silanes, Andrei Shleifer, and Robert Vishny.

Alternative Explanations of Corporate Governance

implicit assumption of the economic theory of the firm – that corporate governance outcomes will be determined by the private behavior of independent economic agents in response to economic incentives. The "law matters" perspective asserts that law is required to shape the incentives of rational actors, and thereby determine the nature of firm-level corporate governance behavior (Shliefer and Wolfenzon 2002).

The empirical evidence regarding this assertion is mixed. A number of countries – such as the United Kingdom and Canada – have historically developed a minority shareholder-oriented governance regime in the absence of significant legal or regulatory incentives. Furthermore, the legal protections for minority shareholders identified as crucial for corporate governance in the articles of LLSV have only been introduced into developed economies in the relatively recent past (Cheffins 2001; Franks et al. 2004; Morck et al. 2005). On the other hand, the transition of the United States away from a blockholder-oriented system of corporate governance in the interwar period was strongly associated with development of supportive law and regulation.[4]

The hypothesis of this book takes a middle path in this debate by arguing that both economic incentives and legislative measures are important determinants of change in firm-level corporate governance outcomes. The interaction of both "bottom-up" factors affecting market incentives (the level of economic rents) and "top down" legal and regulatory reform from Left government causes change in *de facto* corporate governance. However, change in corporate governance law and regulation alone (i.e., without declines in rents) is likely to be relatively ineffective in driving changes in firm-level corporate governance behavior. It was argued in Chapter 2 (Section 2.4) that high economic rents increase the value of the private benefits of control to incumbent blockholders. Blockholders have an incentive to continue to govern corporations without regard to the interests of minority shareholders until the private benefits of control are exceeded by the costs of evading or working around the law (and its enforcement). In addition, blockholders and their allies may devote substantial resources to lobbying for a reversal of such legislative change. In an environment in which the "benefits" are high due to substantial economic rents, the amount of legal change and legal enforcement that must be applied in order to change firm-level behavior by a given amount is likely to be substantially greater than in a low-rent environment. Consequently, a divergence between measures of *de*

---

[4] Key landmarks in this process were the Securities Act of 1933, which based the regulation of new equity issuance on the principle of full disclosure, and the Securities Exchange Act of 1934 – which established the SEC (Securities and Exchange Commission) to regulate securities markets (Hopt 2006: 1179).

jure and *de facto* corporate governance outcomes could emerge in an environment of high economic rents. One way in which such a divergence could arise is explored in the Italian case study of Chapter 10.

A second proposition advanced by LLSV is that corporate governance outcomes are primarily determined by specific kinds of law and regulation, in particular, the corporate and securities law that seeks to guarantee minority shareholder protections. Although general tort law, for example, provides an underlying framework for the enforcement of contracts, LLSV argues that such a generic class of law is insufficient to determine the nature of a corporate governance regime. Equally, law or regulation which is not directly focused on corporate governance, such as labor law, competition law, consumer law, etc., will not be instrumental in driving firm-level corporate governance behavior (La Porta et al. 1998).

This narrow focus on corporate and securities law is criticized by Gourevitch and Shinn (2005), who point to the empirical value of considering the impact of a wider range of law and regulation in determining corporate governance outcomes. In particular, they argue that all laws affecting the overall "degree of coordination" of an economy are relevant, including laws relating to the labor market, competition policy, training and education, the regulation of financial institutions, and pension legislation. Such an outlook draws on Hall and Soskice's view (2001) that corporate governance will be structured to be "complementary" with other component parts of a political economy. In addition, Glaeser et al. (2001) highlight the distinction between "legislation" and "regulation," arguing that the latter is a more important determinant of firm-level corporate governance behavior, as judges (unlike dedicated regulators) do not have the expertise or resources to ensure implementation of specialized statutes relating to investor protection.

The theoretical framework of this book accepts Gourevitch and Shinn's skepticism regarding the privileged position of corporate and securities law. In particular, it implies that any law that might play a role in determining the state of competition in product markets – such as antitrust law, product market regulation, consumer protection law, restrictions on foreign ownership, or laws relating to the operation of public enterprises – could ultimately impact on corporate governance outcomes.

Perhaps the most distinctive component of the "law matters" approach to corporate governance is the hypothesis that legal origin is the key determinant of corporate and securities law orientation, and hence corporate governance outcomes (La Porta et al. 1997, 1998, 2000).[5] According to

---

[5] Although LLSV have been proponents of the legal origin argument, it has ironically been more enthusiastically adopted by financial economists than legal scholars (Roe 2006: 463).

this approach, a key distinction exists between countries that have developed on the basis of common law, and those inheriting a civil law tradition. The former is more likely to give rise to legal environment that encourages the development of the shareholder model of corporate governance, whereas the latter will tend toward law and regulation that favors the blockholder model.

According to the legal origin approach, common law systems are characterized by judicial independence, the importance of precedent, and less emphasis on statutory law and codification than civil law systems. In contrast, the civil law tradition gives rise to a more centralized legal system, with insistence on codification, and consequently a greater potential scope for state-driven political influence (Rajan and Zingales 1999). According to Hayek (1960), the implication of these differences in legal structure is that common law countries are more likely than civil law regimes to support market institutions. As Mahoney (2001: 505) puts it: "There are structural differences between common and civil law, most notably the greater degree of judicial independence in the former and the lower level of scrutiny of executive action in the latter, that provide governments with more scope for alteration of property and contract rights in civil law countries."

However, as a theoretical explanation of corporate governance outcomes, the legal family argument is relatively underspecified. LLSV do not provide a detailed explanation of the mechanism through which common law legal origin gives rise to a more favorable regulatory environment for minority shareholders. Botero et al. (2004) suggest that a lower overall market orientation in civil law countries is generally discouraging of the development of capital markets and the private bonding mechanisms that favor an outsider-oriented corporate governance system. Beck et al. (2003) argue that judge-made law is more flexible and adaptable than statutory law, and this makes it more conducive to the development of financial markets than law emerging from civil law systems. However, neither of these explanations are particularly specific about paths of causation *vis-à-vis* the adoption of law protecting minority shareholders.

Although LLSV (La Porta et al. 1998: 1147) present cross-sectional evidence linking legal family and corporate governance outcomes (measured by ownership concentration), the strength of the correlation between these two variables is highly dependent on the time point chosen to measure the association (LLSV's data relates to the mid-1990s). Roe and Siegel (2007) show that the correlation is much less apparent if evaluated at points in time both before and after the mid-1990s. More generally, the significant historical variation of corporate governance outcomes over the last century suggests that an explanatory variable such as legal origin – which is time invariant – is unlikely to be of much use for an analysis of corporate governance change (Rajan and Zingales 2003).

For example, events such as the shift of US corporate governance away from a blockholder-oriented system in the early twentieth century, the decline in stock market financing of many European countries in the postwar period, and the increased shareholder orientation of European corporate governance in the last ten to fifteen years (described in Chapter 1), are not suggestive of a rigid path dependence in corporate governance arising from legal origin (Rajan and Zingales 2003; Gourevitch and Shinn 2005: 7). Recent historical work undertaken by Lamoreaux and Rosenthal (2004) reveals that the French *code de commerce* in the nineteenth century was in many ways more sophisticated and flexible toward business requirements than its Anglo-American equivalents, notwithstanding its development in a legal environment based on civil law.

The experience in Europe over the last ten to fifteen years demonstrates that civil law countries are perfectly capable of legislating in favor of minority shareholders if they so desire (Gourevitch and Shinn 2005: 87). There is nothing inherent in civil law systems that prevents them from adopting the regulatory parameters of the shareholder model. This perspective is expressed by Tröger (2005: 21) as follows:

Corporate law is not substantially interlocked with other parts of member states' legal systems so as to make the exchange of the regime governing a firm's internal affairs impossible or prohibitively costly. That is not to say that it happens without friction in border areas – mostly to the detriment of third parties – but the point here is that exchange of corporate law regimes between jurisdictions without a common tradition is feasible.

A final noteworthy point is that there no longer exists a substantial divergence in the importance of statutory and judge-made law in modern legal systems. Common law systems rely on a substantial amount of formal legislation, not least with regard to investor protection (Franks et al. 2004: 6). Equally, the legal systems in civil law countries incorporate large amounts of case law. Consequently, it is hard to conceptualize the mechanisms by which the adoption of certain laws becomes more likely in one sort of legal system than another without regard to more political modes of explanation (Berglöf and von Thadden 1999: 10).

3.3 POLITICAL APPROACHES TO CORPORATE GOVERNANCE

Explanations of corporate governance from a political perspective fall into two broad categories. Scholars emphasizing the role of political agency tend to conceive of corporate governance outcomes in terms of political alliances or distributional coalitions between social actors (e.g., Aoki [1986]; Jackson et al. [2005]; Gourevitch and Shinn [2005]). In contrast, neo-institutional approaches focus on the constraining power of institutions. Both of these approaches are considered in turn.

Unlike economic approaches to corporate governance – which invariably view corporate governance outcomes as determined by the agency cost considerations of owners – political approaches often view the firm as open to equal contestation by any social actor. The outcome of this contestation will be determined by the relative power resources of social actors, and the organizational configuration of the firm will reflect the interests of the actor that emerges victorious from this contest. The relative efficiency of differing systems of corporate governance will not necessarily determine the outcome of this process. This perspective is consistent with the work of Jack Knight (1992), who has emphasized the importance of distributive conflict in determining the nature of social institutions. The Nobel laureate economist, Douglass North (1981, 1990), also argues that social institutions – even when they fulfill the function of delivering public goods – will not necessarily be efficient.

One reason why corporate governance may not be subject to efficiency considerations is that – contrary to the view of Jensen and Meckling – agency costs may not play a major role in determining the size of transaction costs. An argument in this vein has been expressed by Mark Roe (1994: 233):

> Corporate governance – even if we knew how to achieve the perfect system – is not the key to economic performance and competitiveness. While extremely pathological governance... will disable firms, within the normal range... macro-economic policies, competition, industry structure, and the education and motivation of managers and employees affect competitiveness and productivity much more than governance alone.

If agency costs are not relevant to transaction costs, then corporate governance outcomes are as likely to be driven by political – or sociological – factors as economic incentives.

Such a perspective leads Gospel and Pendleton, for example, to reject the widely quoted definition of corporate governance presented in Chapter 2: "Corporate governance deals with the ways in which suppliers of finance to corporations assure themselves of getting a return on their investment" (Shleifer and Vishny 1997: 737). Their more distributionally oriented definition is as follows: "Corporate governance is concerned with who controls the firm, in whose interests the firm is governed and the various ways in which control is exercised" (Gospel and Pendleton 2003: 560). Two of the practical implications of the adoption of a political perspective include a greater emphasis on the institutional context of corporate governance, and an increased focus on the role of actors other than owners and managers – particularly employees – in determining corporate governance outcomes.

An analysis of how differing distributional coalitions lead to differing corporate governance outcomes is provided by Peter Gourevitch and James Shinn in *Political Power and Corporate Control* (2005). They discuss corporate governance outcomes in terms of a framework with three social actors – investors, employees, and management – and consider the implications of six possible coalitions between these actors. Their contention is that a "corporatist compromise" – between employees and management (at the expense of owners) – best describes the coalition that has dominated corporate governance outcomes in postwar continental Europe, while a so-called investor model – between owners and management (at the expense of employees) – has prevailed in the United Kingdom and the United States.

One of the weaknesses of Gourevitch and Shinn's framework is that it is difficult to verify if their assertions about the composition of coalitions in differing national contexts are accurate. Many of the coalition combinations suggested by their framework lead to the same outcome in terms of a blockholder or shareholder model of corporate governance, making claims about the precise nature of coalitions in individual countries difficult to falsify. Furthermore, there is no explanation of why particular alliances succeed in the first place, and what factors might lead alliances to change.

An additional potential criticism of their framework is that, although the identification of management as an independent social actor is relevant to an analysis of corporate governance in liberal market economies (where arm's-length ownership gives management the latitude to pursue its own corporate governance agenda), it is less meaningful in the context of blockholder-dominated systems in which blockholders can exert direct control over management.

A further point is that their framework of social actors – consisting of management, employees, and investors – utilizes social categories that are too broad to offer significant explanatory power. Recognition of this weakness leads them to subsequently distinguish between the contrasting material interests of insider and outsider capital, that is, blockholders and diffuse external shareholders, and to identify a cleavage within labor, in terms of those holding equities via claims on pension funds and those whose pension provision is funded directly by companies or the state. Gourevitch and Shinn (2005: 205) argue that the corporate governance interests of the former group may have diverged from those of the rest of the workforce, and may be supportive of an alliance with outsider capital.

Within Gourevitch and Shinn's schema, pension-funded employees play a key role in motivating the formation of a so-called "transparency coalition" between owners and employees. Whereas the interests of shareholders and employees without equity-funded pensions may be viewed as inherently conflictual, employees with such pensions share a common interest with owners in ensuring that firms maximize shareholder value. The concern of both actors is to ensure that management delivers on this objective. In a situation when pension-funded employees come to dominate labor, this could lead to the formation of a distributional coalition of owners and employees against management. This conception builds on work by Martin Höpner and Gregory Jackson in respect of Germany, who argue that such an alliance underlies the development of a hybrid system of corporate governance in which labor is able to retain its previous privileges relating to industrial democracy, for example, codetermination, works councils, etc., at the same time as management is becoming subject to the discipline and external accountability of an outsider-oriented system of corporate governance (Jackson et al. 2005). A similar argument is developed by Perotti and von Thadden (2003). Their formally derived model suggests that minority shareholder protections will be stronger if the median voter owns relatively large amounts of equity, whereas an unequal distribution of wealth will give rise to a blockholder system.

The theoretical framework of this book shares with Gourevitch and Shinn the perspective that some kind of social partnership between capital and labor, that is, a corporatist compromise, has played a key role in corporate governance in nonliberal market economies (although unlike Gourevitch and Shinn, it emphasizes the role of economic rents in this partnership [Barker and Rueda 2007]). Furthermore, Gourevitch and Shinn's highlighting of the possible importance of employees with an equity orientation is incorporated into the hypothesis through their inclusion in the outsider corporate stakeholder group. However, there are several reasons why it seems unlikely that a rising equity orientation amongst workers has been the sole explanation of European corporate governance change over the last ten to fifteen years.

First, with the exception of Switzerland and the Netherlands, private pension fund assets are still relatively insignificant in most nonliberal market economies (see Table 3.1). Furthermore, only a relatively low proportion of

Table 3.1 Assets and equity investment of private pension funds, and public pension expenditure

	Pension fund assets 2003 (US$ million)	Pension fund assets 2003 (% of GDP)	Pension fund assets invested in equities 2003 (%)	Public pension expenditure 2000 (% of GDP)
Austria	10,869	4.3	16.5	14.5
Belgium	10,756	3.5	14.6	10.0
Denmark	58,717	27.7	21.1	10.5
Finland	13,406	8.3	27.0	11.3
France	95,395	5.4	–	12.1
Germany	85,335	3.6	12.7	11.8
Greece	–	–	8.7	12.6
Italy	36,787	2.5	5.8	13.8
Japan	561,437	13.1	–	–
Netherlands	545,239	94.1	44.6	7.9
Norway	10,227	4.6	19.2	–
Portugal	18,243	12.4	19.3	9.8
Spain	54,778	6.5	15.9	9.4
Sweden	23,457	7.8	–	9.0
Switzerland[a]	335,605	125.5	26.5	–
United Kingdom	1,179,718	65.7	53.8	5.5
United States	7,227,959	66.0	29.3	–

Sources: (1) Pension fund data (first three columns): OECD. *Pension Markets in Focus.* June 2005. [a]Data for Switzerland relates to 2002. (2) Public pension expenditure data (final column): Clark (2003: 33). Data relates to 2000.

these funds are invested in corporate ownership (OECD 2005: 6).[6] This reflects a much greater reliance on public pension provision in these countries (see final column). Although demographic trends – driven by an aging population – may change this picture in the future, it appears doubtful that the differing material interests of employees with equity-funded pensions has played a major role in driving the corporate governance changes over the last ten to fifteen years.

Second, the behavior of institutional investors (e.g., pension funds) does not offer much encouragement for the idea of some kind of coalition between investors and workers. A credible form of alliance between workers and pension funds would presumably involve workers seeking to reframe the

---

[6] This partly reflects legal restrictions on the size of pension fund investment in equities in many countries. However, it is noticeable that the actual holdings of equities in pension funds often falls well below maximum permissible limits. For example, as of 2003, German pension funds were allowed to invest up to 45 percent of their portfolios in the equities of listed and unlisted companies, but chose to invest a much smaller proportion (see Table 3.1), suggesting that investor preferences rather than government regulation constrained pension funds' equity orientation (OECD 2005: 7).

investment behavior of pension managers in a manner more consistent with their interests while still in employment. This might include a longer-term investment perspective, and greater direct engagement with corporate management in order to promote issues of broad public concern, such as ethical investment, environmental issues, and vocational training.

Such collaboration between workers and fund managers was predicted by management guru Peter Drucker in the 1970s. Drucker (1976) thought that the growing importance of workers in corporate ownership via pension funds would result in a form of economic system that he described as "pension fund socialism." In such a system, the importance of workers as contributors to pension funds would ensure that pension funds became a tool of workers' interests. However, the subsequent behavior of pension funds in the United Kingdom and the United States did little to bring his prediction to fruition. Although employees in these countries own a much larger proportion of the corporate sector through pension fund investment than in continental Europe, this has not resulted in investment behavior focused on promoting the interests of employees. Clark and Hebb (2004) succinctly describe the nature of the relationship between pension funds and employees as follows: "Like the 'silent majority', it turns out that beneficiaries are often referred to but seldom seen in the world of pension fund management."

So far, the political approach to corporate governance has been discussed in terms of the coalition-forming ability of social actors. However, an equally important neo-institutionalist strand in the political science literature has emphasized how existing institutional forms can constrain and shape economic outcomes through such mechanisms as institutional path dependency, the differing rationality of actors working within differing institutional frameworks, and the veto power of incumbent interests (Zysman 1983; North 1990; Garrett and Lange 1995; Berger and Dore 1996; Keohane and Milner 1996; Hollingsworth and Boyer 1997; Kitschelt et al. 1999; Hall and Soskice 2001; Swank 2002). Deeg and Perez (2000: 142), for example, utilize institutional constraints to explain why there has not been a strong contemporaneous correlation between economic change – such as the abolition of capital controls – and the collapse of the "insider" nature of European political economies. Institutional resilience may also explain why it is possible for economic systems to remain in place – despite their lack of support from powerful distributional coalitions – due to the costs involved in demolishing the existing setup and establishing something new (David 1985: 332; Gourevitch 2003: 318).

A particular constraint on corporate governance change is represented by the notion of "complementarity," which is a central concept of Hall and Soskice's Varieties of Capitalism approach (Aoki 1988; Milgrom and Roberts

1990; Hall and Soskice 2001). A corporate governance system may be viewed as a component of a highly interrelated national production system. According to the logic of this approach, changes in corporate governance are only likely to occur as part of much broader changes in labor relations, education and training, R&D, and other areas that contribute to the operation of an integrated political economy. A corporate governance system that does not sustain coherence with these other components endangers a nation's comparative institutional advantage. The incentive structure generated by the system's internal logic will militate against such an outcome (Aoki and Dore 1994; Hall and Soskice 2001).

The relevance of the complementarity argument *vis-à-vis* corporate governance is supported by the empirical analysis of Hall and Gingerich (2004). They develop an aggregate corporate governance indicator for OECD countries from a principal component analysis of three types of data: minority shareholder protections (La Porta et al. 1998), ownership concentration (La Porta et al. 1998), and the size of the stock market as a percentage of gross domestic product (GDP). An analogous indicator is developed for labor relations, based on measures of the level and degree of wage coordination, and labor market turnover. A high level of cross-sectional correlation is exhibited between the two indicators (0.72). A similarly high correlation (0.78) is recorded between corporate governance and an aggregate measure of social protection (based on the nature of support for the unemployed) (Hall and Gingerich 2004: 21).

However, Gregory Jackson has questioned the notion of "coherence" in respect of economic systems – as emphasized by the varieties of capitalism approach – by observing that complementarity in a particular context is an inherently subjective concept. It may appear that an intrinsic logic is guiding the composition of an economic system, and that this logic stands in the way of any significant change. However, this may simply represent a rationalization of the *status quo*. For example, the institutions of "industrial democracy" in Germany (e.g., codetermination) were strongly criticized in the 1970s (when they were being expanded). Business interests claimed that they would disrupt the logic of the entire German economic model. However, subsequent depictions of *Deutschland AG* frequently cite codetermination as an intrinsic and complementary component of "Rhineland capitalism." What is initially interpreted as incoherency can, therefore, be reinterpreted as complementarity at a later stage. An equally plausible path for economic development is that economic systems evolve in unintended ways, through a process of continual hybridization between new and existing institutions. Only in retrospect do economists or political scientists identify an underlying logic or unifying principle in the entire system (Jackson 2001, Jackson et al. 2005: 41).

Alternative Explanations of Corporate Governance 83

A particular type of political institution that has been linked to corporate governance in the literature is the electoral system. In terms of Lijphart's typology of political institutions (1999), several scholars have noted a correlation between majoritarian institutions and minority shareholder oriented corporate governance outcomes, and between consensus political institutions and blockholder outcomes (Gourevitch et al. 2003; Pagano and Volpin 2005). According to Gourevitch and Shinn (2005: 69), consensus political institutions and blockholder corporate governance are complementary components of a political economy which seeks to promote credible commitments amongst economic actors and a willingness to invest in specific assets. Majoritarian institutions engender more uncertainty in terms of policy formation, and therefore necessitate more flexible corporate behavior. Such adaptability is complementary with more outsider-oriented corporate governance, which encourages management to constantly adapt in response to changing market signals.

Marco Pagano and Paolo Volpin (2005) make the link between the electoral system and corporate governance through a formal median voter model. According to their framework, a proportional representation (PR) electoral system tends to increase the probability of coalition government. This leads to an increase in the focus of government policy on the preferences of homogeneous political groupings. In contrast, majoritarian systems emphasize the importance of pivotal groups that are less politically aligned, due to their key role in determining the balance of power in such an electoral system (Pagano and Volpin 2005: 1006).

Pagano and Volpin utilize these assumptions about the properties of electoral systems to explain differing corporate governance outcomes in a model with three social actors: entrepreneurs, rentiers, and employees, and two political parties. The first social actor, entrepreneurs, are defined as controlling shareholders in companies (i.e., blockholders). Rentiers are noncontrolling shareholders, who live from the returns from their financial wealth (i.e., minority shareholders). Employees have no wealth endowment, and obtain income by selling their labor. In the model, employees and entrepreneurs are assumed to be politically homogeneous social groupings, whose interests are represented by the two representative parties on the Left and Right. In contrast, rentiers are assumed to have dispersed political preferences and to fulfill the role of the pivotal groups of voters (Pagano and Volpin 2005: 1006).

The key result of the model is that in a majoritarian political system, government policy favors the interests of rentiers (e.g., weak employee protection and strong rights for minority shareholders). In such a system, both political parties seek to gain power by offering compromises to gain the support of pivotal voters. In contrast, both parties in a PR system remain loyal to the interests of their core constituents (entrepreneurs and employees), and seek to make post-electoral deals with the other party in a coalition government. The interests of the nonaligned pivotal voters are therefore relatively neglected. Policies are pursued that safeguard the interests of the homogeneous social groupings: strong employee protection (employees) and weak protection for minority shareholders (entrepreneurs) (Pagano and Volpin 2005: 1007).

Both Gourevitch and Shinn (2005), and Pagano and Volpin (2005) present empirical results suggesting a significant level of cross-sectional correlation between political institutions and corporate governance outcomes. In the case of Gourevitch and Shinn, political institutions are measured by Lijphart's measure of political consensuality, whereas Pagano and Volpin use a dummy variable of electoral system proportionality. Both measure corporate governance in regulatory terms, that is, with a measure of minority shareholder protection in each country.

Putting aside issues concerning the realism of the assumptions made by Pagano and Volpin in deriving their results (e.g., that there are only two political parties, and that rentiers are situated in the median portion of the electoral distribution), the difficulty of utilizing electoral institutions in explaining corporate governance outcomes is similar to that relating to the legal origin argument: the largely static nature of the explanatory variable (although there have been some limited recent examples of significant electoral system change; Norris [2004]). In contrast, the explanatory factor proposed by the hypothesis of this book – namely the interaction of partisanship and product market competition – has the advantage of itself exhibiting variation over time. Consequently, I would contend that it offers a more promising basis for explaining temporal change, as well as cross-national variation, in corporate governance.

3.4 SOCIOLOGICAL APPROACHES TO CORPORATE GOVERNANCE

In a recent review of the field of economic sociology, Frank Dobbin (2004: 4) states that "sociology's core insight is that individuals behave according to scripts that are tied to social roles." The sociological approach to corporate governance, therefore, seeks to explain outcomes in terms of social processes rather than utilitarian responses to legal and material incentives. Firms are "embedded" in a society in which norms and conceptions of "appropriateness" play important roles in shaping behavior. Incentives in themselves will not provide a universal explanation of behavior because they will mean different things at different times and in different places, depending on the nature of the specific culture or "frame of understanding" through which they are being interpreted (Blair 2003). Such an approach – focusing on the role of norms and informal constraints on political outcomes – has also influenced political science through the medium of so-called sociological institutionalism (March and Olsen 1984; Hall and Taylor 1996).

Applying the sociological approach to corporate governance, Mizruchi and Bey (2005) do not seek to explain retention of the blockholding model in terms of a materially driven cost–benefit analysis undertaken by company owners or partisan agents (as argued by the hypothesis of this book). Rather, blockholders are part of a social network which is held together by such factors as elite social ties, interlocking directorates, policy-making organizations, financial institutions, the "inner circle" of elite capitalist interests (Useem 1984), and the state. These will not immediately dissipate following short-term reevaluations of agency costs. Furthermore, the resilience of the social norms underpinning such networks will militate against changed corporate governance outcomes based on a purely political contestation between social actors.

Dobbin and Zorn (2005) describe the "shareholder value" strategy adopted by US firms in the early 1980s as a "social construction of interest." According to their argument, three groups of social entrepreneurs – hostile takeover firms, institutional investors, and securities analysts[7] – have succeeded in redefining corporate efficiency in terms of shareholder value maximization, replacing an earlier conception of best practice focused on growth and diversification. The promotion of such a strategy was driven by the self-interest of these actors. However, there was also a need to persuade corporate management and society at large, through a process of rhetoric and social discourse, that shareholder value maximization was an efficient and socially defensible approach (Dobbin 2004). The ultimate factor determining the adoption of a shareholder-oriented system of corporate governance was the ability of the relevant actors to reach a shared understanding about the appropriate "conception of control" (Fligstein 2001). What was of less importance was the underlying truth about the efficiency and fairness of the system, and whether it did indeed minimize agency costs.

---

[7] Richard Swedberg (2005) also stresses the role of management consultants and accounting firms in this policy entrepreneurship role.

Such an interpretation demonstrates the agnosticism displayed by economic sociologists – in common with many political scientists – *vis-à-vis* the role of efficiency in determining economic outcomes (Fligstein and Choo 2005: 62). Social institutions may equally be the result of historical accident or a struggle or discourse between social actors (Granovetter 1985). Concepts such as "efficiency" and "fairness" are often influential as rhetorical devices in the discourse preceding the adoption of economic or political norms of behavior. However, once a shared understanding has been reached amongst relevant actors, they become much less important (Dobbin 2004). This remains the case until the existing system proves itself to be a failure in the eyes of a broad range of society, and the opportunity emerges to begin a new social discourse resulting in a new shared understanding of the way forward (Fligstein 1990).

It is clear that the sociological approach focuses on different types of explanatory factors to those stressed by the hypothesis of this book. My theoretical framework assumes that social actors are rational, self-interested agents that respond to incentives generated both by markets and the prevailing institutional framework. In contrast, the sociological approach stresses changes in norms and conceptions of appropriateness. It should be emphasized that I do not seek to argue that the sociological approach is an invalid means of investigating the issue of corporate governance change. However, I am skeptical that changes in sociological "scripts" are sufficient to provide a full explanation of the significant change in corporate governance of the last ten to fifteen years (a relatively short space of time). In addition, although new corporate governance outcomes may coincide with changed "conceptions of control," it is likely to be difficult to test the causative power of such changed norms. First, they are likely to be difficult to operationalize in any empirical analysis. Second, changed norms may simply reflect rather then cause changes in corporate governance (i.e., they may be endogenous rather than exogenous causative factors).

Given the difficulties involved in incorporating a sociological perspective into the empirical analysis, it is not stressed in the rest of this book. The empirical results presented in subsequent chapters – testing the validity of a hypothesis based on the assumption of social actor rationality – will provide an indication of whether such *a priori* skepticism regarding the explanatory power of a sociological approach is justifiable in practice.

3.5 CORPORATE GOVERNANCE AND NONDOMESTIC FACTORS

The idea of economic and financial openness driving the capital market orientation of the financial system – and by implication the outsider nature of corporate governance – is explored by Raghuram Rajan and Luigi Zingales in *The Great Reversals* (2003).[8] Consistent with the analysis of this book, they argue that incumbent blockholders will oppose an equity-oriented financial system because the latter increases the competitiveness of the business environment. However, if the economy experiences an exogenously driven increase in trade openness or capital mobility – for reasons beyond the control of incumbent players – incumbents are subsequently more willing to accept reform of the financial system, that is, a shift to a financial system based on capital markets, as greater openness will have reduced their "positional rents" (Rajan and Zingales 2003: 7).

The emphasis of Rajan and Zingales on the importance of rents in determining outcomes for the financial system has strong similarities with the claims made by the hypothesis of this book. However, there are several differences in the two approaches. First, Rajan and Zingales assume that openness is synonymous with greater domestic competition. As had been argued in Chapter 2, this need not necessarily be the case (see Section 2.4). Domestic rents may exist at high levels in relatively open economies (and vice versa). In addition, an association between economic openness and financial liberalization is not supported by the findings of Deeg and Perez (2000), who find no correlation between the introduction of capital mobility changes in Spain, France, Italy, and Germany, and the advent of financial sector reform (Deeg and Perez 2000: 142).

Second, Rajan and Zingales assume that the reduction or elimination of rents will cause incumbent blockholders to reverse their previously negative attitude *vis-à-vis* capital markets. However, while it may be true that the elimination of rents creates a political economy in which blockholder's incumbent position is less valuable to them than before, it does not necessarily mean that blockholders will automatically embrace the shareholder model of corporate governance. They still have a material interest in retaining the

---

[8] It should be noted that Rajan and Zingales' paper is not primarily concerned with explaining corporate governance outcomes, but rather the capital market orientation of the financial system. However, it is discussed here based on the assumption that a shift in the financial system toward capital markets is largely equivalent to a shift towards outsider-oriented corporate governance.

private benefits of control. The continued desire of blockholders to retain the private benefits of a self-regulatory system of corporate governance – even in an environment of lower economic rents – accounts for the inertia of conservative political parties *vis-à-vis* pro-shareholder corporate governance reform in the theoretical framework of this book.

A recent study that examines the relationship between globalization and corporate governance is undertaken by Tarun Khanna et al. (2006). They attempt to measure the association between various measures of capital market, product market, and labor market integration between countries – which they use as proxies for "external influence" – and corporate governance. Their conclusion is that countries with a high level of economic integration experience convergence in *de jure* corporate governance regulation, but that such integration has not driven a similar level of convergence in actual (*de facto*) corporate governance practices.

Unfortunately these conclusions are based on a cross-sectional analysis of measures of corporate governance that exhibit significant limitations. Khanna et al.'s measure of *de facto* corporate governance, for example, is constructed from the subjective assessments of analysts at a stockbroking firm (Credit Lyonnais Securities Asia), and relates only to firms in developing countries. Their *de jure* measure is La Porta et al.'s index of shareholder protection (1998), which also has been subject to significant criticism by legal scholars (see Chapter 4 for a detailed discussion of this measure). Nonetheless, as has been discussed, the hypothesis of this book accepts the possibility that *de jure* corporate governance reforms can move ahead of *de facto* change, for example, if policy-makers introduce legislative initiatives when there are still significant economic rents available in product markets (see also the Italian case study in Chapter 10).

A critical political economy perspective on the impact of external factors on corporate governance is presented by Van Apeldoorn and Horn (2007). They contend that corporate governance change is not the outcome of domestic politics or the operation of market-generated incentives, but is driven by transnational social forces favoring neoliberal economic policies operating through supranational institutions. In particular, they argue that the European Commission has been active in promoting a shareholder orientation and the development of a market for corporate control in Europe (Van Apeldoorn and Horn 2007: 212).

The role of the OECD and other international bodies in contributing to a discourse of pro-shareholder corporate governance has been discussed in Chapter 1. However, as was observed in Section 1.2.1, there is little evidence of international institutions being able to push through policy measures at variance with the wishes of domestic policy-makers. Furthermore, the role of

Table 3.2 Main EU directives and regulations concerning company law and corporate governance since 1990

Directive 2007/36/EC of July 11, 2007 on the exercise of certain rights of shareholders in listed companies (14.7.2007).

Directive 2006/68/EC of September 6, 2006 amending Council Directive 77/91/EEC as regards the formation of public limited liability companies and the maintenance and alteration of their capital.

Directive 2005/56/EC of October 26, 2005 on cross-border mergers of limited liability companies.

Directive 2004/25/EC of April 21, 2004 on takeover bids.

Directive 2003/58/EC of July 15, 2003 amending Council Directive 68/151/EEC, as regards disclosure requirements in respect of certain types of companies.

Regulation (EC) No 1606/2002 of the European Parliament and of the Council of July 19, 2002 on the application of international accounting standards.

Directive 2001/86/EC of October 8, 2001 supplementing the Statute for a European company with regard to the involvement of employees.

Regulation (EC) 2001/2157 of October 8, 2001 on the Statute for a European company (SE).

Source: European Commission.

European Union (EU) directives in driving corporate governance change in Europe in the 1990s was negligible. Most EU directives relating to corporate governance have only been introduced since 2002 (see Table 3.2), and several have yet to translate into national law.[9] As noted by Enriques (2006), national regulatory change has been a more significant source of *de jure* corporate governance change than supranational regulatory change during the last ten to fifteen years.

The influence of the EU on national models of corporate governance may have been greatest through directives and policy initiatives not directly addressed at corporate governance. For example, the EU Single Market Programme exerted a significant influence on the competitiveness of European product markets (Høj et al. 2006: 117). According to the theoretical claims of this book, greater competition is a key precondition for corporate governance change. Second, the project of economic and monetary union (EMU)

---

[9] However, since 2001, the European Commission has become active as a promoter of discourse on corporate governance issues. In November 2002, a high level group of company law experts presented recommendations favoring the removal of pyramidal ownership structures, greater shareholder protections, and extension of the market for corporate control. In November 2003, the European Commission issued a report entitled "Modernizing Company Law and Enhancing Corporate Governance in the EU – A Plan to Move Forward," with various recommendations concerning corporate transparency and shareholder protection (Detomasi 2006: 238).

motivated a number of European countries to undertake significant privatization programs during the 1990s as a means of fulfilling the Maastricht convergence criteria on fiscal deficits and debt (OECD 2003: 22; Zohlnhöfer et al. 2008: 103). The introduction of pro-shareholder corporate governance legislation in parallel with this program may have been viewed as a way of increasing the willingness of investors to buy the shares of newly privatized enterprises, thereby enhancing privatization revenues (Gray 1996: 181). The significance of the "EMU effect" is tested through inclusion of a relevant control variable in the quantitative analysis of Chapter 6, and is revisited in the Italian case study of Chapter 10.

4

Measuring Change in Corporate Governance

> Good corporate governance comes down to a lot more than a point system.
>
> Jack and Suzy Welch (2006)

Corporate governance exhibits cross-country variation due to the differing ability of social actors and institutions to exert power and influence over the behavior of corporations. However, the distribution of power in the corporate sector is not something that can be observed and measured directly. In order to undertake an empirical analysis of the hypothesis of corporate governance change outlined in Chapter 2, it is necessary to identify observable and quantifiable proxy measures of corporate governance that are likely to be strongly correlated with underlying but unobservable structures of authority. Despite the extensiveness of the corporate governance literature, there is no universally-accepted means of operationalizing corporate governance on a comparative basis. Consequently, this chapter commences the empirical analysis of the book by evaluating various proxies for corporate governance. A similar procedure is followed in Chapter 5 in respect of product market competition.

As has been described in Chapter 2, this book's theoretical claims are fundamentally concerned with capturing the extent to which the monitoring, oversight, and control of the management of public companies is oriented toward external minority shareholders, that is, outsider capital. This theoretical goal guides the choice of proxies for the dependent variable. The higher the correlation of proxies with actual (albeit unobservable) corporate governance outcomes, the greater will be the accuracy of coefficients obtained from subsequent econometric analysis, that is, they will contain less bias and more valid standard errors due to lower measurement error.

The detailed empirical strategy is undertaken in Chapter 6. However, the broad approach is to apply panel data econometric techniques to a pooled data set covering fifteen nonliberal market economies over the period

1975–2003.[1] It is, therefore, necessary that any potential proxy for corporate governance captures variation over time. This rules out a number of measures that are sometimes utilized in the corporate governance literature – such as ownership concentration and corporate governance ratings – which currently only exist as cross-sectional summaries.

Corporate governance may be evaluated from both a *de facto* and *de jure* perspective, that is, in terms of the actual behavior of companies, or the legislative and regulatory "rules of the game" in which corporations are required to operate (Gourevitch 2003: 315). The primary focus of this book is explanation of actual corporate governance change. However, change in legislation and regulation relating to corporate governance is clearly relevant to firm-level corporate governance behavior. Consequently, this chapter also investigates potential measures of *de jure* corporate governance, particularly Rafael La Porta, Florencio Lopez-de-Silanes, Andrei Shleifer, and Robert Vishny's (LLSV) widely cited antidirector rights index (La Porta et al. 1998).

Each of the potential proxies for corporate governance has strengths and weaknesses. This is a reason why it is useful to triangulate the quantitative analysis with qualitative case study investigations (see Chapters 8–10). However, a further prudent step is to undertake the quantitative analysis with several plausible proxies of corporate governance, rather than base the results entirely on a single measure. This chapter contends that corporate governance may be usefully operationalized with three measures of *de facto* corporate governance: equity share, value traded, and international equity issuance. However, it also concludes that there is currently no satisfactory means by which corporate governance can be measured from a *de jure* perspective. In particular, LLSV's antidirector rights index does not represent a viable measure for utilization in a quantitative analysis.

4.1 MEASURES OF *DE FACTO* CORPORATE GOVERNANCE BEHAVIOR

4.1.1 Ownership concentration and corporate governance ratings

A widely employed measure of corporate governance in empirical research is ownership concentration. This measure permits a comparison of countries

---

[1] The countries included in the sample are: Austria, Belgium, Denmark, Finland, France, Germany, Greece, Italy, Japan, the Netherlands, Norway, Portugal, Spain, Sweden, and Switzerland.

according to the ownership structure of their corporate sectors. High levels of ownership concentration are assumed to imply that corporations are still dominated by blockholders, and hence are more likely to retain a blockholder model of corporate governance. In contrast, a diffuse ownership structure is taken to indicate that blockholders are less significant economic actors, and hence a shareholder model of corporate governance is more likely amongst major corporations.

The results of detailed studies to establish levels of ownership concentration across a wide range of countries have only been available since the late 1990s. The compilation of such data is not a trivial exercise, and involves significant effort to trace the ultimate ownership of thousands of companies, many of which have intentionally complex and opaque financial structures. The first study to undertake this task in a comprehensive manner was published by La Porta, López-de-Silano, and Shleifer in 1999, and contains estimates of ownership concentration relating to the early 1990s for twenty-seven countries (La Porta et al. 1999). The data for several European countries was further refined by Faccio and Lang (2002). Table 4.1 summarizes the outcome of this work in respect of a number of continental European economies, along with the United Kingdom and the

Table 4.1 Ownership concentration (%), early 1990s

United States	15.0
Netherlands	20.0
United Kingdom	23.6
Denmark	37.5
Norway	38.6
Sweden	46.9
Switzerland	48.1
Finland	48.8
Belgium	51.5
Austria	52.8
Spain	55.8
Italy	59.6
Portugal	60.3
Germany	64.6
France	64.8
Greece	75.0

Notes: Ownership Concentration: Percentage of listed firms with individual owners holding stakes in excess of 20% of total market capitalization.

Sources: La Porta et al. (1999) for data relating to United States, Denmark, The Netherlands, and Greece. Faccio and Lang (2002) for other European countries. As quoted in Gourevitch and Shinn (2005: 299). Data relates to the early 1990s.

United States for comparison. The figures show the percentage of listed firms (by value) controlled by blockholders (defined as shareholders with a 20% ownership stake or larger).

Ownership concentration has certain weaknesses as a proxy for the outsider-orientation of a corporate governance regime. For example, the fact that blockholders dominate corporate ownership does not necessarily mean that they are willing or able to exploit or expropriate minority shareholders, or to operate firms in a manner incompatible with external investor interests. Conversely, economies with a diffuse ownership structure may incorporate various mechanisms that work against the interests of external minority shareholders.[2] Furthermore, even after losing their privileged position in the authority structure of the firm, it may take some time for blockholders to dispose of large ownership positions. Such a disposal process requires access to a sufficiently developed capital market through which stakes can be sold at acceptable valuations. This may take time to develop. Furthermore, the disposal of large ownership stakes may require a generational change, as incumbent owners often gain significant status benefits from their control of prominent companies (Agnblad et al. 2001: 252). For these reasons, the structure of ownership in a political economy is likely to exhibit more inertia and path dependence than changes in underlying corporate governance.

However, the main problem with ownership concentration from the perspective of this book is its lack of availability on a time-series basis. Data is only available with respect to large numbers of countries in respect of specific points in time.[3] This restricts its application to studies of a cross-sectional nature, that is, which seek to explain cross-country variation in corporate governance levels, but not variation over time (e.g., La Porta et al. [1999], Roe [2003], Khanna et al. [2006], Aggarwal et al. [2007]). This lack of a temporal dimension, therefore, renders it unsuitable for inclusion in the panel data analysis of Chapters 6 and 7.

A second recently-developed cross-sectional measure of corporate governance was presented in Chapter 1. The so-called GOV index is constructed on the basis of forty-four corporate governance attributes derived from the

---

[2] An example is provided by the Netherlands. The low figure for ownership concentration in Table 4.1 implies that Dutch corporate governance is relatively similar to that of the liberal market economies. However, this impression is misleading, due to widespread operation of a form of synthetic blockholding at many listed corporations. Although company stock is widely held – granting the right to receive dividend payments and other financial returns – voting rights are often vested in company trust offices (*administratiekantoor*), which prevent outsider shareholders exerting effective governance power over firms (Go-Feij 1999).

[3] Some researchers have estimated change in ownership concentration over time (e.g., Franks et al. 2004), but only for a limited number of countries.

ISS (Institutional Shareholder Services) corporate governance rating methodology (Aggarwal et al. 2007). The scores for individual companies are aggregated by country to create a country GOV score (see Table 1.3). However, like ownership concentration, the main practical drawback of the GOV index is its unavailability as a time series. Corporate governance ratings may become a more viable candidate for inclusion in panel data analysis in the future, once they have built up a track record of observations over a reasonable span of years.

4.1.2 Equity share

The first series proposed for utilization as a proxy for corporate governance is national stock market capitalization divided by gross domestic product (GDP), also known as "equity share." A higher equity share is taken to imply a greater orientation toward external minority shareholders, that is, outsider capital. The ability of corporations to issue publicly-traded equity (i.e., equity listed and traded on a stock exchange), and to retain a buoyant share price, requires that firms submit themselves to an increased level of external scrutiny and accountability. In order to be willing to buy and hold the equity of publicly traded companies, external investors need to be persuaded that such companies are being operated in their interests (and not only in the interests of other stakeholders, such as blockholders or employees, or management itself). Consequently, a high proportion of publicly issued equity in GDP is taken to imply that firms have been successful in orienting their governance to the needs of outsider capital and minority stakeholders.

Equity share for four of the countries of the data set is presented in Figure 4.1. These countries are representative of the broader sample in that they all experienced a significant upswing in equity share during the 1990s, although there was substantial national variation in the extent of that upswing. The biggest gainers included Switzerland, Sweden, Finland, and the Netherlands, while equity share grew less buoyantly in Austria, Italy, Norway, Portugal, and Denmark. The series peaked in most countries in 2000/2001, and fell back to lower levels in 2002 and 2003 (albeit remaining substantially higher than in the early 1990s). It has, however, moved back toward its previous highs during the last few years (i.e., during the 2004–6 period).

There are several factors that could affect the use of equity share as a proxy for the blockholder or shareholder stance of corporate governance. First, although a firm may go public as a means of increasing its access to new sources of external finance, controlling stakes may already be held by incumbent blockholders. An indeterminate proportion of national equity markets

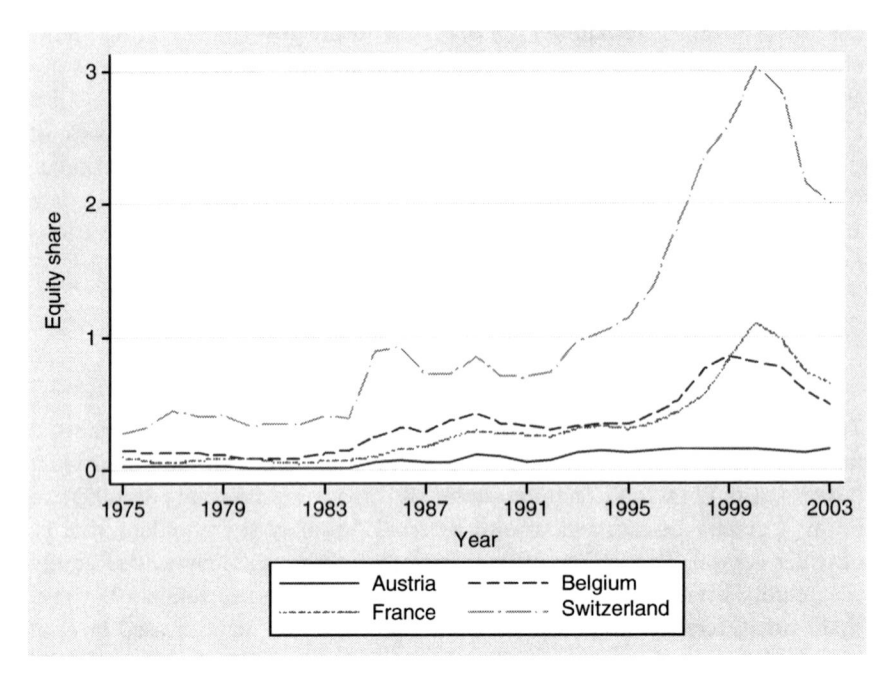

Figure 4.1 Equity share, 1975–2003: Austria, Belgium, France, and Switzerland

may thus represent the sunk investment of insider capital. A high level of equity share may not, therefore, precisely reflect the extent of the outsider orientation of a country's corporate governance.[4]

Second, the relative size of an economy's equity market may be driven by country-specific institutional factors unrelated to corporate governance. In particular, the nature of a country's pension system may affect the magnitude of funds available for equity investment. According to Bonoli (2003), European pension systems can be divided into two groups: "social insurance" countries and "multipillar" countries. In social insurance countries, public arrangements dominate retirement income provision, and the private and occupational pension sectors are relatively small. In multipillar countries, the state provides only a minimum pension while occupational and private arrangements provide a much larger proportion of pension benefits. In

---

[4] One way of overcoming this problem is to use the number of listed companies – rather than their market capitalization – as a proxy for corporate governance. However, this measure suffers from the major disadvantage of not taking into account company size. Countries with a concentrated industrial structure will register low scores for reasons unrelated to their corporate governance orientation (Rajan and Zingales 2003: 11).

order to fund their future pension commitments, multipillar countries are likely to accumulate – through the activities of pension funds and similar non-state savings institutions – larger pools of savings available for equity investment than social insurance countries, which tend to fund pension provision from general taxation.

According to Bonoli's categorization, the Netherlands, Denmark, and Switzerland are examples of European countries with multipillar pension structures, whereas Germany, France, and Spain are social insurance countries (Bonoli 2003; Brooks 2005). Consequently, it is possible that the former group of countries may be structurally inclined toward an equity-oriented financial system regardless of the nature of domestic corporate governance. In the case of Switzerland, the potential supply of funds available for equity investment may also be affected by its status as a leading offshore banking center; this may push the level of equity share to a higher level than merited by the shareholder orientation of corporate governance conditions.

Although these considerations suggest the need for caution in a simplistic application of equity share as a measure of corporate governance orientation, *changes* in equity share are still likely to provide a useful indicator of corporate governance behavior over time. It seems reasonable to assume that change in equity share will be driven primarily by the buying and selling activities of outsider capital (Shleifer and Vishny 1986). In contrast, controlling ownership stakes are likely to be relatively unchanging (given their strategic rather than short-term profit maximizing rationale). Furthermore, the time-constant institutional differences between countries arising, for example, from different types of pension system can be taken into account through the use of dummy variables (or fixed effects) in the panel data estimation process.

A further factor that may affect the efficacy of equity share as a measure of blockholder or shareholder corporate governance is the recent phenomenon of "de-equitization." This occurs when listed firms withdraw their equity from public equity markets. The most high-profile cause of de-equitization in recent years has been driven by the rise of the private equity industry. In order to undertake a so-called leveraged buyout, private equity firms use funds raised from debt markets to purchase the equity of a publicly-listed company. The firm is then taken out of the public market, and managed as a private company. This process may serve to reduce equity share (which relates entirely to publicly-traded equity) without any necessary reduction in the shareholder orientation of corporate governance.

However, the net effect of de-equitization on equity share has (to date) been relatively insignificant in magnitude. Although there is a lack of publicly available data, the European Venture Capital Association report that, in 2005,

Table 4.2 European private equity investment as a percentage of GDP, 2005

Denmark	1.224
Sweden	0.861
Netherlands	0.600
Spain	0.475
Finland	0.471
France	0.453
Switzerland	0.305
Germany	0.247
Norway	0.240
Greece	0.217
Italy	0.203
Portugal	0.180
Belgium	0.159
Austria	0.083

Source: European Venture Capital Association, Thomson Financial, and Pricewaterhouse Coopers.

private equity investment was only a fraction of a percent of GDP in most European economies (see Table 4.2). Given that the average equity share amongst the fifteen countries in the panel in 2003 was 63 percent of GDP, this is a relatively small distortion. In most economies, the impact remained well under 0.5 percent of GDP.

There is a final characteristic of equity share that should be considered. Equity valuations tend to exhibit more volatile cyclical behavior than GDP. In particular, the equity market may experience significant increases or decreases relative to GDP in the short term (e.g., over one to three years) due to fluctuations in interest rates (the "credit cycle"), economic growth, or changes in the general macroeconomic environment (Mendoza and Terrones 2008: 2). A substantial increase in the level of equity market was a feature of the late 1990s; the value of major equity market indices experienced substantial gains in two to three years leading up to March 2000 (the so-called dot-com bubble), and then underwent a substantial downward correction in the subsequent couple of years (Kindleberger and Aliber 2005). This cyclicality is apparent in the latter years of the time series presented in Figure 4.1.

However, at least part of the downturn in equity share observed in 2001 and 2002 is expected to be accounted for by changes in the explanatory variables of my hypothesis, that is, the interaction of partisanship and product market competition. During this period, the Left's participation in European government declined (see Figure 1.2) and the pace of liberalization in product markets reduced (see Chapter 5). Furthermore, fluctuations in equity market valuations that occur for cyclical economic reasons

Table 4.3 Descriptive statistics for equity share (equity market capitalization of listed companies divided by GDP), 1975–2003

	Minimum Value	Maximum Value	Mean	Standard deviation	Number of observations
Austria	0.019	0.170	0.087	0.056	29
Belgium	0.082	0.862	0.350	0.231	29
Denmark	0.077	0.677	0.287	0.180	29
Finland	0.040	2.702	0.471	0.686	29
France	0.052	1.107	0.318	0.294	29
Germany	0.080	0.716	0.247	0.170	29
Greece	0.019	1.421	0.254	0.348	29
Italy	0.026	0.700	0.196	0.181	29
Japan	0.283	1.408	0.668	0.309	29
Netherlands	0.155	1.815	0.610	0.477	29
Norway	0.032	0.399	0.192	0.131	29
Portugal	0.002	0.602	0.171	0.186	27
Spain	0.060	0.810	0.302	0.232	29
Sweden	0.088	1.475	0.530	0.402	29
Switzerland	0.278	3.034	1.083	0.834	29
Overall sample	0.002	3.034	0.385	0.445	433

Sources: World Bank; Beck et al. (2000).

(rather than reflecting changes in corporate governance) can be compensated for through the inclusion of relevant cyclical macroeconomic variables as controls in the econometric analysis, for example, interest rates and GDP growth. Finally, although speculative bubbles may temporarily affect the valuation of equity markets, the market efficiency of sophisticated financial markets in the major industrialized economies tends to ensure that this is a relatively short-lived phenomenon (Malkiel 2003). Consequently, the cyclicality of equity share does not render it unsuitable as a proxy for firm-level corporate governance.

In summary, equity share is likely to be a useful measure of corporate governance in the context of a panel data regression analysis. Table 4.3 presents descriptive statistics for this measure for each of the countries of the sample. The variable is calculated on the basis of average annual stock market capitalizations. The source of post-1989 data is the World Bank Database on Financial Development and Structure constructed by Beck et al. (2000), which was subsequently updated in March 2007. Data relating to years prior to 1989 is obtained from the Global Financial Database, which derives its data from statistical yearbooks published by local stock exchanges and national statistical agencies. Data for most countries is available on an annual basis from the mid-1970s until 2003.[5] The data set provides the possibility of obtaining up to 433 observations across the fifteen countries.

4.1.3 Value of shares traded

The second proxy to be utilized as a measure of *de facto* corporate governance behavior is the total value of shares traded on national stock markets divided by GDP ("value traded"). This data series is commonly used as an indicator of the activity or liquidity of equity markets. It indicates the extent to which the ownership of listed corporations is shifting between different equity market participants, rather than the overall value of ownership stakes (which is captured by equity share).

The rationale of this measure from a corporate governance perspective is based on an assumption about the differing ownership behavior of blockholders and outsider capital. Whereas blockholders own controlling stakes in firms for long-term strategic reasons, outsider capital – such as pension funds, mutual funds, and hedge funds – are active in the buying and selling of shares on stock markets, and are responsible for generating a much larger proportion of annual turnover (Shleifer and Vishny 1986).[6] Consequently, a higher level of value traded in GDP can be taken to imply a greater orientation of corporate ownership toward outsider capital, and hence a closer alignment of the corporate sector to interests of external minority shareholders.

The level of value traded for four countries from the data set is shown in Figure 4.2. As with equity share, the countries shown in the graph indicate a significant increase in outsider orientation amongst European economies during the late 1990s, although a fair degree of cross-national variation is observable in the extent of this change. The countries experiencing the most significant increases in the measure – Finland, Sweden, the Netherlands, and Switzerland – are similar to those highlighted by equity share. In contrast, Norway, Portugal, Denmark, and Italy once again record less significant increases.

In contrast to equity share, stable blockholder ownership positions do not affect the level of this measure. However, changes in the level of value traded may be influenced to some degree by country-specific institutional factors (such as the nature of pension provision), the effect of credit cycles, and

---

[5] The only exception is Portugal, which lacks observations for 1975 and 1976.

[6] There is no hard data concerning the split of European stock market turnover between blockholders and outsider capital. However, Denis and Sarin's analysis (1999) of blockholder-controlled corporations in the United States finds their ownership structure to be far more stable than those of diffusely (i.e., outsider) owned firms.

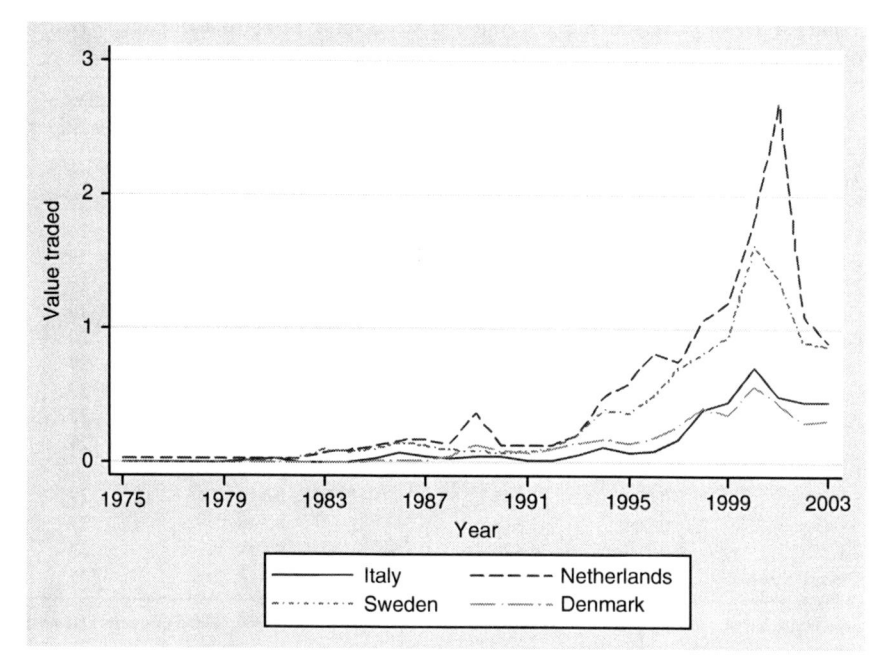

Figure 4.2 Value traded, 1975–2003: Italy, Sweden, the Netherlands, and Denmark

macroeconomic instability. The likely effect of such factors on value traded is less easy to predict than for equity share. For example, cyclical fluctuations in equity markets do not necessarily translate into a lower value of shares traded. Indeed, it is possible for value traded to be higher during a bear market, that is, when levels of equity markets are depressed due to negative market sentiment, than when equity markets are undergoing an upswing. Nonetheless, a significant amount of cyclicality is observable in the data presented in the Figure 4.2 – particularly in the wake of the market downturn in 2000/2001. Consequently, it is still prudent to control for pension systems and cyclical macroeconomic factors – such as interest rates and economic growth – when utilizing value traded in an econometric analysis. As with equity share, it is expected that at least part of the downturn in value traded will be accounted for by changes in the explanatory variables of my hypothesis.

Table 4.4 presents descriptive statistics for value traded for each country in the sample. The data series consists of annual totals of the total value of equity traded in stock markets divided by GDP. The source of the data is the same as that for equity share, and the observations cover the same countries and a similar time frame (albeit with slightly fewer observations for Denmark).

102 Corporate Governance, Competition, and Political Parties

Table 4.4 Descriptive statistics for value traded (value of listed companies traded, divided by GDP), 1975–2003

	Minimum value	Maximum Value	Mean	Standard deviation	Number of observations
Austria	0.001	0.113	0.037	0.037	29
Belgium	0.006	0.235	0.066	0.066	29
Denmark	0.001	0.579	0.161	0.166	24
Finland	0.003	1.723	0.279	0.496	29
France	0.009	0.816	0.192	0.247	29
Germany	0.015	0.751	0.225	0.202	29
Greece	0.000	1.572	0.139	0.328	29
Italy	0.004	0.724	0.135	0.198	29
Japan	0.102	0.946	0.341	0.232	29
Netherlands	0.027	2.690	0.465	0.631	29
Norway	0.001	0.360	0.116	0.124	29
Portugal	0.000	0.511	0.091	0.140	27
Spain	0.004	1.698	0.349	0.540	29
Sweden	0.004	1.628	0.341	0.445	29
Switzerland	0.107	2.476	0.770	0.794	29
Overall sample	0.000	2.690	0.249	0.417	428

Sources: Beck et al. (2000). Updated on March 21, 2007. Data points prior to 1989: Global Financial Database (http://www.globalfinancialdata.com).

4.1.4 International equity issuance

A third proxy to be utilized in the quantitative analysis is the value of international equity issuance as a percentage of GDP ("international equity issuance"). This is data collated by the Bank for International Settlements (BIS), and relates to equity issuance that is specifically targeted toward nondomestic investors. It consists of equity issues falling into three categories: equity issuance from domestic corporations in foreign markets; equity issuance from domestic corporations in foreign currency in the domestic market; and equity issuance from domestic corporations in domestic currency in the domestic market targeted at nondomestic investors. Data refers to both initial public offerings and secondary equity issuance from existing public companies.

Unlike equity share, the level of this proxy is unlikely to be distorted by the equity market activities of blockholders due to its exclusion of issues that are oriented toward domestic ownership groups. The rationale for this proxy is that companies will have to exhibit outsider-friendly governance if they are to raise significant funds in international markets through the issuance of such stock. Its main limitation is that equity issuance activity (the so-called

Measuring Change in Corporate Governance

primary equity market) occurs in cycles, depending on the current state of market sentiment. Issuance boomed in the late 1990s, and then more or less dried up in most markets in 2000 and 2001. These cyclical movements did not necessarily reflect underlying structural changes in corporate governance, but rather the volatilities of the credit cycle, which need to be controlled-for in an empirical analysis.

Another issue relates to country size. A large country may be able to fund a large proportion of its corporate financing requirements from domestic capital markets. Consequently, it may have less need to issue equity that is oriented toward international investors. International equity issuance relative to GDP in such countries may, therefore, incorrectly suggest a relatively weak outsider-orientation. In contrast, a small country may need to raise a high proportion of its corporate finance from international capital markets due to the limited pool of savings available from domestic sources. To allow for the impact that country size may have on international issuance as a measure of corporate governance, it is important to include relevant controls (e.g., absolute size of economy or population) in the econometric analysis.

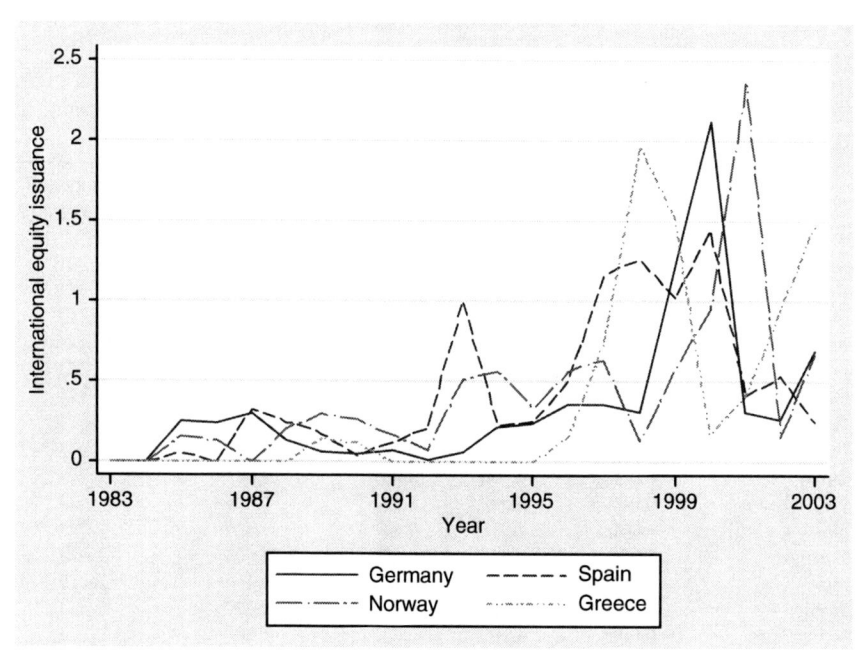

Figure 4.3 International equity issuance, 1983–2003: Germany, Norway, Spain, and Greece

104   Corporate Governance, Competition, and Political Parties

The volatility of the series is apparent from Figure 4.3, which presents data for a further four countries. Although the data suggests a general upward trend in outsider orientation for European economies during the 1990s (which is representative of the data for the other countries), there are considerable short-term fluctuations. There exists a reasonable correlation with the other two series in terms of which countries have experienced the most rapid growth. However, as anticipated, larger European countries – such as Germany and France – register a relatively low level of outsiderness relative to the other proxies. The largest amount of international equity issuance is achieved by the Netherlands and Switzerland. In contrast, the lowest amounts (as a percentage of GDP) are undertaken by Italy, Denmark, and Austria (suggesting a less outsider-oriented corporate governance environment).

Table 4.5 provides descriptive statistics for international equity issuance on a country-by-country basis. The data series covers a shorter period than equity share and value traded (1983–2003), and so provides fewer potential observations for the fifteen countries of the panel than the previous two proxies.

To conclude, this section has made the case for the utilization of three proxies of *de facto* corporate governance in the empirical analysis: equity share, value traded, and international equity issuance. The correlation between the three

Table 4.5 Descriptive statistics for international equity issuance, 1983–2003 (value of equity issuance to international investors as percentage of GDP)

	Minimum value	Maximum value	Mean	Standard deviation	Number of observations
Austria	0.000	0.720	0.209	0.216	21
Belgium	0.000	2.495	0.392	0.632	21
Denmark	0.000	2.272	0.295	0.497	21
Finland	0.000	3.601	0.837	1.065	21
France	0.000	1.300	0.477	0.447	21
Germany	0.000	2.116	0.348	0.490	21
Greece	0.000	1.964	0.365	0.603	21
Italy	0.000	0.857	0.275	0.265	21
Japan	0.000	0.260	0.059	0.087	21
Netherlands	0.000	6.579	1.252	1.625	21
Norway	0.000	2.356	0.417	0.516	21
Portugal	0.000	1.874	0.426	0.629	21
Spain	0.000	1.443	0.440	0.456	21
Sweden	0.000	4.494	0.683	1.029	21
Switzerland	0.000	4.100	1.053	1.267	21
Overall sample	0.000	6.579	0.502	0.814	315

Source: Bank for International Settlements (BIS). Securities statistics (electronic version, as of June 2006).

Table 4.6 Correlation matrix of chosen corporate governance proxies (and ownership concentration)

	Equity share	Value-traded	International equity issuance	Ownership concentration
Equity share	1.000	–	–	–
Value traded	0.885	1.000	–	–
International equity issuance	0.681	0.684	1.000	–
Ownership concentration	−0.677	−0.567	−0.323	1.000

Notes: Table shows value of correlation coefficient (r). Correlations in respect of ownership concentration—for which there is only one observation per country—are calculated utilizing the 1990–5 mean values of the other variables.

chosen proxies is shown in Table 4.6 (along with their cross-sectional correlation with ownership concentration). As can be seen, the equity share and value traded proxies are relatively highly correlated with each other. Equity share and value traded also exhibit a fair degree of correlation with ownership concentration. Perhaps not surprisingly (given its greater volatility), international equity issuance is the least covariant of the three chosen proxies, and is also not strongly correlated with ownership concentration.

4.2 MEASURES OF CORPORATE GOVERNANCE REGULATION

As described in Chapter 2, there are many ways in which insiders may seek to take advantage of the "private benefits of control" (Grossman and Hart 1988). The legal system can be used to counter this risk if market forces are viewed as insufficient to eliminate the moral hazard facing insiders (Clark 1986). However, there is significant variation in the extent to which national law and regulation has sought to constrain the activities of controlling blockholders or management, and make them accountable to minority shareholders. The next section investigates potential measures of corporate governance regulation. It starts by considering LLSV's well-known index of antidirector rights.

4.2.1 LLSV's index of shareholder protection

The most widely utilized measure of *de jure* regulation in the corporate governance literature is the antidirector rights index developed by LLSV

(1998). The index seeks to measure the extent to which the legal framework in forty-nine developed and developing economies restrains the capacity of insiders – such as controlling blockholders or management – to divert corporate wealth to themselves, at the expense of minority shareholders.

It should be noted that regulation relating to shareholder protection represents only one aspect of corporate governance regulation. Other areas of the regulatory framework may also be relevant to the insider–outsider stance of corporate governance, including rules on insider trading, financial disclosure, financial transparency, and accounting standards. However, these areas suffer from the disadvantage that they have not generally been quantified in the form of a numerical index that is available as a time series. Consequently, quantitative studies of corporate governance tend to use measures of shareholder protection as proxies for the changing nature of corporate governance regulation as a whole.

The original antidirector rights index developed by LLSV attempted to provide a cross-sectional snapshot of the situation prevailing in the early to mid-1990s (La Porta et al. 1998). However, the series has been updated and turned into a time series, covering the period 1993–2002, by Pagano and Volpin (2005). The index is constructed as a summary of six possible legal protections available to shareholders *vis-à-vis* company insiders. Each individual protection is evaluated as a dummy variable ($1 = $ protection exists, $0 = $ protection does not exist). Consequently, the total score for each country ranges between 0 and 6, with a high score indicating a high level of minority shareholder protection. The six categories of minority shareholder protections are as follows:

1. Voting by mail: It is often costly or inconvenient for minority shareholders to attend shareholder meetings in person. This may preclude them from voting against proposals put forward by company directors. Although it may be possible for minority shareholders to place their votes in the hands of proxy institutions that vote on their behalf, in practice minority shareholders may simply not bother to vote. They are most likely to cast votes that fully reflect their preferences – and thereby better represent the influence of outsider capital over corporate governance – if postal voting is available. This dummy variable is set to 1 if the law explicitly mandates, or sets as a default rule, that the company must provide a proxy form allowing shareholders to vote on the items on the agenda of a general shareholders' meeting by mail.

2. Obstacles in the way of voting: In many countries, the law permits companies to insist that shareholders deposit their shares with the company, or a financial intermediary, immediately prior to voting at a shareholders'

meeting. The rationale for this requirement is to verify that shareholders have the right to vote at the meeting, and reflects the fact that – in many countries – shares are in bearer rather than registered form (i.e., there is no continually updated register of company shareholders). However, this requirement imposes significant costs on shareholders. While they are waiting for confirmation of their right to vote, shareholders may not sell their shares. Furthermore, the fact that the identity of most minority shareholders is not known prior to the shareholders' meeting makes it difficult for potentially dissenting minority shareholders to form coalitions with a view to opposing the resolutions of company directors. Consequently, the blocking requirement is a barrier to the ability of outsider capital to exert an influence over the corporate governance of the firm. The dummy variable is set equal to 1 if the law neither requires nor explicitly permits shareholders to deposit with the company or another firm any of their shares prior to a general shareholders meeting.

3. Voting rules in the election of company directors: The election of directors through either a system of cumulative voting – whereby all of a shareholder's votes can be placed behind one candidate – or proportional representation increases the potential for minority shareholders to exert significant influence over the composition of the board of directors or the supervisory board. Otherwise, there is a substantial risk that controlling blockholders will use their position of control to appoint board members that entirely represent their own interests. The dummy variable is set equal to 1 if the law explicitly mandates, or sets as a default rule, that directors or supervisory board candidates can be elected either through cumulative voting or proportional representation.

4. Oppressed minority mechanisms: The legal system may provide mechanisms whereby minority shareholders can seek redress against the self-dealing activities of insiders. These might take the form of a legal process in which transactions can be rescinded if they can be shown to be prejudicial to the interests of the firm as a whole. Alternatively, they may offer the right to recover damages arising from prejudicial decision-making by controlling blockholders. These mechanisms go beyond the legal measures available in most countries that relate purely to managerial fraud or gross negligence; they represent an attempt on behalf of the law to increase the accountability of corporate insiders to external minority shareholders. The dummy variable equals 1 if shareholders owning 10 percent or less of the capital stock can challenge (i.e., by either seeking damages or having the transaction rescinded) resolutions that benefit controlling shareholders and damage the company.

5. Preemptive rights: One way in which controlling blockholders might seek to expropriate the wealth of minority shareholders is by issuing new stock, and offering the shares to related parties at below-market prices. This would result in a dilution in the ownership stakes of the original minority shareholders. Such an expropriation can be prevented by a legal requirement to offer new issues of stock to existing shareholders in proportion to their existing shareholdings (a so-called rights issue). This dummy variable equals 1 when the law or listing rules explicitly mandate, or set as a default rule, that existing shareholders are offered the first opportunity to buy new issues of stock.

6. The right to call a shareholders' meeting: Legal requirements differ regarding the ownership proportion that is required in order to call a shareholders' meeting. A lower ownership requirement offers smaller shareholders a greater opportunity to hold insiders to account in the governance of the company. This dummy variable is set to 1 when the equity capital needed to call a shareholders' meeting (directly or through the courts) is less than or equal to 10 percent.

Table 4.7 provides a summary of LLSV's initial evaluation of these legal protections for minority shareholders ca. 1993, and the total index score for each country in the sample (along with values for the United Kingdom and United States for comparison). A notable feature of the scores is the relatively low values awarded to most continental European economies in comparison with common law countries, that is, the United Kingdom and the United States.

The 1998 *Law and Finance* article,[7] in which La Porta, Lopez-de-Silanes, Shleifer, and Vishny presented their antidirector index, is one of the most frequently cited in the comparative law and finance literature (Braendle 2006: 4). Their index has been utilized in a large number of recent empirical studies by respected financial economists (e.g., Dyck and Zingales [2004], Doidge et al. [2005], Licht et al. [2005], Stulz [2005]). However, it has also been subjected to a growing battery of criticism from legal researchers (Coffee 2001; Braendle 2006; Schmidbauer 2006; Spamann 2006; Lele and Siems 2007). A particular source of grievance for many European scholars has been the implication that legal systems with a common law origin (e.g., the United Kingdom, United States, Canada, Australia, and New Zealand) offer better protections for minority shareholders than civil law systems (particularly those of French civil law origin). This has provoked criticism of the index

---

[7] La Porta, Rafael, Florencio Lopez-de-Silanes, Andrei Shleifer, and Robert W. Vishny. 1998. "Law and Finance." *Journal of Political Economy* 106 (4):1113–55.

Table 4.7 Antidirector rights index — original assessment of legal protections of minority shareholder protections relating to the early 1990s by LLSV

	Vote by mail	Shares not blocked	Cumulative voting/PR	Oppressed minority	Pre-emptive rights	Capital to call meeting (%)	Total index score
Austria	0	0	0	0	1	5	2
Belgium	0	0	0	0	0	20	0
Denmark	0	1	0	0	0	10	2
Finland	0	1	0	0	1	10	3
France	1	0	0	0	1	10	3
Germany	0	0	0	0	0	5	1
Greece	0	0	0	0	1	5	2
Italy	0	0	0	0	1	20	1
Japan	0	1	1	1	0	3	4
Netherlands	0	0	0	0	1	10	2
Norway	1	1	0	0	1	10	4
Portugal	0	1	0	0	1	5	3
Spain	0	0	1	1	1	5	4
Sweden	0	1	0	0	1	10	3
Switzerland	0	0	0	0	1	10	2
United Kingdom	1	1	0	1	1	10	5
United States	1	1	1	1	0	10	5

Note: protection exists = 1; protection does not exist = 0.
Source: La Porta et al. (1998).

at a number of levels; from conceptual disagreements regarding the validity of a quantitative measure of law, to more specific disputes regarding the coding of the index.

A general issue concerning LLSV's approach is the difficulty of attempting to summarize the law in the form of quantitative indices (Siems 2005). Law is invariably complex, and riven with caveats and "shades of grey." It may, therefore, be crude or inaccurate (or both) to summarize it with a quantitative score. This may be a particular problem when the nature of the law must be summarized in the form of a binary variable (does shareholder protection exist, yes or no), as is the case with LLSV's index (Braendle 2006).

Furthermore, interpretation of the law is often a highly subjective process. This is a difficult enough matter in a domestic context; however in relation to foreign jurisdictions the problems are magnified. Researchers have to deal with unfamiliar languages, institutions, and legal processes. Recent studies have attempted to overcome some of these problems by assembling teams of locally-based lawyers, and asking them to assess the law in relation to shareholder protections. However, it is invariably necessary to rely on the judgment of individual practitioners, who may not necessarily share a comparable approach in their interpretation of the legal situation or the questions they are being asked to answer (Spamann 2006: 5). The disparity of interpretation regarding the true nature of shareholder protection in different countries has been evident in several recent contributions to the literature. For example, whereas LLSV's index originally assigned an aggregate score of 1 (out of 6) to Germany (see Table 4.7), Braendle's assessment is that it is entitled to a score of 4 (Braendle 2006). Similarly, whereas Austria only scores 2 in LLSV's original index, Schmidbauer (2006) judges it worthy of 4.

The area of most vigorous debate amongst legal scholars regarding LLSV's index has been in respect of the coding of the six index components for particular countries. Critics have been eager to demonstrate that – even on the basis of LLSV's own criteria – the protections available to minority shareholders in civil law countries are not significantly different to those available in countries with a common law legal origin.

When evaluating legal protections, relevant laws can be distinguished in terms of whether their provisions are mandatory, default, or optional in nature. A default rule is where a statute contains enabling provisions which permit, under certain conditions, an opt-out or opt-in from the rule. According to a number of critics, LLSV do not code the components of their index in a consistent manner with respect to these considerations. In some instances, the existence of optional rules is taken as indicative of protection, while in other cases default or mandatory protection is used as the basis for coding a protection in the index. The lack of a systematic approach in this respect has arguably led to an excessively negative assessment of shareholder protections in many non-common law countries, particularly with regard to oppressed minority mechanisms and preemptive rights (Braendle 2006; Schmidbauer 2006; Spamann 2006).

A particularly compelling reason for rejecting the coding of LLSV's index is that three of the LLSV authors – Rafael La Porta, Florencio Lopez-de-Silanes, and Andrei Shleifer – have now themselves revised the coding of the index (in a recent paper with Simeon Djankov of the World Bank). Although their new coding relates to the situation prevailing in May 2003 (rather than ca. 1993), most of the changes arise due to fundamental reassessments of the level of shareholder protection in various countries. In particular, the authors have now attempted to deliver a consistent coding of shareholder protection based on mandatory or default rules (and not optional regulations or legislation with enabling provisions that need not be adopted by a company). Their scores also recognize shareholder protections that may be present in regulation other than company law, including stock market law and regulations, stock market listing rules, civil procedure codes, and the criminal code. Their recoded index has a correlation of +0.6 with the original antidirector rights index, indicating significant revision, although the authors still argue that shareholder protection in common law countries is superior to that provided in the civil law countries of continental Europe (Djankov et al. 2008: 31).

Djankov et al.'s reassessment of the components of LLSV's original index are shown in Table 4.8. The original scores of LLSV are shown in parentheses. It can be seen that some countries – particularly Belgium, Denmark, and Germany – have improved their aggregate scores, whereas the index value of

Table 4.8 Antidirector rights index — revised assessment of shareholder protections (as of 2003)

Country	Vote by mail	Shares not blocked	Cumulative voting/PR	Oppressed minority	Pre-emptive rights	Capital to call meeting (%)	Total index score
Austria	0 (0)	0 (0)	0 (0)	0.5 (0)	1 (1)	5 (5)	2.5 (2)
Belgium	1 (0)	0 (0)	0 (0)	1.0 (0)	1 (0)	20 (20)	3.0 (0)
Canada	1 (1)	1 (1)	0 (1)	1.0 (1)	0 (0)	5 (5)	4.0 (5)
Denmark	0 (0)	1 (1)	0 (0)	1.0 (0)	1 (0)	10 (10)	4.0 (2)
Finland	0 (0)	1 (1)	0 (0)	0.5 (0)	1 (1)	10 (10)	3.5 (3)
France	1 (1)	0 (0)	0 (0)	0.5 (0)	1 (1)	5 (10)	3.5 (3)
Germany	1 (0)	0 (0)	0 (0)	0.5 (0)	1 (0)	5 (5)	3.5 (1)
Greece	0 (0)	0 (0)	0 (0)	0.0 (0)	1 (1)	5 (5)	2.0 (2)
Italy	0 (0)	0 (0)	0 (0)	0.0 (0)	1 (1)	10 (20)	2.0 (1)
Japan	1 (0)	1 (1)	1 (1)	0.5 (1)	0 (0)	3 (3)	4.5 (4)
Netherlands	0 (0)	0 (0)	0 (0)	0.5 (0)	1 (1)	10 (10)	2.5 (2)
Norway	0 (1)	1 (1)	0 (0)	0.5 (0)	1 (1)	5 (10)	3.5 (4)
Portugal	0 (0)	0 (1)	0 (0)	0.5 (0)	1 (1)	5 (5)	2.5 (3)
Spain	1 (0)	0 (0)	1 (1)	1.0 (1)	1 (1)	5 (5)	5.0 (4)
Sweden	0 (0)	1 (1)	0 (0)	0.5 (0)	1 (1)	10 (10)	3.5 (3)
Switzerland	0 (0)	0 (0)	0 (0)	1.0 (0)	1 (1)	10 (10)	3.0 (2)
United Kingdom	1 (1)	1 (1)	0 (0)	1.0 (1)	1 (1)	10 (10)	5.0 (5)
United States	1 (1)	1 (1)	0 (1)	1.0 (1)	0 (0)	–(10)	3.0 (5)

Note: Figures in parentheses are the original assessments (for 1993) of La Porta et al. (1998). Coding: protection exists = 1; protection does not exist = 0. In the case of oppressed minority mechanisms, equals 1 if minority shareholders may challenge a resolution of *both* the shareholders and the board, equals 0.5 if minority shareholders may challenge a resolution of *either* the shareholders or the board. 0 otherwise.

Sources: Djankov et al. (2008) and La Porta et al. (1998).

the United States has been significantly reduced. Other countries – such as Greece and the United Kingdom – have unchanged scores.

4.2.2 An evaluation of available measures of corporate governance regulation

The new LLSV-based index may represent an improvement on the original measure in terms of coding. However, a more fundamental criticism of the antidirector rights index is that its overall structure and composition renders it inadequate as a means of representing the regulatory environment for shareholder protection. For example, Coffee (2001) argues that the six components of LLSV's index offer only an *ad hoc* and partial reflection of the extent of the shareholder protection offered by national legal systems. A number of areas relevant to shareholder protection – such as the type of issues on which shareholders can vote, the employment and remuneration terms of directors, and rules concerning board composition – are not considered by the six components of the index.

It is also asserted that the choice of components reflects a US bias toward corporate governance (Berglöf and von Thadden 1999). For example, the greater prevalence of bearer shares outside common law countries offers shareholders the benefit of anonymity. However, they also give rise to a practical need to block shares prior to a shareholder meeting in order to verify voting rights. This biases downwards the index score of such countries relative to those where registered shares are the norm (e.g., the United Kingdom and the United States), and hence where the blocking of shares prior to a shareholders' meeting is not necessary. Another alleged example of common law bias is provided by the fact that certain legal protections included in the index may not be relevant to particular legal jurisdictions. For example, the ability to use cumulative voting to elect directors may – in the context of a US company – be an important component of shareholder protection. However, in other jurisdictions, similar benefits may be provided by different legal mechanisms or institutional setups, for example, the corporate governance safeguards offered by the European dual board structure. Consequently, shareholders may obtain functionally equivalent protection through the legal system or institutional framework, but this does not necessarily register in LLSV's index (Braendle and Noll 2004).

A particularly significant omission from the antidirector rights index is any measure of law enforcement. The index components relate entirely to the "law on the books." However, the ability to enforce protections in a timely and cost-effective manner is as important to shareholders as the nominal existence of legal protections on the statute book (Azfar et al. 1999; Modigliani and Perotti 2000). In their 1998 article, LLSV provides an estimate of "law and order" enforcement for the forty-nine countries in their sample, based on the assessment of private credit risk agencies in respect of the efficiency of the judicial system, the rule of law, corruption, and the risk of expropriation by the state (La Porta et al. 1998: 1140). However, these protections are not included as components of the antidirector index, and have not been updated by Pagano and Volpin (2005) as part of the process of turning the LLSV index into a time series.

A number of legal researchers have now turned their backs entirely on the LLSV index as a measure of shareholder protection. For example, as part of a major project at the Centre for Business Research at Cambridge, Lele and Siems (2007) have recently created a new set of indices of shareholder protection. These indices are constructed from sixty sub-variables, which assess a much wider range of factors relevant to shareholder protection than LLSV's index. Furthermore, their new index includes variables that consider the extent to which shareholder protections are enforceable. The aggregate

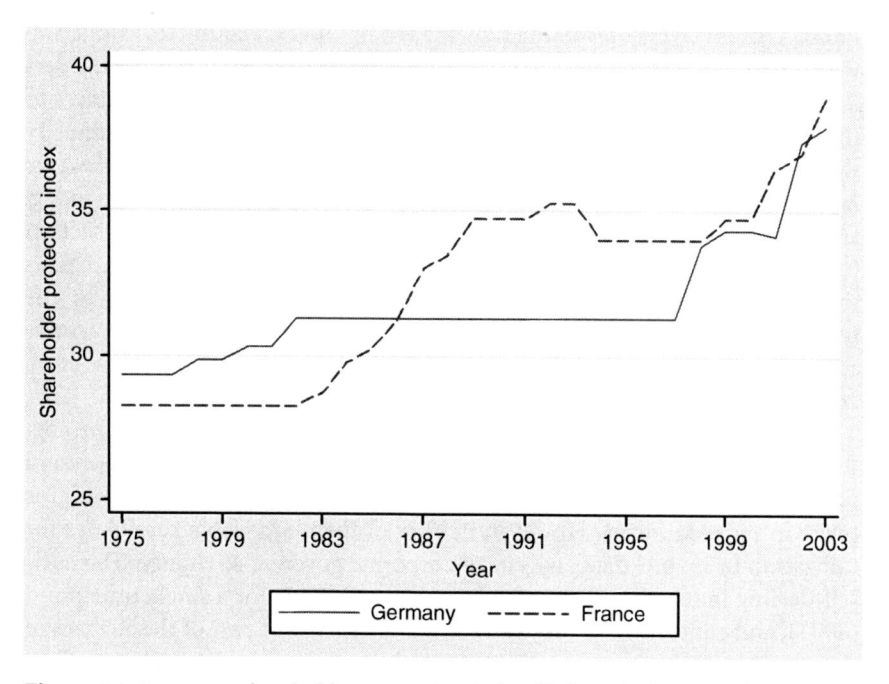

Figure 4.4 Aggregate shareholder protection index (Lele and Siems 2007)

values of their shareholder protection indices for Germany and France are presented in Figure 4.4.

A noteworthy feature of the Lele and Siems indices is that they capture a high level of temporal variation, reflecting the significant volume of European corporate governance reform over the last ten years (see Chapter 1). In contrast, many of the country scores in the time-series version of the antidirector rights index (constructed by Pagano and Volpin) are completely static. The differing story suggested by the two indicators is emphasized by the negative sign of their correlation coefficient (−0.11). Interestingly, there is a much higher level of correlation between Lele and Siems' indices of shareholder protection and the *de facto* proxies of corporate governance outcomes presented earlier in this chapter. For example, the correlation with the international equity issuance proxy is around +0.63. However, a downside of Lele and Siems index from a panel data perspective is that it is currently only available for five countries – the United Kingdom, the United States, Germany, France, and India (only two of which form part of our fifteen-country sample).

La Porta, Lopez-de-Silanes, and Shleifer (along with Simeon Djankov of the World Bank) have also sought to design an improved measure of corporate governance regulation through the creation of a so-called anti-self-dealing index. This involves considering how the law in different countries would deal with a hypothetical self-dealing transaction undertaken by corporate insiders for the purpose of diverting corporate wealth from minority shareholders to themselves. The extent to which national law is available to assist minority shareholders in thwarting this transaction – based on the opinion of lawyers from the Lex Mundi global network of law firms – is quantified in the index. By focusing on how the law as a whole responds to a particular transaction (rather than ascertaining the presence or absence of particular laws or regulations), such a methodology attempts to address concerns relating to the functional equivalence of different types of law, along with the arbitrariness and Anglo-centric choice of variables in the original index (Djankov et al. 2008).

It is apparent that the new approaches to quantifying shareholder protection proposed by Lele and Siems (2007), and Djankov et al. (2008), represent potential improvements over LLSV's original index of antidirector rights (even in recoded form). However, neither of them are viable candidates for utilization in a panel data analysis of corporate governance change. The anti-self-dealing index is available on a cross-country basis for a single time point (2003), and conversion of the index into a time series as part of the analysis of this book does not appear to be a practicable option. In order to be credible, such an exercise would need to be based on the input of a team of lawyers in each of the fifteen legal jurisdictions. Furthermore, the nature of this index – based on an assessment of how the legal system as a whole deals with a specific transaction – is likely to be much more difficult to assess historically than the existence or otherwise of specific rules or law.

Similarly, the extension of Lele and Siem's index of shareholder protection to cover the fifteen countries of the panel represents a logistical challenge beyond the scope of this book. The index is composed of sixty sub-variables, each of which would need to be assessed for each country over a period of many years. In the absence of an international legal research team, a broadening of the coverage of this index for utilization in the panel data analysis is not a feasible possibility.

These considerations lead to the conclusion that a satisfactory measure of *de jure* corporate governance for use in panel data analysis is currently unavailable. The extension by Lele and Siems of their newly constructed indices of shareholder protection to a wider range of countries represents a promising avenue for future research. However, proxies based on LLSV's antidirector rights index – despite their ubiquity in the corporate governance literature – are not viewed as tenable representations of corporate governance regulation on a time-series cross-sectional basis.

5

The Measurement of Product Market Competition

According to the theoretical claims advanced by this book, the presence of economic rents is a key determinant of corporate governance outcomes. Economic rents determine the benefit to blockholders of retaining their positions of control and incumbency, and help secure the support of insider labor for a self-regulatory blockholder system of corporate governance. Economic rents depend, in turn, on the intensity of competition in domestic product markets. However, the operationalization of competition is a complex task. The problem is stated by Høj et al. (2007: 5) as follows: "In practice, the concept of competition is difficult to pin down in measurable terms. Since direct measures are lacking, they must be substituted by proxies." In this chapter, the suitability of a range of potential proxies is evaluated.

As in Chapter 4, potential proxies may be representative of a variable in either a *de facto* or *de jure* sense. *De facto* competition refers to actual competitive conditions prevailing in markets. In contrast, *de jure* competition refers to the nature of the regulatory and legal framework relating to product markets. The theoretical claims of this book are ultimately concerned with the relationship between corporate governance and actual product market competition, as the latter determines the size of economic rents. However, it will be argued that the main potential means of measuring competition from a pure *de facto* perspective – such as real price levels, concentration indices, profit margins, and openness to trade – are often distorted in their ability to signal the underlying nature of competitive conditions. Furthermore, they are invariably available as cross-sectional data series, which precludes their utilization in an analysis of corporate governance change. The chapter concludes that a hybrid measure of product market competition – the Organisation for Economic Co-operation and Development's NMR index, which measures competition from a combined *de jure* and *de facto* perspective – offers the most credible representation of competitive conditions in product markets over time. Consequently, the NMR index is the proxy for product market competition that is used in the panel data analysis of Chapter 6.

5.1 REAL PRICE LEVELS

A potential indicator of *de facto* competitive pressure in an economy is the real price level, that is, the relative level of aggregate prices (Gjersem 2004: 6). The logic of this measure is based on the so-called "Law of One Price," which states that the price of similar goods and services should be equal regardless of national location. Arbitrage activity should ensure that the prices of similar products should converge within a relatively short period of time. However, for the law to hold, goods and services must be bought and sold in a frictionless global market. In the real world, market imperfections or barriers in particular national markets or sectors – arising from a lack of product market competition – may cause prices to diverge on a sustained basis. Consequently, a high level of real prices can be interpreted as reflecting a low level of product market competition, and low real prices as an indicator of more competitive conditions.

The determination of an economy's real price level can also be conceptualized in terms of a Stigler–Peltzman framework of regulatory choice (Stigler 1971; Peltzman 1976). According to this framework, the so-called "regulator" of the economy (a metaphor for the overall political decision-making process) faces a choice of where to set domestic price levels. At a certain (high) level of prices, producer interests will maximize profits (and economic rents), whereas at the perfectly competitive price level, the interests of consumers will be maximized. The regulator has to decide which price level between these two extremes to favor, while recognizing that there is a trade-off in respect of winning the political support of producers and consumers. Too high a price level will win the support of producers, but at the expense of consumer votes. In contrast, a low price level will result in increased consumer support, but producer interests will be less willing to provide financial support or pledge the votes under their control (Rogowski and Kayser 2002: 527).

The standard way to calculate real prices is using Purchasing Power Parities (PPPs). PPPs are ratios of the prices in national currency of the same goods or services in different countries. PPPs are normally calculated (e.g., by the OECD) for individual countries relative to a common base country (e.g., the United States). By dividing PPPs by the nominal exchange rate between the currencies of the two countries, a measure of the real price level in a common currency can be obtained. For example, the PPP ratio of an equivalent basket of products in Finland and the United States was 0.75 in 1980. The nominal exchange rate between the Finnish currency and the US dollar was 0.72. Dividing the PPP by the exchange rate gives a result of 1.04, which implies that the price of similar products in Finland were 4 percent higher than in the United States (Schreyer and Koechlin 2002). The occurrence of an actual exchange rate other than the so-called equilibrium exchange rate (equal to the PPP) always implies that price levels differ in the country under consideration relative to the base country.

PPP data is available from the OECD for all of the developed economies on an annual basis, with the United States as the benchmark country. There are two PPP series available. The first relates to the aggregate prices of all goods and services included in gross domestic product (GDP) (i.e., the components of the GDP deflator). The second refers only to the price of goods and services included in private consumption. Given that the GDP deflator takes account of prices not relevant to domestic product markets (e.g., the price of exports), the private consumption PPP is a more appropriate means of calculating real price levels in the context of the analysis of this book (although the two are likely to give similar results: the correlation coefficient between the two is +0.97). Table 5.1 provides a summary of the data for real prices in respect of private consumption, expressed as an index relative to real prices in the United States.

One of the key criteria for choice of a proxy variable is its likely correlation with underlying but unobservable product market competition. This correlation is brought into doubt if a proxy is likely to be strongly correlated with third variables unrelated to competition. The determinants of real prices are examined in a recent paper by Chang et al. (2008), who undertake a detailed panel data analysis of real prices over the period 1970–2000. The primary purpose of their work is to evaluate the importance of electoral system proportionality in determining real prices. However, their results also reveal the significance of a number of other variables.

Variables found by the study to exhibit significant association with real prices include market openness, population (a proxy for market size), and the proportionality of the electoral system. However, this is not necessarily a cause for concern in respect of utilization of real prices as a proxy for competition. The association between these variables and real prices could result from a mutual correlation with underlying product market competition. For example, a larger economy (as proxied by population size) may be more competitive due to the greater difficulty of coordinating collective action among larger groups of producer interests (Olson 1982). The proportionality of the electoral system may be correlated with real prices due to its impact on the incentives of regulators to favor a more consumer or producer-oriented economic system, which will be strongly related to competition (Rogowski and Kayser 2002). In addition, market openness may be related to competition for reasons discussed in Chapter 2 and in Section 5.4 of this chapter.

The Measurement of Product Market Competition 119

Table 5.1 Real prices levels, private consumption (United States = 100)

Country	1970	1975	1980	1985	1990	1995	2000	2005
Austria	54.7	85.3	104.3	63.5	112.2	129.7	84.2	107.6
Belgium	71.9	107.7	125.1	62.9	109.8	126.1	84.9	107.3
Denmark	80.4	127.6	137.9	82.1	145.0	153.3	104.0	140.1
Finland	71.6	108.7	120.0	84.5	154.8	133.4	90.2	120.5
France	76.3	111.8	129.7	72.5	119.3	126.1	84.3	112.1
Germany	72.4	105.9	122.2	68.2	119.8	140.1	90.4	109.8
Greece	48.8	60.2	68.7	44.5	73.1	85.1	63.8	86.4
Italy	58.7	73.2	86.8	58.6	111.6	92.2	74.4	107.2
Japan	59.1	84.1	101.2	86.0	130.1	185.9	143.8	115.7
Netherlands	65.2	104.7	125.6	68.2	110.2	124.0	85.2	109.7
Norway	99.8	145.8	160.3	106.4	152.1	142.3	102.4	135.4
Portugal	44.4	62.0	57.8	35.3	66.5	81.2	59.9	87.6
Spain	43.3	67.9	87.9	49.4	100.4	94.6	68.4	94.7
Sweden	96.4	133.9	151.1	86.0	148.9	132.1	100.3	123.2
Switzerland	56.5	103.1	124.9	81.0	143.4	168.9	112.4	136.8
United Kingdom	60.9	75.4	111.4	66.5	105.2	98.4	95.7	112.5
United States	100.0	100.0	100.0	100.0	100.0	100.0	100.0	100.0

Source: OECD Statistics database. PPPs for private consumption divided by average nominal US$ exchange rates.

However, a further significant explanatory variable identified by Chang et al.'s study – the level of wealth (as measured by GDP per capita) – is more problematic. It is empirically well established in the economics literature that real price levels tend to be relatively low in poorer countries (Bergstrand 1991). The impact of wealth on real prices can be observed in Table 5.1 with respect to Greece and Portugal (particularly, in the early part of the sample period), where real prices are well below those of most other countries. A plausible explanation for this phenomenon is that labor incomes and costs are lower in poorer countries, and these result in lower aggregate prices. However, this presents a problem for the use of real prices as a proxy for product market competition. A low level of real prices may not necessarily be signaling a high level of product market competition; it could equally be a symptom of low levels of wealth.

A second issue highlighted in Chang et al.'s empirical work arises from the use of market exchange rates in the calculation of real prices. Market exchange rates often change more rapidly and extensively than prices in product markets. For example, following a rapid change in the dollar exchange rate, real prices may suddenly shift from signaling a relatively expensive price level (relative to the United States) to signaling the complete opposite. As can be seen in Table 5.1, this scenario was applicable to most countries in the early to mid-1980s due to the strength of the US dollar (until the Plaza Accord of September 1985).

However, it is inappropriate to infer from these changes that there has been an equivalent change in the underlying state of product market competition. Although producers are presented with an arbitrage opportunity (to produce in the cheaper country and sell in the expensive country), it will take time for suppliers – even in highly competitive market conditions – to take advantage of the resulting price disparities. Only after an indeterminate period of time is it likely that a steady state relationship between real prices and competition will be regained. To account for this concern, Chang et al. utilize the previous year's change in the exchange rate as a control variable in their panel data analysis.

A final problem highlighted by Chang et al.'s analysis relates to taxation. Indirect taxation – which is generally collected via the imposition of a sales tax or value-added tax on consumer purchases – may affect the aggregate price level of an economy. This may serve to distort the signals generated by real prices as a proxy for product market competition. For example, it might be the case that a high level of real prices is a reflection of high indirect taxes rather than a low level of indirect competition (which in turn may arise from the need to finance a greater role for government). Table 5.2 shows that there are significant differences between countries in terms of the magnitude of funds raised from indirect taxation, with the United States, for example, raising much less than the Scandinavian countries.

Table 5.2 Indirect taxation, average 2000–5 (as % GDP)

Country	
Austria	8.0
Belgium	7.1
Denmark	9.7
Finland	8.5
France	7.2
Germany	6.4
Greece	8.4
Italy	6.1
Netherlands	7.3
Norway	8.6
Portugal	7.9
Spain	5.9
Sweden	9.1
Switzerland	4.0
United Kingdom	6.9
United States	2.2

Note: Sales tax plus value-added tax as % GDP.
Source: OECD Revenue Statistics, OECD Statistics.

In summary, differing levels of wealth, indirect taxation, and fluctuations in exchange rates all serve to distort the ability of real prices to act as a proxy for product market competition. For these reasons, real price levels are not adopted as the preferred competition proxy in the empirical analysis of Chapters 6 and 7.

5.2 CONCENTRATION INDICES

The use of concentration as a measure of competition derives from the "structure-conduct-performance" paradigm of industrial economics (Scherer and Ross 1990). A high level of concentration in a sector or an economy is interpreted as indicative of a low level of product market competition. Markets dominated by small numbers of suppliers allow incumbent firms to accumulate market power, and thereby approximate monopolistic price-makers rather than perfectly competitive price-takers. Such firms can exploit their pricing powers to earn supernormal rents at the expense of consumers. Such uncompetitive conditions are often associated with a segmented market structure in which there are significant entry barriers and high sunk costs. In contrast, a large number of market participants – indicated by low levels of concentration indices – are assumed to be indicative of competitive conditions. This is typical of a fragmented market structure in which barriers to entry and sunk costs are low (Oliveira Martins et al. 2002).

Concentration indices – such as the Hirschman–Herfindahl index (the HHI) or the four-firm concentration ratio – are frequently utilized in the literature on industrial organization. However, from both a theoretical and practical perspective, there are drawbacks in using concentration as a proxy for competition (Tirole 1988; Boone 2000). First, an increase in competition tends to raise the market shares of efficient firms at the expense of inefficient firms. This occurs as inefficient firms find themselves unable to compete with more efficient competitors, and exit the market. Such a reallocation of market share serves to increase concentration indices, despite the underlying competitiveness of the market environment. According to Boone et al. (2007:3), this so-called reallocation effect is empirically highly significant, and therefore a major distortion of concentration indices as a measure of competition.

Second, from a practical perspective, time series of concentration indices for national economies are not readily available. Concentration measures are often calculated by antitrust authorities at a sectoral level for the purpose of investigating the competition implications of potential mergers or cases of market abuse (Bishop and Walker 2002). The OECD has also published HHIs

Table 5.3 HHIs of industry concentration in miscellaneous industries, late 1990s

Industry	Austria 1997	Belgium 1997	Finland 1997	Italy 1996	Sweden 1999	United Kingdom 2000	United States 1997
Food products	26	31	150	31	131	27	3
Textiles	88	54	443	7	125	19	7
Clothing	131	493	341	14	244	29	9
Leather products	553	2,566	263	22	360	134	65
Beverages	226	595	2,064	69	1,428	–	192
Rubber products	790	745	775	291	515	–	–
Glass products	440	430	1,154	153	675	–	–
Nonferrous metals	–	1,059	2,372	280	517	–	–
Machinery and equipment	43	96	98	12	70	17	8
Drugs and medicines	490	551	2,175	137	2,042	–	–
Coke and petroleum products	–	1,083	–	1,127	917	–	76
Chemical products	207	75	284	44	375	44	14
Motor vehicles	476	363	429	238	446	90	24
Office and computing equipment	792	387	–	2,208	367	285	18
Electricity and gas	181	889	154	976	156	–	–
Postal and Telecommunications	230	608	559	1,957	653	106	–

Source: OECD (2002).

for individual industries at various points of time (see Gjersam 2004: 49, and Table 5.3). However, there is no consistent times series available for national economies, which could be used in an analysis of corporate governance change. Consequently, the panel data analysis of Chapter 6 is unable to use concentration ratios to proxy for product market competition.

For illustrative purposes, Table 5.3 presents values of HHIs that have been published by the OECD for a selection of industries in various countries. The HHI is defined as the sum of the squares of the market share of each individual firm in a sector or economy. The values relate to the situation prevailing in the late 1990s. Although the situation varies by sector (and the significant gaps in data and country coverage do not permit a definitive assessment), the overall impression is one of relatively high levels of product market competition in the United States and the United Kingdom compared to the nonliberal market economies of continental Europe.

5.3 PROFIT MARGINS

Estimates of profit margins – or price–cost margins – are also used extensively as measures of competition in the empirical industrial organization literature (e.g., Aghion et al. [1999], Nevo [2001], Nickell [1996]). A high level of competition in product markets is assumed to result in low-profit margins, whereas high-profit margins are interpreted as reflecting a market structure in which incumbent producers possess significant market power (and exploit high price–cost margins to generate economic rents).

The main way in which profit margins are calculated in empirical research is through estimation of the so-called markup. The markup is intended to proxy the ratio of price over marginal costs in the calculation of a Lerner index – the ratio of price minus marginal costs over price. Empirical measurement of the Lerner index is problematic, as the marginal costs of firms are not directly observable. Some studies have attempted to calculate the demand and cost functions of individual firms or sectors (e.g., Berry et al. [1995]; Hausman et al. [1994]; Nevo [2001]). However, a recent study by the OECD attempts to calculate markups across a broad range of manufacturing and nonmanufacturing sectors using data from the OECD–STAN database. These sectoral results are aggregated in order to provide a measure of overall manufacturing and nonmanufacturing markups for seventeen countries (Høj et al. 2007). The estimates are presented in Figure 5.1, and represent the average markup over the period 1975–2002.

Estimated markups for manufacturing industries are considerably lower than those for nonmanufacturing sectors. This is not surprising, as manufactured goods are more tradable than nonmanufactured, and therefore have greater exposure to competitive international markets. In contrast, many nonmanufactured products (e.g., services) are difficult to trade internationally or have been subject to various types of regulations that reduce effective competition and generate rents (Høj et al. 2007: 7). Such a sectoral difference in markups suggests that nonmanufacturing sectors are likely to be more important sources of economic rents than manufacturing sectors. Unfortunately, the OECD's markup data is not available as a time series, but only as a cross-sectional average value. Consequently, it is not viable as a proxy for product market competition in the panel data analysis of Chapter 6.

An alternative method of calculating markups is more promising from a time-series perspective, due to the fact that it is obtained from national accounts rather than industry-level data (which tend to be available across time). Cavelaars (2003) shows that the markup can be approximated by the average level of profitability in the economy – or, equivalently, the inverse of

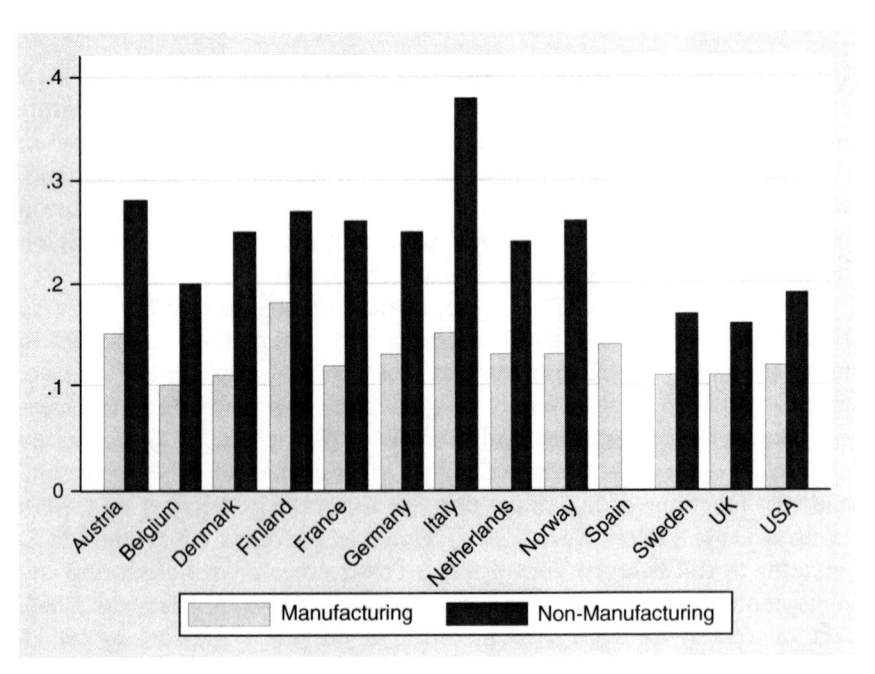

Figure 5.1 Markups in manufacturing and nonmanufacturing (average values, 1975–2002)

Source: Høj et al. (2007: 43).

the share of labor in national income – subject to certain simplifying assumptions about comparable output elasticities of output with respect to labor, and rates of return on capital across countries (Cavelaars 2003: 74).

Such measures of aggregate profitability can be calculated utilizing several types of macroeconomic data. The possibilities are surveyed by Przybyla and Roma (2005) of the European Central Bank, who undertake the calculations in order to analyze the relationship between product market competition and inflation. The first of their suggestions is to calculate the ratio of an economy's operating surplus to either national output or the value of the national capital stock. A second approach involves dividing GDP by the total compensation of employees (the inverse of labor share) (Przybyla and Roma 2005: 12). A further possibility is proposed by Rachel Griffith and her colleagues, who construct a measure of whole economy profitability in terms of total value-added divided by the sum of labor and capital costs (Griffith et al. 2007: 149).

However, there are difficulties in interpreting these profitability measures as proxies for product market competition. First, profit margins are subject to distortion due to the reallocation effect described in respect of concentration indices. For example, an increase in competition will increase the market share of efficient firms with high-profit margins. This will raise the aggregate profit margin, despite the fact that product markets are more competitive than they were before. Second, one of the assumptions made to equate these measures to a Lerner index is that there are constant returns to scale in the production process (Cavelaars 2003: 74). If there exist increasing (decreasing) returns to scale in an economy, then measures of profitability will be biased downward (upward). Third, as well as reflecting levels of competition, profitability could equally be reflective of developments in costs. For example, a downward impulse to costs could be caused by a technologically driven improvement in productivity, or a drop in the price of raw materials. Alternatively, costs could be affected by the ability (or lack of ability) of labor to appropriate quasi-rents from employers (e.g., due to the level of union bargaining power). Hence, change in the average level of profits in an economy could arise from reasons unrelated to competitive pressures in product markets (Blanchard and Giavazzi 2003; Boulhol 2004).

It seems plausible that cost developments (rather than declines in competition) have been a significant factor in driving up rates of profitability in recent years. In several industrialized democracies, labor's share of national income peaked in the mid- to late 1990s. This was followed by a period in which profit's share has tended to increase (Coggan 2004). Nevertheless, there has been some debate as to whether this development has arisen due to the weakening of the bargaining position of labor (e.g., due to an increase in *de facto* labor supply arisen from the increasing globalization of trade and production), or due to improved returns on capital arising from technological change (Bhagwati 2004: 126). However, any attempt to explain this development in terms of a reduction in product market competition seems implausible, particularly in view of the product market liberalization that has occurred in most industrialized economies over the last ten to fifteen years (Griffith et al. 2007).

A final potential distortion of profit share is its cyclicality. Labor income is stickier as an income stream than profit (reflecting the wage stickiness of labor markets). Consequently, during upswings in economic activity, profit's share of GDP increases at a faster rate than that of labor. Equally, during a downswing, profit collapses more rapidly than the remuneration of labor. The result is that profit share experiences cyclical upswings during an overall economic upturn and cyclical declines during a downswing, regardless of changes in product market competitiveness.

Griffith et al. (2007) attempt to correct for these distortions by undertaking various adjustments to their measure of profitability in an analysis of competition and unemployment.[1] However, given the potential problems associated with the measure – and the difficulties involved in overcoming these problems – it remains a matter of doubt as to whether the aggregate profit margin can be viewed as a viable representation of domestic product market competition in an econometric analysis. Consequently, it is not used as a proxy for competition in the panel analysis in Chapters 6 and 7.

5.4 OPENNESS TO TRADE

Openness to trade is often used as a proxy for product market competition in economic and political analysis. Rajan and Zingales (2003), for example, argue that the ability of interest groups to earn "positional rents" in an economy will be significantly reduced by higher levels of trade openness (Rajan and Zingales 2003: 22). According to the logic of this argument, greater openness increases the involvement of foreign producers in domestic product markets, thereby directly increasing competition.

In Chapter 2, it was argued that it is problematic to equate economic openness with the competitiveness of domestic product markets (see

---

[1] For example, they include a measure of the output gap and a time-varying measure of labor market institutions (union density) in their regressions, and account for increasing or decreasing returns to scale by utilizing country-year fixed effects (Griffith et al. 2007: 150).

Section 2.4). Even in relatively open economies, products in tradable sectors account for only 30–40 percent of domestic economic activity (see Table 5.4). Furthermore, the data on markups in Figure 5.1 shows that – even if tradable products are subject to competitive conditions in international markets – this does not necessarily affect the ability of non-traded sectors to generate economic rents (due to the inability of consumers to redirect their purchases away from domestic incumbent producers in such sectors). Despite these issues, trade openness can be measured in a variety of ways, and it is worthwhile to consider if any of these alternative approaches permits product market competition to be operationalized in a credible manner.

A basic distinction in the economics literature is made between "incidence" and "outcome" measures of trade liberalization. Examples of the former include the incidence of tariff and nontariff barriers to trade. However, there are significant practical problems in constructing incidence measure of openness (Pritchett 1996; O'Rourke 1997; Hiscox and Kastner 2002). In respect of tariff barriers, it is difficult to obtain data across many nations and years for potentially thousands of product categories. Furthermore, there is

Table 5.4 Hiscox and Kastner's measure of trade policy orientation versus import penetration

	Trade policy orientation (basic model)	Imports as % GDP
	1980–90 (average)	
Austria	39.63	30.69
Belgium	7.78	55.66
Denmark	27.66	25.95
Finland	33.28	22.10
France	18.49	16.68
Germany	16.55	21.29
Greece	28.99	16.94
Italy	20.79	17.28
Netherlands	8.09	41.62
Norway	32.04	26.75
Portugal	21.69	20.44
Spain	23.43	11.82
Sweden	30.58	25.35
Switzerland	22.22	27.26
United Kingdom	23.31	18.05
United States	22.08	7.47

Note: According to Hiscox and Kastner's measure, lower values are indicative of greater underlying openness.
Source: Hiscox and Kastner (2002: 37), and EU AMECO database.

no simple solution to the issue of how these tariffs should be weighted in an aggregate measure. The same tariff levied on different product categories in different countries could have differing effects on trade flows. In respect of nontariff barriers – which are increasingly important instruments of trade policy – it is difficult to aggregate policy measures that are so qualitatively diverse, for example, import quotas, subsidies, customs and standards regulations, etc., in any sort of meaningful way (Bhagwati 1988).[2]

From an outcome perspective, market openness is most commonly measured in terms of the sum of imports and exports as a percentage of GDP, or in terms of import penetration (imports alone as a percentage of GDP). Given the extremely high correlation of these two series, they can be considered as capturing the same effect. Such measures are commonly employed in empirical work due to the ready availability of data from macroeconomic databases. Examples of recent studies which have utilized trade flows as proxies for product market competition include Bloom and van Reenen (2006), Lane (1997), and Rajan and Zingales (2003).

A problem with adopting these measures as proxies for competition is that they are heavily influenced by country size. For example, the market openness of the United States – according to the import penetration measure – is extremely low. However, the United States contains within its borders a huge internal market, which reduces the necessity of trade with the rest of the world. Low-import penetration does not mean that US product markets are uncompetitive. Indeed, other measures of product market competition discussed in this chapter suggest that US markets are highly competitive. In contrast to the United States, smaller countries will almost inevitably – given the degree of specialization required by modern production techniques – undertake a larger share of economic transactions with customers in nondomestic markets. A smaller country, therefore, is structurally biased toward a higher share of imports and exports in GDP, regardless of levels of competition in domestic product markets or the policy stance of government. The use of openness to trade as a proxy for competition would, therefore, need to control for country size (Hiscox and Kastner 2002).

"Gravity" models of trade attempt to take such factors into account by adjusting trade flows for geographical factors such as the distance from major markets and country size. Their key result is that, *ceteris paribus*,

---

[2] Despite these difficulties, an incidence measure of openness used relatively frequently in the comparative political economy literature is that of Dennis Quinn (1997). This provides an index of *de jure* restrictions on cross-country payments and receipts of goods and invisibles. However, despite an update by Huber et al. (2004), there is still only data for this time series as far as 1999 for most developed countries. Furthermore, there is only coverage up until 1993 for Spain, Portugal, and Greece.

smaller countries that are close to trading partners will tend to trade significantly more than large, isolated countries (Linneman 1966; Aitkin 1973). Furthermore, there tends to be more trade between nearby countries if their factor endowments are very different. Pritchett (1996) seeks to adjust trade openness to take account of these factors by regressing trade openness on population size, size of country (area), and GDP per capita (which is a proxy for capital endowments). He then uses the residuals from the estimation as an adjusted measure of trade openness. Spilimbergo et al. (1999) undertake a similar exercise, but include the distance of an economy from major markets and the distinctiveness of national factor markets in the regression.

A relatively sophisticated gravity model is estimated by Hiscox and Kastner (2002). They estimate two types of gravity model for eighty-two countries across the period 1960–92. Their first formulation models import penetration as a positive function of national income, and a negative function of the distance between trade partners. The second includes measures of factor endowments. Although the latter explains slightly more of the variation in trade flows, the measures of trade policy emerging from the two models are highly correlated. The key variables in each regression are dummy variables specific to each country in each particular year (i.e., a total of $[n-1]*[t-1]$ dummies). Each of these is interpreted as representing the amount by which import share is altered by unobservable factors (i.e., trade policy) in that specific country–year relative to the mean country–year. The values of these dummies are then normalized, with lower values indicative of a greater "free trade" policy orientation.

Table 5.4 shows country rankings of openness in terms of both Hiscox and Kastner's indicator and import penetration (imports as a percentage of GDP). The new indicator is successful in improving the relative position in terms of openness of larger economies such as the United States, and adjusting downward smaller countries such as Austria. Nonetheless, despite adjusting for these factors, the new measure still ranks Belgium, the Netherlands, and Italy as more open than the United States. In light of the country ranking produced by most other measures of competition (which invariably indicate that the United States has the most competitive domestic product markets among developed economies), the gravity measure continues to lack credibility as a proxy for product market competition.

5.5 SURVEY MEASURES OF COMPETITION

Another source of information regarding product market competition derives from a prominent economic survey. The World Economic Forum conducts an annual executive opinion survey among approximately 11,000 management executives around the world, the results of which appear in their *Global Competitiveness Report* (GCR). One of the questions in the survey asks respondents to evaluate the intensity of competition in their local market. The maximum score of 7 is representative of competition which is "intense in most industries, and the market landscape changes over time." The minimum score of 1 corresponds to a situation in which competition is "limited in most industries, and price-cutting is rare." Table 5.5 presents the result of the latest GCR survey, which was conducted in the early part of 2006. Although, there is a reasonable correlation between the results of the survey and other measures of competition, there are several reasons to be skeptical about the survey as an accurate source of insight regarding competitive conditions.

First, the survey is by definition a subjective perception of competitive conditions in local markets, and is unlikely to be based on any rigorous comparative analysis of the situations in different economies. It is hard to imagine that individual respondents have a full picture of competitive conditions across the range of sectors in their local economy (although they may understand the

Table 5.5 Intensity of local competition 2006, GCR survey results (scale from 1 [least] to 7 [most])

Germany	6.2
United Kingdom	6.1
United States	5.9
Sweden	5.9
Belgium	5.8
Netherlands	5.8
Finland	5.7
France	5.7
Austria	5.6
Norway	5.6
Denmark	5.6
Spain	5.3
Switzerland	5.3
Portugal	5.1
Greece	4.7
Italy	4.6

Source: Global Competitiveness Report, 2006/7; World Economic Forum, Geneva.

situation in specific markets), or that they are in a position to relate them in a consistent manner to those of other economies (of which they may have only limited knowledge). Second, incumbent market participants may have a vested interest in taking up the degree of competition in their domestic markets, either due to national pride or a desire to deter competition-promoting intervention from national or European-level regulators. Third, comparison of the level of national scores from international surveys is inherently problematic. Respondents from different countries may interpret the question in different ways, due to cultural factors or the influence of differing business contexts. Consequently, there exist grounds for treating the relative magnitudes of competitiveness suggested by the scores with caution.

An interesting feature of the data in Table 5.5 is the similarity of the scores in many countries. For example, eleven of the sixteen countries have aggregate scores within a range of 0.6 points. In other words, the survey results do not appear to be signaling much difference in product market competition between many developing economies, which is both lacking in plausibility (based on the accumulated evidence of other measures of competition) and suggestive that local executives are either unwilling or unable to report the true nature of local competitiveness in relation to other economies.

5.6 OECD INDICES OF PRODUCT MARKET COMPETITION

Since 1998, the OECD has published an indicator of product market regulation (the PMR index) intended to illustrate broad differences in product market policies in OECD countries (Nicoletti et al. 1999). The overall indicator is constructed from the aggregation of sixteen lower-level indices that reflect the burden of rules and regulations that affect the intensity of domestic competition (see Table 5.6). Each low-level index is given a score between 0 (most encouraging of competition) and 6 (least encouraging of competition). The scores for each subindex are derived from the results of questionnaires sent to national governments, and form part of the OECD's International Regulation Database (Conway et al. 2005).

The practical drawback of the PMR index is that it is currently only available for two years: 1998 and 2003. It is also an entirely *de jure* measure of the "law on the books," and does not take account of actual conditions in product markets, the rigor with which regulations are enforced, or the impact of "informal" rules of behavior, for example, which may be promoted by

Table 5.6 Subindices of the OECD product market regulation indicator (the PMR index)

State controls	Barriers to entrepreneurship	Barriers to trade and investment
Scope of public enterprises	Licenses and permits system	Ownership barriers
Size of public enterprises	Communication and simplification of rules and procedures	Tariffs
Direct state control over business enterprises	Administrative burdens for corporations	Discriminatory procedures
Price controls	Administrative burdens for sole proprietors	Regulatory barriers
Use of command and control (rather than incentive-based) regulation	Sector-specific administrative burdens	
	Legal barriers	
	Antitrust exemptions	

Source: Conway et al. (2005: 8).

professional associations or self-regulatory groups. Nonetheless, the index provides a useful insight into recent trends in the competitiveness of product markets in developed democracies (see Figure 5.2).

Most notably, the index suggests that product market regulation experienced a good deal of convergence in the period between 1998 and 2003. This finding updates previous OECD research, which concluded that convergence among European Union (EU) countries in an earlier period (between 1975 and 1998) had been relatively weak (Nicoletti and Scarpetta 2003: 18). Among the countries in the sample, the PMR index identifies the least competitive as being southern European countries such as Greece and Italy (particularly in 1998). In contrast, by 2003, many northern European countries had achieved levels of product market regulation only slightly more restrictive than those prevailing in liberal market economies (such as the United States and the United Kingdom).

A second OECD competition index – which has been published since 2001 – measures the extent of competition in seven nonmanufacturing sectors of twenty-one OECD countries: the NMR index. According to the OECD, "This indicator provides the broadest coverage of sectors and areas, and the longest time-series currently available for comparing product market regulation across countries" (Conway and Nicoletti 2006: 1). The advantage of the NMR indicator from a practical perspective is that it is currently available in an annualized time-series format over the period 1975–2003, and is therefore a viable candidate for utilization in an analysis of corporate governance change.

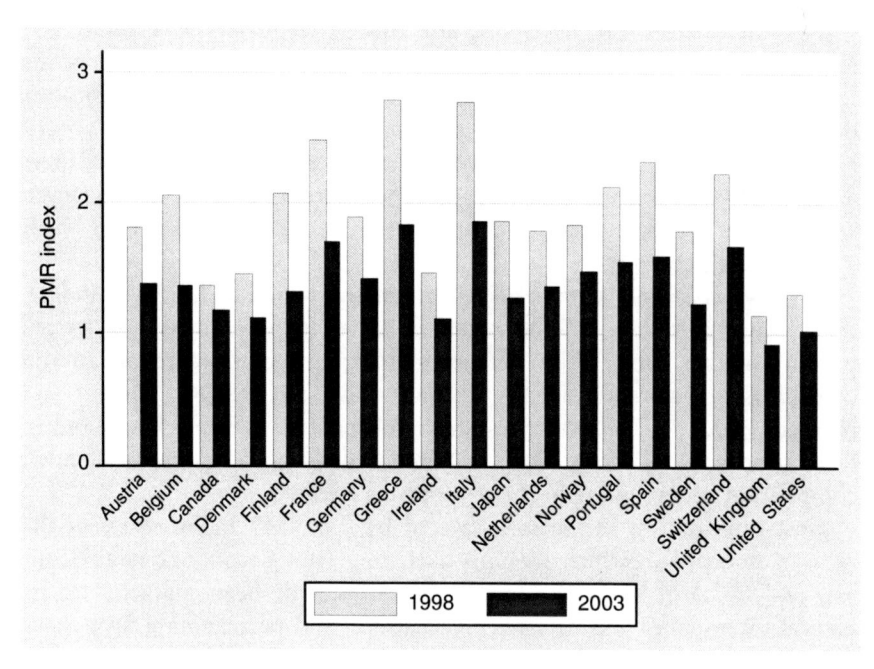

Figure 5.2 The OECD PMR index in 1998 and 2003
Source: Conway et al. (2005).

The objective underlying the formulation of the NMR index is to "capture the extent to which there exist substantive barriers to entrepreneurship and competition in domestic markets where technology and demand conditions would otherwise make competition viable" (Conway and Nicoletti 2006: 2). Its aggregate value summarizes the value of a large number of subindicators that measure the state of regulation and market outcomes from five perspectives: barriers to entry, state involvement in business operations, market structure, vertical integration, and price controls. The NMR index also includes measures of actual market structure in its composition (e.g., market shares of the largest companies, the degree of vertical integration in a sector, etc). Consequently, it is not only a measure of the law and regulation "on the books" (in contrast to the PMR index). Due to this mixed structure, the NMR index may be regarded as a hybrid of a *de jure* and *de facto* measure of competition, which also takes into account the effectiveness of regulatory enforcement and the impact of nonregulatory factors on market outcomes.

The sectors covered by the NMR index fall within the general categories of energy, transportation, and communication. The seven subsectors within these categories are airline transportation, telecommunications, electricity, gas, postal services, rail transport, and road transportation (Conway and Nicoletti 2006). For each sector, low-level indicators (relating to each of the five categories defined earlier) are calculated from a number of subindicators defined as relevant for each sector, and awarded a score of between 0 (most competitive) and 6 (least competitive).[3] The scores of the low-level indicators are aggregated in order to calculate an overall score for each sector. The seven sector scores are then themselves aggregated to calculate the overall NMR index for each country.

Although it is only a partial-economy measure (unlike the PMR index), the NMR index can still be regarded as a credible proxy for overall product market competition. Nonmanufacturing sectors represent around two-thirds of economic activity in most OECD countries (Conway and Nicoletti 2006: 5). The extent to which competition is being liberalized in these sectors is, therefore, likely to weigh heavily on how product market competition is developing in the economy as a whole.

Most importantly, the sectors covered by the NMR index represent the areas of an economy which are most likely to generate economic rents (Conway and Nicoletti 2006: 5). Many have traditionally been characterized by natural monopolies and network externalities, and participating firms have often been burdened with noneconomic objectives (e.g., the provision of a universal service to consumers). Furthermore, until recently, they have been subject to low levels of import penetration, and a very limited potential for entry and exit in respect of new suppliers (Golub 2003). The significantly higher level of profit margins (and hence economic rents) in nonmanufacturing sectors relative to manufacturing sectors is apparent from the cross-sectional data on markups in Figure 5.1 (see Section 5.3).

A further consideration is that the sectors covered by the NMR index are likely to exert significant "knock-on" effects on other sectors. Manufacturing industry and other areas of the economy use their outputs as intermediate inputs in their production processes. For example, an estimated 50–70 percent of the output of the electricity, postal, and telecommunications sectors is utilized as an intermediate output elsewhere in the economy (rather than being delivered directly to the final consumer). Conway and Nicoletti estimate that the knock-on effect of the seven sectors is of particular significance for the Euro-area countries and Japan, although slightly less substantial in the liberal market economies and Scandinavia (Conway and Nicoletti 2006: 21). Consequently, the competitive stance in these sectors can be regarded as a major determinant of the competitive stance of the economy as a whole.

---

[3] The individual subindicators that are used to calculate the low-level indicators for each sector are detailed in the appendix of Conway and Nicoletti (2006).

Table 5.7 The NMR index of product market competition, 1975–2003 (6 = least competitive, 0 = most competitive)

Country	1975	1980	1985	1990	1995	2000	2001	2002	2003
Austria	5.23	5.13	4.90	4.46	3.96	2.96	2.66	2.46	2.41
Belgium	5.48	5.48	5.48	5.34	3.89	2.80	2.54	2.26	2.13
Denmark	5.52	5.52	5.52	4.74	3.51	2.38	1.99	1.74	1.63
Finland	5.48	5.42	5.15	4.62	3.00	2.48	2.47	2.46	2.36
France	6.00	6.00	6.00	5.16	4.82	3.80	3.74	3.32	3.04
Germany	5.25	5.25	5.14	4.60	3.74	2.19	2.03	1.79	1.74
Greece	5.67	5.67	5.67	5.67	5.40	4.99	4.66	4.21	4.15
Italy	5.83	5.83	5.83	5.83	4.93	3.57	3.18	2.67	2.56
Japan	5.07	5.07	5.07	3.52	3.19	2.65	2.38	2.28	2.21
Netherlands	5.56	5.56	5.56	5.56	3.67	1.88	1.81	1.73	1.59
Norway	5.45	5.45	5.02	4.45	3.45	2.82	2.74	2.46	2.34
Portugal	5.92	5.92	5.92	5.31	4.82	3.28	3.05	2.86	2.58
Spain	5.06	5.02	4.99	4.66	4.19	2.77	2.43	2.17	2.03
Sweden	4.55	4.55	4.55	4.36	2.90	2.12	2.08	1.98	1.88
Switzerland	4.10	4.17	4.17	4.17	3.90	3.00	2.94	2.85	2.79
United Kingdom	4.76	4.76	4.33	3.01	1.70	1.17	1.13	1.11	1.05
United States	3.72	3.02	2.48	2.30	1.84	1.51	1.49	1.43	1.44

Note: A lower value of the NMR index indicates a higher level of product market competition.
Source: Conway and Nicoletti (2006).

Table 5.8 Descriptive statistics for the OECD's NMR index of product market competition, 1975–2003 (6 = least competitive, 0 = most competitive)

Country	Minimum value	Maximum value	Mean	Standard deviation	Number of observations
Austria	2.413	5.232	4.350	0.868	29
Belgium	2.133	5.478	4.607	1.133	29
Denmark	1.635	5.523	4.401	1.354	29
Finland	2.361	5.479	4.258	1.211	29
France	3.042	6.000	5.174	0.918	29
Germany	1.736	5.248	4.225	1.239	29
Greece	4.148	5.665	5.424	0.425	29
Italy	2.564	5.826	5.186	1.013	29
Japan	2.207	5.070	3.953	1.047	29
Netherlands	1.594	5.558	4.456	1.475	29
Norway	2.343	5.451	4.281	1.083	29
Portugal	2.578	5.921	5.070	1.030	29
Spain	2.033	5.060	4.320	0.965	29
Sweden	1.876	4.547	3.676	1.031	29
Switzerland	2.788	4.168	3.901	0.455	29
Overall sample	1.594	6.000	4.486	1.149	435

Note: A lower value of the NMR index indicates a higher level of product market competition.
Source: Conway and Nicoletti (2006).

The ability of the NMR index to act as the bellwether of the degree of competition in the economy as a whole is also implied by its high level of correlation with the whole-economy PMR index in the two years in which they overlap. The correlation coefficient is +0.81 in 1998, and +0.72 in 2003. Furthermore, Conway et al. (2005) report that the NMR index has a high level of correlation with Gwartney and Lawson's (2006) index of economy-wide regulation, which is an alternative product market competition index focusing on the extent of business regulation and the presence of government in the business sector (Conway and Nicoletti 2006: 21).

A final point in favor of the NMR index is its widespread use as a proxy for product market competition in both the economics literature and policy circles. For example, it has been used as an explanatory variable in recent studies analyzing the association between competition and domestic and foreign investment (Alesina et al. 2005; Kox and Lejour 2006), productivity (Nicoletti and Scarpetta 2003; Faini et al. 2006), and employment and wages (Amable et al. 2006; Bassanini and Duval 2006). It is also employed for competition-benchmarking purposes in studies by a range of international and national official bodies, including the International Monetary Fund, the European Union, the European Central Bank, the Japanese Cabinet Office, and the UK Department of Trade and Industry (Conway and Nicoletti 2006: 23). The two major studies of structural reform undertaken by the IMF and the OECD – which were discussed in Chapter 2 in order to establish the exogeneity of changes in competition to partisanship – both utilize the NMR index as their measure of product market competition (Helbling et al. 2004; Høj et al. 2006).

For these reasons, the NMR index is viewed as a credible proxy for product market competition, and suitable for use in the panel data analysis of corporate governance change in this book. Actual values of the NMR index on a country-by-country basis over time are presented in Table 5.7, and descriptive statistics are shown in Table 5.8. As with the PMR index, the values of the NMR index also suggest that product market competition has both liberalized and somewhat converged across the fifteen countries of the sample during the course of the time series. However, differences in the pace and extent of this progression are observable between countries. Greece and France retained a relatively uncompetitive market structure, even at the end of the sample period. In contrast, despite commencing the sample period with relatively uncompetitive markets, Denmark, Germany, the Netherlands, and Sweden have undergone significant liberalization. Most of the progress toward greater competition appears to have occurred between 1990 and 2000; something of a slowdown is apparent in the final three years of the time series.

6

A Panel Data Analysis of Corporate Governance Change

The purpose of this chapter is to undertake the main empirical testing of the theoretical claims of the book utilizing a panel data analytical approach.[1] Since the 1990s, panel data analysis has established itself as a key empirical tool in macro-comparative analysis. In the opinion of Bernhard Kittel and Hannes Winner, "[I]t is no exaggeration to say that it has become difficult to defend not using panel data in the analysis of comparative political economy" (Kittel and Winner 2005: 269).

Panel data estimation offers a potential solution to the "small-N, many variables" problem faced by both quantitative and qualitative approaches to comparative politics. By applying panel data econometric techniques to pooled data sets of multiple countries and time periods, it is possible to make inferences on the basis of a much larger number of observations than with a case study approach or a cross-sectional econometric analysis. Furthermore, panel data techniques – unlike cross-sectional approaches – permit an analysis of how variables interact over time, which is particularly relevant to the theoretical claims advanced by this book (which are concerned with corporate governance change). A final advantage is that panel data techniques are available to take account of the inherent heterogeneity in the data-generating processes of different countries, while still identifying the common determinants of cross-national variation and change over time.

In the previous two chapters, the chosen proxies for corporate governance and product market competition were described and justified in detail. This chapter begins by bringing together all of the variables utilized in the quantitative analysis, and justifying the inclusion of the explanatory and control variables that have not yet been discussed.

---

[1] Strictly speaking, the analytical technique used in this chapter is time-series cross-sectional (TSCS) analysis rather than panel data analysis, due to the relatively large size of the data set's time-series dimension relative to the number of countries-that is, relatively large T relative to N (Beck and Katz 2004: 3).

6.1 THE VARIABLES

The hypothesis is tested with annual data for fifteen nonliberal Organisation for Economic Co-operation and Development (OECD) market economies covering the period 1975–2003. A complete panel over this data range would give rise to 435 observations (fifteen countries over twenty-nine years). However, the availability of the data for certain variables limits the analysis to fewer observations in certain regressions (see in detail in the following text). The countries included in the sample are: Austria, Belgium, Denmark, Finland, France, Germany, Greece, Italy, Japan, the Netherlands, Norway, Portugal, Spain, Sweden, and Switzerland.[2] Given that the hypothesis of the book is intended to explain change in the corporate governance of nonliberal market economies (see Section 2.4), observations for liberal market economies, for example, the United States, the United Kingdom, Canada, Ireland, etc., are not included in the data set.

The proxies chosen to represent corporate governance – the dependent variable – have already been discussed in detail in Chapter 4. Table 6.1 provides an overall summary of the data sources and coverage of the three variables: equity share, value traded, and international equity issuance. Table 6.2 presents aggregated descriptive statistics, including means, standard deviations, minimum and maximum values, and the extent of "between" and "within" variation, that is, variation between country units on a cross-sectional basis, and within countries on a temporal basis. Both equity share and value traded benefit are from a large number of observations across the estimation period, and significant "between and within" variation. International equity issuance has fewer observations – the series is not available for the late 1970s and early 1980s – but also exhibits a healthy amount of cross-sectional and temporal variation.

Turning to the explanatory variables, Table 6.3 provides descriptions, and Table 6.4 provides descriptive statistics for the main explanatory and control variables utilized in the analysis. Foremost among the explanatory variables is the chosen proxy for product market competition (which was discussed in Chapter 5), and government partisanship. Given that partisanship is a key variable in the analysis – through its interaction with product market competition – it is now important to give detailed consideration to its operationalization in the empirical analysis.

---

[2] Given that the hypothesis relates to nonliberal market economies, Japan is included in the data set. Its inclusion does not exert any substantive effect over the results (see robustness checks in Chapter 7).

A Panel Data Analysis of Corporate Governance Change

Table 6.1 Data sources and coverage of proxies used for the dependent variable (corporate governance)

Variables	Description	Data coverage	Source
Equity share	Equity market capitalization, divided by GDP	Portugal: 1977–2003. All other countries: 1975–2003	*Post-1989 data*: World Bank Database on Financial Development and Structure (Beck et al. 2000). *Pre-1989 data*: Global Financial Database
Value traded	Value of trading on equity market, divided by GDP	Portugal: 1977–2003 Denmark: 1980–2003 All other countries: 1975–2003	*Post-1989 data*: World Bank Database on Financial Development and Structure (Beck et al. 2000). *Pre-1989 data*: Global Financial Database
International equity issuance	Value of equity issuance to international investors, as percentage of GDP	All countries: 1983–2003	Bank for International Settlements

Note: Details and sources provided in chapter. N.B. Equity share and value traded are simple ratios whereas international equity issuance is a percentage.

Table 6.2 Descriptive statistics of proxies used for the dependent variable (corporate governance)

Variable		Mean	Standard deviation	Minimum	Maximum	Observations
Equity share	Overall	0.385	0.445	0.002	3.034	N = 433
	Between		0.255	0.087	1.083	n = 15
	Within		0.370	−0.420	2.617	T = 28.86
Value traded	Overall	0.249	0.417	0.000	2.690	N = 428
	Between		0.190	0.037	0.770	n = 15
	Within		0.374	−0.414	2.474	T = 28.53
International equity issuance	Overall	0.502	0.814	0.000	6.579	N = 315
	Between		0.323	0.059	1.252	n = 15
	Within		0.752	−0.750	5.829	T = 21

Notes: N = number of observations; n = number of countries; T = average number of observations per country. Details and sources provided in Chapter 4.

Table 6.3 Description of explanatory and control variables

Variables	Description	Data coverage	Source and details
Product market competition	OECD index of product market competition in non-manufacturing sectors: the NMR index (6 = highest, 0 = lowest). A lower value indicates greater product market competition.	All countries: 1975–2003.	Conway and Nicoletti (2006).
Left government	Cabinet composition: social-democratic and labor parties in percentage of total cabinet posts, weighted by days.	Portugal: 1976–2003. Spain: 1977–2003. All other countries: 1975–2003.	Constructed by the author. For party composition, see Table 6.5. For further details, see Section 6.1.
Conservative government	Cabinet composition: conservative parties in percentage of total cabinet posts, weighted by days.	Portugal: 1976–2003. Spain: 1977–2003. All other countries: 1975–2003.	Constructed by the author. For party composition, see Table 6.5. For further details, see Section 6.1.
Pension system	Dummy variable indicating presence of a multi-pillar pension system; otherwise zero.	All countries: 1975–2003.	Based on pension system data compiled by Brooks (2005). For further details, see Section 4.1.2.
Germanic legal origin	Dummy variable, set equal to 1 for countries with Germanic legal origin; otherwise zero.	All countries: 1975–2003.	La Porta et al. (1998).
Scandinavian legal origin	Dummy variable, set equal to 1 for countries with Scandinavian legal origin; otherwise zero.	All countries: 1975–2003.	La Porta et al. (1998).
GDP growth (lagged)	A one-year lag of growth of GDP in real terms, percentage change from previous year.	All countries: 1975–2003.	EU AMECO macroeconomic database.
GDP per capita	GDP per head of population (US$, in thousands).	All countries: 1975–2003.	EU AMECO macroeconomic database.
Interest rates	Ten-year government bond yields (%).	Portugal: 1985–2003.	Global Financial Database.

		All other countries: 1975–2003. Greece: data missing 1989–91.	
Population	Population (thousands).	All countries: 1975–2003.	EU AMECO macroeconomic database.
Electoral system disproportionality	Least squares index of electoral system disproportionality (Gallagher 1991). Higher values indicate less proportional electoral systems.	Spain: 1977–2003. All other countries: 1975–2003.	Calculated by the author from electoral data.
Capital controls	Dummy variable indicating existence of capital account restrictions.	All countries: 1975–2003.	Data up to 2001: Prasad et al. (2003). Extrapolated by the author to 2003.
Public debt effect	Dummy variable, set equal to 1 for EU countries with public debt ratios above 60% of GDP after Maastricht Treaty of 1992; otherwise zero.	All countries: 1975–2003.	Based on OECD data on central government debt.

A common strategy in empirical research is to locate individual political parties at a particular point on the Left–Right spectrum on the basis of expert surveys.[3] Castles and Mair (1984) published the first such survey covering a large number of countries, and a more recent survey has been undertaken by Huber and Inglehart (1995). The starting point for a classification of European parties in this book is based on the expert party categorization schema of Manfred Schmidt (1996), which has been converted into Left–Center–Right partisanship variables by Armingeon et al. (2005). Broadly speaking, parties

---

[3] An alternative approach is to locate parties according to the content of their preelection manifestos. For example, the Manifestos Research Group has coded the content of party election manifestos in relation to a large number of policy categories (Budge et al. 2001; Klingemann et al. 2006). There is, however, a high level of correlation in the placement of parties according to expert surveys and manifesto analyses (Huber and Gabel 2000; Kim and Fording 2002: 192).

Table 6.4 Descriptive statistics for explanatory and control variables

Variable		Mean	Std. Dev.	Min	Max	Observations
Product market competition	Overall	4.486	1.149	1.594	6.000	$N = 435$
	Between		0.514	3.676	5.424	$n = 15$
	Within		1.036	1.623	5.706	$T = 29$
Left government	Overall	40.196	37.117	0.000	100.000	$N = 432$
	Between		18.077	3.456	68.918	$n = 15$
	Within		32.719	−28.722	93.959	$T = 28.8$
Conservative government	Overall	46.676	36.400	0.000	100.000	$N = 432$
	Between		17.847	22.734	91.953	$n = 15$
	Within		32.015	−15.301	117.203	$T = 28.8$
Pension system	Overall	0.108	0.310	0.000	1.000	$N = 435$
	Between		0.206	0.000	0.655	$n = 15$
	Within		0.237	−0.547	0.935	$T = 29$
Germanic legal origin	Overall	0.267	0.443	0.000	1.000	$N = 435$
	Between		0.458	0.000	1.000	$n = 15$
	Within		0.000	0.267	0.267	$T = 29$
Scandinavian legal origin	Overall	0.267	0.443	0.000	1.000	$N = 435$
	Between		0.458	0.000	1.000	$n = 15$
	Within		0.000	0.267	0.267	$T = 29$
GDP growth (lagged)	Overall	2.320	2.045	−7.267	7.503	$N = 435$
	Between		0.491	1.210	3.278	$n = 15$
	Within		1.989	−6.556	7.295	$T = 29$
GDP per capita	Overall	17.598	9.920	2.053	49.348	$N = 435$
	Between		5.839	6.907	27.117	$n = 15$
	Within		8.155	−0.400	42.232	$T = 29$
Interest rates	Overall	8.780	4.186	1.000	27.700	$N = 422$
	Between		2.437	4.241	13.363	$n = 15$
	Within		3.471	−0.103	25.464	$T = 28.133$
Population	Overall	28,437.6	33,187.740	4,007.3	127,619.0	$N = 435$
	Between		34,176.180	4,251.8	121,867.6	$n = 15$
	Within		2,961.466	18,510.0	40,369.9	$T = 29$
Electoral disproportionality	Overall	4.988	4.376	0.469	24.114	$N = 433$
	Between		3.824	1.613	15.630	$n = 15$
	Within		2.335	−4.002	14.241	$T = 28.867$
Capital controls	Overall	0.439	0.497	0.000	1.000	$N = 435$
	Between		0.286	0.000	0.862	$n = 15$
	Within		0.413	−0.423	1.370	$T = 29$
Public debt effect	Overall	0.145	0.352	0.000	1.000	$N = 435$
	Between		0.164	0.000	0.414	$n = 15$
	Within		0.314	−0.269	1.076	$T = 29$

Notes: N = number of observations; n = number of countries; T = average number of observations per country. Details and sources provided in table 6.3.

placed in the Left category are social democratic parties, or parties to the left of social democracy. Right parties are liberal or conservative parties. Parties placed in the center category are centrist parties, including Christian democratic and Catholic parties. Government partisanship variables for Left, Right, and Center parties are constructed by calculating the participation of parties from each of the three categories in government cabinets. Each partisanship variable is expressed as a value between 0 and 100. For example, a value of 45 for the Left partisanship variable indicates that Left parties occupied 45 percent of cabinet posts (weighted by the number of days in office) in a particular year (Armingeon et al. 2005: 2).

However, there are difficulties involved in utilizing Armingeon et al.'s measures of partisanship to test the hypothesis of this book. The Left and Right categorizations map only roughly onto the Left-conservative party distinction that is conceptualized by the analytical framework of Chapter 2. According to that framework, Left and conservative parties are assumed to represent distinctive social constituencies. The core constituents of insider labor are Left parties. A similar role is fulfilled by conservative parties in respect of blockholders. However, Armingeon et al.'s schema includes parties of the extreme Left, for example, Communist parties, and Green parties in its "Left" partisanship measure. It is not clear that insider labor can be regarded as the core constituents of these parties. Furthermore, Armingeon et al.'s "Right" partisanship variable differs from the conception of conservative partisanship outlined in Chapter 2 as it excludes many parties of the Center–Right – particularly Christian democratic parties – which have been custodians of blockholder interests in many European polities. Such parties are often placed by Armingeon et al. in the Center rather than the Right category, for example, the CDU in Germany and the People's Party in Spain. Armingeon et al.'s Right variable also includes some parties of the extreme Right, which are not obvious representatives of blockholder interests. Consequently, it is necessary to make adjustments to the Left–Right partisanship variables constructed by Armingeon et al. in order to align them with the theoretical conceptions of Left and conservative partisanship described in Chapter 2.

With regard to the extreme Left, the participation of Communist parties in European government over the sample period has been negligible.[4] Consequently, their exclusion does not have a big effect on the Left partisanship variable. Green parties have played a somewhat larger role in European government (particularly since 1995). Between 1995 and 2003, they occupied

---

[4] Jean-Claude Gayssot, a member of the French Communist Party (PCF), served as Minister of Transport in Lionel Jospin's government, from 1997 to 2002.

cabinet seats in the governments of four countries: Germany, Finland, Belgium, and France. Even so, the impact of their exclusion from the index of Left partisanship is relatively insubstantial. Overall, the correlation of the new Left partisanship variable (i.e., ex-Green and extreme Left parties) with its original version is around +0.99.

However, the addition of Center–Right Christian democratic parties to Armingeon et al.'s measure of Right partisanship is of greater substantive significance. The criteria utilized in order to add additional parties to the index is a score of above 6 in the expert assessment of Huber and Inglehart (1995), which attributes a score between 0 (most Left) and 10 (most Right) to parties on the basis of ten Left–Right policy criteria.[5] This criterion highlights a number of Center–Right parties – such as the People's Party in Austria, the CDU/CSU in Germany, the Christian Democrats in the Netherlands, and the Popular Party in Spain – which can reasonably be categorized as "conservative" parties, despite previous inclusion in the Center category by Armingeon et al. The addition of these parties to the index results in a new conservative partisanship variable with a correlation of +0.70 with Armingeon et al.'s original measure of Right partisanship. Exclusion of extreme Right parties from the index is of little practical significance, due to the negligible role of such parties in European government over the sample period.

The party breakdowns of the new Left and conservative indices of partisanship are presented in Table 6.5. The placement of any individual party within one of the two categories is ultimately based on a subjective judgment of a party's ideological stance, with which it is possible to disagree. However, it is hoped that this new operationalization is now more closely aligned to the theoretical conception of partisanship described in Chapter 2, and therefore offers a more credible basis on which to evaluate the hypothesis of this book. The variation over time of the new Left and conservative partisanship variables has already been presented in Figure 1.2 (which illustrated the high level of governmental participation of Left parties in the late 1990s; see Section 1.3).

Apart from main dependent and explanatory variables, there are also a number of additional variables that act as control variables in the econometric analysis. These are not included on the basis of expectations arising from the hypothesis of this book. However, the alternative approaches to corporate governance reviewed in Chapter 3 suggest that a range of variables may exert

---

[5] These include: economic or class conflict, xenophobia, centralization of power, conservatism versus change, authoritarianism versus democracy, property rights, isolation versus internationalism, constitutional reform, traditional versus new culture, and national defense (Huber and Inglehart 1995: 78).

A Panel Data Analysis of Corporate Governance Change 145

Table 6.5 Left–conservative positioning of governing political parties in fifteen nonliberal market economies

Nonliberal market economies	Left	Conservative
Austria	Sozialdemokratische Partei Österreichs (SPÖ).	Freiheitliche Partei Österreichs (FPÖ). Österreichische Volkspartei (ÖVP).
Belgium	Social Progressive Alternative/SPIRIT (SP.a/SPIRIT) (until 2001: Flemish Socialist Party). Parti Socialiste Belge (PSB, Francophone).	Liberal Party (LP). Partij voor Vrijheid en Vooruitgang (PVV, Flemish). Flemish Liberals and Democrats (VLD) (former: Party of Liberty and Progress [PVV]). Parti des Réformés et de la Liberté de Wallonie (PRLW). Reform Movement (MR) (in 1999: Fédération PRL-FDF-MCC, former: Francophone Liberals). Independent Catholics (ICAT). Christian Democrat and Flemish (CD and V) (until 2001: Christian People's Party [CVP]). Front Démocratique des Francophones (FDF). Christelijke Vlaamse Volksunie (VU).
Denmark	Social Demokratiet (SD). Left Socialist Party (LSP). Socialistik Folkeparti (SPP, Socialist People's Party).	Venstre (LIB). Det Konservative Folkeparti (CON). Justice Party (JP). Christian People's Party (CPP).
Finland	Suomen Sosialdemokraatinen Puola (SDP, Finnish Social Dem. Party). Suomen Kansan Demokraattinen Liitto (SKDL, communist). Social Democratic League of Workers and Smallholders (TPSL). Vaemmisto Liitto (VAS, Linksallianz).	Kansallinen Kokoomus (KOK, National Coalition). Svenska Folkepartiet (RKP, SFP).
France	Parti Socialiste Français (PSF).	Gaullistes (GAUL). Centre National des Indépendants (IND). Centre Démocratie et Progrès (CDP). Union pour la Nouvelle République (UNR). Union pour un Mouvement Populaire (UMP) (until 2002: Rassemblement Pour la République [RPR]).
Germany	Sozialdemokratische Partei Deutschlands (SPD).	Freie Demokratische Partei Deutschlands (FDP).

(*Continued*)

Table 6.5 Continued

Nonliberal market economies	Left	Conservative
		Christliche Demokratische Union (CDU). Christliche Soziale Union (CSU).
Greece	Pan-Hellenic Social Movement (PASOK).	Political Spring (POLAN). New Democracy (ND). National Radical Union (ERE). Centre Union (from 1977 Union of the Democratic Centre).
Italy	Partito Socialista Italiano di Unità Proletaria (PSIU). Partito Socialista Italiano (PSI). Partito Socialista Unificato (PSU). Partito Socialista Democratico (PSDI). Rinnovamento Italiano (RI). Socialisti democratici italiani (SDI). Democratici di sinistra (PDS). Democratici.	Partito Liberale Italiano (PLI). Forza Italia (FI). Lombard League, Northern League (LN). National Alliance (NA). Democrazia Cristiana (DC). Christian Democratic Centre, United Christian Democrats (CCD, CDU).
Japan	Social Democratic Party (SDP). Democratic Socialist Party (DSP). United Democratic Socialists (UDS).	Liberal Democratic Party (LDP). Japan Renewal Party (JRP). Japan New Party (JNP). New Conservative Party (NCP). Liberal Party (LP).
Netherlands	Partij van de Arbeid (PvdA, Labour Party). Politieke Partij Radicalen (PPR).	Volkspartij voor Vrijheid en Democratie (VVD). Christelijk Historische Unie (CHU). Anti-Revolutionaire Partij (ARP). List Pim Fortuyn. Katholieke Volkspartij (KVP). Christen Democratisch Appel (CDA).
Norway	Labour Party (AP, Det Norske Arbeiderparti).	Conservatives (CON, Hoyre). Liberals (LIB, Venstre). Christian People's Party (CPP, Kristelig Folkeparti).
Portugal	Socialist Party (PSP).	Popular Democrats, Social Democrats (PPD, PSD). Centre Social Democrats, Popular Party (CDS, PP).
Spain	Socialist Party (PSOE).	Centre and Unity (CiU). Popular Alliance, Popular Party (AP/PP).
Sweden	Socialdemokratische Arbetarpartiet (SDA).	Moderata Samlingspartiet (MUP, Moderate Unity Party). Folkepartiet Liberalerna (FP, Liberal Party). Kristen Demokratisk Samling (KDS).
Switzerland	Sozialdemokratische Partei der Schweiz (SPS).	Freisinnig Demokratische Partei (FDP). Schweizerische Volkspartei (SVP).

Source: Constructed by the author (see Section 6.1).

substantive effects on corporate governance outcomes. Furthermore, the discussion of corporate governance proxies in Chapter 4 indicates that it is necessary to include certain control variables to compensate for the distortionary effect of factors on the proxies that are unlikely to be related to corporate governance. It is important to account for the effects of these variables in the regression analysis before drawing conclusions regarding the significance of the interaction of partisanship and product market competition.

To take account of the possible impact of economic factors on corporate governance, three commonly utilized "economic" variables are included in the regressions: gross domestic product (GDP) growth, the level of GDP per capita, and a measure of interest rates. In many studies of corporate governance, GDP growth is analyzed as a dependent variable to be explained by corporate governance (Carlin and Mayer 2003). However, inclusion of GDP growth as a control provides a means of testing the claim that corporate governance is driven by efficiency or economic performance considerations. Such a perspective envisages some kind of link between a superior economic performance and the adoption of minority shareholder-oriented corporate governance.[6] Inclusion of GDP per capita is a way of testing the idea that higher levels of economic development are associated with a greater minority-shareholder orientation (see Section 3.1).

Interest rates have not been explicitly linked to corporate governance by the literature on corporate governance. However, the inclusion of both interest rates and GDP growth provide a way of controlling for the effect of cyclical factors that may exert a short-term effect on the corporate governance proxies, but which are independent of the state of corporate governance (see Sections 4.1.2–4.1.4). The rate of consumer price inflation would provide an alternative means of controlling for these cyclical effects; however, it is likely to be highly correlated with interest rates, and is therefore not included as well. Long-term interest rates in the form of ten-year government bond yields are utilized (rather than short-term rates), as long-term rates are more relevant discount rates in relation to long-term financial assets such as equity securities (Chen et al. 1986).

The regressions control for the possible effects of the legal origin argument (see Section 3.2) through the inclusion of dummy variables that highlight the Germanic or Scandinavian legal origins of a country's legal system. The default option – if a country is coded as zero for each of these two dummy

---

[6] The fact that corporate governance is often considered as an explanatory variable for GDP growth raises an endogeneity concern. This is alleviated by utilizing the GDP growth variable in lagged form in the estimation process. It would appear implausible that corporate governance in the current year could be a determinant of GDP growth in the previous year.

variables – is a French civil law legal tradition. A dummy variable for common law legal origin is not included, as all of the fifteen countries in the data set have civil rather than common law legal traditions.[7]

A measure of electoral system disproportionality – Gallagher's least squares index (Gallagher 1991) – is included to allow for the proportional or majoritarian nature of electoral rules (see Section 3.3). A pension system variable is included to account for the potential impact of a multi-pillar pension system on the corporate governance proxies (see Section 4.1.2). The idea that corporate governance outcomes may be influenced by country size, for example, with smaller countries coming under pressure from larger neighbors (Rajan and Zingales 2003: 35), is controlled for by including population in regressions. A measure of capital mobility is included in the form of a dummy variable that indicates the presence or otherwise of capital account restrictions (Prasad et al. 2003). Finally, a public debt variable is included. This variable is designed to test the idea that countries with high debt levels were forced to pursue a substantial privatization program in order to fulfill the Maastricht convergence criteria (which stipulated a maximum public debt-to-GDP ratio of 60%). According to this argument, countries adopted pro-shareholder corporate governance reform as a means of persuading investors to purchase the shares of companies undergoing privatization (and thereby maximize state revenues; see Section 3.5).

6.2 METHODOLOGY

The interaction of Left (or conservative) government and product market competition can be formalized in terms of the following empirical model:

$$cg_{it} = \beta_0 + \beta_1 \text{Left}_{it} + \beta_2 \text{PMC}_{it} + \beta_3 (\text{Left}_{it} \times \text{PMC}_{it}) \\ + \beta_4 X_{1it} + \ldots + \beta_n X_{nit} + u_{it} \qquad (1)$$

Where β_0 is a general intercept, cg is the corporate governance variable, Left represents the prevalence of Left government, PMC is product market competition, (Left×PMC) is an interaction term between Left government and product market competition, X_1 to X_n represent all other explanatory and

---

[7] The common law countries are the United Kingdom, the United States, Canada, Australia, New Zealand, and Ireland. The Germanic legal origin countries: Germany, Austria, Switzerland, and Japan. The Scandinavian legal origin countries: Sweden, Denmark, Norway, and Finland. The French civil law countries: France, Belgium, the Netherlands, Greece, Italy, Portugal, and Spain (La Porta et al. 1998: 1130).

control variables, β_1 to β_n are the slopes of the explanatory variables, and u is a stochastic error term.

However, a straightforward estimation of such a model gives rise to parameters that are difficult to interpret. For example, the coefficient on Left (β_1) in such a model estimates the effect of Left government when product market competition (PMC) is 0, which is not of much interest. To evaluate partisanship effects at other levels of competition, the normal econometric procedure is to reparameterize the model as follows:

$$cg_{it} = \alpha_0 + \delta_1 \text{Left}_{it} + \delta_2 \text{PMC}_{it} + \delta_3((\text{PMC}_{it} - \text{PMC}_0) \times \text{Left}_{it})$$
$$+ \delta_4 X_{1it} + \ldots \delta_n X_{nit} + u_{it}$$

where PMC_0 represents a specific value of PMC, which is deducted from each observation. Following this adjustment, the parameter on Left (δ_1) can be interpreted as measuring the effect of Left government on corporate governance at that specific level of PMC_0. By reestimating the model with different levels of PMC_0, the significance of Left government in differing environments of product market competition can be compared (Wooldridge 2006: 204; Kam and Franzese 2007: 19).

Before estimating the model, the properties of the data are examined through a series of regression diagnostics. A first set of tests is concerned with the stationarity of the dependent variable. Undertaking regressions on nonstationary time series, that is, where there exists a systematic relationship between the mean, variance, or covariance of the series and time, gives rise to inconsistent estimates and invalid regression diagnostics. In such circumstances, it would be necessary to undertake estimation with either a model specification in first differences or through the application of cointegrating techniques (Kittel and Winner 2005: 278).

Stationarity is tested utilizing the panel unit root tests developed by Levin et al. (2002) and Im et al. (2003). These are pooled versions of the Dickey–Fuller or augmented Dickey–Fuller tests that are commonly used to test for unit roots in individual time series. Both operate under the null hypothesis of nonstationarity. The tests differ from each other in that the Levin–Lin–Chu test assumes a common unit root process across each of the unit series. This is reflected in its alternative hypothesis, which asserts that all of the unit series are stationary. The Im–Pesaran–Shin test operates under an alternative hypothesis that claims at least one, but not necessarily all of the series, are stationary, which may be regarded as a less-restrictive assumption (Im et al. 2003). Both statistics can be evaluated with or without a time trend.

The results of these tests suggest a rejection (at the 5% level) of the null hypothesis of nonstationarity in respect of each of the three proxies for

Table 6.6 Levin–Lin–Chu panel unit root test

	Coefficient	P-value	
Equity share			
Regression without trend	−0.17388	0.0026	Reject unit root null hypothesis
Regression with trend	−0.32944	0.0001	Reject unit root null hypothesis
Value traded			
Regression without trend	−0.15552	0.0090	Reject unit root null hypothesis
Regression with trend	−0.36865	0.0314	Reject unit root null hypothesis
International equity issuance			
Regression without trend	−0.63869	0.0000	Reject unit root null hypothesis
Regression with trend	−0.92956	0.0000	Reject unit root null hypothesis

Notes: Test is applied from the first full year of a balanced panel, based on the natural logarithm of each variable. All tests are undertaken with a one-year lag of the dependent variable.

corporate governance – equity share, value traded, and international equity issuance (see Tables 6.6 and 6.7 in chapter appendix). Despite these results, some caution is warranted, as the power of panel unit root tests can be significantly reduced due to contemporaneous correlation between the units of the panel (Fleissig and Strauss 2001: 155). Notwithstanding this caveat, it is assumed in the rest of the analysis that the dependent variable proxies are stationary, and that it is therefore unnecessary to apply the specialized econometric techniques required for an analysis of nonstationary time series, for example, cointegration techniques or an error-correction model (although a model in first differences will be constructed as a test of robustness in Chapter 7).

Table 6.7 Im–Pesaran–Shin panel unit root test

	T-bar	P-value	
Equity share			
Regression without trend	−2.177	0.003	Reject unit root null hypothesis
Regression with trend	−2.808	0.002	Reject unit root null hypothesis
Value traded			
Regression without trend	−2.413	0.000	Reject unit root null hypothesis
Regression with trend	−3.020	0.000	Reject unit root null hypothesis
International equity issuance			
Regression without trend	−2.681	0.000	Reject unit root null hypothesis
Regression with trend	−3.112	0.000	Reject unit root null hypothesis

Notes: Test is applied from the first full year of a balanced panel, based on the natural logarithm of each variable. All tests are undertaken with a one-year lag of the dependent variable.

A second set of panel data issues concerns the potential variance of errors across units (groupwise heteroscedasticity) and the correlation of model errors across units (spatial correlation). Such data characteristics are a common feature of cross-country panels utilized in comparative political economy. However, both phenomena cause a violation of the spherical errors assumption of the Ordinary Least Squares (OLS) regression model, and give rise to invalid standard errors. Consequently, they prevent accurate hypothesis testing of the coefficients estimated by the OLS model. A Breusch–Pagan LM test of cross-sectional independence and a modified Wald test of groupwise heteroscedasticity suggest that nonspherical residuals are a feature of the data: the null hypotheses of independent errors and homoscedasticity are both rejected (at the 5% level) by the tests.

A way of overcoming these problems has been suggested by Beck and Katz (1995: 638). Their influential approach is to undertake hypothesis testing with panel-corrected standard errors (PCSEs). These more robust estimates of standard error are valid in the presence of groupwise heteroscedasticity and contemporaneous correlation of errors (even in a model estimated by OLS, as long as there is no autocorrelation in the errors). Consequently, all estimation in this chapter is undertaken on the basis of PCSEs.

A third issue for panel data analysis is that a typical data set in comparative political economy does not consist of observations drawn randomly from a large population over time. Rather, it is composed of repeated observations on the same units (i.e., countries). It is possible, therefore, that the data will exhibit some degree of unit and temporal heterogeneity. If unobserved unit and temporal effects are not allowed for in regressions, and there exists correlation between these effects and the explanatory variables included in the model, then estimates will be biased and inconsistent. The calculated coefficients will simply be a weighted average of individual unit specific relationships present in the data, with weighting biased to units with the largest N, largest coefficient values, and smallest standard errors (Bartels 1996).

One way of dealing with the unit heterogeneity problem is to estimate a model in terms of first differences. This eliminates time-invariant unit-specific errors, and allows standard OLS regression techniques to be utilized. However, the drawback of this approach is that the act of differencing data removes information provided by differing levels of observations. Regressions become entirely focused on the relationship between changes in variables. Furthermore, the resulting regressions tend to produce estimates with relatively large standard errors (Beck and Katz 2004: 10). Consequently, a more widely used means of dealing with the unobserved unit effect problem is to undertake regressions with either fixed or random effects.

Fixed effects have the effect of removing any danger of a correlation between unobserved unit-specific errors and explanatory variables. Dummy variables for each unit are added to the right-hand side of the regression equation, and serve to control for these unobserved unit-specific effects. The effect of unit dummies is to "time demean" the observations of each unit, for example, for each country, the country mean value of each variable is deducted from observations. This technique ensures that omitted variable bias arising from unspecified unit heterogeneity is no longer an issue of concern in the panel estimation (Greene 2003: 287). In an analogous manner, dummy variables can also be employed to account for temporal fixed effects (e.g., individual years or decades). The temporal fixed effects allow for the influence of omitted variables that exert a common effect on all countries at the same point in time (e.g., a war or commodity price shock).

Although a mainstay of the comparative political economy empirical literature, fixed effects are confronted by certain limitations. First, the effect of time demeaning is to eliminate the information provided by the cross-sectional variance of variables (Huber and Stephens 2001). The country dummies completely absorb differences in the level of independent variables across countries. In effect, country fixed effects result in a model with a different intercept for each country (although estimated slope parameters are common across all countries). Consequently, estimates from fixed effects regressions relate entirely to the relationship between the intra-unit variations of variables, that is, they are "within" unit estimates (Kittel and Winner 2005: 272). This is a disadvantage if the absolute levels of variables – as well as changes in levels – are of significance for the hypothesis under consideration (Beck and Katz 2004: 5; Plümper et al. 2005: 334). Second, the "within" nature of the estimation means that explanatory variables exhibiting limited temporal variation will have little impact on the determination of coefficients (Kittel and Winner 2005: 272). Third, fixed effects regressions do not permit inclusion of time-invariant variables in regressions, due to the perfect collinearity of such variables with the fixed effects country dummies (Wooldridge 2002). This is a particular issue with respect to the analysis of this chapter, due to the inclusion of time-invariant controls for legal origin.

However, given that the theoretical claims advanced by this book concern the determinants of *change* in European corporate governance, the "within" nature of the fixed effects estimator is well suited to the estimation task. Fixed effects serve to ensure that estimates are not the result of a mixture of influences from both levels and changes in variables, but are entirely driven by changes. With the exception of the legal origin variable, all of the explanatory variables utilized in the analysis exhibit significant temporal variation, and are therefore suitable for inclusion in a fixed effects analysis. Consequently, regressions are undertaken with both country fixed effects and temporal fixed effects. Given their time-invariant nature, it is necessary to evaluate the effect of legal origin in a separate model without country fixed effects, although the results of these regressions will be subject to concerns regarding the possibility of omitted variable bias.

Random effects represent an alternative to fixed effects in the management of unit heterogeneity. These are viable if the researcher has grounds for believing that unobserved country effects are uncorrelated with the explanatory variables. Random effects can be used with time-invariant explanatory variables – unlike fixed effects – and lead to more efficient estimates. They are undertaken with a generalized least squares regression technique, and involve only partial demeaning of unit data. The extent of this demeaning is determined on the basis of an estimated random-effects parameter (rho), whose magnitude determines the similarity of the regression estimates to those of fixed effects (at one extreme) or pooled OLS (at the other).

Despite the potential benefits of random effects, they are not employed in the empirical analysis for two main reasons. First, it is difficult in practice to be confident that omitted variables are uncorrelated with the included explanatory variables. A significant risk remains that the error terms may retain residual correlation with the explanatory variables (e.g., due to a failure to include relevant control variables). Consequently, the use of random rather than fixed effects in the regression increases the risk of severe omitted variable bias, particularly if the value of the random-effects parameter is relatively low (Beck and Katz 2004: 5). Second, it is not possible to calculate PCSEs in the context of a random-effects regression. Due to the presence of groupwise heteroscedasticity and spatial correlation in the model errors, PCSEs are essential for the viability of model hypothesis testing. Consequently, this rules out the use of random effects in subsequent analysis.

A final concern for the estimation strategy concerns the possibility of serial correlation in the model errors. Serial correlation has a similar effect on the validity of hypothesis testing diagnostics as groupwise heteroscedasticity and spatial correlation, although it emerges from the temporal rather than the cross-sectional characteristics of the data generation process (Greene 2003: 592). However, in contrast to groupwise heteroscedasticity and spatial correlation, it is not corrected by the utilization of panel-corrected standard errors. PCSEs are invalid if serial correlation is present. A Wooldridge test of autocorrelation in panel data (Wooldridge 2002) suggests that first-order serial correlation is indeed present in the model residuals.

The advice of Beck and Katz in such a situation is to include a lagged dependent variable (LDV) in model specifications (Beck and Katz 1995). However, this approach has been criticized by researchers for various reasons. First, LDVs are problematic in the context of either fixed or random-effects regressions, as they lead to biased estimates (Nickel 1981; Wooldridge 2002: 270).[8] Second, LDVs may absorb large parts of the trend in the dependent variable, which can lead to downwardly biased coefficients for the other explanatory variables (Achen 2000; Plümper et al. 2005: 349). Third, if the LDV does not fully capture the serial correlation (i.e. there is residual autocorrelation), then OLS estimates will be both biased and inconsistent (Greene 2003: 534).

Luke Keele and Nathan Kelly contend that the use of LDVs is still valid in most practical circumstances. Based on the results of Monte Carlo experiments, they show that, even with residual autocorrelation, biased LDV models still perform well as long as residual autocorrelation is not too great (Keele and Kelly 2006: 203). Furthermore, Beck and Katz (2004) argue – also on the basis of Monte Carlo evidence – that utilization of a LDV with fixed effects leads to reasonable results with TSCS data containing reasonably long time series, for example, at least twenty observations per country (Beck and Katz 2004: 15). Given that this empirical analysis is based on between twenty-one and twenty-eight years of data per country (depending on the proxy utilized for corporate governance), an LDV model is just about viable.

Nonetheless, to avoid any potential concerns regarding the use of LDVs, the regressions are estimated utilizing a Feasible Generalized Least Squares (GLS) procedure – employing a Prais–Winsten transformation of the model residuals – to correct for first-order serial correlation (Wooldridge 2006: 426). In conjunction with PCSEs, this ensures that hypothesis testing is undertaken on a robust basis. An LDV specification is revisited in the context of the robustness testing of Chapter 7 (which models the dynamics of the relationship between corporate governance and partisanship).

6.3 FINDINGS

6.3.1 Direct effects of partisanship

The hypothesis of this book predicts that Left government exerts an effect on corporate governance via its interaction with product market competition. However, before evaluating the empirical evidence for this hypothesis, it is of interest to investigate if there exists a direct relationship between the political complexion of government and corporate governance (i.e., independently of product market competition). As discussed in Chapter 2, the work of Mark Roe (2003) suggests

---

[8] The size of this bias will depend on the sample size and the size of the autoregression coefficient (Kittel and Winner 2005: 278).

that Left government will be positively associated with a blockholder regime. In contrast, Cioffi and Höpner (2006) assert the opposite (i.e., a negative association).

A first set of regressions investigates the validity of these assertions (see Tables 6.8 and 6.9). Partisanship and product market competition are included separately in the regressions, without taking into account the interaction effects. The effect of Left and conservative partisanship is estimated in separate models, in order to ensure that multicollinearity between measures of partisanship does not reduce the efficiency of individual estimates. Three types of regression are estimated for each corporate governance proxy. The first regression includes the legal origin control variables, but excludes any fixed effects due to their perfect collinearity with the time-invariant legal origin dummies. The second regression includes country fixed effects, but excludes the legal origin variables (for the same reason). In the third regression, fixed effects relating to both the unit and time dimension are included, the latter in the form of decade dummy variables.[9] Most variables are included in regressions in logarithmic form, thereby allowing interpretation of model coefficients in terms of elasticities. The exceptions are variables containing a significant number of zero or negative values, for example, dummy-style dichotomous variables, the partisanship variable, and GDP growth, which would lose a significant number of observations following a logarithmic transformation. All regressions are estimated with Feasible GLS with PCSEs.

The results in Tables 6.8 and 6.9 do not provide evidence for a direct relationship between the partisan complexion of government and corporate governance outcomes. Almost none of the coefficients on Left or conservative partisanship are statistically significant (even at the 10% significance level), and the coefficients frequently fluctuate in sign between regressions. There is, therefore, no confirmation of the contention of Mark Roe (2003): that Left government is associated with a blockholder regime. Equally, there is nothing in the results, so far, to support Cioffi and Höpner's (2006) argument that Left government is more likely to be associated with a shareholder approach.

A possible criticism of the regressions in Tables 6.8 and 6.9 is that they are undertaken with contemporaneous values of dependent and explanatory variables. It may be the case that the effect of partisanship on corporate

---

[9] An alternative method of accounting for common temporal shocks is through inclusion of annual fixed effects. However, there are reasons for being cautious of annual dummies. Neyman and Scott (1948) have argued that estimates will be inconsistent if a model contains variables that increase in tandem with the number of observations (the so-called incidental parameter problem). Consequently, following the approach of Chang et al. (2008: 16), decade dummies are utilized rather than annual fixed effects.

Table 6.8 Direct relationship between Left government and corporate governance

Corporate governance proxy	(1) Equity share	(2) Equity share	(3) Equity share	(4) Value traded	(5) Value traded	(6) Value traded	(7) International equity issuance	(8) International equity issuance	(9) International equity issuance
Type of fixed effects included	None	Country	Country and decade	None	Country	Country and decade	None	Country	Country and decade
Left government^	0.0008 (0.0006)	0.0005 (0.0006)	0.0005 (0.0005)	−0.0014 (0.0011)	−0.0011 (0.0011)	−0.0014 (0.0010)	0.0006 (0.0005)	0.0001 (0.0005)	0.0001 (0.0005)
Product market competition	−0.6559^b (0.1060)	−0.4620^a	−0.2553	−1.2767^c	−0.9087^b	−0.8187^a (0.4635)	−0.3335^b	−0.2130	−0.1265
Germanic legal origin^	0.3209 (0.3209)	0.2750	0.3070	0.4590^c	0.4225	0.4635	0.1448 (0.1448)	0.1717	0.2081
	−0.5039^c			−0.6370^c			−0.1462^b		
Scandinavian legal origin^	0.1699 −0.3594			0.2223 −0.7455^b			0.0647 0.0170		
Pension system^	0.2837 0.3616^c (0.1060)	0.0681 (0.0908)	0.0477 (0.0834)	0.3046 0.5249^c (0.1916)	0.3232^b (0.1610)	0.3137^b (0.1499)	0.0876 0.1906^b (0.0892)	0.2031^b (0.0983)	0.1959^b (0.0984)
GDP growth (L1)^	0.0306^b (0.0119)	0.0377^c (0.0125)	0.0393^c (0.0123)	0.0527^c (0.0197)	0.0626^c (0.0208)	0.0675^c (0.0201)	0.0367^c (0.0122)	0.0371^c (0.0126)	0.0399^c (0.0122)
GDP per capita	0.3686^b (0.1803)	0.5431^c (0.1509)	0.4866^b (0.1998)	0.9926^c (0.2564)	1.2250^c (0.2496)	1.0806^c (0.3169)	−0.0869 (0.0762)	−0.1096 (0.0912)	−0.1961^a (0.1176)
Interest rates	−0.6012^c (0.1538)	−0.6512^c (0.1526)	−0.7074^c (0.1508)	−1.0249^c (0.2399)	−1.1381^c (0.2459)	−1.2560^c (0.2360)	−0.2207^b (0.0872)	−0.2560^c (0.0842)	−0.2816^c (0.0837)

Population	0.0417	0.5269	0.4717	0.2069^a	0.9555	0.7705	0.0113	0.7150	0.5698
	(0.0720)	(0.8765)	(0.8026)	(0.1208)	(1.3534)	(1.1941)	(0.0152)	(0.5045)	(0.5115)
Electoral system disproportionality	−0.0144	0.0015	−0.0008	0.0327	−0.0368	−0.0532	0.0277	0.0103	−0.0030
Capital controls^	(0.0511)	(0.0504)	(0.0458)	(0.0844)	(0.0963)	(0.0913)	(0.0316)	(0.0404)	(0.0404)
	−0.1430^b	−0.1792^c	−0.1579^c	−0.3403^c	−0.3973^c	−0.3963^c	−0.1146^b	−0.1271^c	−0.0997^b
	(0.0654)	(0.0651)	(0.0601)	(0.1238)	(0.1272)	(0.1197)	(0.0487)	(0.0456)	(0.0476)
Government debt effect^	−0.0883	−0.0751	−0.0645	−0.1688	−0.1227	−0.1239	0.0041	0.0293	0.0240
Constant	(0.0956)	(0.0916)	(0.0868)	(0.1575)	(0.1513)	(0.1461)	(0.0513)	(0.0535)	(0.0542)
	−0.5878	−7.0087	−6.4006	−3.1490^a	−12.7902	−10.4985	1.2563^c	−5.1991	−3.6421
	(1.0656)	(7.8108)	(7.2186)	(1.6652)	(12.1149)	(10.8458)	(0.4031)	(4.5243)	(4.6660)
Observations	420	420	420	415	415	415	310	310	310
Number of countries	15	15	15	15	15	15	15	15	15

Notes: Standard errors in parentheses. All tests are two-tailed.
All regressions estimated with Feasible GLS and PCSEs.
All regressions estimated in terms of natural logs of variables, except for variables indicated (^).
^{a} significant at 10 percent; ^{b} significant at 5 percent; ^{c} significant at 1 percent.

Table 6.9 Direct relationship between conservative government and corporate governance

	(1)	(2)	(3)	(4)	(5)	(6)	(7)	(8)	(9)
Corporate governance proxy:	Equity share	Equity share	Equity share	Value traded	Value traded	Value traded	International equity issuance	International equity issuance	International equity issuance
Type of fixed effects included	None	Country	Country and decade	None	Country	Country and decade	None	Country	Country and decade
Conservative government^	−0.0005	−0.0003	−0.0003	0.0014	0.0017	0.0018^a	−0.0008	−0.0003	−0.0003
	(0.0007)	(0.0006)	(0.0006)	(0.0012)	(0.0011)	(0.0011)	(0.0006)	(0.0006)	(0.0006)
Product market competition	−0.6424^b	−0.4530	−0.2454	−1.2725^c	−0.8981^b	−0.8233^a	−0.3326^b	−0.2108	−0.1232
	(0.3185)	(0.2764)	(0.3083)	(0.4518)	(0.4225)	(0.4665)	(0.1433)	(0.1709)	(0.2076)
Germanic legal origin^	−0.5066^c			−0.6615^c			−0.1425^b		
	(0.1652)			(0.2169)			(0.0632)		
Scandinavian legal origin^	−0.3560			−0.7467^b			0.0153		
	(0.2860)			(0.3002)			(0.0864)		
Pension system^	0.3655^c	0.0714	0.0534	0.5199^c	0.3429^b	0.3277^b	0.1843^b	0.2002^b	0.1928^b
	(0.1056)	(0.0905)	(0.0832)	(0.1921)	(0.1611)	(0.1510)	(0.0876)	(0.0982)	(0.0983)
GDP growth (L1)^	0.0310^c	0.0378^c	0.0394^c	0.0525^c	0.0631^c	0.0676^c	0.0366^c	0.0368^c	0.0397^c
	(0.0120)	(0.0126)	(0.0124)	(0.0197)	(0.0209)	(0.0202)	(0.0123)	(0.0126)	(0.0122)
GDP per capita	0.3747^b	0.5402^c	0.4839^b	0.9943^c	1.2216^c	1.0757^c	−0.0866	−0.1069	−0.1931^a
	(0.1805)	(0.1525)	(0.2012)	(0.2547)	(0.2499)	(0.3176)	(0.0754)	(0.0911)	(0.1172)
Interest rates	−0.6046^c	−0.6491^c	−0.7067^c	−1.0256^c	−1.1352^c	−1.2473^c	−0.2212^b	−0.2570^c	−0.2833^c

	(1)	(2)	(3)	(4)	(5)	(6)	(7)	(8)	(9)
Population	0.0372	0.5514	0.4913	0.2072[a]	0.9726	0.8176	0.0094	0.6970	0.5524
	(0.1544)	(0.1537)	(0.1518)	(0.2390)	(0.2460)	(0.2364)	(0.0869)	(0.0839)	(0.0834)
Electoral system disproportionality	−0.0151	0.0022	−0.0003	0.0258	−0.0413	−0.0591	0.0264	0.0109	−0.0025
	(0.0710)	(0.8811)	(0.8082)	(0.1207)	(1.3321)	(1.1895)	(0.0150)	(0.4968)	(0.5038)
Capital controls^	−0.1443[b]	−0.1764[c]	−0.1551[c]	−0.3480[c]	−0.4120[c]	−0.4094[c]	−0.1154[b]	−0.1274[c]	−0.0996[b]
	(0.0508)	(0.0507)	(0.0460)	(0.0832)	(0.0963)	(0.0915)	(0.0308)	(0.0401)	(0.0401)
Government debt effect^	−0.0876	−0.0711	−0.0601	−0.1728	−0.1221	−0.1229	0.0027	0.0290	0.0235
	(0.0649)	(0.0646)	(0.0594)	(0.1229)	(0.1258)	(0.1183)	(0.0494)	(0.0459)	(0.0480)
Constant	−0.5149	−7.1992	−6.5436	−3.2535[a]	−13.0731	−11.0559	1.3349[c]	−5.0285	−3.4746
	(0.0957)	(0.0913)	(0.0866)	(0.1577)	(0.1507)	(0.1462)	(0.0505)	(0.0533)	(0.0541)
	(1.0467)	(7.8501)	(7.2652)	(1.6602)	(11.9154)	(10.8012)	(0.3913)	(4.4556)	(4.5980)
Observations	420	420	420	415	415	415	310	310	310
Number of countries	15	15	15	15	15	15	15	15	15

Notes: Standard errors in parentheses. All tests are two-tailed.
All regressions estimated with Feasible GLS and PCSEs.
All regressions estimated in terms of natural logs of variables, except for variables indicated (^).
[a] significant at 10 percent; [b] significant at 5 percent; [c] significant at 1 percent.

160   *Corporate Governance, Competition, and Political Parties*

governance takes time to exert an effect, and consequently may not be discernible in contemporaneous regressions. To check this possibility, the regressions are repeated with various lags on the partisanship explanatory variables. Tables 6.10 and 6.11 present the results of one such regression. In this case, Left and conservative government are included as three-year moving averages (MA 1, 2), that is, an average of the value of the current year and two preceding years. Such a lagged formulation thus allows partisanship a period of several years to impact on corporate governance outcomes.

In contrast to the previous results, the lagged regressions provide some limited evidence of a direct association between partisanship and corporate governance. The partisanship coefficient is significant in respect of one of the proxies for corporate governance (value traded), although it remains insignificant for the remaining two (equity share and international equity issuance). Interestingly, the signs on the statistically significant coefficients are negative for Left government and positive for conservative government, thus providing some backing for Roe's position, that is, the Right government encourages the shareholder model, and Left government the blockholder model, although the evidence is hardly conclusive. The lagged results continue to contradict the claim of Cioffi and Höpner – that the Left rather than conservative government plays a greater role in corporate governance change.

6.3.2 Significance of control variables

The regression results presented in Tables 6.8–6.11 also allow an assessment to be made of the direct impact of product market competition on corporate governance. As has been discussed in Chapter 3, the economic literature predicts a positive relationship between product market competition and the shareholder nature of corporate governance (and hence a negative relationship with the NMR index). All of the regressions produce the expected negative coefficient. However, not all of the coefficients are statistically significant. Most worryingly, competition is only statistically significant (at the 10% level) with fixed country and decade effects (i.e., the model specification with greatest resilience to omitted variable bias) with one of the three corporate governance proxies (value traded). Consequently, change in product market competition does not appear – in itself – to be an overwhelming explanation for change in corporate governance in nonliberal market economies.

Although the hypothesis of this book does not make any claims about the likely significance of other control variables, it is of interest to examine their explanatory power in the regressions. The regressions provide some support for

Table 6.10 Direct relationship between lag of Left government and corporate governance

	(1)	(2)	(3)	(4)	(5)	(6)	(7)	(8)	(9)
Corporate governance proxy	Equity share	Equity share	Equity share	Value traded	Value traded	Value traded	International equity issuance	International equity issuance	International equity issuance
Type of fixed effects included	None	Country	Country and decade	None	Country	Country and decade	None	Country	Country and decade
Left government (three-year MA)^	0.0000	0.0002	0.0004	-0.0042^b	-0.0034^b	-0.0037^c	0.0003	-0.0004	-0.0004
	(0.0010)	(0.0008)	(0.0006)	(0.0017)	(0.0014)	(0.0012)	(0.0006)	(0.0006)	(0.0006)
Product market competition	-0.7034^b	-0.3775	-0.1649	-1.3396^c	-0.6925	-0.5903	-0.3365^b	-0.2077	-0.1260
	(0.3279)	(0.2868)	(0.3110)	(0.4692)	(0.4339)	(0.4465)	(0.1464)	(0.1723)	(0.2078)
Germanic legal origin^	-0.6069^c			-0.9683^c			-0.1441^b		
	(0.1680)			(0.2411)			(0.0650)		
Scandinavian legal origin^	-0.3598			-0.4670			0.0250		
	(0.2624)			(0.3112)			(0.0867)		
Pension system^	0.3073^c	0.0632	0.0330	0.4696^b	0.3940^b	0.4095^c	0.2035^b	0.2177^b	0.2103^b
	(0.1075)	(0.0935)	(0.0846)	(0.1829)	(0.1601)	(0.1415)	(0.0913)	(0.0984)	(0.0986)
GDP growth (L1)^	0.0403^c	0.0494^c	0.0551^c	0.0660^c	0.0852^c	0.0978^c	0.0382^c	0.0375^c	0.0405^c
	(0.0140)	(0.0145)	(0.0140)	(0.0239)	(0.0247)	(0.0234)	(0.0122)	(0.0125)	(0.0121)
GDP per capita	0.4315^b	0.6480^c	0.6278^c	1.0197^c	1.4029^c	1.2144^c	-0.0900	-0.1133	-0.2009^a
	(0.1898)	(0.1659)	(0.2040)	(0.2759)	(0.2766)	(0.3348)	(0.0770)	(0.0918)	(0.1182)
Interest rates	-0.5904^c	-0.6199^c	-0.6833^c	-1.0634^c	-1.1908^c	-1.3515^c	-0.2149^b	-0.2616^c	-0.2874^c
	(0.1593)	(0.1569)	(0.1491)	(0.2485)	(0.2561)	(0.2402)	(0.0885)	(0.0863)	(0.0854)

(Continued)

Table 6.10 Continued

	(1)	(2)	(3)	(4)	(5)	(6)	(7)	(8)	(9)
Corporate governance proxy	Equity share	Equity share	Equity share	Value traded	Value traded	Value traded	International equity issuance	International equity issuance	International equity issuance
Type of fixed effects included	None	Country	Country and decade	None	Country	Country and decade	None	Country	Country and decade
Population	0.0528	1.1321	1.0411	0.3292[c]	1.5667	1.1537	0.0111	0.7422	0.5913
	(0.0676)	(1.0279)	(0.8993)	(0.1259)	(1.4907)	(1.2075)	(0.0149)	(0.5107)	(0.5200)
Electoral. System. Ddisproportionality	−0.0003	−0.0085	−0.0165	0.0256	−0.0627	−0.0847	0.0272	0.0093	−0.0033
	(0.0511)	(0.0523)	(0.0476)	(0.0853)	(0.0954)	(0.0900)	(0.0320)	(0.0401)	(0.0400)
Capital controls^	−0.1790[c]	−0.1967[c]	−0.1857[c]	−0.3855[c]	−0.4580[c]	−0.4823[c]	−0.1110[b]	−0.1218[c]	−0.0936[b]
	(0.0657)	(0.0677)	(0.0616)	(0.1289)	(0.1355)	(0.1255)	(0.0483)	(0.0458)	(0.0474)
Government debt effect^	−0.0802	−0.0725	−0.0614	−0.1852	−0.1336	−0.1344	0.0094	0.0292	0.0233
	(0.0928)	(0.0913)	(0.0843)	(0.1538)	(0.1479)	(0.1407)	(0.0517)	(0.0533)	(0.0542)
Constant	−0.8682	−12.9316	−12.1277	−4.2145[b]	−18.8046	−14.2749	1.2636[c]	−5.4078	−3.7911
	(0.9914)	(9.1892)	(8.0953)	(1.7024)	(13.3919)	(10.9529)	(0.4162)	(4.5842)	(4.7449)
Observations	392	392	392	389	389	389	310	310	310
Number of countries	15	15	15	15	15	15	15	15	15

Notes: Standard errors in parentheses. All tests are two-tailed.
All regressions estimated with Feasible GLS and PCSEs.
All regressions estimated in terms of natural logs of variables, except for variables indicated (^).
Left government is calculated as a three-year moving average (MA) of the current and previous 2 years, that is, MA (1, 2).
[a] significant at 10 percent; [b] significant at 5 percent; [c] significant at 1 percent.

Table 6.11 Direct relationship between lag of conservative government and corporate governance

	(1)	(2)	(3)	(4)	(5)	(6)	(7)	(8)	(9)
Corporate governance proxy	Equity share	Equity share	Equity share	Value traded	Value traded	Value traded	International equity issuance	International equity issuance	International equity issuance
Type of fixed effects included	None	Country	Country and decade	None	Country	Country and decade	None	Country	Country and decade
Conservative governmentt (three-year MA)^	0.0001	−0.0001	−0.0002	0.0041^b	0.0039^c	0.0042^c	−0.0006	0.0002	0.0002
	(0.0011)	(0.0008)	(0.0007)	(0.0017)	(0.0014)	(0.0013)	(0.0007)	(0.0007)	(0.0007)
Product market competition	−0.6935^b	−0.3740	−0.1577	−1.3457^c	−0.7034	−0.6256	−0.3397^b	−0.2099	−0.1282
	(0.3227)	(0.2893)	(0.3131)	(0.4575)	(0.4320)	(0.4510)	(0.1456)	(0.1720)	(0.2078)
Germanic legal origin^	−0.6149^c			−1.0213^c			−0.1432^b		
	(0.1668)			(0.2344)			(0.0643)		
Scandinavian legal origin^	−0.3763			−0.4603			0.0194		
	(0.2618)			(0.3030)			(0.0852)		
Pension system^	0.3146^c	0.0710	0.0440	0.4570^b	0.4114^c	0.4256^c	0.1991^b	0.2129^b	0.2053^b
	(0.1063)	(0.0938)	(0.0849)	(0.1839)	(0.1593)	(0.1420)	(0.0902)	(0.0988)	(0.0990)
GDP growth (L1)^	0.0404^c	0.0489^c	0.0544^c	0.0670^c	0.0861^c	0.0979^c	0.0381^c	0.0375^c	0.0405^c
	(0.0140)	(0.0146)	(0.0140)	(0.0239)	(0.0247)	(0.0235)	(0.0122)	(0.0125)	(0.0121)
GDP per capita	0.4424^b	0.6452^c	0.6217^c	1.0251^c	1.4001^c	1.2145^c	−0.0885	−0.1115	−0.1989^a
	(0.1883)	(0.1685)	(0.2075)	(0.2725)	(0.2755)	(0.3350)	(0.0763)	(0.0914)	(0.1178)

(Continued)

Table 6.11 Continued

	(1)	(2)	(3)	(4)	(5)	(6)	(7)	(8)	(9)
Corporate governance proxy	Equity share	Equity share	Equity share	Value traded	Value traded	Value traded	International equity issuance	International equity issuance	International equity issuance
Type of fixed effects included	None	Country	Country and decade	None	Country	Country and decade	None	Country	Country and decade
Interest rates	−0.5967[c]	−0.6190[c]	−0.6839[c]	−1.0678[c]	−1.1912[c]	−1.3387[c]	−0.2098[b]	−0.2582[c]	−0.2837[c]
	(0.1589)	(0.1579)	(0.1508)	(0.2465)	(0.2551)	(0.2396)	(0.0882)	(0.0858)	(0.0849)
Population	0.0401	1.1512	1.0604	0.3325[c]	1.5618	1.1936	0.0097	0.7376	0.5872
	(0.0674)	(1.0326)	(0.9069)	(0.1262)	(1.4933)	(1.2334)	(0.0147)	(0.5073)	(0.5163)
Electoral system disproportionality	−0.0044	−0.0097	−0.0176	0.0229	−0.0644	−0.0874	0.0246	0.0095	−0.0032
	(0.0507)	(0.0525)	(0.0478)	(0.0840)	(0.0949)	(0.0900)	(0.0315)	(0.0402)	(0.0402)
Capital controls[^]	−0.1849[c]	−0.1959[c]	−0.1845[c]	−0.3925[c]	−0.4674[c]	−0.4895[c]	−0.1143[b]	−0.1238[c]	−0.0962[b]
	(0.0654)	(0.0675)	(0.0615)	(0.1280)	(0.1345)	(0.1241)	(0.0485)	(0.0455)	(0.0473)
Government debt effect[^]	−0.0847	−0.0710	−0.0588	−0.1865	−0.1390	−0.1360	0.0078	0.0299	0.0239
	(0.0925)	(0.0915)	(0.0845)	(0.1537)	(0.1469)	(0.1404)	(0.0512)	(0.0535)	(0.0544)
Constant	−0.7607	−13.0840	−12.2614	−4.5771[c]	−19.0766	−14.9794	1.3105[c]	−5.4011	−3.7894
	(0.9775)	(9.2240)	(8.1535)	(1.7075)	(13.4012)	(11.1712)	(0.4011)	(4.5484)	(4.7072)
Observations	392	392	392	389	389	389	310	310	310
Number of countries	15	15	15	15	15	15	15	15	15

Notes: Standard errors in parentheses. All tests are two-tailed.
All regressions estimated with Feasible GLS and PCSEs.
All regressions estimated in terms of natural logs of variables, except for variables indicated (^).
Conservative government is calculated as a three-year MA of the current and previous 2 years, that is, MA (1, 2).
[a] significant at 10 percent; [b] significant at 5 percent; [c] significant at 1 percent.

legal origin – particularly in its Germanic form – as a significant factor. However, this result should be treated with some caution. Legal origin is only included in the regressions without fixed effects. Consequently, the results of these regressions are potentially subject to omitted variable bias. Furthermore, it is obviously not possible for a time-invariant variable such as legal origin to explain changes in corporate governance (which is the focus of the hypothesis). The tentative conclusion arising from this result, therefore, is that legal origin may play a useful role in explaining comparative corporate governance outcomes, even if it is not helpful in explaining corporate governance change.

The regressions show that the corporate governance proxies are positively associated with economic growth, and negatively associated with the level of interest rates. The coefficients on these variables are unambiguously significant across each of the model specifications. Section 4.1.2 discussed the likely impact of macroeconomic factors (particularly the credit cycle) on the variation of the corporate governance proxies. The existence of this effect is confirmed by the significance of these variables. Their inclusion in the regressions is, therefore, important in order to control for the distorting influence of cyclical macroeconomic factors, and thereby permit the proxies to provide a more accurate indication of outsider corporate governance orientation.

The regression results also show that change in the corporate governance is significantly associated (in a negative direction) with the removal of capital controls. Evidence of a significant positive association with a multi-pillar pension system and levels of economic development (as measured by GDP per capita) is also relatively compelling, although the coefficients are not significant in all model specifications. In contrast, the results do not suggest that corporate governance is associated with the size of the country (as measured by population), the proportionality of the electoral system, or a high level of government debt leading up to economic and monetary union (EMU).

In summary, the first set of regression results – undertaken without the inclusion of interaction effects – provides only limited evidence of a direct association between partisanship and corporate governance change. The same is true of the direct association between product market competition and corporate governance change. A further finding is that GDP growth, interest rates, capital controls, GDP per capita, and the pension system are important control variables for an empirical evaluation of the determinants of corporate governance change.

6.3.3 Interaction of partisanship and product market competition

The next stage in the analysis involves evaluating the relationship between corporate governance and the interaction of Left or conservative government partisanship and product market competition. According to the hypothesis of Chapter 2, Left government is expected to be positively associated with pro-shareholder corporate governance change in an environment of competitive product markets. However, this is not predicted when levels of product market competition are low, when the relationship is expected to be either negative or insignificant. In contrast, conservative government is expected to be negatively or insignificantly associated with corporate governance change at all levels of product market competition.

Tables 6.12 and 6.13 show the results of regressions undertaken with an interaction term (created by multiplying the Left–conservative government partisanship variables and product market competition). This has the effect of substantially increasing the statistical significance of most of the coefficients on partisanship (compared to the results in Tables 6.8 and 6.9). Coefficients on Left government are now positively related to each of the corporate governance proxies, and significant in each model specification. Coefficients on conservative government are negative, and also statistically significant for each of the corporate governance proxies (although only at the 10% level for international equity issuance).

However, as discussed in Section 6.2, the inclusion of a straightforward interaction term (based on simple multiplication of the interacting variables) does not tell a particularly insightful story about the relationship between the interaction of partisanship and competition, and corporate governance. The relationship that is estimated is effectively pertaining to when the value of the NMR index of competition is equal to 0. To see how this relationship changes at different levels of competition, it is necessary to transform the regression equation based on different values of the NMR index. The differing values of the partisanship variable from each of these regressions can be plotted in the form of conditional effects graphs. These show the nature of the relationship between partisanship and corporate governance at differing levels of product market competition. It is not necessary to report the values of the coefficients on control variables for each of the regressions on which the graphs are based, as they are identical to those presented in Tables 6.12 and 6.13 in each case. Only the coefficients on partisanship vary between regressions (Kam and Franzese 2007: 63).

The conditional effects graphs for each of the three proxies of corporate governance are shown in Figures 6.1–6.12. For each proxy, there are graphs summarizing the results of two sets of regressions: a first set estimated

Table 6.12 Relationship of interaction of Left government/product market competition, and corporate governance

Corporate governance proxy	(1) Equity share	(2) Equity share	(3) Equity share	(4) Value traded	(5) Value traded	(6) Value traded	(7) International equity issuance	(8) International equity issuance	(9) International equity issuance
Type of fixed effects included	None	Country	Country and decade	None	Country	Country and decade	None	Country	Country and decade
Left government^	0.0079^c (0.0026)	0.0083^c (0.0023)	0.0082^c (0.0023)	0.0164^c (0.0042)	0.0169^c (0.0041)	0.0163^c (0.0039)	0.0037^b (0.0019)	0.0041^b (0.0019)	0.0040^b (0.0019)
Product market competition	−0.4880 (0.3083)	−0.3318 (0.2597)	−0.1232 (0.2995)	−0.8104^a (0.4207)	−0.5415 (0.3897)	−0.4698 (0.4488)	−0.2388 (0.1483)	−0.0997 (0.1650)	−0.0129 (0.2030)
Interaction term	−0.0016^c (0.0006)	−0.0018^c (0.0005)	−0.0017^c (0.0005)	−0.0041^c (0.0009)	−0.0041^c (0.0009)	−0.0040^c (0.0009)	−0.0008^a (0.0005)	−0.0010^b (0.0004)	−0.0009^b (0.0005)
Germanic legal origin^	−0.5161^c (0.1759)			−0.7226^c (0.2168)			−0.1434^b (0.0653)		
Scandinavian legal origin^	−0.3615 (0.2616)			−0.8684^c (0.2958)			−0.0179 (0.0917)		
Pension system^	0.3665^c (0.1025)	0.0441 (0.0880)	0.0192 (0.0823)	0.5263^c (0.1867)	0.3200^c (0.1528)	0.3114^b (0.1463)	0.1571^a (0.0903)	0.1608 (0.1012)	0.1565 (0.1007)
GDP growth (L1)^	0.0292^b (0.0116)	0.0349^c (0.0121)	0.0363^c (0.0118)	0.0491^c (0.0190)	0.0556^c (0.0200)	0.0592^c (0.0193)	0.0342^c (0.0122)	0.0342^c (0.0126)	0.0371^c (0.0123)
GDP per capita	0.3670^b (0.1788)	0.5349^b (0.1498)	0.4957^b (0.1930)	1.0187^c (0.2465)	1.2775^c (0.2425)	1.1658^c (0.3026)	−0.0852 (0.0755)	−0.0982 (0.0894)	−0.1736 (0.1174)

(Continued)

Table 6.12 Continued

	(1)	(2)	(3)	(4)	(5)	(6)	(7)	(8)	(9)
Corporate governance proxy	Equity share	Equity share	Equity share	Value traded	Value traded	Value traded	International equity issuance	International equity issuance	International equity issuance
Type of fixed effects included	None	Country	Country and decade	None	Country	Country and decade	None	Country	Country and decade
Interest rates	−0.5927[c]	−0.6212[c]	−0.6753[c]	−1.0125[c]	−1.0664[c]	−1.1619[c]	−0.2130[b]	−0.2462[c]	−0.2698[c]
	(0.1496)	(0.1480)	(0.1455)	(0.2262)	(0.2345)	(0.2266)	(0.0856)	(0.0822)	(0.0826)
Population	0.0479	0.3285	0.3204	0.1992[a]	0.1145	0.0250	0.0031	0.6057	0.4893
	(0.0738)	(0.8358)	(0.7717)	(0.1170)	(1.2795)	(1.1264)	(0.0170)	(0.5115)	(0.5102)
Electoral system disproportionality	−0.0148	−0.0039	−0.0086	0.0546	−0.0142	−0.0297	0.0404	0.0264	0.0124
	(0.0513)	(0.0498)	(0.0453)	(0.0877)	(0.0961)	(0.0920)	(0.0310)	(0.0396)	(0.0401)
Capital controls^	−0.1358[b]	−0.1616[c]	−0.1488[b]	−0.3250[c]	−0.3529[c]	−0.3621[c]	−0.0916[a]	−0.0992[b]	−0.0757
	(0.0647)	(0.0627)	(0.0587)	(0.1212)	(0.1254)	(0.1196)	(0.0485)	(0.0446)	(0.0464)
Government debt effect^	−0.0886	−0.0750	−0.0670	−0.1728	−0.1456	−0.1377	0.0004	0.0243	0.0220
	(0.0936)	(0.0888)	(0.0843)	(0.1520)	(0.1449)	(0.1412)	(0.0518)	(0.0543)	(0.0546)
Constant	−0.9089	−5.4200	−5.2952	−3.8156[b]	−5.9566	−4.6652	1.1816[c]	−4.4212	−3.1586
	(1.0672)	(7.4264)	(6.9206)	(1.6168)	(11.4139)	(10.1980)	(0.4019)	(4.5670)	(4.6212)
Observations	420	420	420	415	415	415	310	310	310
Number of countries	15	15	15	15	15	15	15	15	15

Notes: Standard errors in parentheses. All tests are two-tailed.
All regressions estimated with Feasible GLS and PCSEs.
All regressions estimated in terms of natural logs of variables, except for variables indicated (^).
Interaction term = (Left government × Product market competition).
[a] significant at 10 percent; [b] significant at 5 percent; [c] significant at 1 percent.

Table 6.13 Relationship of interaction of conservative government/product market competition, and corporate governance

	(1)	(2)	(3)	(4)	(5)	(6)	(7)	(8)	(9)
Corporate governance proxy	Equity share	Equity share	Equity share	Value traded	Value traded	Value traded	International equity issuance	International equity issuance	International equity issuance
Type of fixed effects included	None	Country	Country and decade	None	Country	Country and decade	None	Country	Country and decade
Conservative government^	−0.0074[c]	−0.0070[c]	−0.0070[c]	−0.0123[c]	−0.0132[c]	−0.0121[c]	−0.0028	−0.0033[a]	−0.0032[a]
	(0.0026)	(0.0022)	(0.0021)	(0.0041)	(0.0039)	(0.0037)	(0.0018)	(0.0017)	(0.0017)
Product market competition	−0.9215[c]	−0.7717[b]	−0.5562[a]	−1.8175[c]	−1.5437[c]	−1.4408[c]	−0.4231[b]	−0.3320[a]	−0.2415
Interaction term	0.0016[c]	0.0016[c]	0.0016[c]	0.0031[c]	0.0035[c]	0.0033[c]	0.1729	0.2001	0.2306
	(0.3438)	(0.3017)	(0.3220)	(0.4567)	(0.4271)	(0.4635)	0.0005	0.0008[a]	0.0007[a]
	(0.0006)	(0.0005)	(0.0005)	(0.0009)	(0.0009)	(0.0008)	(0.0004)	(0.0004)	(0.0004)
Germanic legal origin^	−0.5285[c]			−0.7336[c]			−0.1380[b]		
	(0.1799)			(0.2068)			(0.0646)		
Scandinavian legal origin^	−0.3593			−0.7953[c]			−0.0036		
	(0.2527)			(0.2862)			(0.0927)		
Pension system^	0.3799[c]	0.0505	0.0306	0.5225[c]	0.3668[b]	0.3379[b]	0.1560[a]	0.1702[a]	0.1634
	(0.1004)	(0.0877)	(0.0804)	(0.1898)	(0.1541)	(0.1473)	(0.0898)	(0.1003)	(0.0999)
GDP growth (L1)^	0.0299[b]	0.0362[c]	0.0381[c]	0.0505[c]	0.0593[c]	0.0636[c]	0.0355[c]	0.0353[c]	0.0383[c]
	(0.0117)	(0.0122)	(0.0119)	(0.0193)	(0.0204)	(0.0196)	(0.0124)	(0.0127)	(0.0123)
GDP per capita	0.3983[b]	0.5544[c]	0.5017[b]	1.0432[c]	1.3228[c]	1.1827[c]	−0.0789	−0.0880	−0.1720
	(0.1786)	(0.1520)	(0.1963)	(0.2519)	(0.2479)	(0.3105)	(0.0762)	(0.0915)	(0.1197)
Interest rates	−0.6074[c]	−0.6389[c]	−0.6969[c]	−1.0348[c]	−1.1128[c]	−1.2106[c]	−0.2212[b]	−0.2580[c]	−0.2849[c]

(Continued)

Table 6.13 Continued

Corporate governance proxy	(1) Equity share	(2) Equity share	(3) Equity share	(4) Value traded	(5) Value traded	(6) Value traded	(7) International equity issuance	(8) International equity issuance	(9) International equity issuance
Type of fixed effects included	None	Country	Country and decade	None	Country	Country and decade	None	Country	Country and decade
Population	0.0284 (0.1509)	0.5114 (0.1503)	0.4855 (0.1476)	0.1891[a] (0.2319)	0.4190 (0.2380)	0.4056 (0.2287)	0.0036 (0.0863)	0.6935 (0.0831)	0.5438 (0.0828)
Electoral system disproportionality	−0.0219 (0.0737)	−0.0137 (0.8196)	−0.0193 (0.7699)	0.0394 (0.1144)	−0.0492 (1.1983)	−0.0660 (1.0931)	0.0180 (0.0180)	0.0207 (0.5003)	0.0073 (0.5011)
Capital controls^	−0.1414[b] (0.0512)	−0.1682[c] (0.0498)	−0.1505[c] (0.0451)	−0.3414[c] (0.0854)	−0.4009[c] (0.0951)	−0.3991[c] (0.0906)	−0.1002[b] (0.0303)	−0.1113[b] (0.0400)	−0.0836[a] (0.0401)
	(0.0645)	(0.0630)	(0.0583)	(0.1225)	(0.1253)	(0.1184)	(0.0506)	(0.0464)	(0.0480)
Government debt effect^	−0.0800 (0.0933)	−0.0589 (0.0878)	−0.0503 (0.0836)	−0.1512 (0.1552)	−0.1113 (0.1456)	−0.1088 (0.1434)	0.0039 (0.0508)	0.0331 (0.0538)	0.0277 (0.0546)
Constant	−0.0788 (1.0658)	−6.3999 (7.2826)	−6.0709 (6.9049)	−2.4146 (1.5853)	−7.3917 (10.7427)	−6.7622 (9.9638)	1.4812[c] (0.4335)	−4.8828 (4.5139)	−3.2946 (4.5886)
Observations	420	420	420	415	415	415	310	310	310
Number of countries	15	15	15	15	15	15	15	15	15

Notes: Standard errors in parentheses. All tests are two-tailed.
All regressions estimated with Feasible GLS and PCSEs.
All regressions estimated in terms of natural logs of variables, except for variables indicated (^).
Interaction term = (Conservative government × Product market competition).
[a] significant at 10 percent; [b] significant at 5 percent; [c] significant at 1 percent.

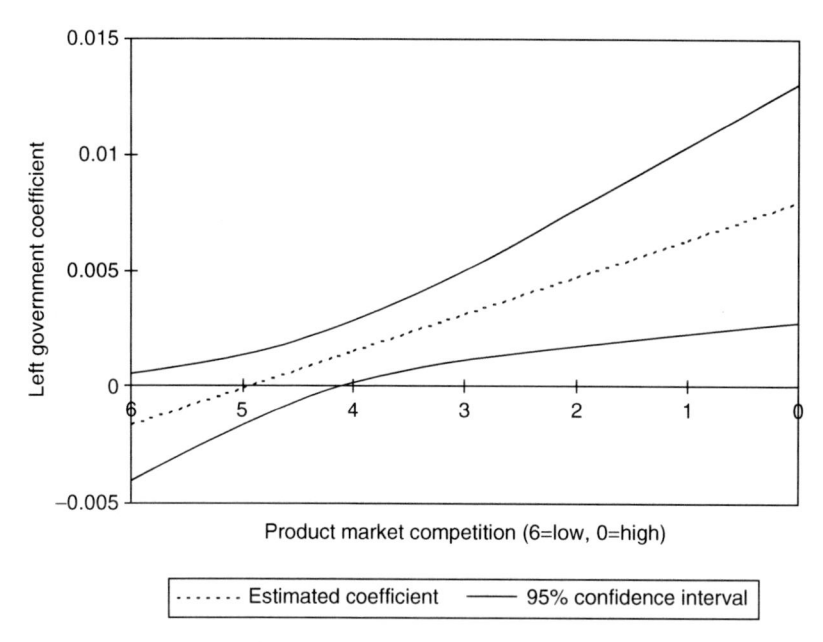

Figure 6.1 Conditional effects of Left government on corporate governance. Dependent variable: equity share. No fixed effects. Legal origin controls

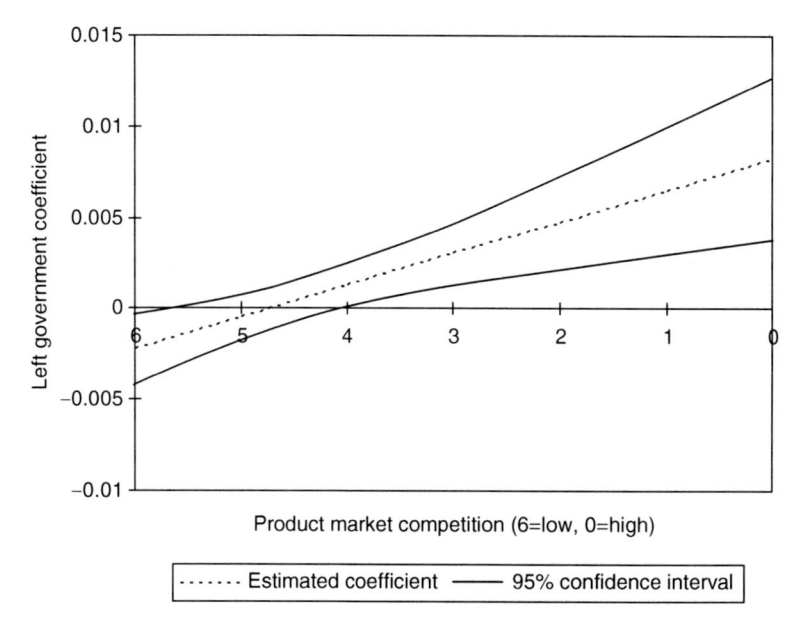

Figure 6.2 Conditional effects of Left government on corporate governance. Dependent variable: equity share. Country and decade fixed effects

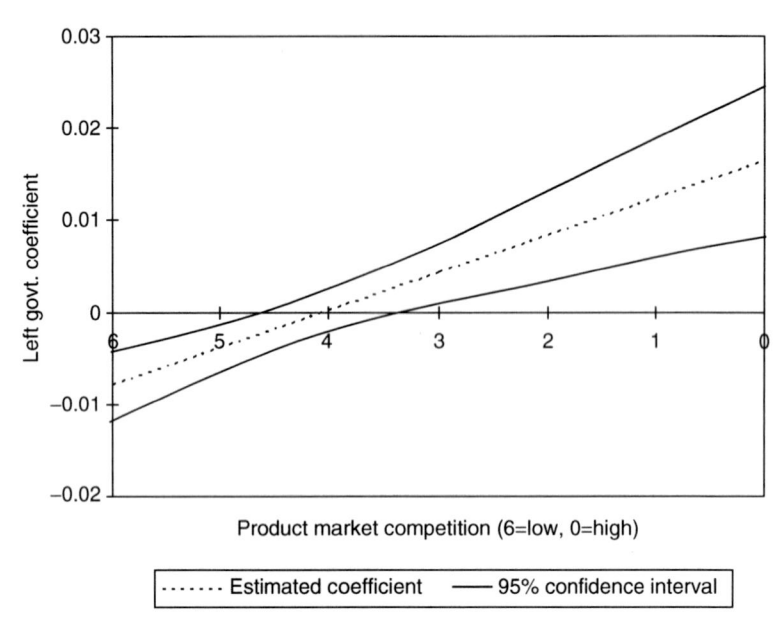

Figure 6.3 Conditional effects of Left government on corporate governance. Dependent variable: value traded. No fixed effects. Legal origin controls

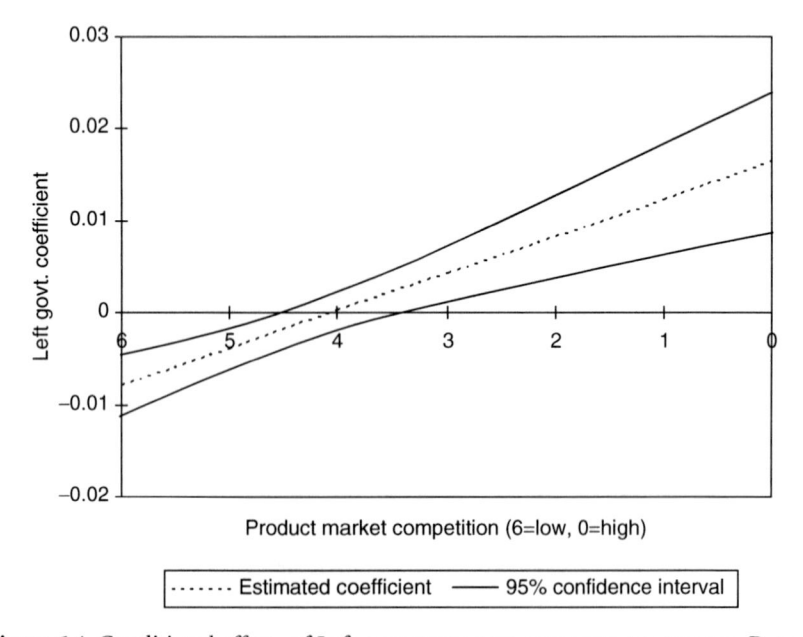

Figure 6.4 Conditional effects of Left government on corporate governance. Dependent variable: value traded. Country and decade fixed effects

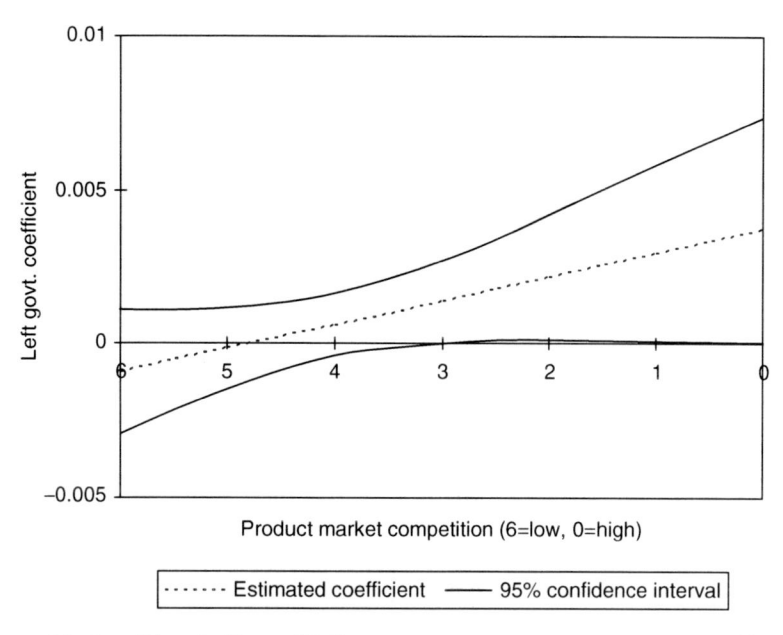

A Panel Data Analysis of Corporate Governance Change 173

Figure 6.5 Conditional effects of Left government on corporate governance. Dependent variable: international equity issuance. No fixed effects. Legal origin controls

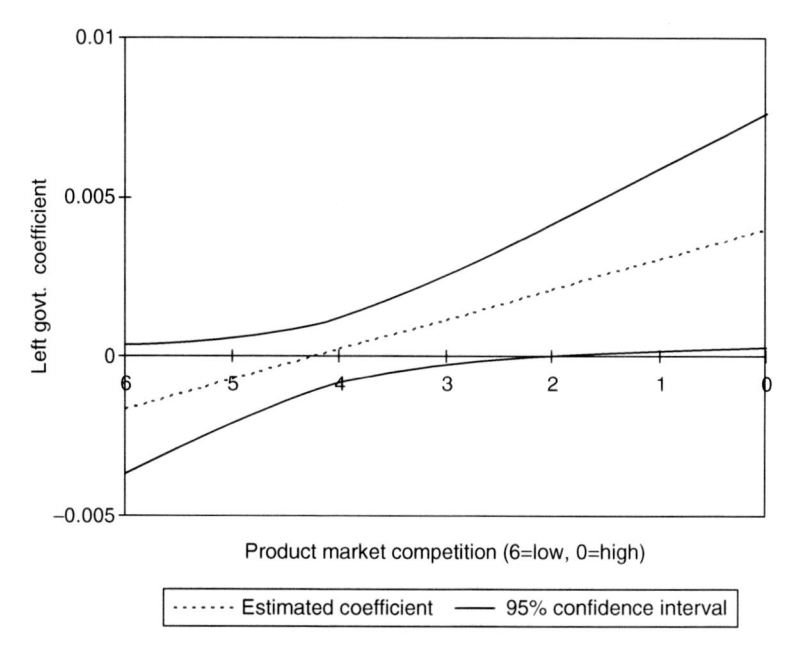

Figure 6.6 Conditional effects of Left government on corporate governance. Dependent variable: international equity issuance. Country and decade fixed effects

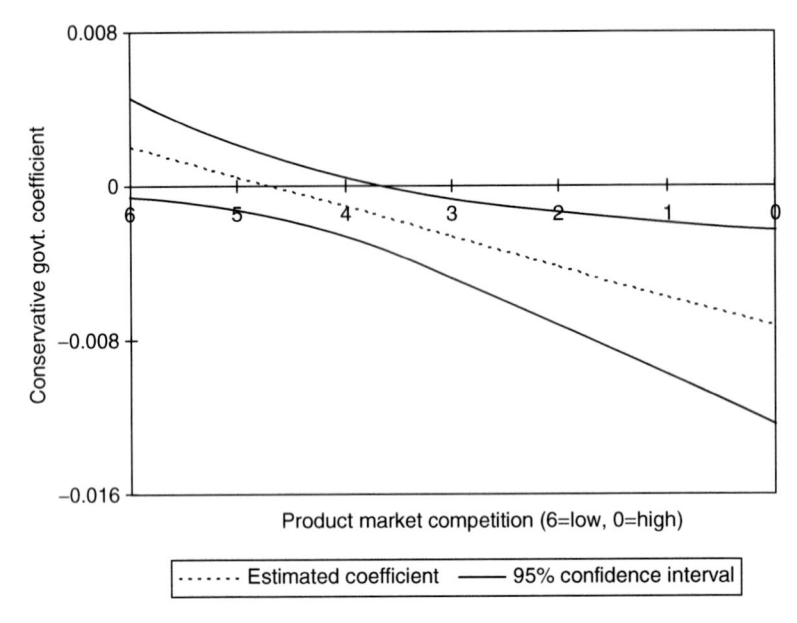

Figure 6.7 Conditional effects of conservative government on corporate governance. Dependent variable: equity share. No fixed effects. Legal origin controls

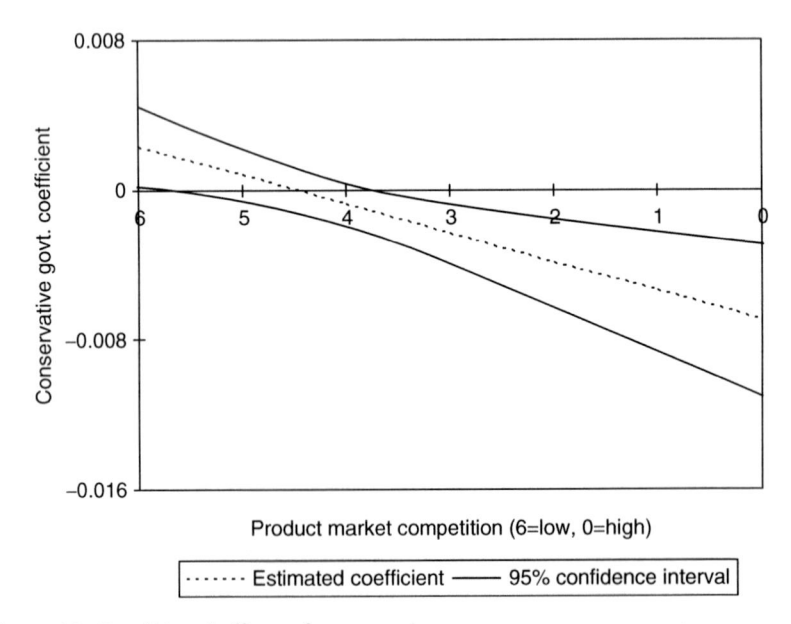

Figure 6.8 Conditional effects of conservative government on corporate governance. Dependent variable: equity share. Country and decade fixed effects

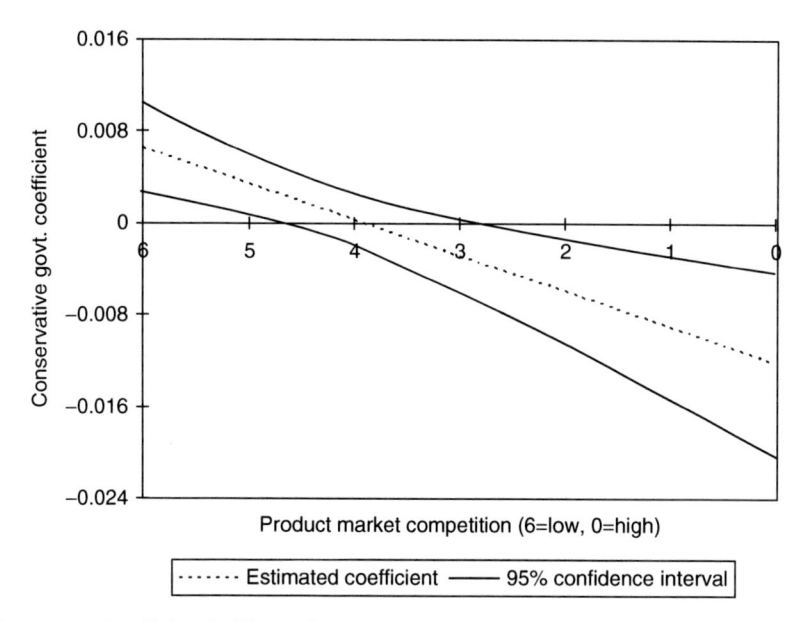

A Panel Data Analysis of Corporate Governance Change

Figure 6.9 Conditional effects of conservative government on corporate governance. Dependent variable: value traded. No fixed effects. Legal origin controls

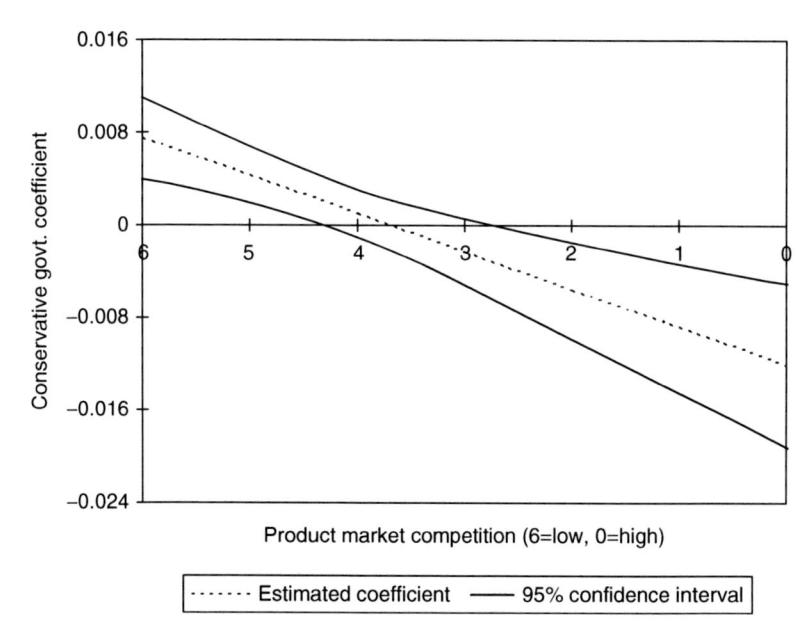

Figure 6.10 Conditional effects of conservative government on corporate governance. Dependent variable: Value traded. Country and decade fixed effects

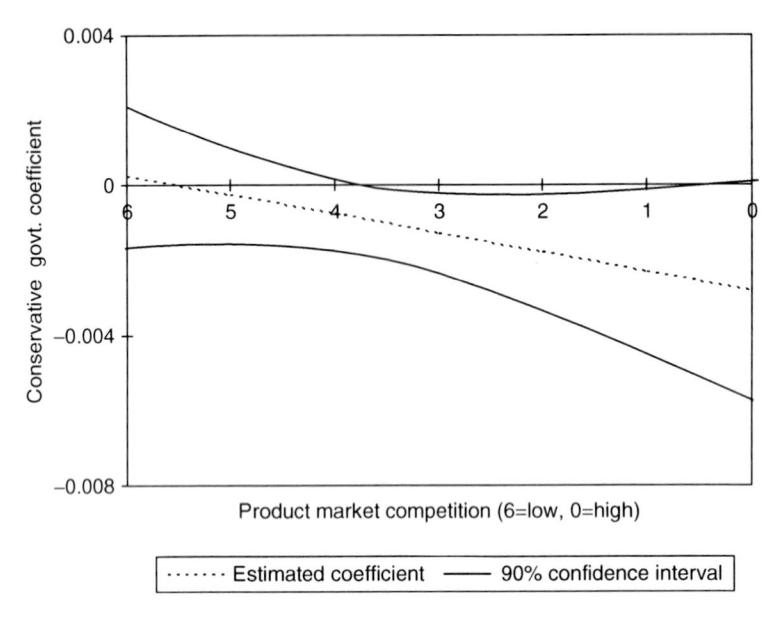

Figure 6.11 Conditional effects of conservative government on corporate governance. Dependent variable: international equity issuance. No fixed effects. Legal origin controls

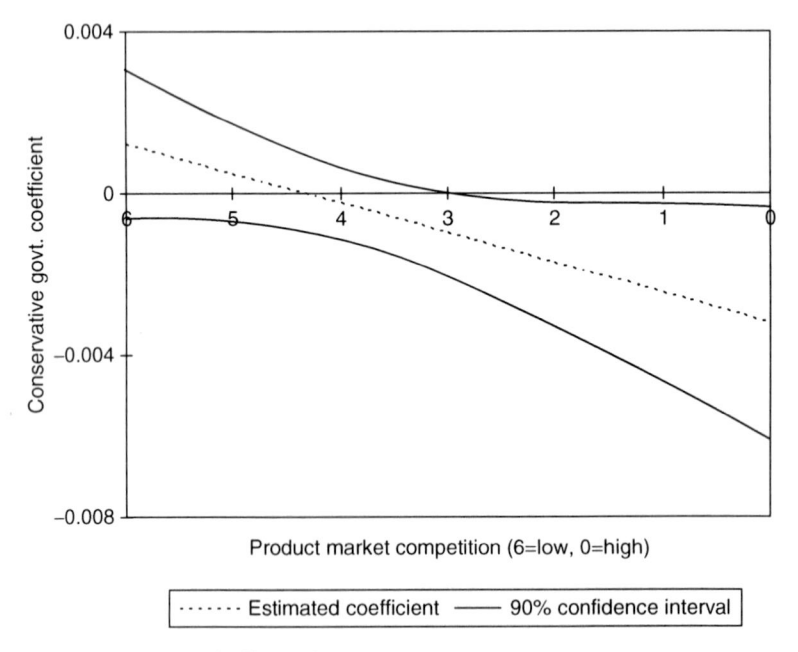

Figure 6.12 Conditional effects of conservative government on corporate governance. Dependent variable: international equity issuance. Country and decade fixed effects

without fixed effects, but with legal origin control variables; and a second set with country and decade fixed effects (but without legal origin control variables). A third set of regressions – estimated with country fixed effects only – was also estimated. However, the results obtained from these regressions tell a similar story to those obtained from the other specifications. Consequently, for reasons of space, the corresponding conditional effects graphs are not shown in this chapter. After presenting the conditional effects of Left government (Figures 6.1–6.6), equivalent results are provided for conservative government (Figures 6.7–6.12).

The results presented in the conditional effects graphs concerning Left government (Figures 6.1–6.6) provide a strong level of support for the theoretical claims of this book. At low levels of product market competition (as indicated by a high value for the NMR index), there exists a negative or statistically insignificant relationship between Left government and the shareholder nature of corporate governance. However, as competition increases, Left government becomes increasingly associated with a pro-shareholder orientation (i.e., the reported coefficient on Left government becomes increasingly positive). This positive impact of the Left on pro-shareholder corporate governance becomes statistically significant below an NMR index value of between 3 and 4 (as indicated by the point at which the lower confidence interval line crosses the horizontal axis of the graphs). These results hold for each of the three corporate governance proxies and across each of the regression specifications (without fixed effects and with legal origin control variables; with country fixed effects; and with country and decade fixed effects).

The international equity issuance proxy yields a slightly less precise result than the other two proxies (as indicated by wider confidence intervals). However, this is not unexpected, given that the series benefits from fewer observations and – as a measure of activity in primary rather than secondary equity markets – is inherently more volatile on a year-to-year basis. The less "persistent" nature of this time series is revisited in the dynamic analysis of Chapter 7. Nonetheless, despite the more challenging nature of this data series, the results obtained in respect of Left partisanship are consistent with those of the other two proxies: Left government – conditional on product market competition – is positively and significantly associated with pro-shareholder corporate governance.

The results relating to conservative government and corporate governance are also consistent with theoretical expectations (Figures 6.7–6.12). At low levels of product market competition, the association between conservative government and corporate governance is generally insignificant from zero (although in the case of the value-traded proxy, a significant positive association is recorded). As competition increases, the association between conservative partisanship and corporate governance develops in the reverse manner to that observed with Left government: The partisanship coefficient becomes negatively associated with the corporate governance proxies, that is, conservative government becomes associated with less shareholder-oriented corporate governance outcomes. In the case of the equity share and value-traded proxies, this negative association is observable at the 5 percent significance level. The international equity issuance proxy provides a slightly less definitive result, with the negative association with conservative partisanship apparent at the 10 percent level of significance.[10]

As argued in Section 6.3.1, it is possible to criticize regressions undertaken with contemporaneous values of variables. It may take time for government to adjust to changes in product market competition, or for its policies to feed through into changes in *de facto* corporate governance outcomes. If this is the case, then a regression between contemporaneous values of corporate governance and the main explanatory variables will not accurately capture the true nature of any underlying relationship. In order to investigate these issues, a second series of models is estimated, containing lagged values of the partisanship variable and the term capturing the interaction between partisanship and product market competition. Various lag structures are tested. However, as before, results relating to three-year MAs of the explanatory variables are presented in the following text, as this lag structure gives rise to the most substantive relationship with corporate governance in respect of the equity share and value traded proxies. According to this model specification, corporate governance is not only associated with change in the interaction of partisanship and competition in the current year, but also with the developments of the previous two years.

The results of these regressions are shown in Figures 6.13–6.18. In the interests of space, the results presented relate only to the model specification with country and decade fixed effects (i.e., the most robust model specification vis-à-vis omitted variable bias). The graphs show both the coefficients obtained from the lagged regressions, and those previously estimated with contemporaneous explanatory variables. In terms of the first two proxies – equity share and value traded – the lagged results are similar to those obtained with the contemporaneous models in terms of coefficient sign and statistical significance. However, the magnitude of the coefficients is substantially larger in the lagged regressions – almost double the size of the contemporaneous coefficients at certain levels of the NMR index. This supports the idea that the

---

[10] For this reason, the confidence intervals shown in Figures 6.11–6.12 (relating to international equity issuance) are 90% confidence intervals rather than 95% confidence intervals.

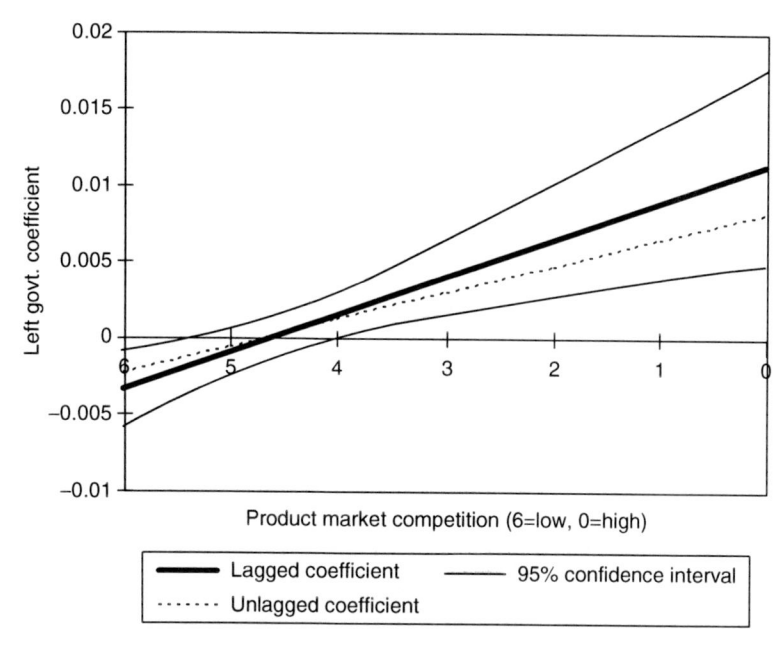

Figure 6.13 Conditional effects of lagged Left government on corporate governance. Dependent variable: equity share. Country and decade fixed effects

Note: The confidence intervals relate to the lagged coefficients.

impact of partisanship on corporate governance may take some time to exert its full effect. In contrast, in respect of the third corporate governance proxy – international equity issuance – the relationship is at its strongest in the contemporaneous rather than the lagged regressions. In the latter case, lags serve to reduce statistical significance and the size of partisanship coefficients. Indeed, the confidence intervals in Figure 6.15 (Left government) and Figure 6.18 (conservative government) suggest that the partisanship coefficients in the lagged regressions are not statistically significant. Once again, this may reflect the volatile and less persistent nature of this data series.

6.3.4 Substantive significance of results

Tables 6.14–6.19 provide an analysis of the substantive significance of the estimated relationships, based on the coefficients obtained from the regression results. They seek to illustrate the effect on corporate governance outcomes of a 5, 10, 25, or 50 point increase in the Left or conservative partisanship variables, that is, Left or conservative parties increasing their share of cabinet posts in government by 5, 10, 25, or 50

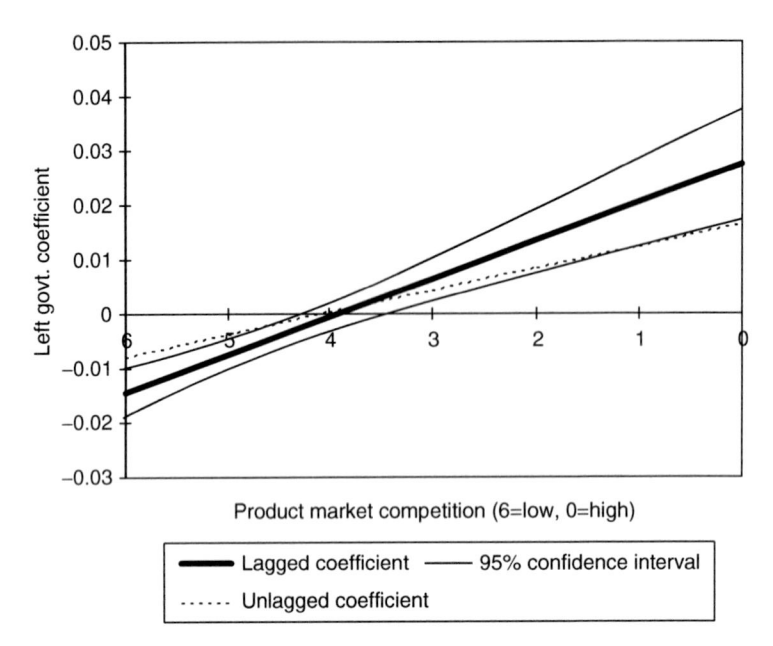

Figure 6.14 Conditional effects of lagged Left government on corporate governance. Dependent variable: value traded. Country and decade fixed effects

Note: The confidence intervals relate to the lagged coefficients.

percent.[11] The impact of such a change in governmental composition is evaluated for each corporate governance proxy at six different levels of product market competition (as measured by the NMR index).

In order to place differing levels of the NMR index into context, Figure 6.19 illustrates its development in three European countries (Germany, Italy, and Sweden) over the sample period. The experience of these three European countries is typical of other European economies since the mid-1970s. Prior to the early 1990s, NMR values of between 4.5 and 6 (the maximum index value) were the norm among the nonliberal market economies. This was followed by declines to below 3 in many countries during the subsequent decade. In some cases, there is evidence of convergence on US levels at the end of the sample period.[12] The United States – whose product

---

[11] It is, of course, possible for the Left and conservative partisanship variables to increase or decrease by any amount between 0 and 100. The above-fixed amounts are simply utilized for the purpose of sensitivity analysis.

[12] The IMF (Helbling et al. 2004) and the OECD (Høj et al. 2006) provide an analysis of the determinants of product market competition change. For a discussion of their results, see Section 2.4.

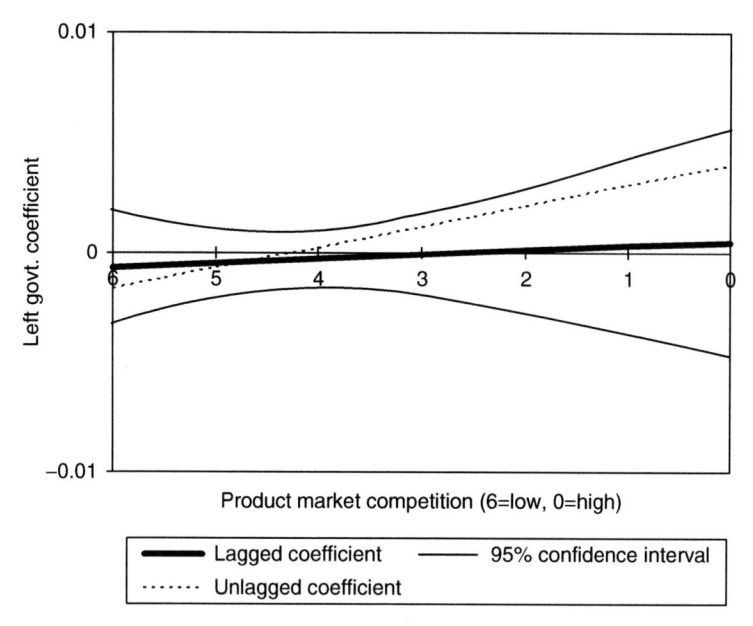

A Panel Data Analysis of Corporate Governance Change 181

Figure 6.15 Conditional effects of lagged Left government on corporate governance. Dependent variable: international equity issuance. Country and decade fixed effects

Note: The confidence intervals relate to the lagged coefficients.

markets are the most competitive among the advanced industrialized democracies – is included in the chart as a "high-competition" benchmark.

The effect of a change in partisanship is evaluated from the starting point of the mean value of each corporate governance proxy.[13] For example, in respect of equity share, the mean value across the sample is 0.39. Tables 6.14 and 6.15 show how this level of equity share would be predicted to change following increases in Left or conservative government at differing levels of competition. A similar procedure is undertaken for the value traded and international equity issuance proxies in Tables 6.16–6.19.

The simulations for each of the proxies suggest that the impact on corporate governance of a small change in the partisan complexion of government (e.g., a 5-point increase in the percentage of cabinet posts held by Left or conservative political parties) is not substantial. Furthermore, even a larger change (e.g., 25 or 50-points) in government composition does not exert a substantive impact if the NMR index lies in the mid- or upper portion of its possible range (e.g., an index value above 3.5). This was the level of

---

[13] This is chosen as the starting point of the simulations for purely illustrative purposes.

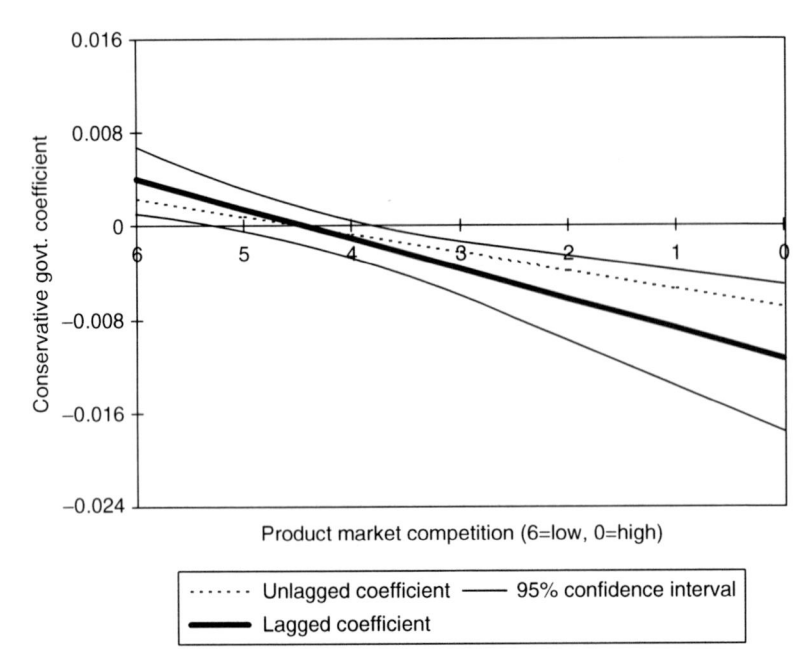

Figure 6.16 Conditional effects of lagged conservative government on corporate governance. Dependent variable: equity share. Country and decade fixed effects

Note: The confidence intervals relate to the lagged coefficients.

competition prevailing in most European economies prior to the mid- and late 1990s.

However, if the NMR index declines below 3 – which has occurred in many sample countries in recent years – then the implications of a 25- or 50-point change in government partisanship for corporate governance become more substantial. In the case of equity share (Tables 6.14 and 6.15), a 50-point increase in the value of Left government in the most competitive market conditions (i.e., an NMR index of 0) would be associated with an increase of equity share from 0.39 (the sample average) to 0.66. With reference to the country ranking in Figure 6.20, this is the equivalent of moving from the position of Belgium to above that of the Netherlands (although still well below the equity share of the United States).[14] The effect of a 50-point increase in conservative government participation would be to reduce equity

---

[14] The United States is included as a point of comparison in Figures 6.20 and 6.21 in order to indicate the equity share/ and value-trade levels of a strongly pro-shareholder system of corporate governance. A similar function is fulfilled by the United Kingdom in Figure 6.22.

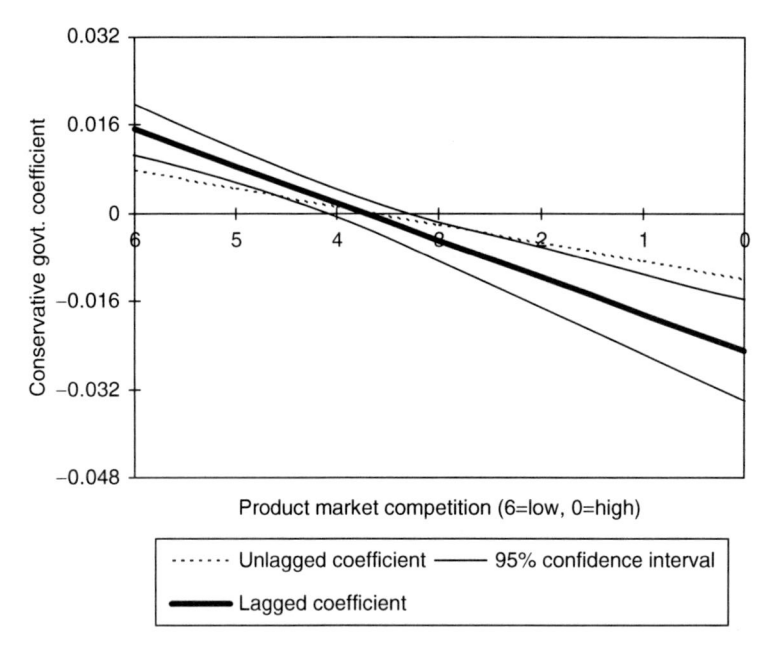

Figure 6.17 Conditional effects of lagged conservative government on corporate governance. Dependent variable: value traded. Country and decade fixed effects

Note: The confidence intervals relate to the lagged coefficients.

share from 0.39 to 0.15 (i.e., a shift from Belgium's position to that occupied by Portugal).

However, such large substantive effects – based on an NMR index of 0 – represent the theoretical upper bounds of possible change in corporate governance. Even in the United States, the NMR index only reached a level if 1.4 at the end of the sample period (i.e., well above 0). At a less competitive NMR index value of 2 – approximately the level prevailing in Germany and Sweden in 2003 – a 50-point change in Left partisanship would be associated with a smaller increase in equity share, from 0.39 to 0.54. In the case of a 50-point increase in conservative government, equity share would decrease from 0.39 to 0.29. These more modest (albeit still substantive) changes imply an upward shift in Belgium's position (in Figure 6.20) to that occupied by Sweden (with Left government), or a downward shift to the position of Denmark (with conservative government).

The estimates obtained with the value traded proxy (Tables 6.16 and 6.17) imply a somewhat larger substantive impact on corporate governance than with equity share. In the extreme competition scenario (i.e., an NMR index

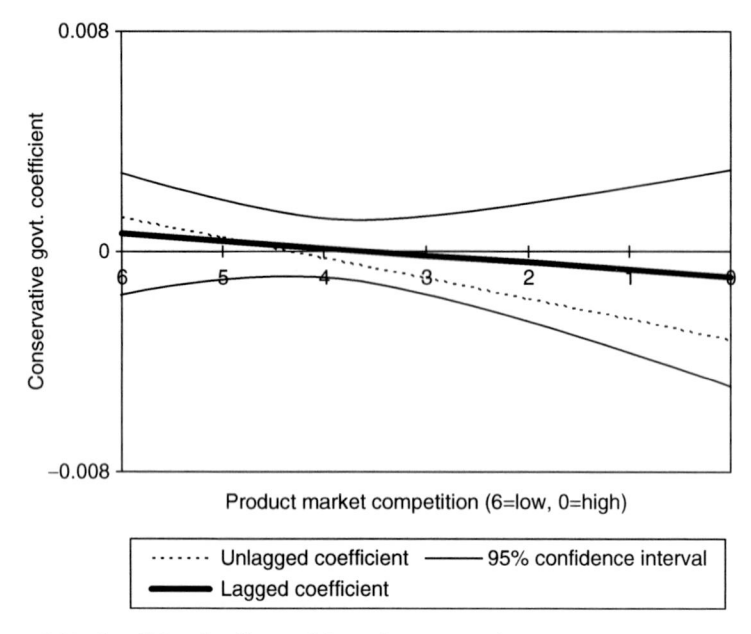

184 Corporate Governance, Competition, and Political Parties

Figure 6.18 Conditional effects of lagged conservative government on corporate governance. Dependent variable: international equity issuance. Country and decade fixed effects

Note: The confidence intervals relate to the lagged coefficients.

Table 6.14 Substantive implications of Left government on corporate governance. Impact on the sample mean of equity share (sample mean = 0.39)

Value of NMR index of product market competition	6	5	4	3	2	1	0
Increase in Left government							
+5 points	0.38[b]	0.39	0.39[b]	0.40[c]	0.40[c]	0.41[c]	0.41[c]
+10 points	0.38[b]	0.39	0.40[b]	0.41[c]	0.42[c]	0.43[c]	0.44[c]
+25 points	0.36[b]	0.38	0.41[b]	0.43[c]	0.46[c]	0.49[c]	0.52[c]
+50 points	0.33[b]	0.37	0.42[b]	0.48[c]	0.54[c]	0.61[c]	0.69[c]

Notes: All values based on regression results with country and decade fixed effects, and refer to effect of change in lagged values (three-year MA) of Left government variable. Lower values of NMR index indicate greater product market competition. Left government variable varies between 0 and 100. Starting value is the sample mean.

[a] significant at 10 percent; [b] significant at 5 percent; [c] significant at 1 percent.

Table 6.15 Substantive implications of conservative government on corporate governance. Impact on the sample mean of equity share (sample mean = 0.39)

Value of NMR index of product market competition	6	5	4	3	2	1	0
Increase in conservative government							
+5 points	0.40^c	0.39	0.39	0.38^c	0.38^c	0.37^c	0.37^c
+10 points	0.41^c	0.40	0.39	0.38^c	0.37^c	0.36^c	0.35^c
+25 points	0.43^c	0.40	0.38	0.36^c	0.33^c	0.31^c	0.29^c
+50 points	0.48^c	0.42	0.37	0.32^c	0.29^c	0.25^c	0.22^c

Notes: All values based on regression results with country and decade fixed effects, and refer to effect of change in lagged values (three-year MA) of conservative government variable. Lower values of NMR index indicate greater product market competition. Conservative government variable varies between 0 and 100. Starting value is sample mean.
^{a} significant at 10 percent; ^{b} significant at 5 percent; ^{c} significant at 1 percent.

Table 6.16 Substantive implications of Left government on corporate governance. Impact on the sample mean of value traded (sample mean: 0.25)

Value of NMR index of product market competition	6	5	4	3	2	1	0
Increase in Left government							
+5 points	0.23^c	0.24^c	0.25	0.26^c	0.27^c	0.28^c	0.29^c
+10 points	0.22^c	0.23^c	0.25	0.27^c	0.29^c	0.31^c	0.33^c
+25 points	0.17^c	0.21^c	0.25	0.29^c	0.35^c	0.42^c	0.50^c
+50 points	0.12^c	0.17^c	0.24	0.35^c	0.49^c	0.70^c	0.99^c

Notes: All values based on regression results with country and decade fixed effects, and refer to effect of change in lagged values (three-year MA) of Left government variable. Lower values of NMR index indicate greater product market competition. Left government variable varies between 0 and 100. Starting value is the mean.
^{a} significant at 10 percent; ^{b} significant at 5 percent; ^{c} significant at 1 percent.

Table 6.17 Substantive implications of conservative government on corporate governance. Impact on the sample mean of value traded (sample mean: 0.25)

Value of NMR index of product market competition	6	5	4	3	2	1	0
Increase in conservative government							
+5 points	0.27^c	0.26^c	0.25	0.24^c	0.24^c	0.23^c	0.22^c
+10 points	0.29^c	0.27^c	0.25	0.24^c	0.22^c	0.21^c	0.19^c
+25 points	0.37^c	0.31^c	0.26	0.22^c	0.19^c	0.16^c	0.13^c
+50 points	0.54^c	0.38^c	0.27	0.20^c	0.14^c	0.10^c	0.07^c

Notes: All values based on regression results with country and decade fixed effects, and refer to effect of change in lagged values (three-year MA) of conservative government variable. Lower values of NMR index indicate greater product market competition. Conservative government variable varies between 0 and 100. Starting value is sample mean.
^{a} significant at 10 percent; ^{b} significant at 5 percent; ^{c} significant at 1 percent.

Table 6.18 Substantive implications of Left government on corporate governance. Impact on the sample mean of international equity issuance (mean value: 0.50)

Value of NMR index of product market competition	6	5	4	3	2	1	0
Increase in Left government							
+5 points	0.49^a	0.49	0.50	0.51	0.52^b	0.52^b	0.53^b
+10 points	0.47^a	0.49	0.50	0.52	0.53^b	0.55^b	0.56^b
+25 points	0.44^a	0.47	0.51	0.54	0.58^b	0.62^b	0.66^b
+50 points	0.38^a	0.44	0.51	0.59	0.67^b	0.75^b	0.83^b

Notes: All values based on regression results with country and decade fixed effects, and refer to effect of contemporaneous (i.e., unlagged) change in Left government variable. Lower values of NMR index indicate greater product market competition. Left government variable varies between 0 and 100. Starting value is sample mean.
^{a} significant at 10 percent; ^{b} significant at 5 percent; ^{c} significant at 1 percent.

Table 6.19 Substantive implications of conservative government on corporate governance. Impact on the sample mean of international equity issuance (mean value: 0.50)

Value of NMR index of product market competition	6	5	4	3	2	1	0
Increase in conservative government							
+5 points	0.51	0.50	0.50	0.49	0.49^a	0.48^a	0.48^a
+10 points	0.52	0.51	0.50	0.49	0.47^a	0.46^a	0.45^a
+25 points	0.55	0.52	0.49	0.46	0.44^a	0.41^a	0.38^a
+50 points	0.60	0.54	0.48	0.43	0.38^a	0.32^a	0.28^a

Notes: All values based on regression results with country and decade fixed effects, and refer to effect of contemporaneous (i.e., unlagged) change in conservative government variable. Lower values of NMR index indicate greater product market competition. Conservative government variable varies between 0 and 100. Starting value is sample mean.
^{a} significant at 10 percent; ^{b} significant at 5 percent; ^{c} significant at 1 percent.

of 0), a 50-point increase in Left government would be associated with an increase in value traded from 0.25 (the sample mean) to 0.99 (i.e., from around the level of Germany, to above that of the United States, see Figure 6.21). A similar increase in conservative government would reduce value traded to almost 0.07 (i.e., from the German level to below that of Norway, the bottom-ranked country). However, in more realistic competitive conditions (with an NMR index of 2), value traded would increase from 0.25 to 0.49 (approximately the level of the Netherlands in Figure 6.21) with Left government, and decrease to 0.14 (close to the level of Italy) with conservative government.

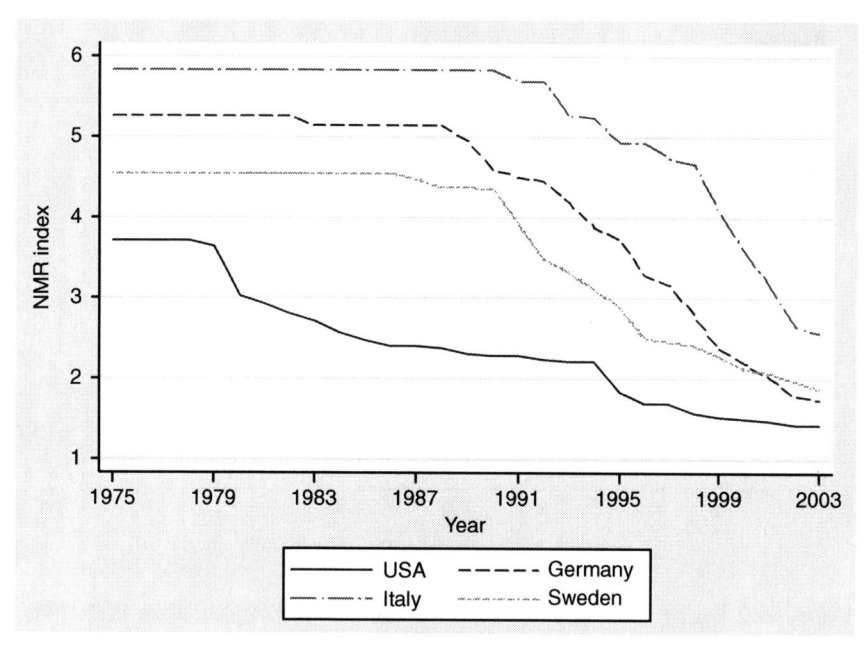

Figure 6.19 Product market competition experiences in three European countries (6 = least competitive, 0 = most competitive)

Note: A lower value of the NMR index indicates a higher level of product market competition.
Source: Conway and Nicoletti (2006).

The estimates obtained with international equity issuance proxy give rise to slightly smaller substantive effects than the other two proxies (Tables 6.18 and 6.19). If the NMR index is equal to 0, a 50-point increase in Left government participation would be associated with an increase in the proxy from 0.5 (the sample mean) to 0.83. This would be the equivalent of shifting France – which occupies a median ranking in terms of the proxy – to a corporate governance ranking above the United Kingdom (see Figure 6.22). An equivalent increase in conservative partisanship in these conditions would be associated with a decline in the proxy from 0.5 to 0.28 (i.e., to roughly the level of Denmark). However, in a more realistic scenario of an NMR index equal to 2, the change is less extreme: a 50-point increase in Left partisanship would be associated with an increase in the proxy from 0.5 to 0.67, while a decrease from 0.5 to

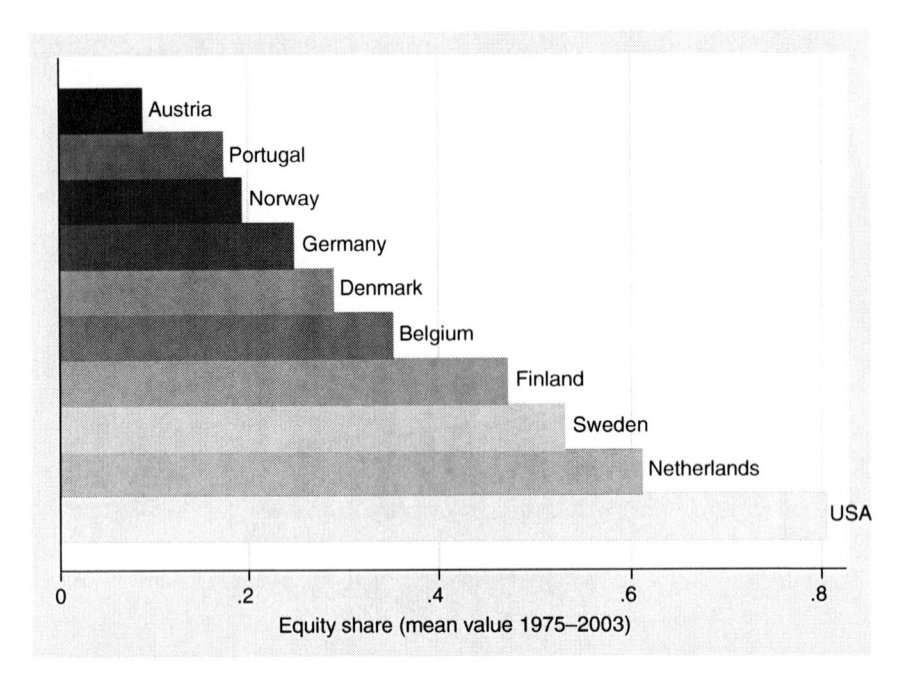

Figure 6.20 Equity share for a range of European countries (mean value 1975–2003)
Note: Equity market capitalization, divided by GDP.
Source: Beck et al. (2000).

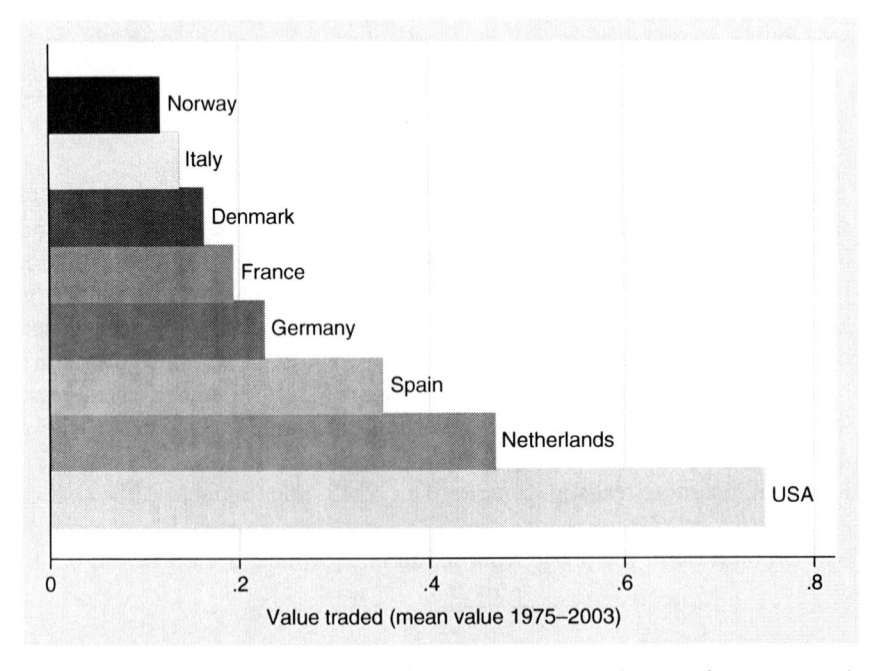

Figure 6.21 Value traded for a range of European countries (mean value 1975–2003)
Note: Value of trading on equity market, divided by GDP.
Source: Beck et al. (2000).

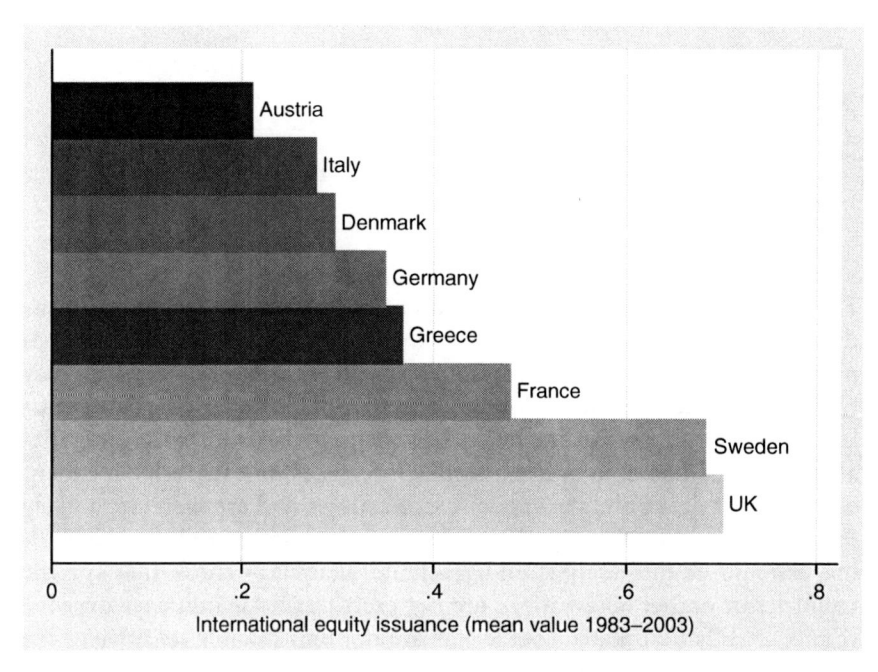

Figure 6.22 International equity issuance for a range of European countries (mean value 1983–2003)
Note: Value of equity issuance to international investors, as percentage of GDP.
Source: Bank for International Settlements (BIS).

0.38 would be the result of a similar increase in conservative government participation. This would shift a median country such as France up or down several positions in the ranking of Figure 6.22. Although not as big a change as with an NMR of 0, this is still far from a negligible impact on corporate governance outcomes.

7

Robustness and Dynamic Modeling

The panel data analysis of Chapter 6 has provided empirical support for the theoretical claims advanced in this book. However, the econometric analysis presented so far draws inferences from a specific sample of data, which may contain observations that are not representative of the underlying data population. The purpose of the first half of this chapter is to confirm the generalizable validity of the results by ensuring that inferences are not overly dependent on particular data points or model specifications, and are therefore a likely feature of the underlying population. Various statistical procedures – including extreme bound analysis and jackknife analysis – check that specific countries or outlier observations are not exerting undue influence over the results, and that estimated coefficients are not unjustifiably sensitive to the inclusion or exclusion of particular control variables.

In the second part of the chapter, the dynamic characteristics of the relationship between partisanship and corporate governance are examined. In Chapter 6, the inclusion of country fixed effects resulted in estimates derived from "within-country" variation of the dependent variable. This enabled the analysis to focus on the determinants of corporate governance change – the focus of the hypothesis of this book – rather than corporate governance levels. In this chapter, a different empirical specification is employed in order to model corporate governance change: a dynamic model in terms of first differences. This alternative specification provides a check of the robustness of the results of Chapter 6, and also enables a comparison to be made of the short- and long-term effects of explanatory variables on corporate governance change.

7.1 TESTS OF ROBUSTNESS

7.1.1 Extreme bound analysis

Presentation of any single set of regression results is potentially open to the criticism that the explanatory variables or control variables could have been chosen differently, or that the relationship might have been specified in an alternative manner. This is described as "model uncertainty" by Leamer (1983), who suggests testing the sensitivity of results to different types of model specification. He terms this procedure "extreme bound analysis," and advocates reestimating the model with different combinations of control variables. The most divergent values of coefficients from these regressions are then compared with the results of the original model. The presumption of this approach is that results which are highly dependent on a particular model specification are less likely to be reflective of an underlying reality in the population, and more likely to reflect the particularities of the specific data sample under analysis.

Such an atheoretical form of "specification search" has been criticized by a number of commentators. For example, McAleer et al. (1985) argue that it makes no sense to exclude a control variable from a regression if theory suggests that its inclusion is justifiable, as the omission of relevant explanatory variables may lead to estimation bias. Ehrlich and Liu (1999) point out that a control variable could be excluded that is jointly statistically significant and highly correlated with the main explanatory variable of interest. This would lead to wide, extreme bounds, and a mistaken inference that the relationship under analysis is "fragile."

According to Leamer's most challenging conception (1983, 1985) of extreme bound analysis, the extreme bound is defined as the highest or lowest estimate from the model reestimations, plus and minus two standard deviations. If the upper bound is positive and the lower bound negative (i.e., it passes through zero), then the relationship cannot be regarded as robust. However, Sala-i-Martin (1997) argues that this definition presents an insurmountable obstacle to most real-world relationships. It is likely that regression results can be found – if enough regressions are run – where the estimated coefficients change sign. According to such a definition, almost no relationship, in practice, is likely to be defined as robust (Sturm and de Haan 2005).

The approach followed in this chapter attempts to chart a middle path between these alternative perspectives. It seems unreasonable to omit large numbers of control variables, as each has been included for justifiable theoretical reasons, and several have proved to be empirically significant determinants of the outcome variable. However, it is of interest to check that the results are not overly sensitive to the inclusion of individual variables. Apart from differing opinions concerning the theoretical justification of variable inclusion, there may be concerns regarding measurement error in the construction of individual variables. Consequently, a compromise approach is pursued by reestimating each of the regressions used to construct the conditional effects graphs – at different levels of product market competition – with each of the eight control variables omitted in turn. The maximum and minimum values of the coefficients on Left and conservative partisanship from these regressions form the extreme bounds, and these are added as lines in the conditional effects graphs alongside the original model coefficients and confidence intervals.

The results of this testing procedure are presented in Figures 7.1–7.6. For reasons of space, extreme bounds are only shown with respect to the models estimated with country and decade fixed effects (the most robust of the three estimation approaches), although the models estimated without fixed effects and with legal origin controls, and country fixed effects only, paint a very similar picture. In respect of each of the corporate governance proxies, omission of any single control variable does not make a major difference to the results. In all cases, the confidence intervals of the extreme bounds indicate that the extreme bounds coefficients remain statistically significant at low levels of the NMR index (with a positive sign for the Left government coefficient, and a negative sign for conservative government), reinforcing the conclusions of Chapter 6.

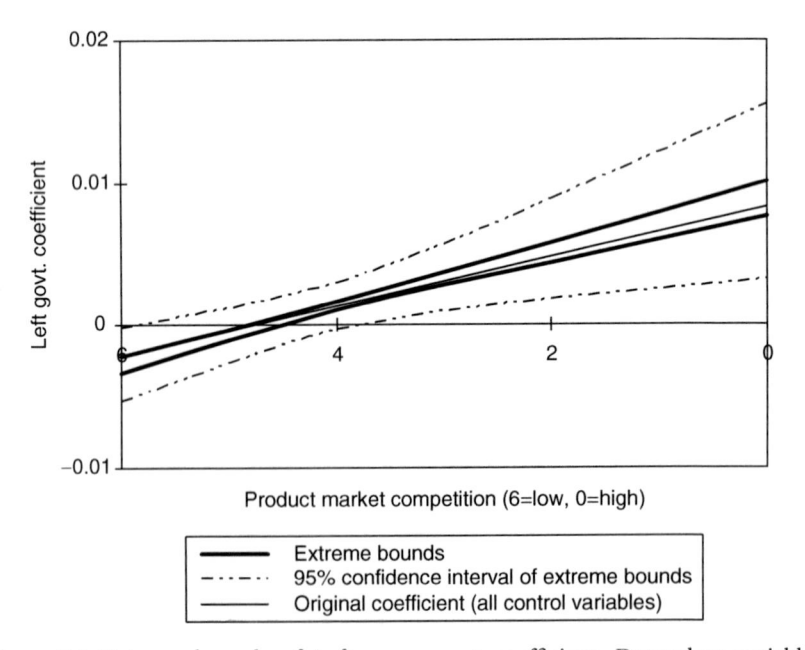

Figure 7.1 Extreme bounds of Left government coefficient. Dependent variable: equity share. Country and decade fixed effects

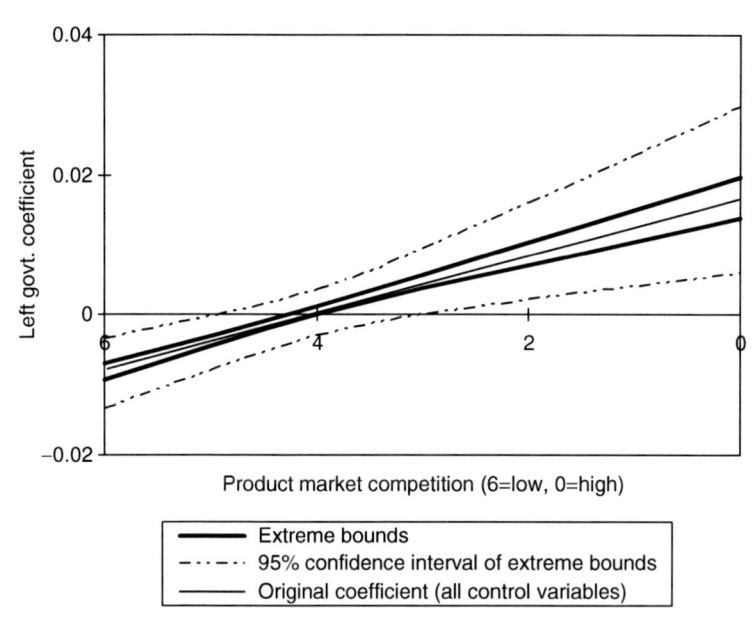

Figure 7.2 Extreme bounds of Left government coefficient. Dependent variable: value traded. Country and decade fixed effects

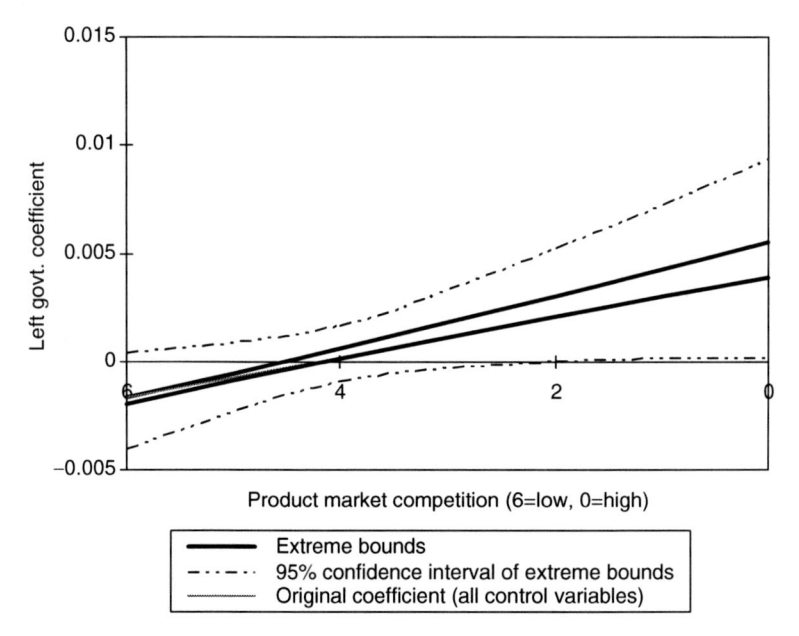

Figure 7.3 Extreme bounds of Left government coefficient. Dependent variable: international equity issuance. Country and decade fixed effects

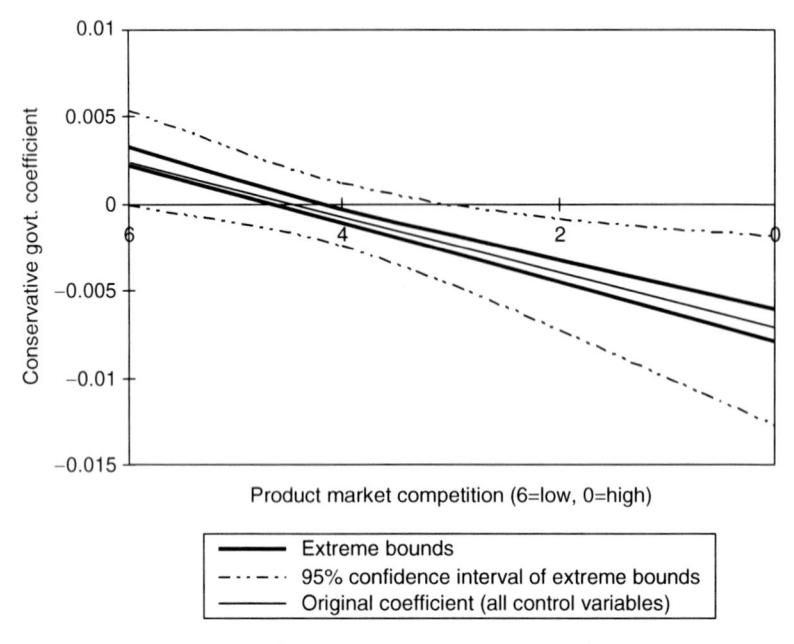

Figure 7.4 Extreme bounds of conservative government coefficient. Dependent variable: equity share. Country and decade fixed effects

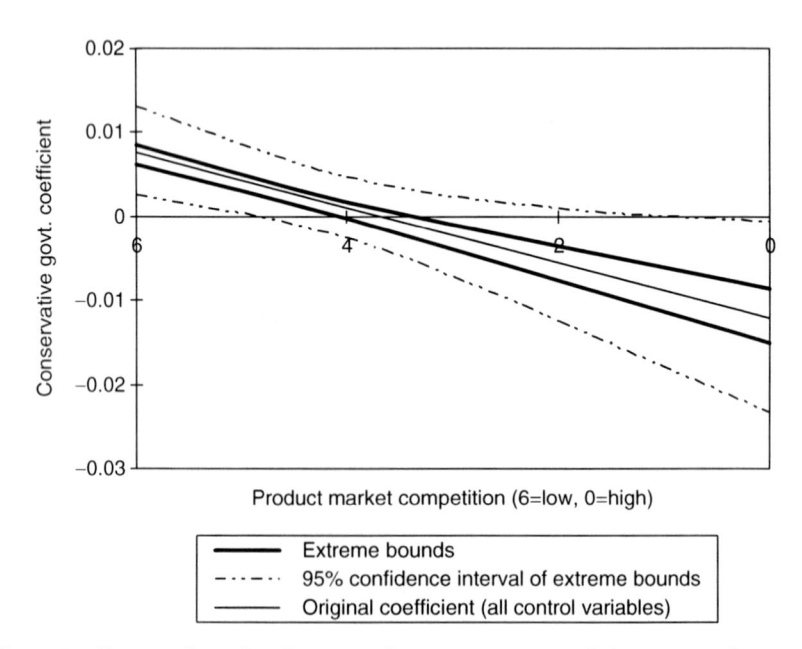

Figure 7.5 Extreme bounds of conservative government coefficient. Dependent variable: value traded. Country and decade fixed effects

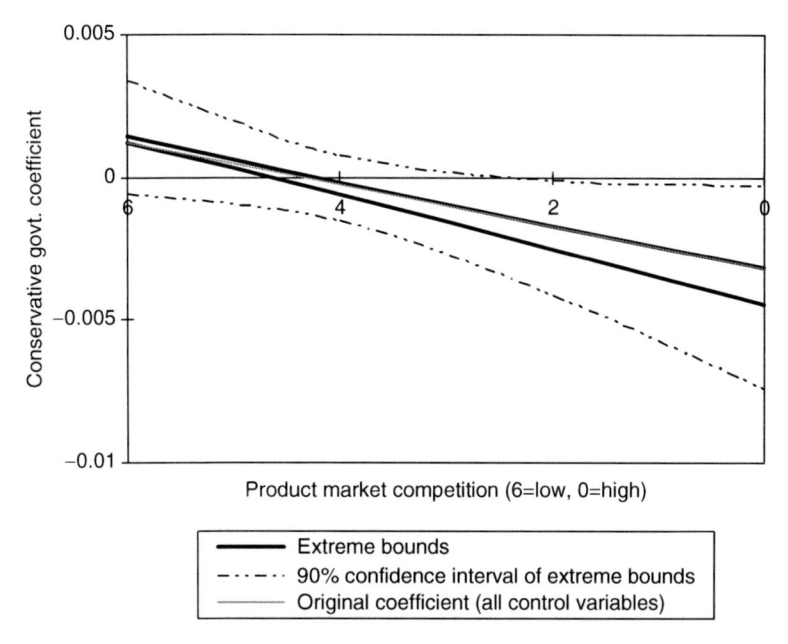

Figure 7.6 Extreme bounds of conservative government coefficient. Dependent variable: international equity issuance. Country and decade fixed effects

Table 7.1 illustrates the control variables whose exclusion gives rise to the extreme bound coefficients. These are identified from regressions relating to the highest possible level of product market competition (i.e., where the NMR index equals zero). Coefficients relating to this level of competition are presented in the table, as they represent the point at which the extreme bounds exhibit maximum divergence from the original model coefficients (on the right-hand-side of conditional effects graphs).

As can be seen from the graphs, the lower extreme bounds for Left government and upper extreme bounds for conservative government tend to be closer to the original coefficient than their opposite extreme bounds. The control variable whose exclusion most frequently exerts the greatest impact on the partisanship coefficient is GDP growth. Omission of this variable often gives rise to the upper extreme bound in respect of Left government, and the lower extreme bound in respect of conservative government (as seen in Table 7.1).

One interpretation of this finding is that the estimated partisanship effect on corporate governance at differing levels of product market competition is being underestimated due to the inclusion of GDP growth as a control. However, omission of GDP growth from the regressions is hard to justify

Table 7.1 Control variables with greatest impact on estimated coefficients

	Variable omitted at maximum coefficient (NMR = 0)	Variable omitted at minimum coefficient (NMR = 0)
Left government coefficient:		
Equity share	Interest rates	GDP per capita
Value traded	GDP growth	GDP per capita
International equity issuance	GDP growth	Electoral system disproportionality
Conservative government coefficient:		
Equity share	GDP per capita	GDP growth
Value traded	GDP per capita	GDP growth
International equity issuance	Electoral system disproportionality	GDP growth

on both theoretical and empirical grounds. GDP growth is present in the regressions to control for the idea that changes in corporate governance may be associated with the differing economic efficiency of corporate governance systems. Together with interest rates, GDP growth also serves to control for the effect of cyclical macroeconomic factors on the corporate governance proxies. Furthermore, it has also proven to be highly statistically significant in the regression results. Consequently, its exclusion from the regression specification is hard to defend, even if its effect is to slightly moderate the substantive magnitude of the estimated coefficients.

7.1.2 Jackknife analysis

An alternative type of robustness test is undertaken through application of so-called Jackknife analysis (Efron and Tibshirani 1993: chapter 11). This involves examining the estimation results after excluding each of the individual countries in the dataset. As before, the resulting maximum and minimum values of the partisanship coefficients are used to construct extreme bounds, which are compared with the coefficients estimated in the fully specified model. The rationale for this analysis is that the generalizable validity of the model is more credible if it is not dependent on the inclusion of data in the data sample relating to a single country (Kittel and Winner 2005: 283).

The results of this procedure are presented in Figures 7.7–7.12. Once again, results are only presented relating to the country and decade fixed effects

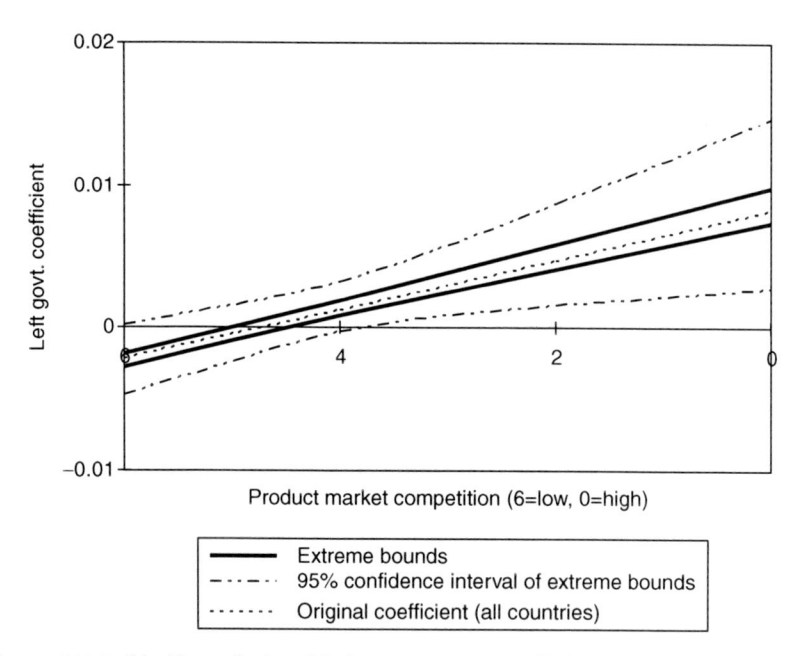

Figure 7.7 Jackknife analysis of Left government coefficient. Dependent variable: equity share. Country and decade fixed effects

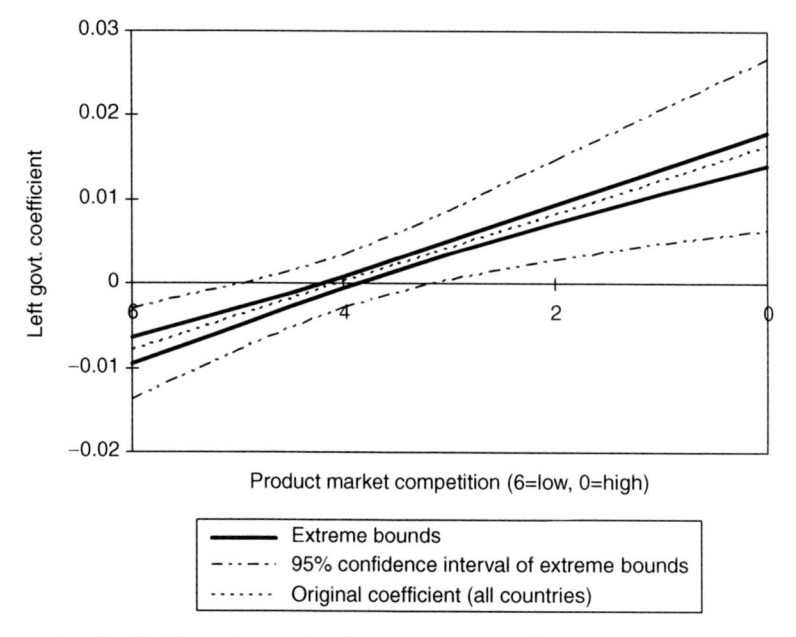

Figure 7.8 Jackknife analysis of Left government coefficient. Dependent variable: value traded. Country and decade fixed effects

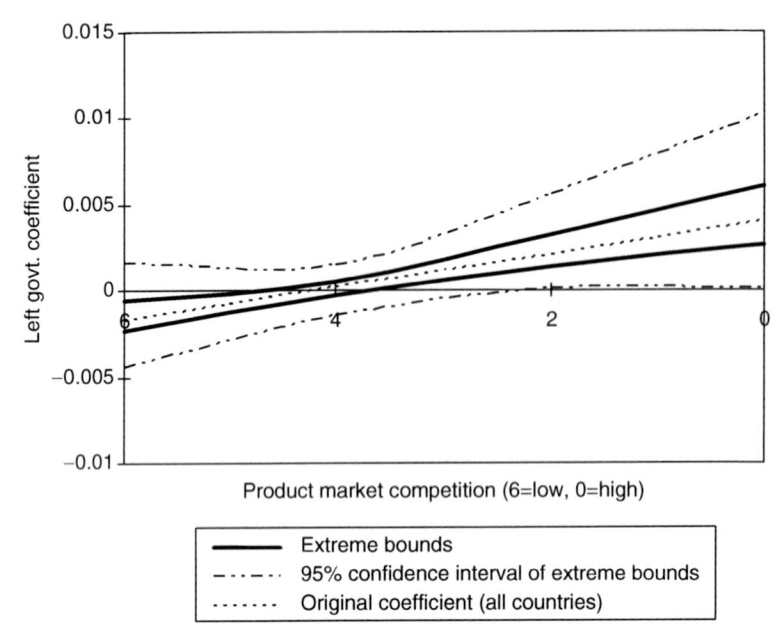

Figure 7.9 Jackknife analysis of Left government coefficient. Dependent variable: international equity issuance. Country and decade fixed effects

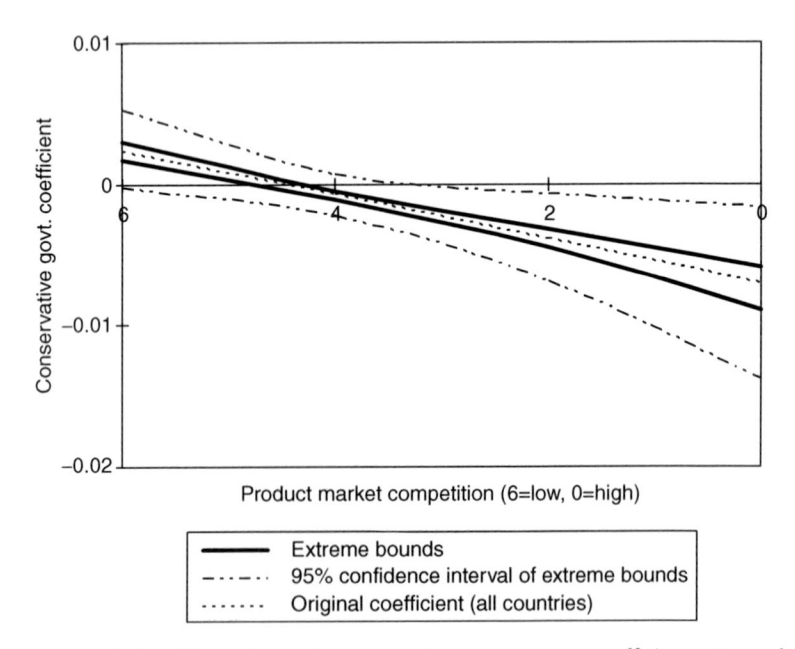

Figure 7.10 Jackknife analysis of conservative government coefficient. Dependent variable: equity share. Country and decade fixed effects

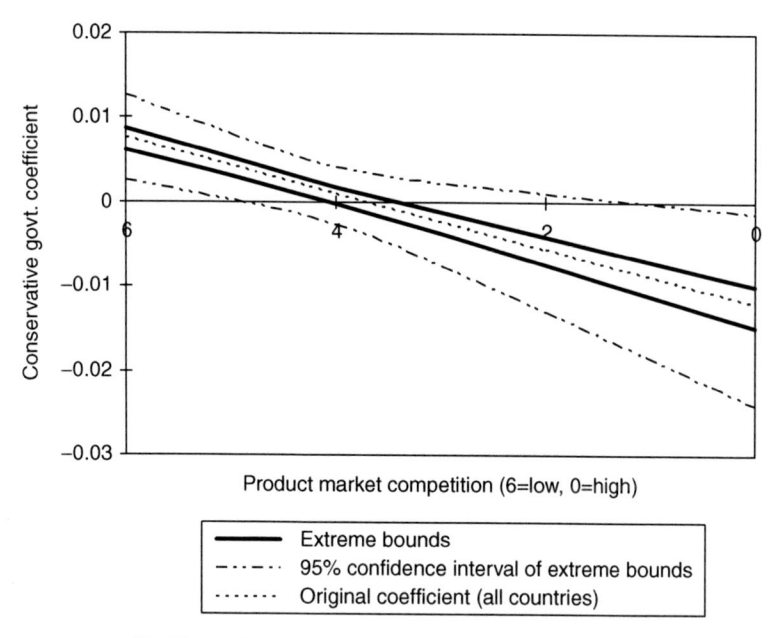

Figure 7.11 Jackknife analysis of conservative government coefficient. Dependent variable: value traded. Country and decade fixed effects

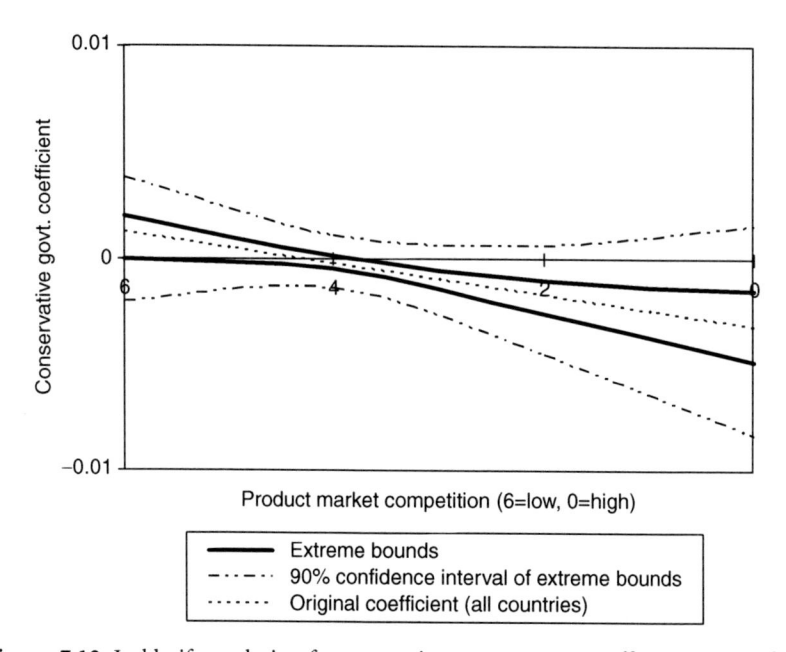

Figure 7.12 Jackknife analysis of conservative government coefficient. Dependent variable: international equity issuance. Country and decade fixed effects

regressions – the other two estimation approaches give rise to a similar outcome. The effect of excluding individual countries on the results is generally small. In particular, the confidence intervals of the extreme bounds show that Left partisanship remains positively significant at low levels of the NMR index with each of the three corporate governance proxies. The significance of the results is not affected by the removal of any individual country from the dataset. This is supportive of the robustness of the results relating to Left partisanship presented in Chapter 6.

However, the procedure does introduce some uncertainty in respect of the conservative partisanship results. Specifically, the confidence intervals of the extreme bounds for the international equity issuance proxy imply that the previously estimated negative coefficients on conservative partisanship (at low levels of the NMR index) are no longer statistically significant if certain countries are removed from the dataset.[1] This is apparent from the upper confidence interval in Figure 7.12, which remains in positive territory at all levels of the NMR index.

Such an outcome suggests a lack of robustness in the conservative partisanship results presented in Figure 6.12. However, the hypothesis of this book only requires that conservative partisanship be negatively or insignificantly related to corporate governance change at high levels of product market competition. An insignificant coefficient on conservative partisanship would, therefore, still be consistent with the hypothesis. The application of jackknife analysis to the other two corporate governance proxies equity share and value traded – continues to imply a negative relationship between conservative partisanship and corporate governance change (at high levels of competition, see Figures 7.10 and 7.11).

Table 7.2 shows which countries are responsible for generating the extreme bound coefficients, following their exclusion from the model. Once again, the table is reflective of regressions undertaken in respect of the highest level of product market competition (NMR index = 0), although generally the same countries are responsible for forming the extreme bound across the conditional effects graph (i.e., at differing levels of competition). The table does not suggest that any single country is responsible for exerting undue influence over the results across all three corporate governance proxies.

---

[1] The two countries whose exclusion from the dataset causes a loss of statistical significance with this proxy are Denmark and Norway.

Table 7.2 Countries with greatest impact on estimated coefficients

	Country omitted at maximum coefficient (NMR = 0)	Country omitted at minimum coefficient (NMR = 0)
Left government coefficient:		
Equity share	Norway	France
Value traded	Germany	Austria
International equity issuance	Sweden	Denmark
Conservative government coefficient		
Equity share	Portugal	Germany
Value traded	Portugal	Spain
International equity issuance	Denmark	Sweden

7.1.3 Influential observations

Having examined the effect of control variables and countries on the robustness of the results, this section examines the impact of individual observations. Any estimation method utilizing least squares techniques is potentially vulnerable to the influence of outliers, that is, a data point with an unusual value, due to the role of residuals in the calculation of parameters. Outliers can result from technical or coding errors, which may require correction. However, they may also represent legitimately occurring extreme observations. If individual observations exert a significant effect over the model results, it may be necessary to evaluate the possibility of reporting model results excluding the outlying observations, and to reconsider the validity of the inferences that have been drawn regarding the nature of the underlying population[2] (Wooldridge 2006: 328).

One of the benefits of expressing variables in logarithmic functional form is its effect of narrowing the range of values for these variables. This makes estimation less sensitive to outlying or extreme observations (Wooldridge 2006: 199). However, following the seminal work of Belsley et al. (1980), a number of statistics have been developed to identify and analyze influential observations. Several of these are presented in Tables 7.3–7.5 in respect of the data sample, with each table listing the most influential 1 percent of observations relating to the regression results for each of the proxies for corporate

---

[2] Such a censoring process can be undertaken by excluding extreme observations directly, or by using regression techniques such as Least Absolute Deviations (LAD). This estimates regression coefficients by minimizing the sum of the absolute deviations of the residuals (rather

Table 7.3 Most influential observations (top 1%). Dependent variable: equity share

Country	Year	Partisanship coefficient	Residual	Studentized residual	Leverage	DFITS	DFBETA
Germany	2003	Conservative	−0.692	−1.850	0.143	−0.756	0.447
Sweden	2003	Left	−0.824	−2.146	0.102	−0.722	−0.312
Sweden	2003	Conservative	−0.822	−2.150	0.101	−0.721	0.312
Portugal	1985	Conservative	−1.642	−4.367	0.100	−1.453	−0.298
Germany	2003	Left	−0.606	−1.587	0.118	−0.580	−0.270
Germany	2002	Conservative	−0.420	−1.113	0.133	−0.435	0.246
Greece	1985	Conservative	−1.219	−3.142	0.063	−0.815	−0.207
Sweden	2002	Left	−0.604	−1.567	0.099	−0.521	−0.203
Sweden	2002	Conservative	−0.585	−1.521	0.097	−0.498	0.182
Greece	1985	Left	−1.293	−3.314	0.058	−0.824	0.166
Japan	2003	Left	−1.088	−2.854	0.107	−0.986	0.166
Denmark	2003	Conservative	−0.331	−0.871	0.119	−0.320	−0.164
Greece	1984	Conservative	−0.968	−2.484	0.064	−0.648	−0.159
Denmark	2003	Left	−0.286	−0.751	0.124	−0.282	0.152
Greece	1984	Left	−1.021	−2.608	0.063	−0.675	0.151
Germany	2002	Left	−0.349	−0.908	0.112	−0.322	−0.144
Greece	1986	Conservative	−1.113	−2.857	0.060	−0.721	−0.137
Greece	1986	Left	−1.154	−2.953	0.060	−0.745	0.137
Greece	1999	Left	1.192	3.070	0.071	0.848	−0.128
Greece	2003	Left	−0.637	−1.658	0.106	−0.570	−0.128
Sweden	1979	Left	−0.710	−1.815	0.071	−0.501	0.127
Sweden	1993	Left	0.313	0.808	0.095	0.262	−0.123
Sweden	1979	Conservative	−0.777	−1.996	0.069	−0.544	−0.117
Sweden	1980	Left	−0.680	−1.722	0.055	−0.414	0.116
Portugal	1985	Left	−1.753	−4.643	0.095	−1.502	0.116
Denmark	2000	Left	−0.417	−1.085	0.107	−0.375	−0.114
Germany	1999	Conservative	0.303	0.796	0.120	0.294	−0.112
Spain	2001	Conservative	0.395	1.014	0.077	0.292	0.110
Japan	1990	Conservative	0.516	1.326	0.076	0.381	0.107
Norway	1999	Left	0.330	0.844	0.079	0.247	−0.107

governance. Results for Left and conservative partisanship are brought together into the same table. Consequently, individual observations may appear in the tables on multiple occasions if they are influential at different levels of product market competition, and for both Left and conservative model coefficients.

Inclusion and ranking in the tables are determined on the basis of each observation's DFBETA statistic (Belsley et al. 1980). This measures the extent

than the sum of squared residuals), thereby giving less weight to outlying observations. However, use of LAD estimators is problematic, as its estimator properties are justified only asymptotically, and require fulfillment of more restrictive data assumptions than OLS in order to guarantee consistency (Wooldridge 2006: 332).

Table 7.4 Most influential observations (top 1%). Dependent variable: value traded

Country	Year	Partisanship coefficient	Residual	Studentized residual	Leverage	DFITS	DFBETA
Germany	2003	Conservative	−0.756	−1.017	0.144	−0.416	0.244
Portugal	1985	Conservative	−2.141	−2.833	0.100	−0.946	−0.198
Greece	1984	Conservative	−2.150	−2.787	0.064	−0.729	−0.180
Norway	1980	Left	−1.978	−2.551	0.060	−0.643	0.177
Greece	1985	Conservative	−2.029	−2.627	0.063	−0.682	−0.175
Sweden	1979	Left	−1.819	−2.359	0.072	−0.660	0.172
Greece	1984	Left	−2.194	−2.841	0.063	−0.737	0.168
Switzerland	1975	Left	2.245	3.018	0.129	1.159	0.166
Austria	2002	Conservative	−1.024	−1.325	0.075	−0.378	−0.163
Sweden	2003	Left	−0.823	−1.080	0.104	−0.368	−0.161
Germany	2003	Left	−0.711	−0.940	0.118	−0.344	−0.158
Spain	2001	Conservative	1.111	1.440	0.077	0.415	0.156
Sweden	1979	Conservative	−1.942	−2.523	0.071	−0.696	−0.152
Sweden	2003	Conservative	−0.782	−1.027	0.103	−0.348	0.152
Greece	1999	Left	2.747	3.594	0.071	0.993	−0.150
Austria	1987	Conservative	2.211	2.853	0.054	0.684	−0.144
Greece	1985	Left	−2.168	−2.799	0.058	−0.697	0.142
Norway	1982	Conservative	−1.863	−2.420	0.071	−0.671	0.139
Denmark	2002	Left	0.506	0.669	0.120	0.247	−0.136
Norway	1999	Left	0.831	1.076	0.079	0.315	−0.134
Spain	2002	Conservative	0.949	1.231	0.079	0.361	0.133
Norway	1976	Left	−1.125	−1.461	0.082	−0.437	0.129
Spain	2002	Left	1.026	1.327	0.076	0.381	−0.128
Austria	2003	Conservative	−1.109	−1.448	0.091	−0.458	−0.127
Austria	2003	Left	−0.972	−1.268	0.092	−0.405	0.125
Austria	1987	Left	2.245	2.892	0.053	0.687	0.124
Austria	2002	Left	−1.002	−1.291	0.069	−0.353	0.123
Sweden	1978	Left	−1.371	−1.766	0.066	−0.469	0.122
Spain	2001	Left	1.129	1.457	0.072	0.406	−0.121
Norway	1980	Conservative	−2.065	−2.664	0.056	−0.649	−0.115

to which the estimated partisanship coefficients (presented in the conditional effects graphs) shift when the observation is included or excluded from the regression, scaled by the estimated standard error of the coefficient. A widely quoted rule of thumb suggests that a DFBETA greater than unity in absolute value is a cause for concern, since this observation shifts the value of the estimated coefficient by more than one standard error (Agresti and Finlay 1997: 539; Baum 2006: 130). However, as the DFBETA statistic tends to decrease as the sample size increases, it is also worthwhile to examine observations with lower values. Belsley et al. (1980) suggest that observations where $|DFBETA| > 2/\sqrt{N}$ are worthy of scrutiny as potential outliers. This cutoff point equates to around 5 percent of the observations in the dataset

204   *Corporate Governance, Competition, and Political Parties*

Table 7.5 Most influential observations (top 1%). Dependent variable: international equity issuance

Country	Year	Partisanship coefficient	Residual	Studentized residual	Leverage	DFITS	DFBETA
Denmark	2003	Left	−0.529	−2.184	0.147	−0.906	0.496
Sweden	2003	Conservative	−0.662	−2.728	0.134	−1.073	0.456
Sweden	2003	Left	−0.655	−2.689	0.131	−1.043	−0.431
Denmark	2003	Conservative	−0.526	−2.162	0.137	−0.861	−0.423
Germany	2002	Conservative	−0.429	−1.769	0.146	−0.730	0.395
Finland	2003	Conservative	−0.761	−3.048	0.077	−0.883	0.282
Norway	2001	Left	0.648	2.589	0.083	0.781	0.264
Germany	2002	Left	−0.389	−1.581	0.125	−0.599	−0.260
Germany	2000	Conservative	0.468	1.901	0.119	0.698	−0.259
Sweden	2000	Left	0.632	2.585	0.124	0.974	0.252
Sweden	2000	Conservative	0.631	2.585	0.125	0.978	−0.252
Germany	2000	Left	0.491	1.981	0.110	0.698	0.238
Germany	2001	Conservative	−0.337	−1.370	0.128	−0.525	0.235
Denmark	1994	Left	0.801	3.249	0.099	1.077	−0.234
Sweden	1999	Conservative	−0.570	−2.332	0.125	−0.883	0.225
Denmark	2001	Left	−0.458	−1.833	0.098	−0.602	−0.212
Spain	1993	Left	0.538	2.142	0.085	0.651	0.184
Germany	2001	Left	−0.309	−1.249	0.118	−0.456	−0.182
Denmark	1994	Conservative	0.793	3.220	0.099	1.067	0.181
Portugal	2001	Conservative	−0.620	−2.493	0.094	−0.801	0.180
Sweden	1998	Conservative	−0.451	−1.817	0.104	−0.619	0.177
Sweden	1994	Left	0.275	1.109	0.116	0.401	−0.174
Norway	1998	Left	−0.353	−1.405	0.089	−0.439	0.173
Sweden	1998	Leftb	−0.447	−1.795	0.104	−0.611	−0.173
Spain	1993	Conservative	0.529	2.112	0.086	0.648	−0.171
Sweden	1999	Left	−0.564	−2.292	0.120	−0.844	−0.171
Norway	2001	Conservative	0.659	2.627	0.077	0.757	−0.159
Norway	2002	Conservative	−0.252	−1.010	0.102	−0.340	−0.158
Norway	2002	Left	−0.272	−1.084	0.097	−0.355	0.153
Denmark	2002	Left	−0.168	−0.685	0.135	−0.271	0.152

(i.e., with a DFBETA in excess of 0.1 in absolute value). However, for reasons of space, the tables in the following text present the top 1 percent of observations in terms of influence over the regressions results relating to partisanship.

As well as the DFBETA, the table also shows the residual of each observation, that is, the distance between the value of the dependent variable predicted by the model and the actual value of the dependent variable. This is a measure of the extent to which the model is successful in predicting the value of the outcome variable in respect of that particular observation. The studentized residual is a standardized value of the residual, and corresponds to the t-statistic that would be obtained by including a dummy variable in the regression coded 1 for that observation and 0 otherwise. Consequently, a significant value is an indication of whether an observation significantly shifts the *y*-intercept. Absolute values of the studentized residual of between 2 and 3 are relatively large, indicating poor model fit. However, 5 percent of residuals will fall into this range entirely by chance, and may not therefore be considered as problematic outliers. A value above 3 in absolute value may, however, be worthy of investigation as a potential outlier.

The influence of an observation is not solely dependent on the size of its residual. The second component of influence is the leverage (or hat-value) of the observation. This relates to the values of the explanatory variables rather than the dependent variable, and measures how far they fall from their sample means. Other things being equal, an observation with higher leverage will exert greater influence over the model results. The mean value of leverage in the sample equals p/n, where p is the number of parameters in the model. In the case of our sample, this implies that any observation with leverage in excess of around 0.06 (in the case of equity share and value traded) and 0.08 (in the case of international equity issuance) will impact the results proportionately more than the average observation. As a rule of thumb, relatively large leverage is indicated by a value in excess of three times the mean value, that is, in excess of 0.18 for equity share and value traded and 0.24 for international equity issuance (Agresti and Finlay 1997: 539).

Finally, the DFITS statistic summarizes the influence of the observation on the overall fit of the model (as opposed to a specific coefficient, which is indicated by DFBETA). It examines the change in the model's predicted value following addition and deletion of individual observations.[3] A larger absolute value indicates greater influence, with a value in excess of 1 indicating substantial influence and a possible outlier. A high value of DFITS and DFBETA can be caused by either a high residual, high leverage, or a combination of the two.

The influence statistics in Tables 7.3–7.5 show that none of the observations in the dataset give rise to a DFBETA in excess of 1 (or even 0.5), suggesting that none of the observations is an extreme outlier or the result of incorrectly coded data. However, certain observations are obviously more influential than others. For example, the observations for Denmark and Sweden in 2003 appear at the top of the ranking in respect of the international equity issuance proxy. The German observation for 2003 is also the most influential with equity share and value traded. The significance of

---

[3] Alternatives to the DFITS value – with the similar objective of measuring the influence of observations on overall fit – are Cook's distance and Welsch's distance (Cook and Weisberg 1982: 135; Welsch 1982).

these observations is also reflected in the relatively high values of their DFITS statistics. However, the high values of their leverage statistics suggest that the influence of the Danish and German observations is driven more by values of corresponding explanatory variables in 2003 than by poor model fit. This may partly be due to the historically untypical values – for Denmark and Germany – of the conservative and Left partisanship explanatory variables in that year (reflecting a conservative government in Denmark and a Left government in Germany). However, although this may create high leverage for these observations, it is hard to argue – from a theoretical perspective – that such observations should be excluded from the model estimation. Such values for Left or conservative government – although far from their sample means – are an entirely plausible possibility, and should therefore be taken into account in the estimation process. This conclusion is consistent with the approach of Belsley et al. (1980), who argue that an influential observation should only be dropped if it is the result of an uncorrectable error, and not simply because it represents an extreme or "inconvenient" observation.

Observations whose influence over the results derives from poor model fit (i.e., high residuals) primarily belong to Greece and Portugal (although the Danish observation for 1994 is a poor fit with international equity issuance, and the Swiss observation for 1975 produces a high residual for value traded). It could be argued, therefore, that it would be useful to reestimate the model excluding Greece and Portugal, given that the applicability of the theoretical claims of the hypothesis to these countries seems less than to other nonliberal market economies. However, once again, their exclusion would be hard to justify from a theoretical perspective. Furthermore, the preceding jackknife analysis reveals that exclusion of Greece or Portugal in their entirety from the estimation makes negligible difference to the regression results. Neither country gives rise to the coefficients forming the extreme bounds that are generated by the jackknife procedure.

7.2 DYNAMIC MODELING OF CORPORATE GOVERNANCE

It is often the case in social science that there exists a substantial difference between the long-run and short-run effects of explanatory variables on outcome variables. This may occur due to a high level of persistence or inertia in the level of dependent variables, which therefore may not respond immediately to changes in explanatory variables. The results obtained in Chapter 6 from regressions with country fixed effects are based on the temporal variation of the corporate governance proxies.[4] Consequently, they yield coefficients relating to their short-run association with the interaction of partisanship and product market competition. This contrasts with results that would be obtained from a purely cross-sectional regression, which would reflect the long-run association of explanatory and dependent variables.

In order to differentiate between short-run and long-run effects, the dynamics of the relationship can be modeled by including a lagged dependent variable (LDV) as an explanatory variable in the model specification. Whereas the short-run effect – or impact multiplier – is indicated by the value of the estimated partisanship coefficient, the long-run effect is given by $\frac{\beta}{1-\phi}$, where β is the estimated partisanship coefficient and ϕ is the coefficient on the lagged dependent variable, that is, the autoregression coefficient. Including a LDV may also assist in ridding the model of first-order serial correlation (Beck and Katz 2004: 20).

Unfortunately, including a LDV in a model with country fixed effects leads to biased estimates (Nickel 1981). The fixed effects transformation involves subtracting each unit's average value from each observation. This causes the transformed value of the LDV to become correlated with the transformed error, thereby giving rise to bias. There is some disagreement in the literature regarding the extent to which this poses substantive estimation problems. According to a Monte Carlo study by Judson and Owen (1999), the bias can be as great as 20 percent, even with a time-series dimension exceeding thirty observations. Consequently, the authors recommend the use of alternative instrumental variable (IV) or generalized method of moments (GMM) estimators for datasets with less than thirty years of observations (Kennedy 2003: 313). Beck and Katz (2004) are more sanguine on the use of LDVs in panels with between twenty and thirty time-series observations. While acknowledging the risk of bias, Beck and Katz argue – also based on Monte Carlo evidence – that such an estimator will be more efficient than more sophisticated techniques that depend on the identification of viable instruments to replace the LDV (Beck and Katz 2004: 29).

One way of addressing the problem of "Nickel bias" is to express the regression equation in terms of first differences, thereby eliminating unit heterogeneity (and sweeping the time-invariant country fixed effects out of the estimation). This is shown by the transformation of model (1) into model

---

[4] The fixed effects strip out the information provided by the absolute levels of variables – see Section 6.2.

(2), where y_{it-1} is the lagged dependent variable, ρ is the autoregression coefficient, x_{it} is a vector of explanatory variables that vary over units and time, β_2 is a vector of coefficients on x, u_i represents time-invariant unit-level heterogeneity, and ϵ_{it} is the error term. Following first differencing, both of the time-invariant variables from equation (1) – the constant (β_1) and the unit effects u_i – disappear from the model.

$$y_{it} = \beta_1 + \rho y_{it-1} + x_{it}\beta_2 + u_i + \varepsilon_{it} \qquad (1)$$

$$\Delta y_{it} = \rho \Delta y_{it-1} + \Delta x_{it}\beta_2 + \Delta \varepsilon_{it} \qquad (2)$$

However, Anderson and Hsiao (1981, 1982) show that the transformed equation (2) still retains a correlation between the first difference of the LDV ($y_{it-1} - y_{it-2}$) and the first difference of the error term ($u_{it} - u_{it-1}$). This leads them to suggest the replacement of the first difference of the LDV with an instrument: either $y_{it-2} - y_{it-3}$, or y_{t-1}, both of which are correlated with $y_{it-1} - y_{it-2}$, but not with $u_{it} - u_{it-1}$. However, Arellano (1989) and Arellano and Bover (1995) show – based on the results of Monte Carlo experiments – that both of these potential instruments lead to biases and large standard errors, particularly with smaller samples (e.g., $T < 20$) and values of the autoregressive coefficient close to 1 (i.e., high inertia). Furthermore, Arellano and Bond (1991) observe that the Anderson–Hsiao estimator is inefficient, as it does not take account of the available instruments created by the panel structure, for example, all of the available lagged endogenous and exogenous variables.

The Arellano–Bond estimator is a GMM estimator that specifies the model as a system of equations – one per period – and allows the instruments contained in each equation to differ (e.g., in later periods, more lagged values of the instruments are available). The instruments include suitable lags of the levels of the endogenous variables, which enter the equation in differenced form, as well as the exogenous regressors. The estimator can easily generate a large number of instruments, since by period t all lags prior to, say, $(t - 2)$ might be considered as instruments. If T is relatively large, the use of all possible instruments may lead to downwardly biased (albeit efficient) regression estimates (Ziliak 1997). Consequently, it may be necessary to limit the maximum number of lags of an instrument that are used in the estimation. This is undertaken with the help of a Sargan test of overidentifying conditions (Wawro 2002). However, more recent Monte Carlo work by Blundell and Bond (1998) shows that the Arellano–Bond estimator can perform badly in a small sample, high autoregressive parameter (e.g., $\rho \geq 0.8$) context, that is, the same environment in which the Anderson–Hsiao estimator is inefficient. Such data characteristics may necessitate the use of more computationally sophisticated GMM estimators, that is, the forward orthogonal deviations estimator proposed by Arellano and Bover (1995).

The choice of dynamic estimation technique in this chapter is made with reference to the specific data characteristics of the proxies for corporate governance. Although a model with a LDV and fixed effects may be feasible – following the findings of Beck and Katz (2004) –for the equity share and value-traded proxies (both of which have around twenty-eight years of observations per country), this is more doubtful in respect of international equity issuance (where $T = 21$). Consequently, to reduce the risk of bias, a GMM estimator is preferred. Furthermore, given that none of the proxies exhibit very high levels of persistence (i.e., the autoregression coefficient for each of the proxies is less than 0.8), use of the Arellano–Bond estimator is a viable option, and capable of greater efficiency than the Anderson–Hsiao estimator.

The results of an Arellano–Bond dynamic model estimation are presented in the form of conditional effects graphs in Figures 7.13–7.18. The model is estimated robustly to generate standard error estimates that are consistent in the presence of heteroscedasticity and autocorrelation within panels. The results reflect a specification in which the use of lagged values of the endogenous and exogenous variables is limited to $(t - 3)$. The Arellano–Bond test for

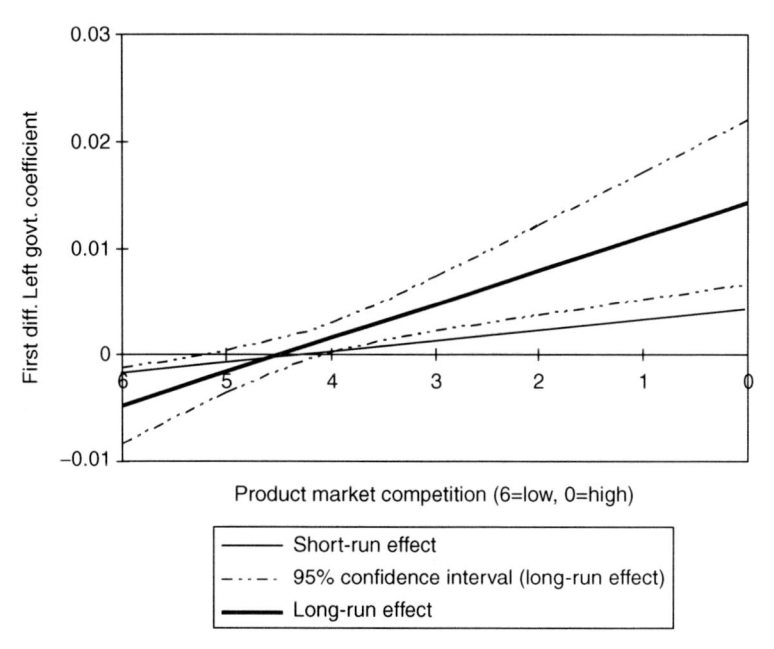

Figure 7.13 Dynamic impact of Left government on corporate governance (first differences). Dependent variable: equity share

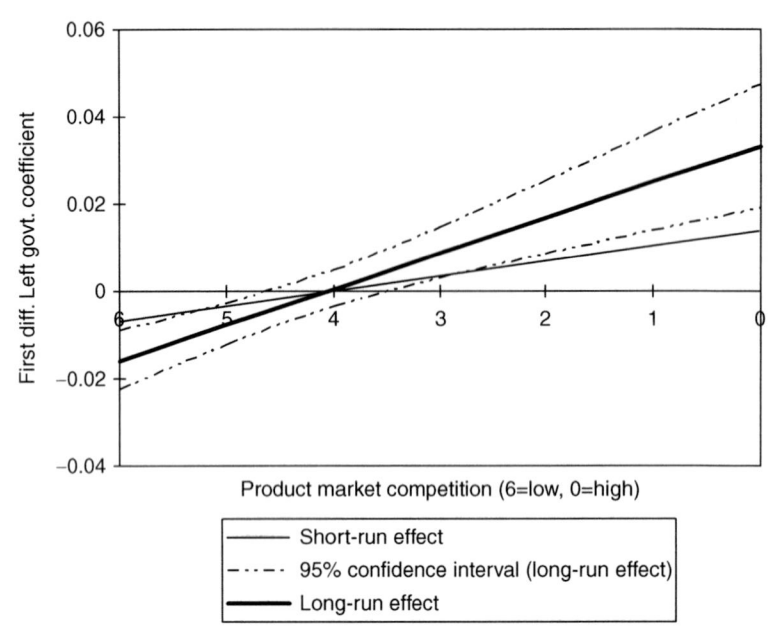

Figure 7.14 Dynamic impact of Left government on corporate governance (first differences). Dependent variable: value traded

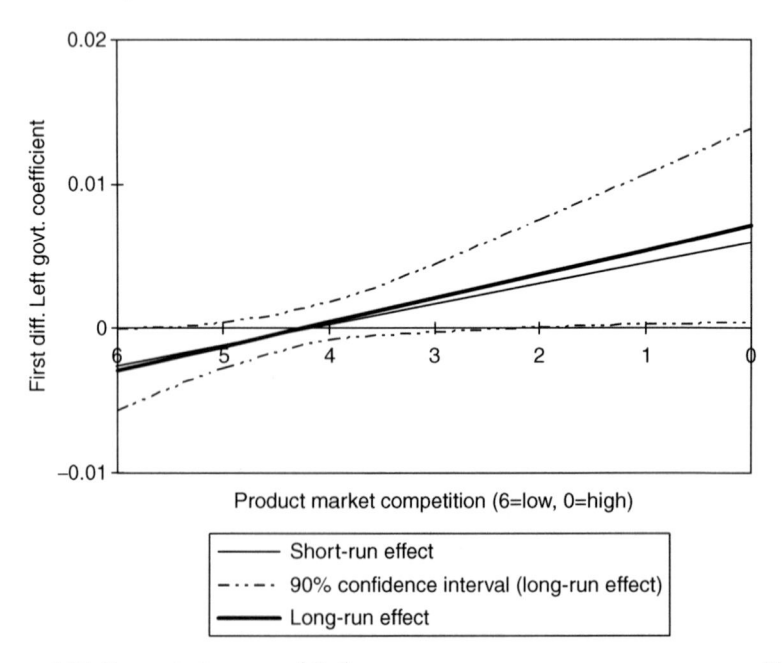

Figure 7.15 Dynamic impact of Left government on corporate governance (first differences). Dependent variable: international equity issuance

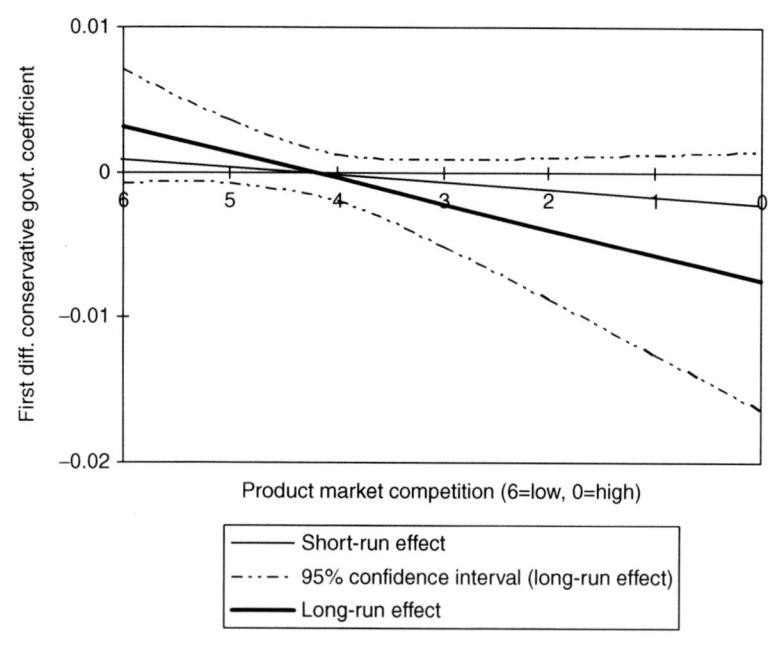

Figure 7.16 Dynamic impact of conservative government on corporate governance (first differences). Dependent variable: equity share

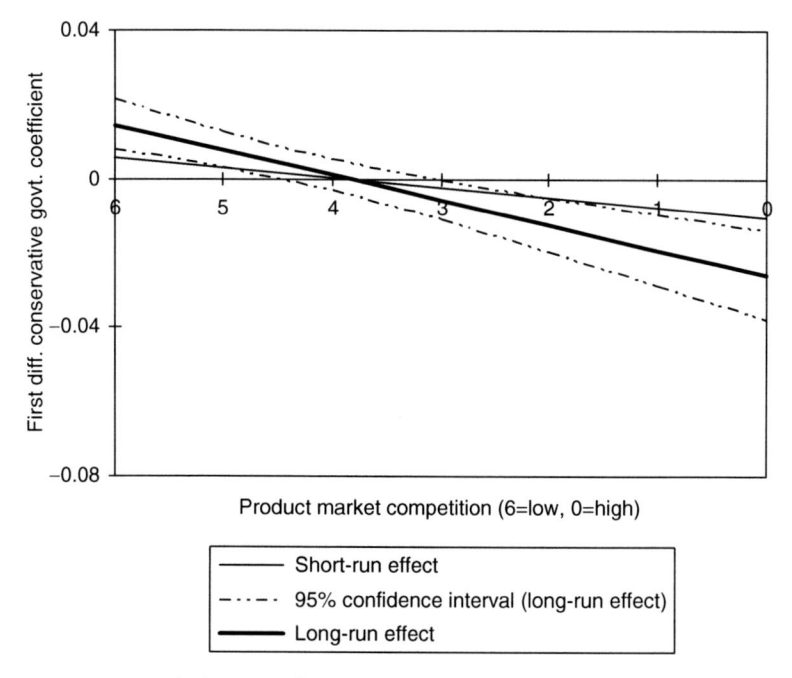

Figure 7.17 Dynamic impact of conservative government on corporate governance (first differences). Dependent variable: value traded

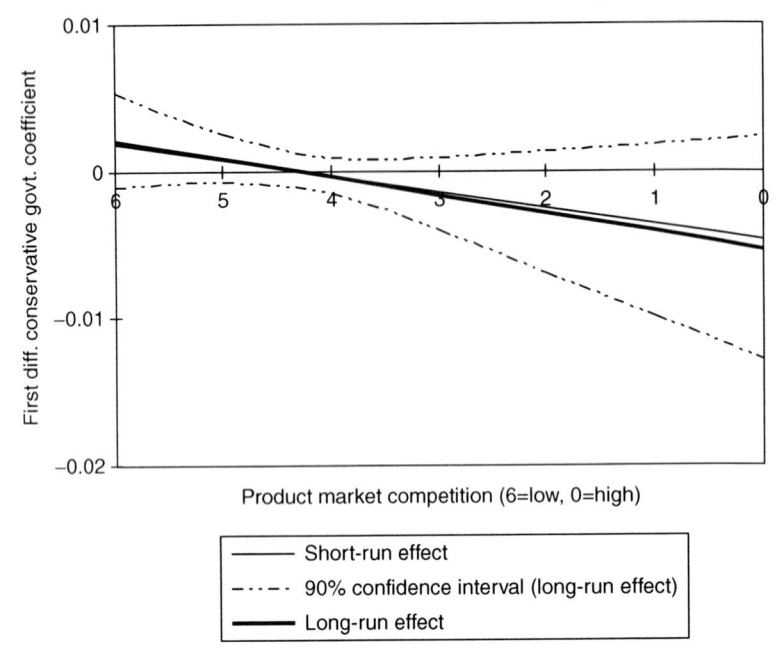

Figure 7.18 Dynamic impact of conservative government on corporate governance (first differences). Dependent variable: international equity issuance

autocorrelation is applied to the residuals; the result of the higher-order autocorrelation component of this test suggests that these lags are not endogenous, and are therefore acting as viable instruments.

The coefficients of these regressions require slightly different interpretation to those of Chapter 6, as they relate to a model in first differences rather than levels. Nonetheless, the short-run effects suggest a relationship between the interaction of partisanship and competition, and corporate governance that is consistent with the previous empirical analysis. In respect of each of the corporate governance proxies, more Left government is significantly associated with more shareholder-oriented corporate governance at higher levels of product market competition, but with the opposite at lower levels of competition (Figures 7.13–7.15).

However, the results with a specification in first differences raise further doubts concerning the significance of the coefficient on the conservative government variable. In the case of the value traded proxy, an increase in conservative government remains negatively associated with corporate governance change at higher levels of competition (Figure 7.17), which is identical to the results of Chapter 6. However, with the other two corporate governance proxies – equity share and international equity issuance – this negative relationship is no longer statistically significant (as indicated by the upper confidence intervals remaining above the horizontal axis in Figures 7.16 and 7.18). Along with the results of the jackknife analysis in Section 7.1.2, this outcome gives further credence to the possibility that the relationship between conservative partisanship and corporate governance change (at high levels of competition) is insignificant rather than negative in nature.

The three corporate governance proxies paint differing pictures in respect of the difference between short-run and long-run effects. Both equity share and value traded imply that long-run effects are more than double those of the short-run impact multipliers, suggesting that the contemporaneous coefficients estimated in Chapter 6 represent only part of the story. However, the long-run effects estimated in respect of the international equity issuance proxy are similar to the short-run effects. Such differing results reflect the differing nature of the proxies as data series, and are consistent with the differing results obtained from models with lags in Chapter 6 (Section 6.3.1).[5] International equity issuance is a relatively volatile flow variable that gives rise to an autoregression coefficient in the first-difference model of less than 0.2. In contrast, equity share is a stock variable, exhibiting a greater degree of persistence over time ($\rho = 0.7$). Consequently, the contemporaneous association between the explanatory variables and international equity issuance is likely to represent the full extent of the relationship, whereas this is not the case in respect of equity share and value traded.

---

[5] The substantive impact of the long-run effects is consistent with that of the lagged coefficients for equity share and value-traded, and the contemporaneous coefficients for international equity issuance. An analysis of the substantive impact of the long-run effects would, therefore, tell a similar story to that presented in Section 6.3.4.

8

Qualitative Analysis: Introduction to the Case Studies

8.1 RATIONALE FOR THE CASE STUDIES

In the previous chapters, the theoretical claims of the book were examined from a macro-comparative perspective, utilizing panel data econometric methods. Such a large-N quantitative analysis of corporate governance change in nonliberal market economies represents the main empirical focus of this book. However, in the remaining chapters, the aim is to increase the depth and concreteness of the analysis through presentation of two country case studies.

A methodological approach involving the qualitative comparison of specific events and experiences in a small number of countries – described by Lijphart (1971) as "the comparative method" – is potentially complementary to an empirical analysis based on "the statistical method," in which a large number of countries are analyzed utilizing (primarily) quantitative techniques (King et al. 1994). Both methodologies are concerned with the evaluation of relevant evidence in relation to potentially falsifiable knowledge claims. Both approaches, therefore, have a potential role in fulfilling the broad objective of political science, which is defined by Gabriel Almond (1996) as "the creation of knowledge, defined as inferences or generalizations about politics drawn from evidence."

The utilization of case studies in this book is primarily motivated by a desire to benefit from some of the relative strengths of the case study method vis-à-vis those of other methodological approaches. In particular, it is hoped that case studies will permit a more detailed evaluation of the context and processes by which causal variables exert their effect on dependent variables, especially in terms of the intentionality of relevant social actors (Taylor 1970). In contrast, a "large-N" statistical approach is primarily adapted to establishing the magnitude and significance of covariation between variables, and may not necessarily be conclusive in verifying the operation of causal mechanisms that are claimed to underlie empirical relationships (Hedstrom and Swedburg 1998; Gerring 2004: 348).

Equally, however, it should be recognized that the case study approach suffers from certain weaknesses. It is often problematic to make strong inferences about a broad class of countries from a small number of cases. In particular, a focus on individual units or countries is vulnerable to the criticism that the experience of that particular country is not representative of others in the class under investigation. A related problem is that many hypothesized relationships are probabilistic rather than invariant in nature. The ability of specific cases to definitively falsify probabilistic relationships is inherently limited, as the individual case under examination may form part of the "error term" that forms part of the "true" underlying relationship (Gerring 2004: 349).

A further series of concerns relates to the lack of systematic procedures for undertaking case study research. The subjectivity involved in collating and presenting case study evidence may give rise to suspicions that inferences are biased, unfair, or incomplete (Yin 2003: 9). Furthermore, it is sometimes difficult for the case study method to rule out rival explanations of empirical phenomena. This contrasts with statistical analysis, which allows explicit inclusion of relevant control variables (Landman 2003: 25). Some degree of qualitative control may be possible through "most similar" and "most different" systems design (Przeworski and Teune 1970; Faure 1994). However, in many instances, the number of control variables that can be convincingly accounted for through such techniques is likely to be limited.

Taken together, these types of concern lead Robert Yin (2003: iii) to observe that "the case study has long been (and continues to be) stereotyped as a weak sibling among social science methods." Nonetheless, while remaining cognizant of the pros and cons of case studies, the approach taken in this book is to recognize that quantitatively derived results may be usefully complemented by an analysis of the contextual conditions in individual countries, that is case studies. In particular, confidence in the empirical basis of theoretical claims is likely to be increased if both methodological approaches are able to independently yield consistent conclusions (in contrast to a situation in which the hypothesis is justified on the basis of one approach alone). Such a "triangulation" of empirical methodologies is increasingly viewed as an important safeguard of the integrity of social scientific research (King et al. 1994). The aspiration of this book is summarized succinctly by John Gerring (2004: 353): "If both case study and cross-unit methods have much to recommend them, then both ought to be pursued – perhaps not in equal measure, but at least with equal diligence and respect."

8.2 CHOICE OF COUNTRY CASES

According to the theoretical claims of this book, partisanship is associated with change in *de facto* corporate governance outcomes through its interaction with economic rents. The case study technique offers an opportunity to understand in more detail the specific processes by which differing levels of economic rents translate into changes in the corporate governance preferences of relevant social actors in individual country settings. There are at least two ways in which such "process tracing" may be accomplished. First, a longitudinal case study can be undertaken of a country that has experienced significant changes in levels of product market competition over time. This allows the corporate governance preferences of social actors during periods of "low competition" to be compared with those of similar actors within the same country at a later point in time, when levels of competition are significantly higher. A second approach is to evaluate the experiences of two countries that contemporaneously exhibit different levels of product market competition (i.e., on a cross-sectional basis), and compare the differing corporate governance preferences of relevant social actors in the two countries.

The intention of Chapters 9 and 10 is to present case study evidence utilizing both of these approaches. Given the constraints of space, the emphasis is placed on examining the experience of Left government rather than conservative government, as the former is assumed to be the main force behind corporate governance change by the hypothesis of this book. For the longitudinal case study, the strategy involves identifying a nonliberal market economy that has enjoyed a significant increase in product market competition over time, and which has also experienced periods of Left government during both the "low" and the "high" competition periods. According to the hypothesis, the latter period is expected to be more strongly associated with pro-shareholder corporate governance change than the low-competition period, driven by the changing corporate governance preferences of both Left parties in government and their core constituents.

For the cross-sectionally motivated case study, the aim is to identify a second country that has experienced a less significant decline in economic rents, but which enjoyed Left government at roughly the same point in time. According to theoretical expectations, the Left and its core constituents in the second country have less incentive to reform corporate governance. In addition, the availability of economic rents makes it more difficult to translate *de jure* corporate governance reforms into changes in firm-level corporate governance outcomes. Indeed, it is possible that a gap may emerge between the shareholder-orientation of regulation and firm-level behavior, as the resources required to enforce *de jure* change will be higher in a high-rent environment (see Chapter 2, section 2.4). For both these reasons, the high-rent country is expected to be less associated with *de facto* corporate governance change than the low-rent country, despite the presence of Left government.

Table 8.1 shows how product market competition has developed over time in each of the fifteen nonliberal market economies utilized in the quantitative analysis. Once again, the measure of competition is the Organisation for Economic Development and Co-operation's (OECD) NMR index (the proxy for competition utilized in the quantitative analysis).[1] Whilst most countries experienced very little change in competitive conditions prior to 1985, product markets began to liberalize in the late 1980s and early 1990s, although the rate of change and the endpoint in the final year of the sample period (2003) varied by country.

According to the results presented in Chapter 6, Left government becomes significantly associated with more outsider-oriented corporate governance when the NMR index declines below a value of around 3. With regard to the conditional effects graphs of pervious chapters, this is indicated by the point at which the lower bound confidence interval passes through the horizontal axis. Figure 8.1 illustrates this crossover point with regard to the set of results obtained for the value-traded proxy.

This "threshold" level of competition is used to create a short-list of appropriate candidates for the case studies. It can be observed from Table 8.2 – which provides a summary of the Left's involvement in European government since 1990 – that there are five countries in the sample that experienced significant periods of Left government in the period following attainment of the threshold level of product market competition: Denmark, Finland, Germany, the Netherlands, and Sweden. These countries represent potential candidates for the longitudinal case study of corporate governance change over time. For the comparative case study, France, Italy, Greece, and Portugal all experienced Left government at an approximately comparable time (i.e., the late 1990s) to that of the countries in the first group, but in the context of lower (subthreshold) product market competition, that is values of the NMR index that had not exceeded the threshold value. These represent candidates for the second case study.

---

[1] A detailed discussion of the NMR index is provided in Chapter 5.

Table 8.1 Levels of product market competition (NMR index, 0 = highest, 6 = lowest)

	1975	1985	1990	1995	1996	1997	1998	1999	2000	2001	2002	2003
Austria	5.2	4.9	4.5	4.0	3.9	3.9	3.9	3.3	3.0	2.7	2.5	2.4
Belgium	5.5	5.5	5.3	3.9	3.8	3.7	3.4	3.1	2.8	2.5	2.3	2.1
Denmark	5.5	5.5	4.7	3.5	3.4	3.1	3.0	2.6	2.4	2.0	1.7	1.6
Finland	5.5	5.1	4.6	3.0	2.9	2.7	2.7	2.5	2.5	2.5	2.5	2.4
France	6.0	6.0	5.2	4.8	4.8	4.6	4.3	4.0	3.8	3.7	3.3	3.0
Germany	5.2	5.1	4.6	3.7	3.3	3.2	2.8	2.4	2.2	2.0	1.8	1.7
Greece	5.7	5.7	5.7	5.4	5.4	5.3	5.3	5.1	5.0	4.7	4.2	4.1
Italy	5.8	5.8	5.8	4.9	4.9	4.7	4.7	4.1	3.6	3.2	2.7	2.6
Japan	5.1	5.1	3.5	3.2	3.1	3.1	2.9	2.8	2.6	2.4	2.3	2.2
Netherlands	5.6	5.6	5.6	3.7	3.3	3.1	2.9	2.4	1.9	1.8	1.7	1.6
Norway	5.5	5.0	4.5	3.4	3.3	3.3	3.2	2.9	2.8	2.7	2.5	2.3
Portugal	5.9	5.9	5.3	4.8	4.6	4.5	4.4	4.0	3.3	3.1	2.9	2.6
Spain	5.1	5.0	4.7	4.2	4.0	3.7	3.5	2.9	2.8	2.4	2.2	2.0
Sweden	4.5	4.5	4.4	2.9	2.5	2.5	2.4	2.3	2.1	2.1	2.0	1.9
Switzerland	4.1	4.2	4.2	3.9	3.9	3.8	3.7	3.2	3.0	2.9	2.9	2.8

Note: A higher index value indicates a lower level of product market competition.

Source: Conway and Nicoletti (2006).

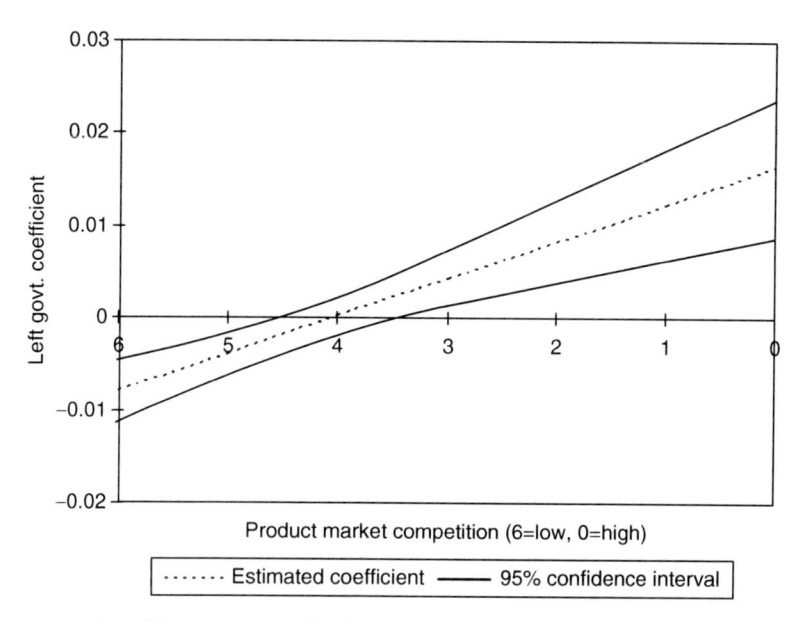

Qualitative Analysis: Introduction to the Case Studies 219

Figure 8.1 Conditional effects of Left government on corporate governance. Dependent variable: value traded. Country and decade fixed effects

The choice of a pair of cases – one from each group – is not greatly facilitated by considerations emerging from the "most similar systems design" approach of Przeworski and Teune (1970). The composition of the first group is dominated by northern European countries, which are typically classified by political economists as coordinated market economies (CMEs) (Hall and Soskice 2001). The second group consists primarily of southern European countries, which are often categorized under the banner of a separate variety of capitalism, for example as "Mediterranean" or mixed market economies (Rhodes 1997; Hall and Soskice 2001). Consequently, it is not really possible to bring together two countries that exhibit strong similarities, thereby allowing the dimensions of similarity to be controlled-for during the process of comparison.

The decision to choose Germany and Italy for the case studies is based primarily on their status as two of the three "big" political economies of continental Europe (although France could equally have been chosen for the second case). Although size does not necessarily ensure that the experience of these two cases will be typical of other European countries, it probably means that they represent more "critical" cases for the evaluation of the hypothesis. The choice of two similarly large countries also goes some way to controlling

220 Corporate Governance, Competition, and Political Parties

Table 8.2 The Left in European government: before and after achievement of "threshold" product market competition

	Year in which NMR index falls below 3	Significant Left government after this date (and prior to end of sample period)?	Left participation in government since 1990
Austria	2000	No	Until 1999: Coalition of the Social Democratic Party of Austria (SPÖ) and Austrian People's Party (ÖVP). Chancellors: Franz Vranitzky (SPÖ, 1986–97); Viktor Klima (SPÖ, 1997–9).
Belgium	2000	No	Since 1999: Junior partners in "Rainbow coalition" with Flemish and French-speaking Liberals, and (until 2003) Greens. Prime Minister: Guy Verhofstadt (VLD).
Denmark	1998	Yes	Social Democrat (SD)-led coalition (1993–2001). Prime Minister: Poul Nyrup Rasmussen (SD).
Finland	1996	Yes	Social Democrat (SDP)-led coalition (1995–2003). Prime Minister: Paavo Lipponen (SDP).
France	Not attained	No	Prior to 1993: Socialist (PSF)-led government. Prime Ministers: Michel Rocard (1988–91); Édith Cresson (1991/2); Pierre Bérégovoy (1992/3). 1997–2002: Socialist (PSF)-led government. Prime Minister: Lionel Jospin (1997–2002).
Germany	1998	Yes	1998–2005: Social Democratic Party (SPD) and Green Party coalition. Chancellor: Gerhard Schröder (SPD).
Greece	Not attained	No	1993–2004: PASOK government. Prime Ministers: Andreas Papandreou (until 1996); Costas Simitis.
Italy	2002	No	1992/3: Socialist-led coalition. Prime Minister: Giuliano Amato. 1996–2001: Center–left coalitions: Prime Ministers: Romano Prodi (1996–8); Massimo D'Alema (1998–2000); Giuliano Amato (2000/1).
Netherlands	1998	Yes	1994–2002: Labour Party (PvdA)-led coalition. Prime Minister: Wim Kok (PvdA).

Norway	1999	No	1990–7: Labour Party (AP) government. Prime Ministers: Gro Harlem Brundtland (1990–6); Thorbjørn Jagland (1996–7). 2000/1: Labour Party (AP) government. Prime Minister: Jens Stoltenberg.
Portugal	2002	No	1995–2002: Socialist Party (PSP) government. Prime Minister: António Guterres.
Spain	1999	No	Until 1996: Spanish Socialist Workers' Party (PSOE) government. Prime Minister (from 1982): Felipe González.
Sweden	1995	Yes	Social Democratic Party (SDA)-led coalition (1996–2006). Prime Minister: Göran Persson (SDA).
Switzerland	2001	No	Minority member of permanent grand coalition.

Source: Constructed by the author.

for country size as a potential alternative explanatory variable. In addition, the Italian case is of particular interest due to the disparity of its *de facto* and *de jure* corporate governance experiences. Italy illuminates an important facet of the hypothesis of Chapter 2 that legislative and regulatory reform translates more directly into firm-level corporate governance change in the absence of high levels of economic rents.

The contrasting competitiveness of product markets in Italy and Germany in the late 1990s is further emphasized by a second OECD index of product market competition discussed in Chapter 5 – the product market regulation (PMR) index. As of 1998, this placed Germany in a mid-ranking position amongst OECD countries (see Figure 8.2). Although German product markets were less competitive than those of liberal market economies, such as the United Kingdom and the United States, they were significantly more competitive than those of Italy, which registered the least competitive score of the sample. Progress in liberalizing German product markets was noted in an OECD report on structural reform in the German economy, published in September 1998. The OECD (1998: 129) concluded that "with respect to extending competition to previously protected sectors, significant progress has been made." In contrast, an OECD report on Italian competition, published at around the same time, concluded that "Italy remains among the

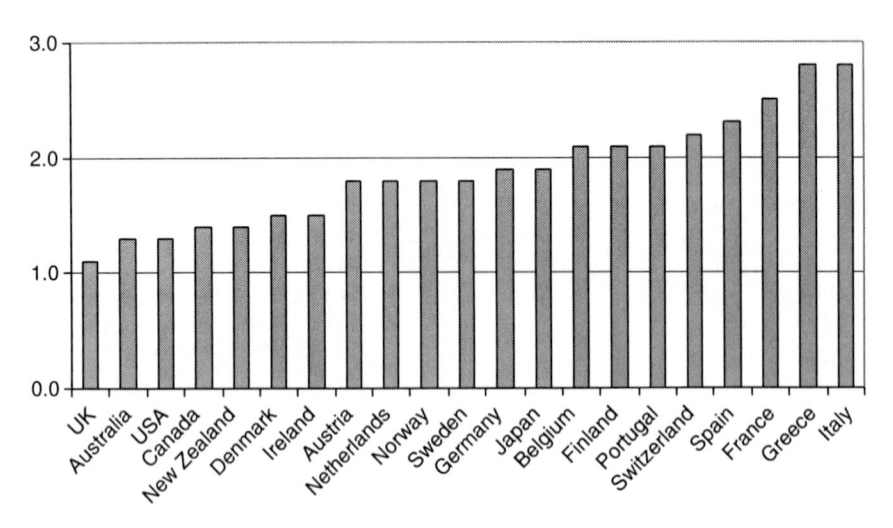

Figure 8.2 PMR index of "whole economy" product market competition, 1998

countries whose economic environment presents the greatest obstacles to competition" (OECD 2000b: 8).

In short, Germany and Italy provide examples of two nonliberal market economies with common experiences of Left government in the late 1990s, but contrasting experiences in terms of product market competition. Such cases are expected to give rise to differing outcomes in terms of the dependent variable – corporate governance change – and therefore represent interesting tests of the viability of the hypothesis. Both of the case studies are primarily constructed from an analysis of the relevant secondary literature, although evidence from primary policy documents and parliamentary debates is referred to where it is available.

9

The Case of Germany: From Blockholding to Hybrid Corporate Governance Regime

In this chapter, the theoretical claims of the book are related to the experience of corporate governance change in Germany over the last two decades. Germany is often viewed as the archetypal example of an insider-controlled and stakeholder-oriented system of corporate governance (Franks and Mayer 1994; Schmidt 2004: 402). However, in this chapter it is argued that change in the competitive landscape of incumbent blockholders has interacted with a significant period of Left government to generate a substantial shift in a pro-shareholder direction. This has not caused a wholesale transformation of German corporate governance into an ideal-type shareholder model. Although minority shareholders have improved their position, they have not yet emerged as supreme corporate stakeholders. Rather there has been a redistribution of power among company owners, from blockholders to minority shareholders. The result is a hybrid (Jackson 2003: 262) model of corporate governance, which combines elements of both the blockholder and shareholder systems.

Although the hypothesis of this book makes general claims about the determinants of corporate governance change across all nonliberal market economies, corporate governance change in specific countries takes place along paths that reflect the particularities of national institutions and historical experiences. Consequently, the following discussion begins with a description of the distinctive nature of the postwar political economy in Germany, and the model of corporate governance with which it was associated. This is followed by an analysis of the most important means, in the German context, by which falling economic rents impacted on the politics of corporate governance during the 1990s: the changing business model of the private universal banks. Section 9.4 interprets this political debate in terms of the changing preferences of political actors and their core constituents, and seeks to explain these changed preferences in relation to the declining level of economic rents in the German economy.

9.1 THE CORPORATE GOVERNANCE OF DEUTSCHLAND AG

The power structure of the postwar system of "organized free enterprise"[1] in Germany may be depicted in terms of two distinctive elements: First, an interlocking corporate network of major companies, dominated by blockholders. Second, a strong position for insider labor, deriving from legislation that provided employees with protections to counterbalance the ownership rights of blockholders (Ziegler 2000: 198; Hackethal et al. 2005: 390). This structure enabled both blockholders and employees to benefit from economic rents available to firms, the latter in the form of high levels of job security, high wages, and employment benefits. In contrast, minority shareholders have not played a significant role in German corporate governance (at least until relatively recently), and have occupied a vulnerable and unrepresented position in the corporate power structure. In the rest of this section, the position of each of these three groups of corporate stakeholders – blockholders, insider labor, and minority shareholders – is examined in more detail.

The German corporate sector has traditionally been populated by several types of corporate actor. These have included large pyramidal business groups, which are often privately owned or controlled by family interests; stock-market-listed corporations, which in principle are open to ownership participation from minority shareholders, but in practice have been controlled by large private universal banks or other financial institutions; and small-and-medium-sized enterprises (SMEs), for example, members of the *Mittelstand*, which have tended to remain under the direct control of family or entrepreneurial interests. What all of these enterprise types have shared is an ownership structure dominated by blockholders rather than minority shareholders (Fohlin 2005: 10).

Key structural features of the German corporate network have been interlocking shareholdings and interlocking directorates (Windolf and Beyer 1996; Beyer 1998; Windolf and Nollert 2001). Such interlinkages are typical of blockholder-dominated economies in a number of countries, particularly in continental Europe. However, the postwar German network was distinctive in the extent of its interlinkages across the entire system – not just particular sectors or groups of firms – and the central coordinating role played by

---

[1] This expression is used by Andrew Shonfield (1965) and John Zysman (1983: 252) to capture the nature of the postwar German economy.

financial institutions (Zysman 1983: 72). This contrasted, for example, with the Japanese *keiretsu*, which were relatively isolated networks of corporate and financial actors. Within the German corporate network of 1996, financial companies such as Deutsche Bank and Dresdner Bank were both actively and passively involved with a variety of companies, and there existed important reciprocal cross-shareholdings between the financial institutions themselves. Deutsche Bank, for example, held shares in Allianz, and Allianz-owned shares in Deutsche Bank. However, cross-shareholdings between nonfinancial companies were relatively few in number, emphasizing the hierarchical dominance of financial companies over the corporate network (Höpner and Krempel 2004: 340).

A consequence of the close links between major companies was the encouragement of cooperative rather than competitive industrial behavior within the network. This gave rise to a number of positive externalities. For example, Reinhard Schmidt (2004) writes that "the insider control system encourages firm-specific investments by lenders, employees and large shareholders." However, it also served to embed a "quasi cartel," which protected a small group of elite blockholders against the influence of economic actors lying outside the network (Zysman 1983: 252; Höpner and Krempel 2004). The benefits obtained from the German economic system, therefore, derived "in part... from the economic benefits of having a smoothly running and relatively efficient system. But in part they may also come from the 'exploitation' of those shareholders who are not insiders, that is, the small shareholders and possibly also some institutional investors" (Schmidt 2004: 403).

Although accounts of the German financial system tend to focus on the role of the private universal banks (of which the big three have been Deutsche Bank, Dresdner Bank, and Commerzbank[2]), several other types of banking institutions have also fulfilled an important role in the German financial system. Of particular note are the public savings banks (including the *Landesbanken*), and credit cooperatives. Indeed, of the 3,000 monetary financial institutions in Germany at the end of 2000, 20 percent were public savings banks and around 60 percent were in the cooperative banking sector, although many of the latter were extremely small institutions (Hackethal 2004: 74). Unlike private universal banks, public savings banks and credit cooperatives have been explicitly charged, alongside their commercial activities, with the task of promoting public policy goals. These have included ensuring that peripheral geographical regions are adequately served by financial institutions, and the implementation of industrial policy. In addition, the financial

---

[2] The big three were joined by a fourth – Bayerische Hypo-und Vereinsbank (HVB) – in 1999, following the merger of two large Bavarian banks (Hackethal 2005: 75).

needs of small- and medium-sized *Mittelstand* firms have traditionally been served by these smaller savings and cooperative banks rather than by big universal banks (Lütz 2005: 141).[3]

However, the private universal banks have played the defining blockholder role in the German insider corporate network due to their *Hausbank* relationships with the larger industrial corporations. The foundations of these relationships have been multiple ties of ownership, board memberships, and the provision of loans. In place of an emphasis on corporate transparency (as in the liberal market economies), the German corporate governance regime has traditionally relied on large banks to monitor and discipline corporate managers behind closed doors.[4] Long-term relationships between bankers and corporate managers have reduced pressures for maximizing short-term financial returns and encouraged long-term growth strategies by industrial enterprises. Such long-term relationships have been facilitated by the access of banks to insider information about firms' activities. Furthermore, banks have represented other shareholders as delegated monitors of management, either through proxy votes at shareholder meetings (*Depotstimmrecht*) or via the seats on supervisory boards. Crucially, at times of corporate crisis, it has been the private universal banks that have played the central role in coordinating rescue operations on behalf of both state authorities and other corporate interests (Lütz 2005: 142).

In short, the tight interlinkages of the German corporate network have ensured that corporate governance has been dominated by a relatively small number of elite blockholder actors. Blockholder interests have primarily been coordinated by the private universal banks, even in those instances where the banks have not held controlling ownership stakes directly. However, the control of insider capital over corporate governance has not been absolute. As will now be described, blockholders have been constrained in the German system by the ability of employees to exert influence over corporate behavior. This has arisen due to the ability of labor to translate political power into supportive company and labor law, particularly in respect of codetermination rights.

---

[3] Smaller companies are generally not publicly traded, and tend to remain owned by family blockholders. The main relationship of the banks with such firms is, therefore, through lending relationships rather than sharing ownership (Elsas and Krahnen 2004: 197).

[4] The monitoring role of the large banks has been widely admired, even in liberal market economies. For example, Nicholas Crafts writes that "there are good reasons to choose the German rather than the British style of capital markets...in practice, the effectiveness of German banks as monitors of company performance...makes the German system unambiguously superior" (Crafts 1992: 409).

Labor codetermination (*Mitbestimmung*) incorporates employees into corporate governance through a replication of Germany's highly organized collective bargaining arrangements at the level of each individual firm. It operates at two levels: through employee involvement in works councils, which generally occurs at the level of the plant; and supervisory board representation, at the level of the corporation as a whole (Wiedemann 1980; Katzenstein 1987). These rights have been entrenched by legislation, the most notable example of which is the Codetermination Act of 1976, which stipulates that most large corporations (with more than 2,000 employees) must appoint an equal number of shareholder and employee representatives to their supervisory boards (Prigge 1998).

According to German company law, public corporations (*Aktiengesellschaft* or AG) are required to have a dual board structure in which the supervisory board is separate from the management board, with no overlapping membership. The supervisory board (*Aufsichtsrat*) appoints and supervises the managing board (*Vorstand*) and formulates (or at least approves) major corporate policies and strategies. The significant role of employees on the supervisory board is, therefore, a potentially important mechanism by which labor can exert influence over corporate governance. However, in practice, such a channel of influence has been limited due to the tendency of blockholders and managers to formulate corporate strategy on a bilateral basis, and thereby bypass supervisory boards in decision-making wherever possible. This has served to undermine the power of labor at the supervisory board level (Roe 2003: 72).

Furthermore, although German codetermination legislation relating to supervisory board participation is the most extensive in Europe, it still only covers less than half of the private sector workforce. Many employees – particularly those working for small- and medium-sized companies (e.g., the *Mittelstand*) – are not employed in public-listed corporations. Furthermore, a number of large companies (particularly those active in the service sector) are either subject to the less-stringent requirements of earlier (i.e., pre-1976) codetermination legislation (which requires only one-third employee representation on supervisory boards) or are able to opt out of board codetermination obligations altogether (Thimm 1980; Ziegler 2000: 200).

Despite its symbolic significance, the practical importance of board-level codetermination has generally been less than that of works council codetermination (Wiedemann 1980: 80–2). The Works Constitution Act of 1972 provided for the election of works councils in facilities or plants of business enterprises with five or more permanent employees. However, many large firms voluntarily instituted enterprise works councils covering entire corporate groups to ensure stable and cooperative labor relations (Streeck 1996: 36;

Thelen 2001: 85). Works councils have wielded substantial influence within the workplace due to their power to demand information on corporate activities, and be consulted on major corporate decisions (e.g., hirings, lay-offs, and overtime). In addition, they have the power to demand compensation for economic injury to employees caused by managerial policy decisions in certain instances (Ziegler 2000: 199). Assmann (1990) argues that works council codetermination has played a crucial role in coordinating labor relations in workplaces staffed by highly skilled and productive employees, and has been the main mechanism by which labor has protected its interests vis-à-vis corporate management (at least until the 1990s).

Although blockholder and employee stakeholders have been able to exert a high level of influence over corporate governance in Germany, the same cannot be said of minority shareholders. Whereas an important aspect of the shareholder model of corporate governance is that board members represent the interests of all types of shareholder – including minority shareholders – this has not been true of German supervisory boards. The main members of supervisory boards have been the representatives of blockholders – particularly banks – and employees (exercising their codetermination rights). The interests of investors with noncontrolling ownership stakes have not been explicitly represented.[5]

Furthermore, the "insider" status of blockholders and insider labor has granted them a privileged flow of information regarding the activities of corporate management. In contrast, corporate activities have been much more opaque to noninsider actors. In a regulatory environment with less-stringent requirements concerning financial reporting and disclosure, it has been problematic for minority shareholders to monitor the behavior of corporate management, and ensure that they are managing the firm in order to generate a satisfactory return for all investors. Furthermore, German law provided – until relatively recently – few effective avenues for private litigation to enforce minority shareholder rights (Rieckers and Spindler 2004: 355).

Such a lack of concern for potential or actual outsider investors did little to promote the development of securities markets, which until the early 1990s were fragmented across eight regional and self-regulating stock exchanges. Capital markets played a relatively limited role in the functioning of companies, which were able to rely on banks to fulfill their ongoing external financing needs, primarily through bank loans. Equally, banks were eager to

---

[5] It should be noted that lobbying groups have attempted to represent the interests of small shareholders from outside the company. For example, the SdK (*Schutzgemeinschaft der Kapitalanleger*) has been in operation since 1959. However, such groups have not been major social actors in the German political economy.

foster this dependency – at the expense of the development of securities markets – in order to ensure that external social actors did not gain ownership rights over significant components of the German company network.

9.2 ECONOMIC RENTS AND GERMAN CORPORATE STRATEGY

A central claim of this book is that greater product market competition exerts a significant effect on the behavior of blockholders and insider labor. In the absence of economic rents, blockholders become more concerned with ensuring their commercial viability, and less willing and able to secure the cooperation of erstwhile social partners, such as insider labor, through the sharing of economic rents. This provokes a political reaction in terms of corporate governance policy from the party political representatives of insider labor. In this section, the specific impact of growing competitive pressures on German blockholders, insider labor, and private universal banks during the 1990s is examined.

The period after 1992 marked a clear end to the postwar *Wirtschaftswunder* of high economic growth, and high and stable employment levels in Germany. In response to the post-unification boom in the early 1990s, the Bundesbank imposed a restrictive monetary policy, which exerted a dampening effect on the domestic demand for the output of German companies for much of the decade (DIW 1996). The ability of fiscal policy to counter this downturn was constrained by the need to transfer substantial resources to the new eastern Länder (around 4% of GDP per year in the late 1990s)[6] (Grahl and Teague 2004: 558). At the level of the firm, German management had to cope with the highest labor cost burden of any industrialized country, mainly due to high levels of nonwage labor costs which had risen substantially during the 1970s and 1980s (from 56% of direct wages in 1972, to 82% in 1998). Even taking into account Germany's outstanding record in terms of productivity and productivity growth, this translated into one of the highest levels of unit labor costs among developed economies (Tüselmann and Heise 2000: 168;

---

[6] German unification did not exert a direct effect on corporate governance, as the corporate institutional framework of Deutschland AG was transferred in its entirety onto the defunct industrial structure of Eastern Germany. However, the economic downturn arising from unification may have increased the pressure on employers to rethink their relationships with insider labor (Streeck and Hassel 2003: 101).

Hassel and Williamson 2004). The accumulated unit labor cost disadvantage between 1989 and 1998 amounted to roughly 17 percent relative to the average of other major Organisation for Economic Co-operation and Development (OECD) countries (IW 1999). This exerted a chronic squeeze on the profit margins of German companies.

German companies had faced a difficult macroeconomic environment before, for example, following the global oil price shock of the early 1970s, but had adjusted in a manner that retained the integrity of the German economic and social model. However, the difference this time was that depressed demand was combined with a substantial increase in the competitiveness of product markets. Between the mid-1980s and late1990s, the level of NMR index – the proxy utilized to measure product market competition in the quantitative analysis chapters – almost halved, suggesting a significant increase in product market competition (see Table 8.1). This finding is supported by the work of Albach et al. (1999), which seeks to assess the financial situation of German-listed corporations from a bottom-up perspective, that is, through the analysis of the balance sheets of individual companies. Based on the development of their "variance of sales" index, which aggregates the market conditions faced by individual companies, they conclude that product market competition in Germany experienced a major increase in the early 1990s (Albach et al. 1999: 514). Consequently, it is plausible to conclude that German companies entered the downturn of the early 1990s without the protection of economic rents that had cushioned them during the 1970s and 1980s.

The response of German corporations to this challenge was not necessarily to embrace the shareholder model of corporate governance (at least not initially). However, it did lead them to become noticeably more aggressive in pursuit of their short-term financial interests, and less willing to engage in cooperative behavior with social partners (Williams 2000; Streeck 2001; Grahl and Teague 2004: 562). Major enterprises threatened exit from Germany as a production base (particularly to Central Europe), often as a means of negotiating reduced labor costs (Tüselmann and Heise 2000: 168). Firms adopted more aggressive means of rationalizing their operations – such as mergers, disposals, and acquisitions – rather than sticking to the gradualist adjustment strategy which had characterized their earlier response to difficult market conditions (see Table 9.1). The German chemicals and pharmaceutical sector – a mainstay of the German economy – provided a prominent example of this more aggressive restructuring approach. Many of the main pharmaceutical enterprises (e.g., Hoechst, Bayer, and BASF) shifted their R&D activity overseas during the 1990s (particularly to the United States). Hoechst subsequently merged with the French company Rhone-Poulenc, and BASF sold its entire pharmaceutical division to a US company in 2000 (Vitols 2001: 367).

Table 9.1 Number of mergers and acquisitions in Germany

Year	Number of mergers and acquisitions
1980	635
1981	618
1982	603
1983	506
1984	575
1985	709
1986	802
1987	887
1988	1,159
1989	1,414
1990	1,548
1991	2,007
1992	1,743
1993	1,514
1994	1,564
1995	1,530
1996	1,434
1997	1,751
1998	1,888

Source: OECD (1999a).

A further example of changing corporate behavior is provided by Tony Edward's case study (2004) of Volkswagen. Prior to the 1990s, Volkswagen had operated as a classic example of a blockholder and stakeholder corporation. The regional government of Lower Saxony held a blockholding stake of almost 20 percent of the voting shares in the company (which served to counter any potential takeover risk), and there was a long history of cooperation between workers and management. However, the arrival of Ferdinand Piëch as CEO of the company in 1993 resulted in the adoption of a more financially driven management style. Targets were adopted for return on capital, and wage increases for employees were held well below increases in productivity. The result was that the share of value-added going to employees fell from 90 percent to 70 percent over the course of the 1990s. It is important to note, however, that this did not result in the distribution of higher returns to minority shareholders. The resources generated by the more financially driven approach were used to pay off debt and build up reserves. In other words, resources were accumulated to sustain the independence and discretionary power of company insiders, that is, blockholders and management, at the expense of other company stakeholders, such as insider labor and minority shareholders (Edwards 2004: 527).

Despite strong employment protection law and codetermination arrangements, the greater financial orientation of corporate behavior had major negative implications for insider labor. Employers responded to the difficult conditions by steadily reducing employment levels.[7] Table 9.2 shows that, by the end of the 1990s, employment reduction rates in Germany were not dissimilar to those in liberal market economies, and significantly higher than in many nonliberal market economies (Jackson 2005: 424). By 1997, the overall unemployment rate had risen to well above 9 percent, with over a third of the total unemployed on a long-term basis (Tüselmann and Heise 2000: 168).

As well as experiencing reduced employment, insider labor found it increasingly difficult to counter the rise of a financial orientation among firms due to a fragmentation of its bargaining position within the German system

Table 9.2 Rates of employment reduction for selected countries, 1999–2001

	Employment reduction rate (Average value, 1999–2001)
Australia	0.093
Canada	0.096
France	0.069
Germany	0.101
Japan	0.041
Netherlands	0.065
Spain	0.077
Sweden	0.095
Switzerland	0.091
United Kingdom	0.129
United States	0.106

Note: The employment reduction rate is the proportion of firms implementing a 10 percent reduction in employment within a twelve-month period. Relates to listed firms with more than 2,000 employees.
Source: Jackson (2005: 424).

---

[7] It should be noted that much of the employment adjustment in the 1990s was achieved through "benevolent" methods of workforce reduction, such as early retirement rather than compulsory redundancies. However, this "externalization" of labor costs placed significant burdens on the German welfare state (Streeck 1997; Jackson 2005: 424). Greater unemployment also increased the burden of nonwage costs on employers, which further reduced their scope to share economic rents with insider labor (Streeck and Hassel 2003: 107).

of industrial relations. After four decades of relative stability, trade union density began to decline during the 1990s, from around 36 percent in the early 1990s to about 28 percent by 2003 (Grahl and Teague 2004: 564). Furthermore, sector level collective bargaining – which had previously served to stabilize employment relations across the economy – began to erode during the 1990s (Ziegler 2000: 210; Thelen and Kume 2003: 187; Ulman and Gerlach 2003). A notable development was the increased use of "opening clauses," particularly by smaller companies, which permitted an opt-out from industry wage deals in cases of poor commercial circumstances (Grahl and Teague 2004: 565).

Third, and of most direct relevance for corporate governance, codetermination arrangements became increasingly undermined. Growing numbers of SMEs fell outside the ambit of codetermination legislation (representing around 60% of employees). Furthermore, in the face of a rising fear of unemployment, firm-level works councils became increasingly focused on facilitating the agenda of management, for example, in terms of improving corporate efficiency and flexibility, rather than protecting the rights of employees (Kommission Mitbestimmung 1998; Hassel 1999; Höpner 2002: 32). This led Lane (2003) to describe works councils – by the end of the 1990s – as little more than "empty shells."

The position of insider labor in the late 1990s was such, therefore, that it was no longer benefiting from a share of economic rents from blockholders through either high wage levels or stable employment relationships. Furthermore, it was increasingly unable to resist a shift in corporate behavior in a direction that ignored their interests. This breakdown of social partnership between blockholders and insider labor during the 1990s led Streeck and Höpner (2003: 15) to conclude that "the release of corporations from social obligations is very advanced in Germany, and it is irreversible."

Although the impact of declining economic rents was felt on blockholder-controlled companies and insider labor across the German economy, a further important catalyst for corporate governance change emerged from developments in the financial sector. Competitive pressures began to impact on the private universal banks in the late 1980s (Fischer and Pfeil 2004: 319). The net interest margin[8] earned by banks on their traditional lending business with *Hausbank* corporate clients began to decline to levels that were insufficient to

---

[8] Net interest margin is the difference between the interest income received by banks from loans, and the interest payable by banks in order to acquire funds for lending (e.g., to deposit account holders). It is analogous to the gross margin of nonfinancial companies. Hackethal (2004: 74) notes that declining net interest margins on traditional lending business have been a common feature of banking systems throughout most developed economies since the late-1980s.

compensate for the cost and riskiness of capital.[9] This caused the banks to reassess their entire business strategy, and, in particular, their commitment to a central coordinating role at the heart of the German corporate network (Weber 2002).

There were a number of reasons for the decline in profitability of traditional lending activities. On the funding side of the balance sheet, universal banks were affected by a shift in savings patterns among savers that began in the second half of the 1980s (see Table 9.3). Savers increasingly preferred to place their surplus funds in securities and financial products provided by insurance companies, rather than leaving them in bank deposit accounts. Consequently, there was increased competition for a rapidly shrinking pool of bank deposits. This trend gathered momentum during the 1990s, particularly following the privatization of Deutsche Telecom in 1996 (which further stimulated the interest of private investors in share ownership).

Furthermore, these changes occurred in the context of a market structure in which large numbers of financial institutions competed for saver's funds. This was reflected in the number of banking branches attempting to secure deposits, which were 0.61 per thousand people in Germany (as of 1985),

Table 9.3 Flows into financial assets by German households

	Billion (€)		Share of financial assets (%)	
	1991–5	1996–2000	1991–5	1996–2000
Cash and bank deposits, of which	263.6	106.2	35.9	15.9
Cash and sight deposits	78.4	95.8	10.7	14.4
Time deposits	21.9	−25.8	3.0	−3.9
Savings deposits	165.3	50.4	22.5	7.6
Savings bonds	−2.1	−14.1	−0.3	−2.1
Investment in securities, of which	195.6	212.0	26.6	31.8
Fixed-income securities	74.8	4.3	10.2	0.6
Shares	7.6	39.1	1.0	5.9
Investment certificates	113.2	168.7	15.4	25.3
Other participating interests	22.7	16.4	3.1	2.5
Claims on insurance companies	207.9	293.9	28.3	44.1
Other claims	43.8	38.0	6.0	5.7
Total	733.6	666.5	100.0	100.0

Source: Capital finance account of the Deutsche Bundesbank, quoted in Weber (2002).

---

[9] According to Hackethal, Schmidt, and Tyrell, the net interest margin of private commercial banks in Germany fell from around 2.3 percent during the 1980s to just over 1 percent by the end of the 1990s (Hackethal et al. 2005: 403).

compared to an average of 0.49 in the European Union (EU) as a whole (Hackethal 2004: 88). Although the smallest cooperative banks consolidated during the 1980s and 1990s, such a fragmented and overbanked market structure made it difficult for the large private universal banks to win a significant market share, particularly as they were competing against quasi-public institutions (e.g., credit cooperatives or *Landesbanken*) enjoying some degree of state subsidy (see later). Consequently, the combined market share of retail deposits of the big four universal banks in 2000 was less than 14 percent, much less than that of equivalent banks in other European countries (Hackethal 2004: 76). Due to the growing difficulties of obtaining retail funding in such an overbanked environment, the universal banks were forced to turn to capital markets for funding, which were a more expensive source of funds than retail deposits (Westrup 2007: 1101).

At the same time, the profit margin obtainable by lending to corporate clients was under downward pressure. Large German corporations – the traditional clients of the private universal banks – found it increasingly viable to use capital markets as a source of external funds. In addition, foreign banks were increasing their lending to German corporations, often through the overseas affiliates of German multinational companies (a form of borrowing offering tax advantages). There was also an increase in the volume of lending undertaken by public savings banks (e.g., the *Landesbanken*), which were able to raise funds more cheaply than private-sector banks due to state guarantees that boosted their credit ratings. Such competition for the traditional banking business of corporations pushed down lending margins. Compounding these problems was the poor overall environment for lending growth, given the overall weakness of the German economy in the 1990s (Weber 2002).

All these changes served to reduce the attractiveness of traditional lending activities to private universal banks. The banks responded to the situation in a number of ways. An initial step was for banks to encroach onto the business territory of insurance companies (according to the logic of the so-called *bancassurance* business model, which advocated the combining of banking and insurance activities). This challenged established norms regarding "spheres of influence" within the corporate network, and transmitted the competitive pressures felt in banking into the insurance sector. For example, in 1988 Deutsche Bank announced its intention to establish its own life insurance company, which provoked a fiercely negative reaction in the insurance sector (Büschgen 1995: 794). According to Höpner (2003), increasing competitiveness between financial actors prompted the gradual dissolution of interlocking directorates and personal ties between financial institutions from the mid-1980s onward (Höpner 2003: 137). It also catalyzed a reorientation of insurance companies, comparable to that undertaken by the large universal banks. Beyer (2002) has described how the largest German insurer, Allianz, transformed its investment style from one of stable industrial ownership toward active asset management during the 1990s. Allianz is nowadays more comparable to an Anglo-American mutual fund than a strategic actor in old-style "Germany Inc" (Beyer 2002).

A second response from private universal banks was to adopt an aggressive posture *vis-à-vis* the public savings banks. The latter became viewed as competitors rather than social partners (Fischer and Pfeil 2004: 34). For example, in 1994, the German Banking Association (*Bundesverband deutscher Banken*, BDB) – the main lobbying organization of the private universal banks – filed a formal objection with the European Commission accusing the state government of North Rhine-Westphalia of illegally subsidizing the Westdeutsche Landesbank (WestLB). This complaint related to assistance that the regional state government had offered WestLB in 1992 in the form of publicly owned housing assets at a "noncommercial" rate of interest. This was submitted to the EU in defiance of the wishes of the German federal government, which argued that the public savings banks were providers of "services of general economic interest" that should be exempt from EU rules on competition and state aid. However, this argument was rejected by the European Commission, and, in July 2001, the Schröder government agreed to remove all public guarantees from the *Landesbanken* (by July 2005). Ongoing pressure from the private universal banks also led the Commission, in November 2002, to open antisubsidy cases against five other *Landesbanken*. In September 2004, they were required to repay state government subsidies of €4.3 billion (Lütz 2005: 143).

However, the most significant response of the private universal banks to the decline in the returns offered by their traditional lending business was a switch of business strategy toward more lucrative investment banking activities, which were a source of high returns for US and UK banks (Vitols 2001: 347; Cioffi 2002; Hackethal et al. 2005). Investment banking is primarily concerned with the financing of corporations through the issuance and trading of securities on capital markets (rather than through bank loans). It also derives fee income from advising corporate clients in respect of mergers and acquisitions. The decline in traditional lending is illustrated by the changing composition of German bank's balance sheets in Table 9.4.

In general, investment banking conflicts with traditional *Hausbank* activities because cross-shareholdings and interlocking directorates create conflicts of interest in the provision of objective advice on investment banking transactions (Dziobek and Garrett 1998; Beyer and Höpner 2003: 185). Such a conflict led to controversy in 1997, when Deutsche Bank acted as a financial advisor to the steelmaker Krupp in its hostile takeover bid for Thyssen,

Table 9.4 Development of balance sheets of German universal banks, 1990–2001

Balance sheet positions	Percentage share of business	
	1990	2001
Lending to domestic banks	19.4	16.9
Lending to foreign banks	7.6	8.2
Lending to domestic nonbanks, of which	51.1	42.3
Enterprises and self-employed persons	27.3	20.3
Private individuals	14.6	14.5
Public authorities	8.8	7.3
Lending to foreign nonbanks	2.7	5.4
Securities portfolios, of which	11.6	18.5
Domestic securities, of which	10.8	14.0
Bank bonds	7.5	9.1
Public bonds	2.3	1.8
Investment certificates, other securities	0.3	2.3
Foreign securities, of which	0.7	4.6
Nonbank bonds	0.4	3.0

Source: Deutsche Bundesbank: Statistical Supplements to the Monthly Reports, various years. Quoted in Weber (2002).

despite occupying a seat on the target's supervisory board (Jackson 2003: 282). Furthermore, investment banking is directly concerned with promoting the interests of all capital market actors – including outsider capital – and is therefore incompatible with the championing of an insider corporate network (Hellwig 2000: 127). Consequently, a shift in business strategy toward investment banking by the former "guardians" of the German corporate network was a major blow for the long-term prospects of an insider system of corporate governance in Germany.

During the 1990s, both Deutsche Bank and Dresdner Bank acquired British and US investment banking subsidiaries,[10] while Commerzbank began a major expansion of its in-house investment banking subsidiary in London (Hackethal 2004: 76). Equity cross-shareholdings in industrial companies were siphoned off into subsidiary companies, as a prelude to disposal and as a means of removing them from mainstream business activities.[11] Less

---

[10] Deutsche Bank acquired the British merchant bank, Morgan Grenfell, in 1989, and the US bank, Bankers Trust, in 1997. Dresdner Bank acquired Kleinwort Benson, a British merchant bank, in 1995.

[11] The attractiveness of equity cross-shareholdings to banks was further reduced by revisions to the Basel accords on the capital adequacy of banks (Basel II). The new regulations required banks to hold more capital than before in order to protect against the riskiness of holding equity securities on their balance sheets (Bank for International Settlements 2001).

emphasis was placed upon obtaining savings deposits and granting industrial loans, and the banks pulled out of previously long-term lending relationships with corporate clients that did not offer acceptable risk-adjusted returns on equity.

At the same time, the BDB (the German Banker's Association) – encouraged the German government to support the promotion of Frankfurt as a national financial center (Lütz 1998; Cioffi 2006: 550). As discussed in Section 9.1, German capital markets had previously been fragmented through the operation of numerous regional stock markets. The growth of a unified national capital market centered on Frankfurt was seen by the banks as essential to the development of capital markets in Germany, which, in turn, was viewed as an important prerequisite for the competitiveness of the banks in global investment banking (Dyson 2002: 100).

The change of business strategy adopted by banks in the 1990s was associated with a steady erosion of the links between banks and industry. Banks reduced their blockholdings in other corporations through financial devices such as Deutsche Bank's 1997 issue of a long-term convertible bond linked to its holdings in Daimler-Benz (in order to avoid capital gains tax). Divestment of large stakes were further encouraged by the tax reform of the Social Democratic government in 2002, which fully exempted the capital gains of cross-shareholding divestments from tax. Both Deutsche Bank and Dresdner Bank began to disengage from their network of interlocking directorates. Deutsche Bank's retreat from the monitoring of nonfinancial firms was especially noteworthy. In 1996, 29 of the supervisory board chairmen of the 100 biggest firms were representatives of the Deutsche Bank. Only two years later, this number had declined to seventeen. In 2001, Deutsche Bank announced that it would resign from the supervisory board chairmanships of external companies altogether (Beyer and Höpner 2003: 184). This disengagement was also reflected in a decline in capital interlinkages. The number of capital ties between the 100 largest companies dropped from 168 in 1996, to 80 by 2000 (i.e., a 50% decline within four years). During the same period, the amount of net value-added represented by capital links declined to 86 percent of the 1996 amount. This reduction was most significant between financial and industrial companies (Höpner and Krempel 2004: 349).

Most importantly, the private universal banks renounced their willingness to champion the corporate network at the expense of their own profitability, for example, for the achievement of political stability or wider social goals (Beyer and Höpner 2003; Grahl and Teague 2004: 564). According to Höpner and Jackson, the last time that the banks actively intervened to fulfill a role unconnected with their own profitability was in 1992/3, when Deutsche Bank increased its shareholding in the tire producer Continental. This was undertaken in order to help the company's management rebuff a hostile takeover bid by the Italian company Pirelli (Höpner and Jackson 2001). However, by 1996 the banks were unwilling to prevent the collapse of Bremer Vulkan – Germany's largest shipbuilder – sparking mass demonstrations and protests, and a loss of 22,000 jobs. In 1999, the government was only able to secure limited bank support for a rescue of construction giant Philip Holzmann AG (and only then in conjunction with a state aid package) (Höpner and Krempel 2004). Reluctant bank support was sustained until 2002, when the banks forced the ailing company into administration, despite the efforts of regional and federal political leaders to secure a further bailout. The Holzmann collapse was the largest postwar collapse of a German company, and resulted in the loss of 24,000 jobs. The episode was emblematic of the major shift in the role that the private universal banks perceived for themselves in the "modern" German political economy (Hackethal et al. 2005: 404).

Initially, the close relationships between the public banks, credit cooperatives, and small- and medium-sized companies appeared to be unruffled by the pressures affecting private universal banks (Deeg 1999). Although the economics of lending at private universal banks began to deteriorate in the early 1990s, they did not weaken perceptibly at savings banks and *Landesbanken* until the second half of the 1990s. In fact, the savings banks claimed to have protected the German *Mittelstand* from a "credit crunch," in the face of the retreat of the large private universal banks. However, in recent years, the ability of the public savings bank sector to sustain traditional lending activities has been affected by the loss of their state guarantees and the new Basel II banking capital regulations (Fischer and Pfeil 2004: 344). A shortage of bank lending has led smaller firms to experiment with new sources of finance, for example, private equity, "mezzanine capital," asset-backed finance, and leasing (*Financial Times* 2004). These developments will increasingly expose SMEs to nonbank sources of corporate finance, and further erode the traditional relationships that underpin the German corporate network (Lane 2003: 18).

9.3 THE POLITICS OF CORPORATE GOVERNANCE IN GERMANY

One of the difficulties in examining the interlinkages of politics and corporate governance in specific countries is that corporate governance is rarely a policy area that appears in party manifestos or policy documents. It is generally regarded as a technically arcane or specialist field of policy, for which it is not necessary to establish explicit or high-profile policy positions in order to win the support of voters. For this reason, partisan stances on corporate governance are not monitored in cross-country expert analyses of manifestos undertaken by political scientists (e.g., Budge et al. [2001]). However, it is possible to detect trends in the attitude of political parties (and their core constituents, such as insider labor) to corporate governance issues. In the German case, the primary sources of information cited in this section are the policy documents of trade union economic experts, and the content of party political debates in the Bundestag relating to the introduction of legislation on corporate governance in the late 1990s and early 2000s.

Of the main German political parties, the Christian Democratic Union (CDU) – which along with its Bavarian sister party, the Christian Social Union (CSU), dominated the government of postwar Germany until the end of the 1960s – has traditionally been the most loyal political guardian of the German corporate network, and the most reflective of blockholder interests (Streeck 1997; Ziegler 2000: 203; Cioffi 2006: 551; Cioffi and Höpner 2006). The second main party of the political Right – the Free Democratic Party (FDP) – has tended to express a less supportive view of a corporate sector built on an interlocking capital network (Lambsdorff 1989: 81–2). However, the inability of the FDP to win more than around 6–12 percent of the vote in postwar federal elections has regulated them to a junior role among German conservative parties (although they have often participated in government as a part of coalitions with either the CDU or Social Democrats).

The main party of the Left – the Social Democratic Party of Germany (SPD) – has not traditionally (i.e., before the 1990s) been a notable advocate of pro-shareholder corporate governance. Prior to the Red–Green coalition of 1998, the main period of postwar SPD-led government occurred between 1969 and 1982, under the chancellorships of Willy Brandt and Helmut Schmidt.[12] The SPD approach to corporate affairs during their period of government in the 1970s was to secure workers' interests through employment protection legislation and the strengthening of works and board-level codetermination rights. However, such traditional pro-labor policies have coexisted with an alternative "anti-concentration" strand of thinking in German Social Democracy, which has proved in recent years to be surprisingly compatible with a pro-shareholder orientation (Cioffi 2006: 552).

In the 1920s, many German Social Democrats – based on their interpretation of Marxist economic ideology – developed a strong antipathy toward the

---

[12] Although the SPD also participated in a "grand coalition" with the CDU in the late 1960s, under the Chancellorship of Kurt Georg Kiesinger (CDU).

emerging German model of capitalist organization of interlocking capital ownership stakes and high levels of producer collusion (Höpner 2003: 27). An influential view was expressed by Lenin, who viewed the German economic model as a particularly undesirable variant of capitalism due to its cartelistic tendencies. The resulting economic concentration increased the capacity of capitalists to exploit the working class. In particular, Lenin highlighted the role played by banks in the system, and warned that they represented a dangerous conglomeration of economic power (Lenin 1985 [1917]: 45). These considerations justified the dismantling of the interlocking capital network – along with the banks – as an intermediate step on the road to full-blown socialism, a view that was subsequently described as "state monopoly capitalism theory" (*Staatsmonopolistischer Kapitalismus*) (Huffschmid 1995: 2; Esser 1998: 620).

During the postwar period, an antieconomic concentration perspective continued to be expressed by many on the Left. The involvement of the German corporate network – particularly the banks – with the Nazi regime discredited organized capitalism in the eyes of many trade unionists and social democrats. In their Düsseldorf manifesto of 1963, the trade unions called for the disentanglement of the corporate sector, the abolition of tax policies promoting corporate networks, and a reduction in the economic role played by banks (Haferkamp 1966: 10; Leminsky and Otto 1974: 252). This view was reflected by the SPD in its Berlin manifesto of 1989: "In order to repress the power of banks and insurance companies, we favor the disentanglement of capital ties between companies" (Sozialdemokratische Partei Deutschlands 1998: 46).

However, such an "anti-concentration" perspective was resisted by the SPD-led governments of Willy Brandt (1969–74) and Helmut Schmidt (1974–82). During these administrations, there was some discussion of reducing the power of the private universal banks. For example, the bankruptcy of the private bank Herstatt in 1974 led to the establishment of a commission on banking issues. The commission published its report in 1979, in which it suggested that banks should be forbidden to own more than 25 percent of industrial companies (Studienkommission 1979: 267). According to Höpner and Krempel (2004: 348), the government of Helmut Schmidt gave serious consideration to the idea of implementing this recommendation. However, by the time of the CDU election victory in 1982, it was still not on the statute books (Eglau 1989: 78).

Rather than attacking the power of organized capital, the SPD governments of the 1970s sought to increase the rights of employees as a counterweight to blockholder power. The Works Constitution Act of 1972 and the Codetermination Act of 1976 – discussed earlier in this chapter – were both examples of attempts to directly strengthen the position of employees within corporations. In addition, the government worked in partnership with the private universal banks in pursuit of social objectives. Banks and insurance companies were expected to intervene in cases where strategically or socially important corporations were in crisis situations or potentially vulnerable to foreign takeover, for example, high-profile cases relating to Mercedes,[13] AEG, and Gerling in the 1970s (Büschgen 1995: 596; Beyer 2002; Beyer and Höpner 2003: 190; Streeck and Höpner 2003). Furthermore, at a time when the world economy was experiencing significant economic difficulties (following the first oil price shock of 1973), the duty of the German corporate network from an SPD and insider labor perspective was to absorb and retain greater amounts of labor than would be justified according to a pure profit-maximizing strategy, in order to buffer employees from the disruptive effects of the economic downturn. Reflecting this restraint, Gregory Jackson estimates that the elasticity of employment in response to output changes in Germany was typically around one quarter of that of the United States during the postwar period (Jackson 2001: 124).

Consequently, although influential ideological strands in postwar social democracy emphasized the dangers of concentrations of economic power inherent in the blockholder model – particularly those represented by the banks – this was not the path followed by the Left in government in the 1970s. Codetermination and employment protection were viewed as the most viable policies to secure the interests of insider labor. These were practical means of resolving cross-class differences, as they secured workers' interests with minimal disruption to the existing production structure. Blockholders accepted such measures as the price to pay for the continuation of a blockholder-dominated self-regulatory system. Furthermore, it gave rise to positive externalities, for example, the maintenance of good industrial relations, and the encouragement of long-term commitments between social actors (a point which is emphasized in the Varieties of Capitalism literature). The effect of the SPD-led governments of the 1970s, therefore, was to cement a corporatist compromise between blockholders and insider labor *vis-à-vis* the existing blockholder model of corporate governance.

Corporate governance faded from the political radar in the 1980s. The SPD in opposition continued to profess a less positive view of the role of the banks and blockholders in the German economy than the CDU (Ziegler 2000: 203). But this was not an issue of active political debate. However, three factors gave renewed impetus to corporate governance in the mid-1990s. First and most

---

[13] In this notable instance, in 1974, Deutsche Bank temporarily became the majority shareholder of Mercedes-Benz with a 57.5 percent share block, following intervention at the behest of Helmut Schmidt (Büschgen 1995: 657).

importantly, a number of corporate scandals and failures came to light, for example, at Metallgesellschaft (1993), Bremer Vulkan (1996), Balsam (1994), and Jürgen Schneider AG (1994) (Vitols 2003: 253). These brought into question the ability of the existing corporate governance framework – particularly the central monitoring role of banks – to control corporate activities, and prompted a public debate on how to improve governance practices (Ziegler 2000: 203; Jackson 2003: 268). Second, the banks began to press for the development of Frankfurt as a major financial center, and sought centralization and reform of securities regulations in order to support this objective. Third, the fiscal requirements of German participation in economic and monetary union (EMU) provided an incentive for the government to engage in a large-scale program of privatization. Corporate governance became an issue of concern for government as part of the process of ensuring that the shares of privatized enterprises would be attractive to investors, thereby raising the maximum possible revenue for the state (Ziegler 2000: 206).

The response of the CDU-led government of Helmut Kohl to these new challenges was extremely limited. Some minimalist steps were taken in a more regulatory-oriented direction to placate public criticism relating to the various corporate scandals. In particular, the Second Financial Market Promotion Act of 1994 established a supervisory agency for security trading (*Bundesaufsichtsamt für den Wertpapierhandel*, BaWe) under the jurisdiction of the Federal Ministry of Finance. The main task of the new agency was the policing of new insider trading laws, and ensuring that banks and investment businesses complied with new centrally defined rules of conduct. In addition, the CDU-led government agreed in 1994 – following intense lobbying by the private universal banks – to transfer responsibility for monitoring capital markets to the federal government (from regional government), a measure which was also seen as necessary for the success of the privatization program (Lütz 1998). However, there was no appetite to engineer a substantive shift toward a shareholder system of corporate governance (Höpner 2003: 20; Cioffi 2006: 551).

Such a limited response to the issues highlighted by the corporate scandals was viewed as inadequate by policy representatives of insider labor. Economic experts at trade unions were concerned that the existing German system – based on the self-regulation of blockholders – was increasingly untenable from an insider labor perspective. The greater financial orientation of companies, the emasculation of codetermination, the reduced bargaining power of trade unions, and the unwillingness of banks to monitor management gave rise to a "corporate governance vacuum," which permitted blockholders and management to pursue their agendas independently of other social actors. The German corporate model had operated in a satisfactory manner in previous decades, despite underlying concerns regarding concentrations of economic power. However, its viability had depended on blockholders operating in a "socially enlightened" manner. If this was no longer the case, then a more robust response to the corporate scandals was required (Küller 1997: 529; Höpner 2002: 167).

Trade union officials began to accept that many aspects of pro-minority shareholder regulation were consistent with the interests of insider labor. The basis for this new viewpoint was dissatisfaction over German accounting rules. These were unhelpful to the operation of codetermination, as they reduced the transparency of corporate activities and performance (Schäfer 2000: 91). According to the German commercial code (*Handelsgesetzbuch*, HGB), management was able to exercise wide discretion over the level of reported corporate earnings, which could be adjusted in individual years through the creation or drawing down of reserves. This made it difficult for employees to understand the true financial position of the firm, and therefore play a meaningful role in codetermination. The ability to manipulate earnings was also increasingly used by management to negotiate lower wage settlements. Furthermore, during a number of the corporate collapses of the 1990s, for example, at Holzmann, the management had used reserves to cover up problems and to pursue high-risk projects, with negative implications for the job security of employees. Consequently, trade unions began to argue in favor of a shift to the international accounting standards (IAS) favored by minority shareholders, as they offered much less scope to manage corporate earnings via the use of reserves (Scheibe-Lange and Prangenberg 1997).

However, this soon led to a wider recognition among union officials of the value of pro-shareholder regulation in restraining the power of blockholders and their management. Hans-Detlev Küller, a top official of the Confederation of German Trade Unions (*Deutsche Gewerkschaftsbund*, DGB) argued that a lack of shareholder orientation among German companies was leading to their systematic undervaluation on equity markets, which competitively disadvantaged them *vis-à-vis* their Anglo-American peers. According to Küller, this was not in the long-term interests of German employees, as it made them vulnerable to takeover or restructuring (Küller 1997: 528). Heinz Putzhammer and Roland Köstler – both on the executive board of the DGB – observed that many employees were now small shareholders, and therefore deserved appropriate minority shareholder protection. Hans-Detlev Küller summed up the new attitude of many trade unions officials to corporate governance by asserting that "if the shareholder value approach is able to contribute to a reduction in the risk potential [of firms], this can only be in the interests of employees" (Küller 1997: 529).

Perhaps, the most explicit indication of how trade union thinking on corporate governance had evolved in the late 1990s to early 2000s was provided by the DGB's written response to the EU Commission's draft action plan on company law and corporate governance in 2003 (DGB 2003). In their submission, the DGB expressed unreserved support for measures that protected the interests of minority shareholders, and which enhanced their ability to participate and exercise power at shareholder meetings. The submission argued in favor of enhanced transparency in financial reporting, and for the publication of information concerning management remuneration and the underlying ownership of firms. The use of the pyramidal ownership structures – utilized by blockholders as a tool of control over corporations – was condemned. The DGB also encouraged the appointment of independent directors that could represent the interests of small shareholders (in addition to employees) on company boards, and the creation of independent audit committees. Finally, it supported the notion of shareholder democracy (one-share, one-vote) through the abolition of multiple voting shares. Such a position statement was testimony to the close identification of insider labor with many aspects of the pro-shareholder approach by the late 1990s to early 2000s.

The new politics of corporate governance emerged at the party political level during parliamentary debates prior to the enactment of the 1998 Control and Transparency Law (KonTraG)[14] in the final months of the Kohl administration. In 1997, a working group had been established within the CDU–FDP government to consider proposals for "careful corrections" to the governance of supervisory boards (in the light of ongoing public disquiet surrounding a number of corporate scandals and failures).[15] The initial recommendations of the working group were modest, and included proposals that supervisory boards should meet more often, that board members should be required to disclose their seats on other boards, and that ownership stakes of banks in industrial enterprises of greater than 5 percent should be publicly disclosed. Once again, the intention was to head off any pressure for a wide-ranging reform of blockholder self-regulation through the introduction of few additional regulatory safeguards over corporate behavior (Ziegler 2000: 203).

However, deliberations over new legislation were the catalyst for the SPD to introduce a range of counterproposals on corporate governance (Cioffi 2002). The SPD advocated a shift to a more shareholder-oriented corporate governance regime, and proposed measures to strengthen the rights and protections of

---

[14] *Gesetz zur Kontrolle und Transparenz im Unternehmensbereich* (KonTraG).

[15] Rainer Funke, parliamentary state secretary of the Justice Ministry, quoted in the *Financial Times*, (February 27, 1997: 11).

minority shareholders. Such proposals were packaged together with a number of radical "anti-bank" proposals to appeal to the SPD's "anti-concentration" political constituents, including a policy of limiting bank's ownership stakes in other enterprises to 5 percent, and ending the practice of proxy voting by banks (i.e., where banks used the voting rights of shares owned by their customers). As the private universal banks were themselves keen to withdraw from their coordinating role in the German corporate network, these were not proposals that the banks sought to oppose (Ziegler 2000: 203).

Such a profound reshaping of the German corporate network – through the empowerment of minority shareholders at the expense of blockholders – was anathema to the Christian Democrats (Ziegler 2000). However, the SPD proposals put the CDU on the defensive side; the SPD's more vigorous approach to corporate governance reform found support among a number of the traditional allies of the CDU, including its junior coalition partner (the FDP), the bosses of the private universal banks, and a number of major German multinationals.[16] However, a major reform of company law was not supported by employer associations and the bulk of owners and managers of small- and medium-sized corporate enterprises in the German company network, which represented a core political constituency of the Christian Democrats. Although such actors had acquiesced in the earlier securities law reform – which primarily affected the stock market activities of the largest listed corporations and banks – many rejected more wide-ranging company law reforms that would significantly reduce their autonomy from small shareholders. Opposition to further reform was particularly intense among owners and managers of the *Mittelstand*, who feared that further reforms would threaten family control of firms and their stable sources of credit within the established corporate network (Cioffi 2006).

The contrasting viewpoints of the political parties were expressed openly when draft legislation was debated by members of parliament in the Bundestag in March 1998. The FDP argued in favor of pro-shareholder reforms, and expressed regret that they could not push their senior coalition partner – the Christian Democrats – more strongly in that direction. The primary FDP speaker in the debate – Otto Graf Lamsdorff – argued that Germany was a "rent-seeking" society, and would benefit in terms of efficiency from the greater discipline imposed by minority shareholders and capital markets. In contrast, Joachim Gres – on behalf of the CDU – argued in favor of "constancy" in the

---

[16] Notable examples of bosses of German multinationals favoring some degree of pro-shareholder reform in the 1990s included Paul Achleitner (Allianz), Rolf E. Breuer (Deutsche Bank), Gerhard Cromme (ThyssenKrupp), Heinrich von Pierer (Siemens), and Jürgen Schrempp (DaimlerChrysler) (Beyer and Höpner 2003).

corporate structure, and denied that "Germany Inc" was based on a quasi-cartel structure. Another leading CDU spokesman – Harmut Schauerte – rejected the idea of proposals to limit the power of the banks.

The CDU position was attacked by the main speakers of the SPD – Hans-Martin Bury and Eckehard Pick – who called the proposed legislation a "placebo law," designed to appease the public following a series of corporate scandals, but not motivated by a desire for significant change. They criticized the German corporate network – particularly the interlocking directorates, the lack of transparency, the power of the banks, and the lack of exposure to capital market pressures – which served to hold back innovation. This perspective was supported by Margarete Wolf of the Green Party, and by Uwe-Ernst Heuer of the postcommunist PDS (Party of Democratic Socialism), both of whom argued that greater capital market discipline was needed in order to break down the interlocking German corporate network (Deutscher Bundestag 1998: 20354).

Outside the Bundestag, the SPD position was firmly rooted in the support of the trade unions, including the Confederation of German Trade Unions (Ziegler 2000: 204). In fact, the DGB argued that the proposed measures should go beyond listed companies, and also apply to the governance of smaller private firms, the activities of which were often opaque to outsiders. Such a lack of transparency hindered the activities of works councils in these enterprises (Bolt 2000; Köstler 2000; Höpner 2002: 170).

In order to diffuse the pro-shareholder offensive of the SPD (while retaining the support of core constituents), the CDU-led government introduced compromise legislation, which accepted a number of the SPD proposals – such as the legalization of share buybacks and stock options, and the abolition of unequal voting rights on shares. Symbolically, the new proposals also dropped the notion of the firm as a stakeholder entity, a concept that had been retained in German company law since the Stock Corporation Act of 1937 (and reaffirmed by the Federal constitutional court in 1979). These concessions were used to head off the more radical proposals of the SPD regarding reduced ownership rights for banks. The final legislation also stopped banks from voting the proxy votes of their clients if their own ownership stake exceeds 5 percent, and improved bank's disclosure regarding their shareholdings and directorates in other firms (Höpner 2003: 21).

Despite the best efforts of the CDU, the KonTraG – which passed through the Bundestag in March 1998 – represented the most significant change in German company law since 1965 (Cioffi 2006: 552). It allowed the SPD to score a significant political victory. On the one hand, they were able to use their pro-shareholder approach to present themselves as economic modernizers, and thereby reach out to new sources of support (particularly middle-class votes).

On the other, they retained the support of their core constituents – insider labor – by arguing that pro-shareholder corporate governance would undermine the interlocking and self-regulatory blockholder network and curb the concentrated economic power of blockholders. As the only party supporting the existing self-regulatory institutions of Deutschland AG, the CDU were left looking like apologists for privileged and unaccountable vested interests, an impression which contributed to their defeat in the federal elections of September 1998 (Cioffi 2006: 551).

The incoming SPD–Green government of 1998 was faced with a choice regarding how best to further curb the powers of blockholders (Höpner 2003: 23). The more radical approach – favored by many in the SPD – was to implement the earlier proposals regarding limitations on the ownership stakes of banks in industrial enterprises. A second possibility – which had been proposed during the KonTraG debate by the FDP – was to lower or abolish existing taxes on sales of corporate cross-shareholdings. Economic liberals tended to favor the latter policy pathway, as direct limitations on bank ownership were viewed as an excessively blunt and socialistic means of influencing the economic behavior of private market actors.[17]

Initially, however, it was not possible to make a definitive decision on this issue, due to a power struggle within the SPD between economic modernizers – led by the Chancellor, Gerhard Schröder – and traditionalists, such as SPD Chairman Oskar Lafontaine, who had taken the position of Finance Minister in the new government. However, the modernizers quickly moved to consolidate their power, and in March 1999, Oskar Lafontaine resigned from the cabinet.[18] The new finance minister and ally of Gerhard Schröder, Hans Eichel, then proceeded to pursue the more market-oriented solution to the problem of interlocking capital, and drafted a new tax law – known as the "Eichel Plan" – that completely abolished all capital gains tax on sales of cross-shareholdings, thereby lifting a major obstacle to the dissolution of the corporate network, and further facilitating the ability of the banks to withdraw from corporate gover-

---

[17] Based on the comments of Otto Graf Lambsdorff in the debate on the KonTraG, minutes of the Bundestag debate 13/220, March 5, 1998.

[18] The resignation of Lafontaine removed a major obstacle to a significant reorientation of Social Democratic policy across a range of policy areas. While the manifesto for the 1998 election had emphasized traditional SPD policy approaches – such as continued support of the welfare state, lower taxes for lower earners, employment protection, and social security for the unemployed – Schröder now proposed a radical new supply-side agenda. This included reductions in company taxation and employer's nonwage employment costs, reform of pensions and health care, and a commitment to a balanced budget by 2004. The broad objectives were laid out in his publication on the Third Way (*Die Neue Mitte*, cowritten with Tony Blair), and in more detail in the "Future 2000" program (*Zukunfts Programm 2000*), both launched in June 1999 (Hering 2004: 102).

nance oversight. The plan was strongly opposed by the CDU. The CDU/CSU candidate for Chancellor in the 2002 election – Edmund Stoiber – announced that he would reverse the law if elected as Chancellor (Höpner 2003: 25). There was also some disgruntlement on the Left, given that the measure would offer a large tax break to large corporations. However, traditionalist elements of the SPD parliamentary party were persuaded that this was a price worth paying, given its likely effect of dissipating concentrations of economic power in the German corporate structure.[19] As a result, the proposal passed through the Bundestag and promulgated into law in 2000.[20]

A revealing example of the differing partisan approaches to corporate regulatory reform was provided by the move of the Schröder government to create a new financial regulator in January 2001. The new regulatory body, the *Bundesanstalt für Finanzdienstleistungsaufsicht* (BaFin), was formed from the merger of three existing regulatory bodies.[21] The need for a single market regulator with greater powers was accepted across party lines, given the increasing overlap of different areas of financial services, and the lack of effectiveness of the securities market regulator (BaWe) created by the Kohl government. However, it was assumed by many commentators that this task would be assumed by the Bundesbank, which had indicated its desire to play a greater role in financial regulation (following its loss of powers over monetary policy to the European Central Bank). The controversial step of the SPD-led government was to ignore the Bundesbank's requests and establish a new institution, with direct accountability to the government and the Bundestag.[22] This step was condemned by the Bundesbank itself, which stated that "banking oversight is not suitable for the business of politics,"[23] a position that was strongly supported by the CDU and FDP in Bundestag debates and

---

[19] The left-wing of the SPD was initially suspicious of the economic modernization agenda of Gerhard Schröder, particularly as it coincided with the departure of Lafontaine from the cabinet, and the marginalization of the Left from the inner decision-making circles of the SPD (Bannas 2000). However, during the course of 2000, the Left became increasingly supportive of the new "pragmatic" approach of the government. The newly formed Democratic Left Forum – a grouping of left-leaning members of the Bundestag (led by Andrea Nahles) – was a focus of this increased willingness to cooperate with the Schröder reform program (Hering 2004: 113).

[20] 2000 Corporate Income Tax Law (*Steuersenkungsgesetz*).

[21] These included the banking regulator (*Bundesaufsichtamt für das Kreditwesen*, BaKred), the securities market regulator (*Bundesaufsichtsamt für den Wertpapierhandel*, BaWe), and the insurance regulator (*Bundesaufsichtsamt für das Versicherungswesen*, BaV).

[22] BaFin is now overseen by an Administrative Council of twenty-one members, including representatives from relevant government ministries and the Bundestag. The Bundestag also has the right to require BaFin management to appear before relevant parliamentary committees (Westrup 2007: 1101).

[23] Comments of Edgar Meister, member of the Vorstand of the Bundesbank, *Frankfurter Allgemeine Zeitung*, January 26, 2001.

parliamentary committee discussions over the next two years (Schüler 2004: 12). In contrast, the SPD-led government argued that the creation of BaFin was an important means of increasing the accountability of the financial system to political institutions. This would not have been achieved if regulatory power had been given to the Bundesbank, whose constitutional standing placed it outside the ambit of either ministerial or parliamentary control (Westrup 2007: 1096).

A further major piece of corporate governance legislation introduced by the Schröder government was the Securities Acquisition and Takeover law of 2001. This aimed to facilitate the development of a market for corporate control in Germany. Such a proposal came at a time when takeovers were becoming an increasingly contentious political issue. The hostile takeover of Mannesmann by the British firm Vodafone in 2000 had been the largest ever takeover of a German company by a foreign buyer, and had been made possible by the corporate governance changes implemented in the KonTraG law (Höpner and Jackson 2001). However, it had ignited a populist backlash against takeovers, particularly when the magnitude of severance payments to the ousted Mannesmann management was made public. This led the prosecutor's office in Düsseldorf to launch a case against the supervisory board members that had approved these payments, the most prominent of which was the CEO of Deutsche Bank, Josef Ackermann (Kolla 2004). Alongside the controversy generated by the Mannesmann affair, attempts by the European Commission to launch a European Takeover Directive foundered in the European Parliament in July 2001, with German Christian Democrat Members of European Parliament (MEPs) playing a major role in that defeat. Both these developments created a difficult environment for the introduction of takeover legislation in October 2001.

The measures proposed by SPD-led government were less radical than those contained in the European takeover directive. In particular, they permitted defensive measures, for example, poison pills, by a target company if such measures had been approved by shareholders during the preceding eighteen months, and if the defensive measures were ratified in advance of use by the supervisory board. Such proposals were acceptable to the trade unions, as the involvement of the supervisory board in this process allowed labor a role in codetermining any decision to implement defensive measures (Höpner 2003: 26). Nonetheless, the law was far from being an "antitakeover" law, and significantly facilitated the undertaking of hostile takeovers in Germany. In contrast, the CDU contended that the proposed legislation did not allow companies sufficient means to defend themselves, and proposed an increase in shareholder approval period to thirty-six months.[24] Despite these objections, the statute passed into law in November 2001.[25]

Alongside the introduction of specific measures concerning the taxing of cross-shareholding and the encouragement of a market for corporate control, the Schröder government also sought to undertake a fundamental reevaluation of German corporate governance, and consider how it could be repositioned away from the blockholder status quo. Soon after coming to power, two official commissions on corporate governance were established – consisting of both academic experts and representatives of employer and employee interests groups (the Baums commission[26] and the Cromme commission[27]). A noteworthy precondition for these discussions was the recognition that the codetermination rights of employees were not up for debate. Indeed, around the same time, the Works Constitution Act of 2001 was introduced to strengthen the position of works councils in corporate decision-making (Thelen and Kume 2003; Vitols 2003: 13; Hackethal et al. 2005: 390). The implicit remit of both commissions was clear: to identify a code of "best practice" that strengthened minority shareholders at the expense of blockholders, while respecting the position of insider labor in the power structure of the firm (Zumbansen 2007: 485).

Following a series of broad-based recommendations from the Baums commission, the Cromme commission was mandated, in 2001, with the more practical task of drafting a proposed code of corporate governance. This was modeled on the OECD principles, and proposed behavioral norms for German corporations on issues such as corporate disclosure, transparency, the role and functioning of boards, and the appointment and responsibility of auditors. Adherence to these recommendations by companies served to provide minority shareholders with rights and protections roughly equivalent to those enjoyed by their peers in a liberal market economy. Although the code was not made mandatory – contrary to the wishes of trade union negotiators on the Cromme commission – the government passed a law in 2002 requiring public limited companies to either comply or explain their deviation from these principles in their annual reports (Höpner 2003: 22).[28]

---

[24] See the report of the Parliamentary Financial Committee (*Beschlussempfehlung und Bericht des Finanzausschusses, Drucksache 14/7477*), November 14, 2001.

[25] 2001 Takeover Law (*Gesetz zur Regelung von öffentlichen Angeboten zum Erwerb von Wertpapieren und Unternehmensübernahmen*).

[26] Theodor Baums, ed., *Bericht der Regierungskommission Corporate Governance. Unternehmensführung, Unternehmenskontrolle, Modernisierung des Aktienrechts* (Cologne, Otto Schmidt 2001).

[27] Gerhard Cromme (Chairman), German Corporate Governance Code, drafted by the German Corporate Governance Commission, Berlin, February 26, 2002.

[28] 2002 Corporate Sector Transparency and Publicity Act (*Gesetz zur Transparenz und Publizität im Unternehmensbereich*, TransPuG).

By 2003, the SPD-led government had moved Germany a long way in the direction of a shareholder system of corporate governance. The corporate governance ratings calculated by Aggarwal et al. ([2007]; see Table 1.3) suggest that German corporations had achieved shareholder orientations well above those of many other European countries. Securities law largely attained the international standards of liberal market economies, and the interests of minority investors were protected to an extent unimaginable a decade earlier.[29] Large German companies operated with much higher levels of transparency, and in accordance with international norms of financial reporting. The guardians of the blockholder self-regulatory network – the private universal banks – had transformed themselves into profit-oriented institutions with no particular social or corporate monitoring role. Although corporate Germany still retained a higher level of ownership concentration than a typical liberal market economy,[30] the German corporate network of interlocking capital and directorates appeared to be undergoing a gradual process of dissolution (Beyer and Höpner 2003: 184; Hackethal et al. 2005: 390). Significantly, all of these changes occurred while sustaining the corporate governance role of insider labor (Vitols 2003: 13). In the words of Beyer and Höpner, "In the 1990s, intensified institutional change in Germany departed from the logic of organized capitalism" (Beyer and Höpner 2003: 180).

9.4 EXPLAINING CORPORATE GOVERNANCE CHANGE IN GERMANY

Section 9.3 has described how the Left in government – over a five-year period in the late 1990s to early 2000s – implemented major corporate governance changes in a shareholder direction, contrary to the preferences of their main political opponents, the Christian Democrats. How does such a pattern of change accord with the hypothesis of corporate governance change – concerning the interaction of partisanship and product market competition – presented in this book?

---

[29] Eric Nowak describes what has been achieved as follows: "Germany in 2003 has a modern and investor-oriented capital market law that is definitely able to meet international standards, and can even cope with the US regulatory framework governed by the SEC" (Nowak 2004: 448).

[30] Nonetheless, the *Financial Times* reported in 2005 that international shareholders had acquired more than 50 percent of the available free-floating shares of the firms in the DAX index of thirty largest German companies. This contrasted with negligible foreign ownership in 1990 (*Financial Times*, April 1, 2005).

This chapter has argued that differences in the levels of economic rents provide an explanation for the differing corporate governance preferences of Left governments in the 1970s and the late 1990s. In a high-rent environment, the Social Democratic governments of the 1970s were content to work with blockholder interests within the context of legally enshrined codetermination arrangements. Notwithstanding long-held concerns regarding the concentration of economic power implied by a heavily interlinked corporate network, Left parties and insider labor perceived benefits in working within the existing corporate framework. Some of these benefits were secured by legislation, for example, employment protection, codetermination rights, etc. However, many were obtained via the "enlightened" behavior of blockholder enterprises, for example, higher wages, the shielding of employees from economic volatility, and the willingness of banks to intervene to rescue ailing companies and support employment.

The evidence presented in this case study also suggests that the attitude of insider labor and Left political parties toward blockholders became significantly more negative in the 1990s. The declining availability of economic rents rendered blockholders – particularly the universal banks – less willing to secure the acquiescence of insider labor (through the sharing of economic rents), with the consequence that insider labor (and the Left) perceived blockholders as uncooperative social partners. The accommodation with blockholder interests pursued by SPD governments in the 1970s hence became increasingly untenable. The breakdown of this corporatist compromise between social actors has been succinctly described by Reinhard Schmidt:

The traditional German corporate governance system relied to a large extent on compatible mutual expectations, on long-term cooperation, and on implicit deals with a give-and-take between parties that know each other and to a certain extent trust each other. Recent developments suggest the basis for this kind of cooperation has disappeared (Schmidt 2004: 419).

The political opportunity that was grasped by policy entrepreneurs in the SPD was to link a growing antipathy toward blockholders and banks among insider labor with the adoption of pro-shareholder governance reforms. Pro-shareholder corporate governance reforms were also likely to appeal to influential elements within the "outsider" stakeholder group, for example, the middle class, which were growing in electoral significance in the 1990s. Such reforms could also be sold to the Left's core constituents as representing an effective means of undermining the concentrations of power in the German corporate network. Furthermore, they shifted regulatory power over corporate governance from blockholders to the state, which increased the accountability of corporate governance to political actors (Westrup 2007: 1112). In contrast, the ability of the Christian Democrats to adopt pro-shareholder policies was constrained by the continued importance of blockholder interests among their core constituents (Cioffi 2006: 557). Ultimately, it was easier for the SPD to reconcile its core constituents to pro-shareholder reform than the CDU. This allowed it to reach out to outsiders as economic modernizers more effectively than the CDU, and win political support for a pro-shareholder stance (Cioffi and Höpner 2006).

In summary, the hypothesis of this book – concerning the interaction of Left government and product market competition in the determination of corporate governance change – appears to hold up well in a longitudinal analysis of German corporate governance change. In terms of the analytical framework of Chapter 2, the changes that occurred during the 1998–2003 period served to redistribute power from blockholders to outsiders. However, such a shift has not necessarily implied that Germany has converged on a pure shareholder system of corporate governance. Such a change would require minority shareholders to have assumed a supreme position *vis-à-vis* other stakeholders (Schmidt 2004: 406).

The continued importance of insider labor represents a political obstacle to the achievement of such an ideal-type corporate governance system (Jackson 2003: 297). Although insider labor has been a key actor involved in the empowerment of minority shareholders at the expense of blockholders, it is unlikely to support further pro-shareholder measures that undermine its own position in corporate authority structures.[31] For example, a fully functioning market for corporate control – based entirely on the ownership preferences of outsider capital (and without the safeguards of the 2001 takeover law) – would represent a threat to labor codetermination of enterprises, as supervisory boards would no longer be able to approve takeover defenses (Höpner 2003: 8). Consequently, it would be implausible to expect insider labor to support measures that went further in that direction.[32]

---

[31] For example, in 2005, Gerhard Schröder appointed a commission – at the request of employer associations – to examine the continued viability of codetermination. However, discussions terminated in November 2006 when the chairman of the commission – Kurt Biedenkopf – announced that agreement could not be reached between employer and employee groups. In particular, the Confederation of German Trade Unions (DGB) could not accept the proposals of the Confederation of German Employers' Associations (*Bundesvereinigung der deutschen Arbeitgeberverbände*, BDA) and the Federation of German Industries (*Bundesvereinigung der Deutschen Industrie*, BDI) for a reduction in employee representation on supervisory boards from one-half to one-third (Vogel 2007).

[32] Although the Social Democrats and Greens remained in government until 2005, corporate governance faded as a major political issue in Germany after 2003. There has also been little appetite for further corporate governance reform since the advent of the "grand coalition" of the CDU and SPD in November 2005 (Cioffi 2006: 556). This suggests that the limits of pro-shareholder corporate governance reform for the Left may already have been reached.

However, for the time being at least, a new social equilibrium between contesting social actors has been reached (Hackethal et al. 2005: 405). This has resulted in a "hybrid" regime[33] of corporate governance, which combines elements of the shareholder and blockholder ideal types, but is distinct from both (Vitols 2003: 6; Deeg 2001; Jackson et al. 2005: 42). The shareholder is now stronger in Germany, but not yet victorious.

---

[33] This new style of corporate governance is described by Sigurt Vitols as "negotiated shareholder value" (Vitols 2003: 16).

10

The Case of Italy: Everything Changes, Everything Stays the Same

"If we want things to stay as they are, things will have to change."
From *The Leopard* (*Il Gattopardo*) by Giuseppe Tomasi di Lampedusa (1958).

On the face of it, the German and Italian experiences of corporate governance reform in the late 1990s exhibit certain similarities. Both took place under the aegis of Left governments, and both appeared to involve a shift in a pro-shareholder direction. However, corporate governance outcomes in the two countries differed in one key respect. Whereas in Germany the introduction of new law and regulation translated into significant firm-level corporate governance change, this was not the case in Italy. An insider-oriented system of corporate governance remained in place, with blockholders sustaining their dominant position vis-à-vis minority shareholders.

For Pepper Culpepper (2007: 796), the impotence of *de jure* corporate governance reform in Italy poses significant problems for political explanations of corporate governance. Most political theories view policy change as a key intermediate step in the causal pathway from the political preferences of social actors to actual economic or political outcomes. For example, Gourevitch and Shinn's framework (2005) describes how changes in political coalitions of social actors leads to changes in policy, which in turn affects actual outcomes. Similarly, the argument presented by Cioffi and Höpner (2006) assumes that Left government tends to favor pro-shareholder corporate governance, which in turn impacts on *de facto* corporate behavior due to the policy initiatives of Left government.

The Italian experience also appears to represent a paradox for the argument of this book. On the one hand, the absence of firm-level corporate governance change in Italy is consistent with its theoretical expectations. Italian product markets were significantly less competitive than those of Germany in the late 1990s, with the implication that high levels of economic rents were still available to producers. Consequently, an outcome of limited *de facto* corporate governance change – notwithstanding the incumbency of the Left in

The Case of Italy: Everything Changes, Everything Stays the Same 257

government – is in line with the predictions of the hypothesis. On the other hand, pro-shareholder regulatory measures were introduced in Italy, apparently under the banner of a Center–Left government. Such an apparent divergence between *de facto* and *de jure* outcomes demands an explanation.

According to the hypothesis outlined in Chapter 2, firm-level corporate governance is unlikely to shift in a shareholder direction in an environment of high economic rents for two reasons. First, the sharing of economic rents between blockholders and insider labor ensures that partisan actors remain favorably disposed toward the blockholder model. In particular, Left parties are willing to tolerate a self-regulatory blockholder system due to the fact that their core constituents (insider labor) also benefit from such a system (e.g., through greater employment stability and higher wages). Second, it is more difficult for governments to translate *de jure* corporate governance reform into changes in *de facto* outcomes in a high-rent environment. High economic rents increase the private benefits of control to blockholders, and therefore make them less willing to relinquish power over their firms to minority shareholders. Consequently, the intensity of regulatory reform needed to achieve a given level of *de facto* corporate governance change – particularly in relation to the resources required to enforce that regulation – will be greater than in an economy with lower levels of economic rents.

In this chapter, it is argued that high levels of economic rents inhibited actual corporate governance change for both of these reasons. Pro-shareholder corporate governance reform was not the policy preference of insider labor or Left political actors (unlike in Germany). Pro-shareholder legislation did appear, but for reasons exogenous to party politics. Empowered by the widely supported objective of securing Italian participation in economic and monetary union (EMU), technocratic actors temporarily dominated the policy-making process during the 1990s, and were able to push through shareholder-friendly legislation on the grounds of its ability to assist in the fulfillment of the Maastricht convergence criteria (Deeg 2005: 541). However, this was a largely cosmetic exercise. Due to both a lack of underlying support from party actors and their core constituents, and a judicial system with limited enforcement capabilities, the introduction of additional pro-shareholder regulation did not make a substantive difference to *de facto* corporate governance outcomes. Nonetheless, it achieved its primary purpose of helping to secure Italian entry into EMU.

This chapter is structured differently from the previous case study in that there is no intention to trace the changing corporate governance preferences of political actors and their core constituents over time (i.e., in the form of a historical or longitudinal case study). Rather, the objective is to offer a cross-sectional comparison with the German experience of corporate governance reform in the late 1990s (when both countries experienced apparently similar stripes of government). The rest of the chapter is structured as follows. In the first section, the distinctive nature of postwar Italian corporate governance is outlined, particularly in relation to that of Germany. This is followed by a description of the corporate governance reforms of the Prodi government in the late 1990s, and an evaluation of their impact on firm-level corporate governance behavior. In the third section, the context of Italy's bid for EMU membership is examined. The purpose of this section is to demonstrate how technocrats came to dominate Italian politics in the early to mid-1990s at the expense of party political actors, and to emphasize the overriding importance of the EMU factor in the design of economic policy. In the final section, the strength of this exogenous factor is used to explain why pro-shareholder corporate governance was introduced in Italy, even in an environment of uncompetitive product markets. The chapter concludes by arguing that higher levels of competition remain a key precondition for the realization of a greater outsider orientation in the actual corporate governance behavior of Italian corporations.

10.1 THE NATURE OF POSTWAR CORPORATE GOVERNANCE IN ITALY

"The Italian economic model, characterized by family capitalism, a weak state, enormous budget deficits, and an amazing vitality among SMEs, is unique, except for perhaps the economy of the Chinese diaspora" (Albert 1993). Michel Albert's description of Italian capitalism provides an indication of the difficulties involved in classifying the Italian political economy relative to that of other industrialized democracies. In terms of Hall and Soskice's Varieties of Capitalism schema, Italy is placed in the "mixed" or "Mediterranean" category (along with France, Spain, Portugal, and Greece), whose typical features are a relatively large agricultural sector, a high level of state intervention, and relatively liberal arrangements in labor relations (Rhodes 1997; Hall and Soskice 2001: 19). However, Italy exhibits considerable variation in economic structure between regions, sectors, and types of firm (Contarino 2000: 175).

Since the early 1970s, the Italian corporate sector has been characterized by a production structure with a notably large number of small producers, a moderate number of medium-sized enterprises, and a relatively small number of large corporations (OECD 2000b: 158). According to De Cecco (2007), such an industrial structure partly arose due to the application of strict employment protection laws in the 1970s, which applied to larger firms (employing more than fifteen workers) but not smaller enterprises. This created an incentive to break down production into small units, and to specialize in low-technology, light industrial goods, particularly in the export-oriented textile and fashion sectors. Such sectors benefited from an abundance of relatively cheap and well-trained labor, and were assisted in their export activities – at least until the 1990s – by a policy of periodic currency devaluations (De Cecco 2007: 767).

A central role in the Italian corporate governance system has been played by families (Aganin and Volpin 2003; Pagano and Trento 2002; Melis 2006). This has been true of both small- and -medium-sized companies (SMEs), and larger companies. The former (as in most countries) are overwhelmingly directly owned and controlled by families or founding entrepreneurs. The latter – although more likely to be listed and traded on stock markets (with minority shareholders amongst their ownership base) – have often also remained under the control of prominent families (the so-called *salotto buono*, such as the Agnelli, Pirelli, and Marzotto dynasties of northern Italy). Family-owned holding companies have sustained a high level of control over Italian listed companies either by retaining large direct ownership positions in individual enterprises, or through techniques such as pyramidal ownership structures and nonvoting shares, which permit the retention of control with relatively small ownership stakes. The latter mechanisms of control – although not unique to Italy – have been particularly evident in the Italian corporate sector relative to other European economies (Bianchi et al. 2001: 154). According to Amatori and Colli (2000: 14), almost all of the firms listed on the Italian stock market, as of the early 1990s, were effectively controlled by nine large industrial holding groups through a mixture of these types of control mechanisms.

Reflecting the dominance of blockholders, the boards of large public companies have mainly been staffed by insiders – such as family members, former managers, and other allies – whose loyalty has been cemented by cross-shareholdings or shareholder alliances. Corporate strategies and activities have remained opaque to external actors. Furthermore, minority shareholders have had few rights or means of representing their interests on boards. Even more so than in Germany, the Italian corporate system has exhibited the classic characteristics of an insider of corporate governance, that is, elite blockholder interests seeking to sustain their self-regulation of corporate enterprises, with a minimum of interference from other actors, such as minority shareholders or even the state (Segreto 1997; Deeg 2005).

Given such an insider-oriented business environment, it is not surprising that capital markets remained relatively undeveloped in postwar Italy. According to Amatori and Colli, only 217 firms were listed on the stock market at the end of the 1980s, and the stock market's share of national income was low compared to other developed economies (Amatori and Colli 2000: 12; see Chapter 4, Section 4.1.2). Rather than turn to capital markets for the investment capital, firm's main sources of external funding were family members or allies within relevant insider networks (Cobham et al. 1999: 327). Furthermore, the government bond market in Italy – inflated by many years of government deficits – tended to absorb the economy's surplus savings, thereby "crowding out" the development of a public equity market (Guiso and Jappelli 2000).

Although the German and Italian systems both gave rise to "patient capital," in which corporate managers were shielded from the necessity of short-term shareholder value maximization, key differences have characterized the corporate environments of the two countries. First, the state played a more significant direct role in corporate ownership in Italy for much of the postwar period. From the early 1930s onward, large direct shareholdings in Italian companies were held through its holding company, IRI (*Istituto per la Ricostruzione Industriale*), particularly in the energy, steel, chemicals, and banking sectors. Even in the early 1990s, all of the major commercial banks were still under state ownership, along with the extensive savings bank sector (Della Sala 2004: 1045).

Second, Italian banks have no tradition of close *Hausbank* or tutelage relationships with industrial corporations. In contrast to the universal banking model of the large German banks, banks in Italy were heavily restricted in their activities by extensive state regulations for much of the postwar period. These restrictions required them to focus on the provision of short-term loans, with longer-term loans being the province of state-directed special credit institutes. Such a limited role for banks was also caused (until 1993) by state prohibitions regarding bank ownership of shares in nonfinancial companies, and a ban on the participation of bank representatives on company boards.[1] Consequently, banks have not played the same kind of monitoring role in Italian corporate governance as in Germany. The monitoring role has been undertaken by controlling shareholders directly, or by other associated members of corporate networks (Amatori and Colli 2000: 12; De Cecco 2007: 778).

A notable exception to the generalizations mentioned earlier about the weakness of commercial banks was provided by the Milanese investment bank, Mediobanca. From the 1960s onward, this unique institution operated as an independent coordinator and deal-maker for many blockholder inter-

---

[1] Bank ownership of company shares was effectively prohibited by the banking reform of 1936 (De Cecco and Ferri 2001).

The Case of Italy: Everything Changes, Everything Stays the Same

ests, particularly the cluster of major industrial firms in northern Italy known as the "Northern Galaxy." The founder of Mediobanca (Enrico Cuccia) was, until his death in 2000, one of the most influential operators in the secretive world of postwar Italian capitalism. Although owned for many years by state-controlled banks, Mediobanca was partially privatized in the late 1980s. However, this did not displace it from its central role in Italian capitalism; privatization simply allowed blockholder allies to buy direct ownership stakes, and contribute representatives to the Mediobanca board of directors (Deeg 2005: 528).

A final area of difference between the Italian and German corporate governance systems relates to the differing organizational structure of insider labor in the two countries. Reflecting the organizational fragmentation of the corporate sector, Italian organized labor has lacked cohesiveness and organizational unity (Rigby and Aledo 2001). Partisan and ideological divisions have made it difficult for the three trade union confederations – the CGIL (*Confederazione Generale Italiana del Lavoro*, which was traditionally linked to the Communist Party), the CISL (*Confederazione Italiana Sindacati Lavoratori*, the Christian Democrats), and the UIL (*Unione Italiana del Lavoro*, the Socialist Party) – to present a united front in their negotiations with employers. Despite attempts in the 1970s to develop national-level corporatist structures of collective bargaining (*concertazione*) along the lines of the German model, the divergent perspectives of labor actors led to their formal abandonment in the early 1980s. In addition, there was no tradition of formal labor participation in corporate decision-making through codetermination mechanisms, either at the level of the board or the plant (Trento 2005: 227).

However, this has not meant that insider labor in Italy has been a powerless social actor. First, employment protection legislation in Italy is amongst the most stringent of all Organisation for Economic Co-operation and Development (OECD) countries (see Chapter 2, Figure 2.4). The Worker's Statute (*Statuto dei Diritti dei Lavoratori*) of 1970 established a high level of job security for workers (following a period of substantial industrial unrest), while the *Cassa Integrazione Straordinaria* measure of 1975 provided employees with significant income protection in the event of corporate restructuring. In addition, the scala *mobile* reform, also enacted in 1975, guaranteed 100 percent indexation of worker's wages (Locke and Baccaro 1996: 5). Second, trade unions have exercised considerable influence over firms on a decentralized basis through local-level bargaining. During the late 1970s and 1980s, a number of new firm or regional-level union organizations emerged (e.g., the so-called autonomous unions and the *Comitati di Base*), which engaged in wide-ranging negotiations with employers in respect of restructuring and shifts in work organization. Such unions often represented the functional equivalent of works councils in Germany, although their activities also served to undermine the national-level bargaining position of the three main union confederations (Baglioni and Milani 1990; Locke and Baccaro 1996: 9).

Insider labor was, therefore, able to secure its interests (and hence a share of economic rents) through a mixture of legislative protections and decentralized bargaining (rather than through institutionalized corporatist negotiations structures, as in Germany) (Molina 2006: 647). Furthermore, despite a lack of cohesion, Italian unions have benefited from an even greater degree of disunity amongst Italian employers. The employer's peak association (Confindustria) has traditionally been riven by divisions of interest – particularly between large companies and SMEs – and has consequently been ineffective in lobbying against the attempts of the trade union confederations (which have enjoyed strong connections with political parties) to secure protections for insider labor through the legislative process (Molina and Rhodes 2007b: 241).

10.2 REFORM OF ITALIAN CORPORATE GOVERNANCE?

The most significant legislative reform in Italian corporate governance of the 1990s was the Uniform Code for the Governance of Capital Markets[2] of 1998, known as the Draghi Law. This legislation was based on the report of a government commission on corporate governance under the chairmanship of Mario Draghi (the Director-General of the Italian Treasury). The key measures of the new law were as follows (Deeg 2005: 522):

- A lowering to 2 percent of the threshold at which equity shareholdings should be made public and reported to the stock market regulator.
- An obligation to make public the existence of shareholder agreements, that is, pacts pledging several large shareholders to create an effective blocking or controlling group, and the banning of antitakeover pacts.
- The regulation of insider trading.
- The enabling of investors to solicit and vote proxies at shareholders meetings.
- A lowering of the size of ownership stake – from 20 percent to 10 percent – at which minority shareholders could force a special shareholders' meeting.
- An increase in the role of external auditors in monitoring management.

[2] *Testo Unico delle disposizioni in materiali di mercati finanziari*, Legislative Decree 24/02/98, No. 58. The Law was passed in February 1998, and came into effect in July 1998 (Deeg 2005: 545).

The securities regulator – CONSOB (*Commisione Nazionale per le Società e la Borsa*) – was given formal powers to implement the law. Furthermore, in 1999, an Italian corporate governance code (the Preda Code) was issued by the Italian Stock Exchange (*Borsa Italiana*) on a non-compulsory "comply or explain" basis. The code addressed an issue not covered by the Draghi law, namely, the structure and remuneration of company boards of directors. It was subsequently revised and reissued in 2002 (Melis 2006: 55).

The legislative change of the late 1990s – particularly the Draghi law – strengthened the formal rights and protections of minority shareholders in Italian companies. However, the extent of the reform measures should not be exaggerated. The Draghi law also contained anti-shareholder elements, for example, allowing management to adopt takeover defenses (albeit with shareholder approval), which had not previously been permissible (Portolano 2000). Furthermore, class actions on behalf of minority shareholders remained inadmissible in Italy, and there were still no procedures in civil law whereby investors could recover money lost through corporate malfeasance (Delaney 2004; Djankov et al. 2008).

According to Djankov et al. (2008), Italy's score for LLSV's antidirector rights index was still only 2.0 in 2003 (i.e., well after the Draghi reforms), compared with a value of 3.5 for Germany and 5.0 for the United Kingdom.[3] Italy failed to record a shareholder-friendly score in four of the six subcategories of the index (vote by mail, shares not deposited, cumulative voting, and oppressed minority mechanisms).[4] A significant difference remaining between the Italian and German regulatory frameworks was that shareholder meetings could be called with 5 percent of shareholder votes in Germany, compared with a 10 percent requirement in Italy. In addition, nonvoting or unequal voting shares, giving rise to a deviation from the principle of "one-share one-vote," were outlawed as part of the late 1990s reforms in Germany, but remained a legal and widely used control mechanism in Italy.

Another source of regulatory weakness in Italy related to the mechanisms specified by the Preda code regarding board membership. Although recom-

---

[3] Aganin and Volpin (2003) have claimed that Italy went from a score of 1 to 5, a level similar to that of the United Kingdom and the United States (Aganin and Volpin 2003; Pagano and Volpin 2005). However, Djankov et al. (2008) argue that this fails to distinguish between legislation that "enables" shareholder protections to be adopted by company bylaws, and those that "require" such protections to be enforced. It should be noted that LLSV's index of antidirector rights has shortcomings as an aggregate measure of shareholder protection, which are discussed in Chapter 4.

[4] For a detailed description and critique of La Porta et al.'s antidirector rights index (1998), see Chapter 4, sections 4.2.1 and 4.2.2.

mending the inclusion of an "adequate" number of independent board members, the code did not specify how many this would mean in practice, or advise splitting the roles of chairman and managing director (despite the fact that Italian corporations – in contrast to those in Germany – had a unitary board structure). Nor was there a stipulation for a separate nomination committee to determine the membership of boards (unlike in the German code of corporate governance). These omissions assumed particular importance during the Parmalat scandal in 2003 (discussed later), and led the *Financial Times* to conclude that "the board thus remains a weak check and balance on management [in Italy]" (*Financial Times* April 12, 2004).

However, despite these caveats, the Draghi reforms still represented an overall improvement in the *de jure* position of minority shareholders in Italy. Of more concern than the policy changes themselves was the fact that firm-level corporate governance behavior exhibited little response to the new legislation (Enriques 2003; Della Sala 2004; Ferrarini 2004; Deeg 2005: 523; Ferrarini et al. 2005; Ventoruzzo 2005; Culpepper 2007: 795; Mengoli et al. 2007). Despite the Draghi law and other related measures, incumbent blockholders continued to dominate Italian corporations and pay little regard to the interests of minority shareholders. Legal changes failed to provide sufficient incentive for them to relinquish this position, either through a divestment of their ownership stakes or by encouraging a greater shareholder orientation on behalf of their corporate managers.

In order to illustrate the continued dominance of blockholders, Table 10.1 presents the results of an analysis of the ownership structure of the thirty largest Italian corporations by Pepper Culpepper (2007). This shows that, although overall corporate ownership became more widely dispersed between 1996 and 2005, this decline was entirely due to the impact of privatized firms. In contrast, non-privatized companies remained dominated by blockholders to the same extent as in the 1990s (Culpepper 2007: 791). In other words, the only blockholder that reduced its position of ownership and control over the period was the state. Such a finding is supported by Corrado and Zollo (2006). These authors undertook a structural network analysis of Italian ownership networks, comparing the situation in 1990 to that of 2000, and found that the impact of the corporate governance reforms on ownership networks (other than those of the newly privatized entities) was, at most, marginal (Corrado and Zollo 2006: 342).

Melis (2006), however, reports that certain changes have occurred in the ownership structure of Italian listed companies over the last decade. Based on data from the securities regulator (CONSOB), he finds that the number of listed companies owned by shareholders with more than 50 percent of

The Case of Italy: Everything Changes, Everything Stays the Same

Table 10.1 Average ownership concentration of thirty largest Italian companies, 1996–2005

	1996	2000	2004/5	Change (%) 1996–2004/5
Ownership concentration	43.7	35.6	33.0	−24.5
Ownership concentration excluding privatized companies	32.4	34.4	33.2	+2.5

Source: Culpepper (2007: 791). Original data collected from company reports and the Amadeus database for 2000 and 2004/5; most data from 1996 comes from the database of La Porta et al. (1999).

company shares, that is, majority controlled, declined from 67 percent to 33 percent between 1996 and 2004. However, the number of firms under the "effective control" of blockholders – that is, where the largest shareholder owns less than 50 percent of the shares, but still effectively controls the company – more than tripled over the same period. Such effective control was made possible through shareholder alliances between large shareholders. In such cases, the controlling shareholder owns less than 50 percent of the shares, but can rely on the support of other large shareholders to retain control over the firm. Such shareholder alliances are sometimes formalized through explicit documented agreements. However, contrary to the stipulations of the Draghi reforms, they are more frequently informal in nature. Analogously to pyramidal holding company structure and nonvoting shares, such arrangements allow blockholders to reduce the size of their ownership stakes in individual companies without suffering any loss of control (Melis 2006: 49; Michaels 2007).[5]

A similar increase in the use of shareholder alliances is reported by Bianchi and Bianco (2006). According to their study, use of the traditional methods of sustaining blockholder control – majority ownership stakes, pyramidal ownership structures, and nonvoting shares – declined between 1990 and 2005. However, shareholder coalitions have substantially increased in importance. As of 2005, they estimate them to be in operation with respect to almost 50 percent of listed companies. The use of shareholder coalitions has been particularly prevalent amongst newly privatized companies (such as banks), which have less ownership concentration than non-privatized companies – as

---

[5] In a study of seventy-four shareholder agreements between 1998 and 2003, Gianfrate (2007) found that alliances controlled an average of 50 percent of the voting shares of each company, and 90 percent of the board memberships.

illustrated in Table 10.1 – but are equally controlled by blockholders due to the presence of shareholder alliances. Consequently, although recently privatized enterprises may appear to represent an area of the economy in which the earlier stranglehold of blockholders has waned, such an impression is illusory due to the existence of shareholder agreements (Bianchi and Bianco 2006: 6–17). These observations support Cullpepper's conclusion (2007: 796) that "Italy was in 1995, and remains in 2007, a system in which a small number of shareholders continue to exercise control over most of the companies listed on the stock exchange."

The dominance of blockholders has been bolstered by lack of governmental capacity to enforce new legislation. According to Deeg (2005: 537), the new corporate governance code and transparency rules were largely ignored by listed firms. The ability of the regulatory authorities – particularly CONSOB and the Bank of Italy – to enforce minority shareholder protection was limited, and widely criticized by foreign investors (Edmondson 2004; Israely 2004). CONSOB was poorly staffed and funded, and unable to impose fines, investigate insider trading, demand internal documents from firms under investigation, or bring criminal charges on its own account (Barber 2004; McHugh 2004).[6] Furthermore, Kapner finds evidence that it was not just a question of too few resources; the regulator was, as a matter of principal, reluctant to enforce the legal rules protecting minority shareholders against blockholders (Kapner 2002). The prevailing view amongst minority shareholders (particularly foreign investors) remains that it is both difficult and costly to defend shareholder rights through the regulators and the courts (Kruse 2007: 766). This is reflected in the fact that the "new" legislation has yet to be tested in court to any significant extent (Kapner 2003; Barucci and Falini 2005).

The collapse of Parmalat in 2003 provides a case study of the inability of minority shareholders to enforce the rights obtained from the Draghi reforms. Parmalat was an internationally significant dairy company quoted on the Milan stock exchange. As of 2000, it was amongst the thirty largest corporations in Italy. The Tanzi family owned a 50.02 percent stake in a pyramidal holding company, Parmalat Finanzana, which in turn controlled the rest of the Parmalat corporate empire. However, Parmalat collapsed in 2003 when it emerged that the Tanzi family had fraudulently extracted around €13 billion from the company over a period of years (Delaney 2004). Parmalat

---

[6] At the time of the Parmalat scandal in 2003, CONSOB had a staff of about 400, less than 20 percent of the number employed at the United Kingdom's Financial Services Authority (Barber 2004). However, since 2006, the reputation of CONSOB has been improving amongst market participants (Michaels and Barber 2006).

– like most other Italian companies – did not comply with the provisions of the Preda code regarding internal controls and independent directors (Melis 2006: 66). Furthermore, it proved extremely difficult for both private and public actors to hold controlling shareholders to account through enforcement of the new corporate governance laws (Ferrarini 2004; Ferrarini and Giudici 2006). Enriques (2003), for example, provides evidence that the court in Milan (the foremost court in Italy for corporate law cases) was loath to rule against controlling shareholders during the crisis. This finding is consistent with Enriques' earlier analysis of corporate law proceedings in Milan, where he found the court to be highly deferential to the interests of controlling shareholders (Enriques 2002). Similar legal problems emerged in respect of the bankruptcy of Cirio – another large food company – that collapsed in 2002 (Culpepper 2007: 792).

The Draghi changes also did little to promote the development of an open market for corporate control in Italy. Olivetti's takeover of Telecom Italia in 1999 was initially seen as an encouraging sign. Telecom Italia had been formed in 1994 from the merger of several state-owned telecommunications companies. Following privatization in 1997, Telecom Italia's management had been criticized due to its lack of commercial direction. The takeover by Olivetti – a much smaller Italian technology company – was seen as symbolic of a new way of doing business in Italy. Dwayne Woods (2000: 153) writes, for example, that "Olivetti's successful takeover of Telecom Italia was an astonishing feat that represents a significant change in Italian and European capitalism."

However, on closer examination, the Telecom Italia takeover was fully consistent with the "old ways of doing things." Following the privatization in 1997, the state retained a 3.4 percent "golden share" in the company, and placed a further 9 percent of the shares with "reliable" shareholders such as the Agnelli family and several public banks. These ownership stakes allowed the Italian government to rebuff a foreign bid for the ailing company – from Deutsche Telecom – in favor of a highly speculative bid from Olivetti, whose market capitalization was seven times smaller than that of Telecom Italia. Olivetti's key advantage in the eyes of authorities was that it was a domestic player. Subsequently, Olivetti was able to gain control of Telecom Italia with only 3.2 percent of the shares through an elaborate pyramidal structure. A key player in ensuring the success of Olivetti's bid was Mediobanca, one of the key coordinators of Italian blockholder capitalism. The Telecom Italia takeover, therefore, hardly represented the emergence of an open market for corporate control in Italy, but rather a realignment of resources within the existing Italian corporate structure (McCann 2000: 57).

The ineffectiveness of legislation designed to promote an effective market for corporate control was further emphasized by the Fazio affair in 2005.

During that year, it emerged that the long-serving Governor of the Bank of Italy – Antonio Fazio – had used his office to veto the takeover of an Italian bank (*Banca Antonveneta*) by ABN AMRO, a Dutch bank, in favor of a domestic acquirer (*Banca Popolare Italiana*). Such favoritism ignited significant criticism from the European Commission and the European Central Bank and, in December 2005, Fazio resigned from the Governorship (notwithstanding the lifetime tenure attached to the position)[7] (Barber 2006).

Given the impotence of the new corporate governance legislation, should one conclude that Italian capitalism is entirely unchanged relative to the early 1990s? That conclusion would be exaggerated, as there have been two substantive changes to the corporate structure. First, although the state retains levers of influence throughout the corporate sector, for example, through "golden shares," privatization has substantially reduced the direct ownership role of the state in the economy. This is obviously a major change. Second, the banking sector has undergone a major restructuring. In 1992, the public sector controlled 70 percent of bank assets. However, as a result of privatization, this declined to 12 percent by 1999. Furthermore, the shift to the private sector was associated with a substantial consolidation of the banking sector into a small number of large financial groups.[8] However, neither of these changes has exerted a substantial effect on corporate governance behavior. As has been discussed, privatization led to a slight increase in ownership concentration amongst newly privatized firms. But this did not translate into greater power for minority shareholders. With respect to the restructuring of the banking system, the effect was limited by the fact that banks anyway never played a central role in coordinating blockholder interests in Italy (unlike in Germany) (Deeg 2005: 541).

Since the fall of the Prodi government in October 1998, the progress of corporate governance reform in Italy has been slow. Even the Parmalat affair of 2003 – the worst corporate governance scandal yet experienced in Europe – has had a limited effect in catalyzing further reforms (Cova 2005). A measure introduced in 2004 allowed companies greater choice over their style of board structure. Companies can now choose between the traditional Italian model, with a board of statutory auditors; a British-style

---

[7] Despite a high level of support from within the Berlusconi-led coalition, Fazio's position eventually became untenable. In mid-December 2005, the European Commission issued the Italian government with a "letter of formal notice," which required Rome to explain its regulatory framework for banking takeovers, the first step in the process of launching a legal challenge at the European Court of Justice (*Financial Times*, December 13, 2005).

[8] As of 2007, these had consolidated into two large groups: the Unicredit Group (created from the merger of Unicredito Italiano and Banca Commerciale Italiana) and Intesa Sanpaolo SpA (created from the merger of Banca Intesa and Sanpaolo IMI) (De Cecco 2007: 779).

board, with an independent audit committee; or a German dual board (Ventoruzzo 2005). However, Melis reports that few companies have used the law to change the structure of their boards, and the measure does nothing to address the fundamental problems raised by the Parmalat collapse (Melis 2006: 63). Other initiatives undertaken by the Center–Right Berlusconi government – such as the government's partial decriminalization of false accounting, the reduction of the statute of limitations from 4.5 to 3 years, and the elimination of the estate tax – are more designed to support blockholders than promote pro-shareholder reform (Moretti 2003; Deeg 2005: 536). The second administration of Romano Prodi – in power from May 2006 until January 2008 – was also unable to enact further significant corporate governance reform.

10.3 EMU AND THE EMPOWERMENT OF THE TECHNOCRATS

At the start of the 1990s, the Italian political system was convulsed by three major shocks. First, the exposure of the widespread corruption of the political class – known as *Tagentopoli* – which culminated in the *Mani pulite* ("clean hands") investigation of 1992, and destroyed many of the mainstream political parties. Second, the collapse of international communism, which allowed the main party of the Italian Left to transform itself into a political force that could realistically participate in government. And finally, the adoption of a new electoral system – following a referendum in 1993 – which shifted Italy from proportional to more majoritarian electoral rules, and increased the incentive of both the Left and Right to polarize into competing coalitions in order to win political power[9] (Tocci 2000: 78; Bardi 2007: 711).

The combined effect of these changes was to permit the emergence of new political actors on both the Left and Right of the political spectrum. On the Center–Right, the Christian Democratic Party (*Democrazia Cristiana, DC*) – which dominated postwar Italian government prior to the 1990s – was fatally wounded by the political scandals, and dissolved into various smaller political groupings.[10] The opportunity created by its demise was grasped by media oligarch Silvio Berlusconi, who created *Forza Italia* as a new party of the

---

[9] The 1993 reform assigned three-quarters of seats through single-member plurality districts, with the remainder allocated by proportional representation. A 4 percent national threshold was set for parliamentary representation (Bardi 2007: 711).

[10] A similar fate befell the other political parties – the so-called *Pentapartito* – that supported the Christian Democrats in coalition government prior to the early 1990s: the Italian Socialist

Center–Right in December 1993. On the Left, the Communist Party (*Partito Comunista Italiano, PCI*) – which despite significant historical support[11] had been blocked by the Christian Democrats from postwar governmental involvement – also dissolved into two new parties in 1991: the Communist Refoundation Party (*Partito della Rifondazione Comunista, PRC*) and the more moderate Democratic Party of the Left (*Partito Democratico della Sinistra, PDS*). By 1996, the PDS was in a position to form a key component of a Center–Left governmental coalition, a role that would have been inconceivable for its predecessor in the pre-Cold War era.

However, another major effect of the domestic political turmoil of the early 1990s was to reinforce the importance of Italy's participation in European integration. It was matter of some pride that Italy had been the only southern European country to be involved in the European project right from the start, as one of the seven original signatories of the Treaty of Rome in 1957. During the 1980s, European Union (EU) participation became an increasingly important symbol of modernity and stability in the Italian political consciousness. At a time when Italians felt growing disillusionment with domestic political institutions, the EU was representative of political legitimacy. Association with the EU was therefore valued across all sections of the population (Dyson and Featherstone 1996: 298; Quaglia and Radaelli 2007: 924). Public opinion surveys in the 1980s showed Italy to be one of the most pro-European of EC member states (Giuliani 2000).[12] Even the Communist Party (PCI), which had previously been euro-skeptical, embraced European integration in the 1980s (Maggiorani 1998). Italy's participation at the forefront of EU integration was, therefore, a matter of bipartisan agreement, with support across a wide range of political and economic cleavages in Italian society (Quaglia and Radaelli 2007: 928).

A group amongst which a pro-European ethos was particularly strong was the technocratic elite at the top of major economic institutions, such as the Bank of Italy (*Banca d'Italia*) and the Treasury (*Tesoro*). Since the 1970s, this group had been forced to deal with the negative macroeconomic conse-

---

Party (*Partito Socialista Italiano*), the Italian Socialist Democratic Party (*Partito Socialista Democratico Italiano*), the Italian Liberal Party (*Partito Liberale Italiano*), and the Italian Republican Party (*Partito Repubblicano Italiano*).

[11] During the 1970s, the PCI typically won the support of around a third of voters, making it the most significant communist party in a Western democracy.

[12] On a scale ranging from −100 to +100, Italian support for EMU was the largest in the whole EU (with a score of + 55), compared to + 31 in France and −7 in Germany. Data from European Commission, reported in *Economist* Supplement, "A Survey on Italy" (November 8, 1997) (data for the year 1997).

quences of a dysfunctional political system, such as currency instability, high inflation, and escalating fiscal deficits. Despairing of finding domestic solutions to these endemic problems, the technocrats enthusiastically embraced the notion of *vincolo esterno* ("external constraint"), whereby a widespread consensus in favor of EU integration could be exploited to impose an external discipline on the domestic opponents of economic policy reform (Dyson and Featherstone 1996: 274; 1999). Their ability to impose such an approach on the Italian political economy gained impetus following the decision of France and Germany to push ahead with EMU in the late 1980s.[13] Popular support for Italy's participation in EMU, along with the paralysis of the political class in the wake of the *Tagentopoli* scandal, offered the technocrats a unique opportunity to take control of economic policy, and overcome veto players that had previously stymied economic reforms (Bull and Rhodes 2007: 659).

This began during the negotiations over the Maastricht Treaty. A significant issue for the Italian team was the prospect of a tough set of economic convergence criteria for EMU qualification. The Delors report on monetary union had urged that "binding rules... [consisting of] effective upper limits on budget deficits of individual countries" be established for EMU participation, as "uncoordinated and divergent national budgetary policies would undermine monetary stability and generate imbalances in the real and financial sectors of the Community" (Kenen 1995: 14). The need for fiscal criteria was emphasized by German, Dutch, Danish, and British negotiators during the intergovernmental conference, with the result that a reference value of 60 percent was defined for the public debt-to-GDP ratio, and a 3 percent maximum for the fiscal deficit-to-GDP ratio (Moravcsik 1998).[14] This represented a major obstacle for Italy, where the debt-to-GDP ratio reached 120 percent in the early 1990s, and annual fiscal deficits were well into double figures[15] (De Cecco 2007: 764).

Although the domestic political implications were hardly to be exaggerated, the Italian negotiators had no hesitation in accepting the convergence criteria. It was a politically legitimate decision to make, given the overwhelming

---

[13] The broad objective of EMU was stated by member states at the Hanover Summit in June 1988, and defined in more detail by the European Commission in the Delors report of 1989. Detailed negotiations on EMU took place during the intergovernmental conference beginning in December 1990, which concluded at the European Council meeting in Maastricht in December 1991. The Maastricht Treaty was formally signed in February 1992, and – as well as defining the road map for EMU – also led to the transformation of the European Community into the European Union.

[14] The 60 percent debt figure was chosen as it was close to the average value of the EU 15's debt level at that time (Savage 2001: 46).

[15] Between 1990 and 1995, the Italian fiscal deficit averaged 10.2 percent of GDP (ECB 2008).

popular consensus in favor of Italian participation in EMU, on the one hand and it represented an ideal means of implementing the *vincolo esterno* approach which they believed was the only way to save Italy from economic disaster, on the other. As foreign minister Carli (1993: 435) expressed it shortly after the Maastricht Treaty: "Our agenda at the table of the Inter-Governmental Conference on European Union represented an alternative solution to problems which we were not able to tackle via the normal channels of government and parliament." Regardless of whether domestic political actors recognized the distributional implications of accepting the Maastricht criteria at the time, there was little that such actors could do to halt the process. The EMU negotiations, therefore, represented a key moment in which power over the domestic policy agenda shifted from the increasingly discredited *Partitocrazia* to a small group of nonpartisan technocratic actors, whose importance in attaining the popularly demanded objective of EMU entry granted them – for a while at least – a much greater degree of political legitimacy than traditional party political actors (Dyson and Featherstone 1996: 290; De Cecco 2007: 770).

During the subsequent six years, Italian economic policy almost entirely focused on the objective of fulfilling the Maastricht criteria. The qualification strategy consisted of three main elements. First, a substantial program of fiscal and budgetary retrenchment, including the imposition of a one-off $3.7 billion "eurotax" in 1997 (Savage 2001: 48). Second, a large-scale program of privatization, which raised more funds for the public exchequer than any other privatization program of the 1990s (Deeg 2005: 531).[16] Third, an anti-inflationary policy of *concertazione* ("concertation"), involving tripartite negotiations over wage settlements with unions and employer associations (Ferrera and Gualmini 2004). A series of short-lived governments in the early to mid-1990s used the catalyst of EMU as a means of "pushing through" reforms in these areas against political opposition that otherwise would have been politically difficult to overcome (Sbragia 2001; Radaelli 2003; Bull and Baudner 2004; Quaglia and Radaelli 2007: 929). The central role of the technocrats in these policies was given explicit political expression in the "technical" governments of Carlo Azeglio Ciampi (1993/4) – who prior to assuming the premiership was Governor of the Bank of Italy – and Lamberto Dini (1995/6), who had also been at the central bank. However, a key role in economic policy continued to be played by Mario Draghi, who remained Director-General of the Italian Treasury throughout the 1990s, and was appointed Chairman of the Italian Committee for Privatizations in 1993, with overall responsibility for the privatization program.

---

[16] Privatization raised €90 billion between 1992 and 1999, €20 billion of which derived from the privatization of Telecom Italia in 1997 (Amatori and Colli 2000: 26).

The Case of Italy: Everything Changes, Everything Stays the Same 273

The election of the Center–Left *Ulivo* ("Olive Tree") coalition led by Romano Prodi in May 1996 came at a particularly crucial time in the EMU convergence process. At that stage, it seemed quite likely that Italy would not succeed in participating in the first wave of EMU, scheduled for 1999. The budget deficit for 1996 was expected to exceed 7 percent of gross domestic product (GDP), well above the 3 percent reference value of the Maastricht criteria. Italy's own commissioner at the European Commission in Brussels – Mario Monti – predicted that Italy was unlikely to qualify, while Giovanni Agnelli – the leading corporate oligarch and former head of Italy's largest corporation, Fiat – commented that "only a miracle" would save Italy from remaining outside the initial euro-zone formation (Parker 1997: 136).

Despite this skepticism, the overwhelming priority of the Prodi government was to take the necessary measures to ensure EMU participation, and this involved reducing the fiscal deficit and public debt "at all costs" (Parker 1997: 129). The stakes were further raised when it became clear that there was no prospect of a postponement of the starting date of EMU, and that both Spain and Portugal would also join from the start (Radaelli 2003). A frenetic program of emergency budgets and parliamentary votes of confidence – including Prodi's temporary resignation ahead of the 1998 budget – were required in order to push through tax increases, spending cuts, and gain approval for privatization transactions (e.g., the sales of Autostrade and Rome airport). The measures also included a substantial transfer of gold reserves between the Bank of Italy and the Italian exchange office (Savage 2001: 48). At the same time, ministers and officials exerted considerable diplomatic effort in persuading the other EU member states and the EU institutions (particularly the Commission) that Italy would be able to make the necessary adjustments, and meet the convergence criteria. Often this was undertaken in the face of significant foreign skepticism. German finance Minister Theo Waigel, for example, complained that many of the measures being taken, such as the eurotax, were simply an attempt to "cook the books" (Paterson and Smart 1997).

10.4 CORPORATE GOVERNANCE REFORM: PARTISAN POLITICS OR ELITE PROJECT?

Although ostensibly a creature of the Center–Left, the Prodi government was still essentially a technocratic administration. Simon Parker (1997) notes the high level of continuity with the earlier "technical" administrations of Carlo Azeglio Ciampi and Lamberto Dini, both of whom were appointed to key positions in the Prodi government, Finance Minister and Foreign Minister respectively. Furthermore, Romano Prodi himself was a career economist and technocrat, having only recently assumed an explicitly political role.[17] This meant that the three top positions in the Prodi government were occupied by people who had not been career politicians before the 1996 elections (Parker 1997: 127).

Prodi's entry into politics occurred through his creation of "The Olive Tree" (*l'Ulivo*) electoral concept, which sought to unite a heterogeneous group of political forces, ranging from Greens to ex-Christian Democrats (Hellman 1997: 84). The Olive Tree was a Center–Left imitation of Silvio Berlusconi's "Pole of Freedoms" (*Polo delle Libertà*) coalition brand, which Berlusconi created to exploit the bipolarizing tendencies of the new electoral system at the 1994 election. Unlike Berlusconi, Prodi did not have his own political party or support base. Nonetheless, his technocratic status was viewed as an asset by the parties of the Left – particularly the PDS – which were hampered by a lack of legitimacy due to their links to the former Communist party (Diamanti 2007: 737). As Parker puts it, the Left "reasonably calculated that ex-Christian Democracy voters would not turn around 180 degrees in their voting habits, but they may be persuaded to support a trusted public figure who was identifiably part of the Catholic political tradition without necessarily being a political professional" (Parker 1997: 125).

Consequently, although the Prodi government had the broad support of the Left *vis-à-vis* the policy objective of the Maastricht convergence conditions, it was by no means obvious that the policies being implemented by Prodi were directly reflective of the political preferences of Left political actors or their core constituents. Despite emerging from the 1996 elections with the largest share of the vote within the Olive Tree coalition, the PDS "tactically surrendered the premiership to a technician who served to alter the character of the coalition from a left-wing movement to a technical force that was more appealing to the electorate" (Tocci 2000: 73).

The corporate governance law of 1998 – which passed into law by means of delegated legislation – represented a clear example of the implementation of the technocratic policy agenda. The man appointed by Prodi to design the blueprint for a new law on corporate governance in 1997 (Mario Draghi) was also the official with primary responsibility for ensuring the success of the privatization program and the realization of EMU entry (Deeg 2005: 522).[18] Furthermore, as Draghi himself observed, corporate governance reform had

---

[17] From 1982–9, and again between 1993/4, Prodi was director of the state holding company, IRI, and was heavily involved in the privatization of *Credito Italiano* and *Banca Commerciale Italiana* in 1993.

[18] This contrasted with the situation in Germany, where the impetus for corporate governance reform emerged from within political parties, particularly the Social Democrats.

The Case of Italy: Everything Changes, Everything Stays the Same 275

been defined by the Italian Treasury as a technical component of the privatization process since the start of the privatization program in 1993 (Draghi 2000: 262). As Chairman of the Privatization Commission, Draghi was aware that foreign investors and small private investors were potentially important buyers of the shares of companies undergoing privatization. However, in order to encourage them to invest in the newly privatized entities, it was necessary to increase their confidence in their rights as minority shareholders. In particular, they needed to feel less vulnerable to the risks that had traditionally deterred small and foreign investors from buying shares in Italian corporations, that is, expropriation from large or controlling shareholders. The imminence of the EMU qualification deadline – and of a large number of privatization transactions – made the implementation of such reforms an important component of the EMU qualification process for both Prodi and Draghi.

However, it should not be assumed that the Italian Treasury favored a shift to a fully fledged system of shareholder corporate governance. The preferred end point was a German-style system, in which universal banks played a central role – through large and stable ownership stakes – in monitoring and controlling the management of industrial companies (Onado 1996: 100; Deeg 2005: 531). However, this objective required first the privatization of state banks, and their consolidation into groups that could fulfill such a universal banking function. In Draghi's words, a key objective of the privatization process was "to give an important role to the commercial banks, both in the placement phase and in the formation of stable shareholder groups. The banking system had therefore to be privatized first to be a credible partner in the privatization of industrial corporations" (Bank of Italy 1995: 174; Draghi 2000: 262). This strategy was also behind the banking law of 1993 that allowed banks to issue bonds, extend medium and long-term credit, and acquire ownership stakes in nonfinancial firms (Deeg 2005: 531). It was also reflected in the subsequent highly protective stance of successive Italian administrations *vis-à-vis* foreign takeovers of major domestic banks (e.g., the Fazio affair discussed previously).

There is also little evidence that insider labor supported the Draghi reforms (except as a means of securing EMU entry) (McCann 2007). Whereas in Germany, trade union experts had increasingly recognized during the 1990s that pro-shareholder reform was likely to help fulfill the interests of insider labor, such a viewpoint had not developed within Italian unions prior to the passage of the Draghi legislation (Culpepper 2007: 795). Indeed, there was very little awareness within Italian trade unions of corporate governance as a policy area in the mid-1990s, possibly because major corporate scandals had yet to highlight the issue as in Germany. According to Friedman (1998), the three main union confederations expressed no public reaction to the enactment of the law by legislative decree in February 1998. Culpepper concludes that "whether or not the Italian reforms [of corporate governance] could have been passed without the tacit support of labor remains a speculative question. Yet it seems on the basis of the evidence that the labor component of the transparency coalition is a permissive factor, rather than a causally central one" (Culpepper 2007: 795).

However, should the silence of labor unions on corporate governance reform in February 1998 be interpreted as suggestive of tacit approval? There is a good deal of circumstantial evidence to suggest otherwise. During the 1990s, Italian unions exhibited a willingness to temporarily suppress their traditional militancy in order to achieve the national objective of EMU membership. In particular, the EMU factor catalyzed the return of attempts at concertation, which had previously been abandoned in 1984 due to a lack of union cooperation (Contarino 2000: 177). As a result of the exogenous EMU factor – and also due to the demise of the Christian Democratic and Socialist parties, which served to temporarily depoliticize industrial relations – "technocratic and Center–Left governments were able to reach negotiated agreements with the unions, which could be presented to their members not as unilateral concessions, but as contributions to national economic salvation, to which others were also contributing" (Contarino 2000: 177).

However, the contingency of insider labor support on the EMU factor became apparent after the acceptance of Italy into EMU in mid-1998. The commitment of the unions to concertation evaporated by the end of the year, and the main terms of the final concertation pact of 1998 were never implemented (Bull and Rhodes 2007: 666). Unity amongst the main trade union confederations crumbled, with the CGIL (the largest of the three main union confederations) rejecting further dialogue with the government and employers on reforms aimed at increasing labor market flexibility. Furthermore, the CGIL subsequently expressed wide-ranging criticism of the economic liberalization measures of the earlier Prodi government (including the company law reforms), despite not having voiced such opposition during the period when Prodi was in power (Della Sala 2004: 1053). This was followed, in the summer of 1999, by the expression of opposition to the idea of promoting shareholding amongst employees, which was hardly suggestive of a pro-shareholder stance (Trentini and Lombardia 1999).

In short, insider labor's acquiescence in pro-shareholder corporate governance reform in February 1998 seems more likely to have reflected the suppressive effect of the exogenous EMU factor than implicit support for enhancing the rights of minority shareholders. Insider labor was willing to go along with technocratic policy prescriptions – in areas such as corporate

The Case of Italy: Everything Changes, Everything Stays the Same

governance and industrial relations – during a temporary period of national emergency. Hine and Vassallo (2000: 41) note that, by the time of Italy's acceptance into EMU, the attitude of all the three trade union confederations toward Prodi was "extremely cool," with the consequence that there was little objection to his removal from office in the latter part of 1998.

As has been mentioned in Chapter 9, one of the difficulties in establishing the role of corporate governance in party politics is the topic's lack of salience in party policy documents, speeches, and manifestos. In the case of the Italian government of 1996–2001, this is further complicated by the large number of disparate parties that were involved in the Center–Left coalition (see Table 10.2). In addition, whereas corporate governance reforms in Germany were extensively debated by party actors in the Bundestag, the Italian legislation was enacted by administrative decrees that did not require parliamentary debate or approval, thereby further serving to obfuscate partisan attitudes to the issue (Friedman 1998).

Cioffi and Höpner (2006) point to several statements in newspapers made by Massimo D'Alema – leader of the PDS, and the largest coalition party – as evidence that corporate governance reform was a partisan objective of the Italian Left. For example, in interview with the *Financial Times* in December 1997, D'Alema was quoted as stating that "[w]e are carrying out privatizations but we still have not done enough to create a proper financial market," and also regretting that "we do not have guarantees for small shareholders, no

Table 10.2 Political parties supporting the Olive Tree coalition government of 1996

Political party	Vote, 1996 election (%)	Seats in Chamber of Deputies (%)
Democratic Party of the Left (*Partito democratico della Sinistra*, PDS)	21.1	
Italian People's Party (*Partito Popolare Italiano*, PPI) South Tyrolean People's Party (*Südtiroler Volkspartei*, SVP) Italian Republican Party (*Partito Repubblicano Italiano*, PRI) Democratic Union (*Unione Democratica*, UD)	6.8	45.2
Italian Renewal (*Rinnovamento Italiano*, RI) Italian Socialists (*Socialisti Italiani*, SI) Patto Segni (Segni Pact, PATTO)	4.3	
Federation of the Greens (*Federazione dei Verdi*)	2.5	
Communist Refoundation Party (*Partito della Rifondazione Comunista*, PRC)[a]	8.6	5.6

[a] Not formally part of the Olive Tree coalition.

rules for public companies."[19] However, at this stage, D'Alema was already a key member of Prodi's coalition government, and would hardly be expected – a few months before the passing of the Draghi law and the EMU entry decision – to make remarks that were unsupportive of his own government's economic policy. Prior to his appointment as Prime Minister in October 1998, D'Alema was anyway not directly concerned with the economic policy. As Chairman of the Bicameral Commission on Constitutional Reform, his main responsibility in government was leading negotiations with the other political parties on the reform of Italy's dysfunctional political institutions (Hine and Vassallo 2000: 38).

It was undoubtedly the case that the PDS – after emerging as one of the two heirs of the Italian Communist Party (PCI) in 1991 – was shifting from the Left to the Center ground of Italian politics during the mid-1990s.[20] In its 1996 election manifesto, it expressed acceptance of the market economy and stressed the need to reform the welfare state (Hopkin and Ignazi 2008: 8). A textual analysis of the 1996 manifesto data with regard to a range of economic policy issues reveals almost no difference in the Left-Right stance of the PDS, the Olive Tree coalition as a whole, and the Conservative *Pole of Freedoms* coalition with whom they contested the election (Campus 2001: 10; Pelizzo 2003: 73).

However, there is no evidence from policy documents or its preelection policy platform of an intention on behalf of the PDS to implement policy initiatives favoring minority shareholders (Bellucci 1999; Blim 2000; Campus 2001; Giannetti and Mulé 2006; Hopkin and Ignazi 2008).[21] Furthermore, pro-shareholder corporate governance initiatives were not a feature of D'Alema's own premiership of the Center–Left coalition (October 1998 to April 2000), which took place after the European Commission had confirmed Italy's success in qualifying for EMU in May 1998.[22] Corporate governance

---

[19] Paul Betts and James Blitz "At the Head of Italy's Table, The *Financial Times* Interview: Massimo D'Alema," *Financial Times*, December 22, 1997.
[20] This transition culminated in the merger of the PDS with the remains of the former Christian Democrats (DC) and the Socialist Party (PSI) in 1998, to form the *Democratici di Sinistra* (DS – Democrats of the Left).
[21] Giannetti and Mulé (2006) and Hopkin and Ignazi (2008) provide analyses of the policy evolution of the PDS and the DS during the 1990s. Campus (2001) evaluates party platforms at the 1996 election. Pelizzo (2003) charts the policy positions of Italian parties based on party manifesto data. Bellucci (1999) offers an interpretation of party positions on economic issues at the 1994 and 1996 elections.
[22] In their 2006 article, Cioffi and Höpner make a factual error when they state that "the most important corporate governance reforms [in Italy], however, were the D'Alema government's 'Draghi reforms' in 1998" (Cioffi and Höpner 2006: 11). The Draghi law was enacted in February 1998, during Romano Prodi's premiership, and eight months before the administration of Massimo D'Alema.

reform appears to have been a policy area based on the EMU factor rather than the partisan objectives of the PDS. Nathalie Tocci describes the relationship between Italian political parties and policies at that time as follows: "The strict convergence criteria to be attained by January 1999 prevented governments from enacting trivial *leggine* and forced elites to tackle professionally major issues on the economic agenda. Whether parties truly believed in the pursuit of these objectives and used Maastricht as a legitimizing device or whether they unwillingly accepted the criteria from above remains an open question" (Tocci 2000: 77).

Less ambiguity surrounds the attitude of the second largest party supporting the Center–Left government – the Communist Refoundation Party (*Rifondazione Comunista*, PRC) – toward the Draghi reforms. The PRC was not formally part of the governing coalition. However, it cooperated with the Olive Tree during the electoral campaign in 1996, and the government was dependent on its support for achievement of a majority in the Chamber of Deputies (the lower house). Although initially supportive of the broad objective of EMU entry, the policies employed to achieve that objective – including corporate governance reform – became increasingly difficult for the PRC to tolerate.[23] As Blim (2000: 174) put it, "fiscal austerity, pension reform, privatization, and sound money caused consternation and discomfort in the ranks... something had to be achieved to justify their continued support of Prodi." The PRC voiced strong opposition to pro-shareholder reform in the run-up to the enactment of the Draghi law in February 1998 (Blitz 1997; Deeg 2005: 534). Although placated for several months by government promises to introduce a thirty-five-hour working week (Friedman 1998), the PRC finally terminated its support of the government as soon as Italy had been accepted into EMU.[24] It was clear that the PRC was not an enthusiastic supporter of pro-shareholder reform (or other EMU-related economic reforms, e.g., pension reform), and it is implausible to presume that it would have supported such a policy initiative in the absence of the EMU *vincolo esterno*.

---

[23] Like the PDS, the PRC emerged out of the Italian Communist Party (PCI) in 1991. According to the textual manifesto analysis of Campus (2001), the PRC was the only major political party in the 1996 election with a distinctively "Left" position on a left–right scale relating to economic policy (Campus 2001: 10).

[24] The subsequent D'Alema administration had to ally with a group of ex-Christian Democrat deputies – which had fought the 1996 election under the conservative *Pole of Freedoms* coalition banner – in order to stay in power.

10.5 CONCLUSION: ECONOMIC RENTS AND ITALIAN CORPORATE GOVERNANCE

The previous sections have argued that the pro-shareholder reforms enacted in Italy in the late 1990s were primarily explained by an exogenous EMU effect, not by an underlying preference of partisan actors or insider labor for pro-shareholder reform. This largely concurs with Deeg's conclusion that the Italian corporate governance reform "can be fairly described as an elite project, driven in good part by external pressures to conform with EU directives, to qualify for EMU, and to be competitive in a rapidly integrating European financial and corporate space" (Deeg 2005: 541).

In the German case, the impetus for corporate governance reform came from party political actors (the SPD) and their insider labor core constituents. In contrast, insider labor in Italy did not view pro-shareholder reform as a necessary means of reforming the behavior of corporations. Labor's position *vis-à-vis* employers continued to be underpinned by strong employment protection and effective decentralized bargaining arrangements. Consequently, Left political actors showed no signs of embracing the cause of shareholder protection. The source of the pro-shareholder regulation that did emerge was the EMU *vincolo esterno*, which necessitated the introduction of cosmetic regulatory reform by technocratic actors (but without any serious intention to enforce that reform). The eventual admission of Italy into EMU permitted what Hine and Vassallo have called "the return of politics," that is, a return to prominence of the *Partitocrazia*, and the downgrading of technocratic influence on policy (Hine and Vassallo 2000). As Molina and Rhodes (2007a: 806) express it, "The removal of the EMU *vincolo esterno* released social and political actors to pursue their own interests and agendas." As soon as the objective of EMU membership had been achieved, support for further pro-shareholder measures amongst insider labor and Left political actors largely disappeared, and there was little subsequent emphasis placed on introducing or enforcing regulation, for example, through the courts or the securities regulator. Such a finding supports the hypothesis of this book, which argues that partisanship is only likely to function as a driver of corporate governance change in an environment of relatively low economic rents, for example, the situation experienced by Germany in the late 1990s.

Bianchi and Bianco also identify another reason why nominal Italian regulatory reform in the late 1990s failed to translate into *de facto* change

(Bianchi and Bianco 2006: 18–19; Micossi 2006). High economic rents increased the value of the private benefits of control of companies to Italian blockholders. Blockholders retained an incentive to continue governing corporations in line with blockholder norms of corporate governance, that is, without regard to the interests of minority shareholders, until the private benefits of control were exceeded by the costs of defying the law. In an environment in which the benefits were high due to substantial economic rents, and the costs were low due to "the notorious dysfunctions of the Italian judicial system" (Ferrarini 2005: 29),[25] it was not surprising that nominal reforms failed to make much impact on actual blockholder behavior. Culppeper (2007: 793) makes the point as follows: "Controlling shareholders maintain many resources they can use to keep laws on the books from compromising their effective control of companies, particularly when the enforcement capacities of public and private actors remain weak."

In the absence of an exogenous catalyst for legislative initiatives in corporate governance – such as the EMU *vincolo esterno* – economic rents remain a key determinant of both *de jure* and *de facto* corporate governance change in Italy. The experience of the last decade suggests that reforming corporate governance without prior reform of product markets is likely to be ineffective (unless substantial resources are devoted to enforcement). Blockholders will continue to look for ways to circumvent the interests of minority shareholders in order to continue benefiting disproportionately from economic rents. Furthermore, as long as insider labor is satisfied with its ability to secure a share of economic rents from blockholders though statutory employment protections or bargaining arrangements, they are unlikely to sponsor major initiatives on corporate governance within Left political parties. In contrast, the introduction of pro-shareholder reform in a more competitive environment – as in Germany in the late 1990s – has a greater chance of success, as both blockholders and insider labor have less to lose, and are therefore less likely to be resistant of such changes.

Consequently, Gourevitch and Shinn (2005) and Cioffi and Höpner (2006) are still correct to view change in corporate governance policy as an intermediate step on the way to changes in actual corporate outcomes. But economic rents are a prerequisite for effective reform at the company level. In the case of Germany, economic rents were not an obstacle to significant actual corporate

---

[25] La Porta et al. (1998) provide a score for the efficiency of national judicial systems (ranging from 0 to 10). The score for Italy is 6.75. This compares with scores of 10.0 for the United Kingdom and the United States, 9.0 for Germany, 8.0 for France, and 7.0 for Greece. The Italian score is, however, slightly higher than that of Portugal (5.50) and Spain (6.25) (La Porta et al. 1998: 1142).

governance change. In the Italian case, economic rents made the policy channel ineffective – despite the apparent similarity of a "modernizing" Center–Left government. Resistance to the shareholder model is likely to remain in evidence as long as economic rents inflate the private benefits of control for Italian corporate insiders.

11

Conclusions

This final chapter has a number of objectives. First, it provides a summary of the analysis that has been undertaken in the rest of the book, and draws conclusions regarding the viability of the hypothesis advanced in Chapter 2. Second, it explores possible limitations of the analysis, and considers what aspects of corporate governance change are not addressed by the book. Finally, it offers some reflections on the book's broader implications for policy-makers and the future of corporate governance.

Chapter 1 presented evidence of an increasingly shareholder-oriented approach to corporate governance in the nonliberal market economies of continental Europe over the last ten to fifteen years. It was also noted that Left parties enjoyed a strong presence in government over the same period. This presented a puzzle, as intuitive expectations regarding the economic policy preferences of political parties – and also Mark Roe's theory (2003) of the political determinants of corporate governance – imply that pro-shareholder corporate governance reform is more likely to be a feature of conservative than Left government.

Chapter 2 offered a theoretical framework to explain this puzzle. The theory incorporated the insight of John Cioffi and Martin Höpner (2006) that Left parties have sought to appeal to new groups of voters through pro-shareholder policy initiatives, whereas the ability of conservative parties to move in that direction has been constrained by links to incumbent corporate interests. However, whereas Cioffi and Höpner accounted for this development in terms of a greater capacity for electoral opportunism on behalf of Left parties, the hypothesis proposed in this book sought to explain party behavior according to the differing material interests of relevant social actors.

An analytical framework was outlined with three corporate stakeholders – blockholders, insider labor, and outsiders – with differing corporate governance preferences. Blockholders and insider labor were assumed to be relatively homogeneous social groupings, and represented the core political constituents of conservative and Left parties respectively. Outsiders did not have their own party, and represented a potential source of new votes for both parties. However, they required a commitment to pro-shareholder corporate governance policies in order to win their support. As long as economic rents were substantial in a political economy (due to low levels of product market competition), neither the Left nor conservative parties were willing to solicit the support of outsiders in this way, as both of their core constituents benefited from the sharing of economic rents. However, if economic rents were insubstantial, insider labor would no longer have an interest in sustaining a self-regulatory blockholder model of corporate governance. Indeed, it would view the blockholder model as an undesirable source of power for concentrated, unaccountable, and potentially adversarial capitalist interests, that is, blockholders.

Consequently, in such circumstances, it would become possible for political entrepreneurs in Left parties to persuade insider labor core constituents of the merits of pro-shareholder corporate governance reform. Such a policy approach had the double advantage of both countering the power of blockholders and appealing to new sources of electoral support. In contrast, conservative parties would remain the apologists of the blockholder model – even in the absence of economic rents – in order to retain the private benefits of control for blockholders.

Chapter 3 contrasted the proposed hypothesis with existing explanations of corporate governance in a range of academic disciplines. An important difference between competing approaches concerned the role played by economic efficiency in determining corporate governance outcomes. It was argued that, although the hypothesis advanced in the book is based on the rational behavior of social actors, acting according to their material interests, it is not assumed that corporate governance outcomes will necessarily converge on the most efficient (e.g., in terms of minimizing the cost of capital for the firm). Nor is it assumed that there is a necessary equality between *de jure* and *de facto* corporate governance outcomes (as argued by many legal scholars). Indeed, if economic rents are substantial in a political economy, then the introduction of corporate governance regulation may have only a limited effect on firm-level corporate governance behavior (unless underpinned by substantial enforcement resources) due to the greater value to blockholders of the private benefits of control.

The empirical testing of the hypothesis was primarily undertaken through a macro-comparative statistical analysis. Chapters 4 and 5 evaluated ways in which two of the key variables – corporate governance and product market competition – could be operationalized in such an analysis. Both of these variables share the characteristic of not being directly observable. Consequently, it is necessary to identify suitable proxy variables. Given the pros and cons of different measures of corporate governance, it was decided to undertake the empirical analysis with three plausible proxies – equity share, value traded, and international equity issuance – rather than to base conclusions on a single measure. However, other potential measures of corporate governance – such as ownership concentration, corporate governance ratings, and measures of corporate governance regulation – were not utilized for various conceptual and practical reasons. The Organisation for Economic Co-operation and Development's NMR index was chosen as the most plausible measure of product market competition, an assessment reflected in its widespread utilization in the empirical economics literature.

In Chapter 6, the hypothesis was formalized in terms of an empirical model that specified the interaction of partisanship and product market competition as the main explanatory variable. This model was employed in a panel data econometric analysis of corporate governance change with a data set of fifteen nonliberal market economies covering the period 1975–2003. The results of this analysis suggested that the interaction of partisanship and competition was a highly significant determinant of corporate governance change. In particular, significant shifts in a pro-shareholder direction were associated with Left government – but not conservative government – in the context of high levels of competition. In contrast, neither Left nor conservative government was associated with corporate governance change in a low-competition environment. The robustness tests of Chapter 7 confirmed that these conclusions were not sensitive to the inclusion of particular countries or observations in the data set, or the choice of individual control variables. The reestimation of the model in terms of first-differences (i.e., a dynamic model specification) gave rise to similar results.

Case studies of Germany and Italy in Chapters 9 and 10 contributed a qualitative dimension to the testing of the hypothesis. Germany represents a country which experienced a significant increase in product market competition by the late 1990s. A declining level of support for the status quo blockholder model of corporate governance emerged amongst insider labor and Left party actors during the same period. At the same time, the private universal banks withdrew from their postwar role as guardians of the German corporate network. The reduced willingness of blockholders to compromise with insider labor in the operation of firms – due to the reduced availability of economic rents – made it possible for SPD party modernizers to win support for pro-shareholder reform that redistributed power from blockholders to outsider capital.

In contrast, Italy had achieved less competitive product markets than Germany by the late 1990s, suggesting that producers continued to benefit from economic rents. It had also experienced much less firm-level corporate governance change in a shareholder direction, as predicted by the hypothesis of this book. However, the distinctive feature of the Italian case was the disparity between *de jure* and *de facto* corporate governance change. Whereas pro-shareholder legislative reform was introduced by the Prodi government in the late 1990s – as a part of Italy's drive to achieve membership of economic and monetary union (EMU) – this did not exert much impact on firm-level behavior. Such a disparity supported the argument of Chapter 2 that economic rents represent an obstacle to the successful implementation of legislative corporate governance reform, as they increase the private benefits of control to blockholders. In such circumstance, significant resources must be expended on legislative enforcement in order to achieve a given level of corporate governance change (which did not occur in the Italian case).

In summary, the empirical evidence examined in this book is highly supportive of the idea that economic rents play a key role in determining the degree of association between partisanship and corporate governance change in nonliberal market economies. Economic rents represent the missing ingredient in the pattern of partisanship proposed by Cioffi and Höpner (2006). Although the empirical analysis has supported Cioffi and Höpner's assertion that Left governments have exhibited a greater propensity than conservative parties to promote pro-shareholder reform, the evidence also suggests that this association is conditional on economic rents. Economic rents are the key factor that mould the preferences of the Left *vis-à-vis* corporate governance policy, and determine the ability of such policy to translate into changes in firm-level corporate governance outcomes.

These conclusions emphasize the fact that corporate governance change has occurred in individual countries as a result of nationally located developments in product markets and domestic politics. This runs counter to the idea that similar outcomes would have occurred in any case – regardless of competitive conditions in product markets and their interaction with the partisan complexion of governments – due to the diffusion of an international consensus concerning "best practice" in corporate governance.[1] Rather, the results show that corporate governance change was contingent on a combination of particular national economic and political circumstances. Where these prerequisites were not in place, substantial firm-level corporate governance change was less likely to occur.

What are the possible shortcomings of the analysis that has been undertaken? It is worth stressing that the quality of the inferences drawn from a statistical analysis are crucially dependent on the quality of the underlying data. In particular, the results presented in this book have depended on the

---

[1] The role of external governments, international institutions, and international communities of experts in diffusing "best practice" in economic policy – and in propagating emulation and learning effects – has recently been explored by Simmons et al. (2008).

choice of empirical proxies to represent key dependent and explanatory variables. One of the specific problems involved in an analysis of corporate governance change is the lack of availability of several commonly utilized proxies in time-series form. For example, ownership concentration and corporate governance ratings are potentially useful measures of corporate governance orientation, but are only currently available on a cross-sectional basis (or for a limited number of years and/or countries). Similarly, a lack of credible proxies for *de jure* corporate governance regulation in time-series format also rules out the inclusion of a measure of corporate governance regulation in the data set.

However, while development of longitudinal data for ownership concentration is likely to remain hampered by the practical difficulties of establishing the ownership structure of a large number of companies over time, it is likely that improved time-series of corporate governance ratings and shareholder protection indices will become available in coming years (e.g., from the CBR project at Cambridge), thereby permitting corroboration of the hypothesis on the basis of alternative corporate governance proxies.

This book has emphasized a macro-comparative statistical approach in its empirical analysis. Qualitative research has played a lesser role, and has taken the form of two country case studies, chosen to occupy contrasting positions in terms of levels of the explanatory variable (i.e., a high-competition country and a low-competition country). Furthermore, the source of data for these studies has mainly been relevant contributions to the secondary academic literature and available policy documents. An alternative research design might have increased the number of country case studies – exploring a wider range of outcomes in terms of the explanatory variable – and sought evidence from primary empirical sources, for example, interviews with relevant social actors.

The advantage of initially undertaking a macro-comparative approach, however, is that it permits the generalizable validity of the hypothesis to be established across a range of countries. In contrast, a limitation of the case study approach is that – even after examination of a number of cases – the general applicability of the theoretical claims may still be in doubt. Ideally, future work will bring together the existing analysis with further country cases in order to define the specific pathways of causation that connect economic rents with partisanship in individual countries.

The focus of this book has been on identifying the determinants of change from a blockholder to a shareholder model of corporate governance. This represents a relevant dimension along which to chart the course of recent corporate governance change in nonliberal market economies. However, such a definition of corporate governance change is not necessarily relevant to liberal market economies (LMEs), for example, the United Kingdom or the United States. In a LME context, blockholders have long ceased to be major social actors or corporate stakeholders, and shareholding is dominated by institutional or foreign investors with diffuse ownership stakes.[2] The main corporate governance debates tend to revolve around the uneasy relationship between shareholders and corporate managers. Managers are able to assert themselves as independent actors to a much greater extent in the absence of controlling shareholders. Consequently, an analysis of corporate governance change that encompassed LMEs would require a conceptual framework in which managers appeared as distinct corporate stakeholders, contrary to the approach of this book.

There are two other types of corporate governance change that are not addressed in this study. The first arises from the growing importance of private equity in corporate ownership. The analysis of this book has associated concentrated ownership stakes with incumbent capitalist interests. However, the private equity investment model turns this assumption on its head. It involves professional money managers taking concentrated ownership stakes in individual companies, and then withdrawing companies from their public listings on stock markets, often as a prelude to a major corporate reorganization. While proponents of private equity claim that this governance model is enhancing of both efficiency and employment levels in the long run, critics argue that "private equity, with its investor friendly emphasis, is fundamentally subversive of continental Europe's stakeholder models of capitalism" (Plender 2007). Equally, it runs counter to the tenets of the shareholder model, as corporations disappear into a "black hole", in which there exists a low level of transparency to corporate outsiders.

As was shown in Chapter 2, leveraged buyout activity by private equity investors is still a relatively small-scale phenomenon in the European corporate sector, and is partly dependent on cyclical economic factors (e.g., the price and availability of debt finance).[3] Nonetheless, it has already provoked a hostile reaction amongst many European politicians. For example, in April 2005, the Chairman of the German Social Democratic Party (Franz Münterfering) described private equity companies as "locusts" that "destroy everything and move on," a sentiment that was widely supported in German opinion polls and echoed by other European politicians.[4] It is ironic to note that – despite advocating pro-shareholder corporate governance as a means of unseating

---

[2] It should be noted, however, that several high profile companies in LMEs are still controlled by blockholders, including Microsoft, Wal-Mart, and the Ford Motor Company.

[3] For example, since the advent of the global credit crunch in 2008, leveraged buyout activity has more or less ground to a halt.

[4] For example, the Swedish Prime Minister, Göran Persson, criticized the potential takeover of Volvo by private equity investors in September 2006, commenting that "these venture capitalists will break the national capital structures into pieces" (Ibison 2006).

incumbent domestic elites – outsider capital should itself seek to benefit from blockholding in the context of private equity. The rise of private equity also suggests that the shareholder model of corporate governance – in which corporate activities are open to the scrutiny and discipline of public capital markets – is not necessarily viewed as the only (or most efficient) way to govern corporations by outsider capital.

A second type of corporate governance change arises from the entry onto the global corporate scene of so-called sovereign wealth funds (SWFs). SWFs are government investment institutions (mainly from developing economies)[5] with substantial pools of resources to invest in the global economy.[6] Whereas this book has assumed that the main objective of outsider capital is the maximization of risk-adjusted financial returns, uncertainties regarding SWFs arise from their potential to influence corporate activities on the basis of political considerations. This would be problematic in cases where nations with only a limited commitment to democratic governance at home were exploiting the market mechanisms of liberal democracies – through ownership stakes taken by SWFs – in the pursuit of foreign policy objectives (Beffa and Ragot 2008).

Prior to his return to the US administration, Lawrence Summers expressed his concerns in relation to SWFs as follows: "The logic of the capitalist system depends on shareholders causing companies to act so as to maximize the value of their shares. It is far from obvious that this will over time be the only motivation of governments as shareholders" (Summers 2007). Summer's remarks raise different – albeit equally important – questions in the light of the substantial equity stakes that domestic governments have taken in major financial companies as a result of the financial crisis of 2008/9. The manner in which governments will seek to manage these ownership stakes – and the extent to which their behavior as company owners will also undermine the "logic of the capitalist system" – remains unclear.

This book has sought to provide an explanation of the dynamics of corporate governance change in the nonliberal market economies of Europe over the last two decades. In addition to considering its relevance to past developments, it is of interest to consider if the book's findings have implications for economic policy or future trends in corporate governance.

---

[5] The six countries with the largest SWFs (as of 2007) are (in order of size): the United Arab Emirates, Norway, Singapore, Saudi Arabia, Kuwait, and China (Kimmitt 2008).

[6] The International Monetary Fund (IMF) estimates that sovereign wealth funds control around $3 trillion in resources (as of 2007). This exceeds the $1.5 trillion managed by hedge funds worldwide, but is still relatively small compared to the $53 trillion managed by institutional investors, such as pension funds, endowments, insurance companies, and mutual funds (Johnson 2007).

A first implication of the analysis is that – contrary to the perspective of the "law matters" school described in Chapter 3 – policy-makers wishing to encourage a pro-shareholder corporate governance regime should first seek to improve the competitiveness of product markets. The introduction of shareholder-oriented company and securities law may appear – at first sight – to be a more direct means of establishing the shareholder model. However, if economic rents remain available to producers, both capital and labor market actors will lack the incentive to mobilize political support behind pro-shareholder reform. Furthermore, it will be difficult to implement at the company level due to the resistance of incumbent blockholders.

Second, there is nothing inevitable about the continued advance of the shareholder model of corporate governance. The analytical framework of this book has shown that pro-shareholder corporate governance reform is contingent on the competitiveness of product markets. However, it is not implausible to imagine that the trend of recent years toward increased product market competition could stall or even shift into reverse.

For example, at the time of writing, a major financial and economic crisis is leading national governments to consider new ways of protecting domestic industries and jobs. A policy response involving tariffs, subsidies, capital controls, or a greater role for publicly owned enterprises in economic activity could distort the competitive functioning of product markets. In such circumstances, economic rents could, once again, become a prominent feature of national economies, with the implication that the political and economic incentives to proceed further in the direction of pro-shareholder reform would diminish.

Finally, although this book has focused on the specific case of Europe, its analytical approach is potentially applicable to any political economy in which the starting point is the blockholder model of corporate governance. In practical terms, this means that it is relevant to the corporate governance systems of most countries outside of the English-speaking world. The blockholder model remains a more ubiquitous model of corporate governance than the Anglo-American shareholder model. Furthermore, in many economies – particularly those of developing economies – there are low levels of competition in domestic product markets. Consequently, economic rents are likely to play a major role in shaping corporate governance policy and behavior in many non-European regions of the world.

This work ends with the thought that, although corporate governance is in the midst of a period of significant change, the firm remains a pivotal institutional form in the framework of a modern economy. It is still the main means by which societies mobilize resources and create wealth. However, the firm is an evolving concept, and its objectives and authority structure are open to dispute. Corporate governance is, therefore, likely to remain an important area of research in comparative political economy, as scholars seek to understand the shifting interlinkages between politics and corporations in a rapidly evolving economic landscape.

Bibliography

Abowd, John M., and David S. Kaplan. 1999. "Executive Compensation: Six Questions That Need Answering." *Journal of Economic Perspectives* 13 (4): 145–68.

Achen, Christopher F. 2000. Why Lagged Dependent Variables Can Suppress the Explanatory Power of Other Independent Variables. Paper read at *The Annual Meeting of the Political Methodology Section of the American Political Science Association*, July 20–22, at Los Angeles.

Aganin, Alexander, and Paolo Volpin. 2003. "History of Corporate Ownership in Italy." ECGI Finance Working Paper (17).

Aggarwal, Reena, Isil Erel, René Stulz, and Rohan Williamson. 2007. "Differences in Governance Practices between U.S. And Foreign Firms: Measurement, Causes, and Consequences." *NBER Working Paper* (13288).

Aghion, P., M. Dewatripont, and P. Rey. 1999. "Competition, Financial Discipline and Growth." *Review of Economic Studies* 66 (4): 825–52.

Agnblad, J., E. Berglof, P. Hogfeldt, and H. Svancar. 2001. "Ownership and Control in Sweden: Strong Owners, Weak Minorities, and Social Control." In *The Control of Corporate Europe*, eds. F. Barca and M. Becht. New York: Oxford University Press.

Agresti, Alan, and Barbara Finlay. 1997. *Statistical Methods for the Social Sciences*. 3rd edn. Upper Saddle River, NJ: Prentice Hall.

Aguilera, Ruth V., and Gregory Jackson. 2003. "The Cross-National Diversity of Corporate Governance: Dimensions and Determinants." *Academy of Management Review* 28 (3): 447–65.

Aitkin, Norman D. 1973. "The Effect of the EEC and EFTA on European Trade. A Temporal Cross-Section Analysis." *American Economic Review* 63 (5): 881–92.

Albach, Horst, Thomas Brandt, ManFred Fleischer and Jianping Yang. "Soziale Marktwirtschaft: Eine Erfolgsgeschichte. 50 Jahre Bundesrepublik Deutschland im Lichte von Industriebilanzen." In *Eine lernende Demokratie. 50 Jahre Bundesrepublik Deutschland*, eds. M. Kaase and G. Schmid. Berlin: Edition Sigma/WZB Jahrbuch.

Albert, Michel. 1993. *Capitalism Against Capitalism*. London: Whurr.

Alchian, Armen A., and R. Kessel. 1962. "Competition, Monopoly, and the Pursuit of Money." In *Aspects of Labor Economics*, edn. NBER. Princeton, N. J.: Princeton University Press.

—— 1950. "Uncertainty, Evolution, and Economic Theory." *Journal of Political Economy* 58: 211–21.

—— and Harold Demsetz. 1972. "Production, Information Costs, and Economic Organization." *American Economic Review* 62 (5): 777–95.

Alesina, Alberto, S. Ardagna, G. Nicoletti, and F. Schiantarelli. 2005. "Regulation and Investment." *Journal of the European Economic Association* 3 (4): 791–825.

—— and Francesco Giavazzi. 2006. *The Future of Europe: Reform or Decline*. Cambridge, MA/London: MIT Press.

Bibliography

—— S. Ardagna, G. Nicoletti, and F. Schiantarelli, Nouriel Roubini, and Gerald D. Cohen. 1997. *Political Cycles and the Macroeconomy*. Cambridge, MA/London: MIT Press.

Allan, James P., and Lyle Scruggs. 2004. "Political Partisanship and Welfare State Reform in Advanced Industrial Societies." *American Journal of Political Science* 48 (3): 496–512.

Allen, Franklin and Douglas Gale. 2000. *Comparing Financial Systems*. Cambridge, MA: MIT Press.

Almond, Gabriel A. 1996. "Political Science: The History of the Discipline." In *A New Handbook of Political Science*, eds. R. E. Goodin and H.-D. Klingemann. Oxford: Oxford University Press.

Alt, James E. 1985. "Political Parties, World Demand, and Unemployment: Domestic and International Sources of Economic Activity." *American Political Science Review* 79 (4): 1016–40.

—— 2002. "Comparative Political Economy: Credibility, Accountability, and Institutions." In *Political Science: The State of the Discipline*, eds. I. Katznelson and H. V. Milner. New York/London/Washington, DC: Norton/American Political Science Association.

—— and R. C. Lowry. 2000. "A Dynamic Model of State Budget Outcomes under Divided Partisan Government." *Journal of Politics* 62 (4): 1035–69.

Alvarez, R. Michael, Geoffey Garrett, and Peter Lange. 1991. "Government Partisanship, Labor Organization, and Macroeconomic Performance." *American Political Science Review* (85): 539–56.

Amable, Bruno, Lilas Demmou, and Donatella Gatti. 2006. "Institutions, Unemployment and Inactivity in the OECD Countries." *PSE Working Papers* (No. 16).

Amatori, Franco, and Andrea Colli. 2000. "Corporate Governance: The Italian Story." *Unpublished Paper*: Bocconi University.

Anderson, T. W., and Cheng Hsiao. 1981. "Estimation of Dynamic Models with Error Components." *Journal of the American Statistical Association* 76 (375): 598–606.

—— 1982. "Formulation and Estimation of Dynamic Models Using Panel Data." *Journal of Econometrics* 18: 47–82.

Aoki, Masahiko. 1986. "Horizontal vs. Vertical Information Structure of the Firm." *American Economic Review* 76: 971–83.

—— 1988. *Information, Incentives, and Bargaining in the Japanese Economy*. Cambridge: Cambridge University Press.

—— and Ronald Philip Dore. 1994. *The Japanese Firm: The Sources of Competitive Strength*. Oxford: Oxford University Press.

Arellano, Manuel. 1989. *A Note on the Anderson-Hsiao Estimator for Panel Data*. Oxford: Institute of Economics and Statistics, University of Oxford.

—— and Stephen Bond. 1991. "Some Tests of Specification for Panel Data: Monte Carlo Evidence and an Application to Employment Equations." *Review of Economic Studies* 58 (2): 277–97.

—— and Olympia Bover. 1995. "Another Look at the Instrumental Variable Estimation of Error-Components Models." *Journal of Econometrics* 68 (1): 29.

Armingeon, Klaus, Philipp Leimgruber, Michelle Beyeler, and Sarah Menegale. 2005. "Comparative Political Dataset, 1960–2003." *University of Berne*.

Armour, John, and David A. Skeel. 2006. "Who Writes the Rules for Hostile Takeovers, and Why? – The Peculiar Divergence of US and UK Takeover Regulation." *ECGI Working Paper Series in Law* (73/2006).

Arrow, Kenneth J., and Gerard Debreu. 1954. "Existence of an Equilibrium for a Competitive Economy." *Econometrica* 22 (3): 265–90.

Assmann, Heinz-Dieter 1990. "Microcorporatist Structures in German Law on Groups of Companies." In *Regulating Corporate Groups in Europe*, eds. D. Sugarman, G. Teubner, and European University Institute. Baden-Baden: Nomos.

Azfar, Omar, Thornton Matheson, and Mancur Olson. 1999. "Market-Mobilized Capital." *IRIS Center Working Paper* (233).

Baglioni, Guido and Rinaldo Milani. 1990. *La Contrattazione Collettiva Nelle Aziende Industriali in Italia*. Milan: Franco Angeli.

Bakan, Joel. 2004. *The Corporation: The Pathological Pursuit of Profit and Power*. London: Constable.

Balling, Morten, Claus Holm, and Thomas Poulsen. 2005. "Corporate Governance Ratings as a Means to Reduce Asymmetric Information." *Financial Reporting Research Group Wworking Ppaper Sseries, Aarhus School of Business* (R-2005–04).

Baltagi, Badi H. 2001. *Econometric Analysis of Panel Data*. 2nd edn. Chichester: John Wiley & Sons.

Bank for International Settlements. 2001. "The Basel II Capital Accord: An Overview." *Economic and Financial Review — European Economics and Financial Centre* 8 (3): 103–48.

Bank of Italy. 1995. *Annual Report for 1995*. Rome: Bank of Italy.

Bannas, Günter. 2000. "Murren in der SPD-Fraktion. Schröders Regierungsstil geht zu Lasten der Legislative." *FAZ*, July 29.

Barber, Tony. 2004. "Consob 'Could Have Done Little To Prevent Scandal'." *Financial Times*, January 21.

—— 2006. "The Good News: Non-sweaty Shoes and Shareholders' Rights." *Financial Times*, March 20.

Barca, Fabrizio, and Marco Becht, eds. 2001. *The Control of Corporate Europe*. New York: Oxford University Press.

Bardi, Luciano. 2007. "Electoral Change and its Impact on the Party System in Italy." *West European Politics* 30 (4): 711–32.

Barker, Roger M., and David Rueda. 2007. "The Labor Market Determinants of Corporate Governance Reform." *CLPE Research Paper No. 5/2007*.

Bartels, Larry M. 1996. "Pooling Disparate Observations." *American Journal of Political Science* 40 (3): 905–42.

Barucci, Emilio and Jury Falini. 2005. "Determinants of Corporate Governance in the Italian Financial Market." *Economic Notes* 34 (3): 371–405.

Bassanini, Andrea and Romain Duval. 2006. "Employment Patterns in OECD countries: Reassessing the Role of Policies and Institutions." *OECD Economics Department Working Papers* (No. 486).

Baum, Christopher F. 2006. *An Introduction to Modern Econometrics Using Stata*. College Station, TX: Stata Press.

Beal, Edwin F. 1955. "Origins of Codetermination." *Industrial and Labor Relations Review* 8 (4): 483–98.

Bebchuk, Lucian A., and Jesse M. Friedn. 2004. *Pay Without Performance: The Unfulfilled Promise of Executive Compensation.* Cambridge, MA/: Harvard University Press.

Becht, Marco, and Colin Mayer. 2001. "Introduction." In *The Control of Corporate Europe*, eds. F. Barca and M. Becht. Oxford: Oxford University Press.

Beck, Nathaniel, and Jonathan Katz. 1995. "What to Do (and Not to Do) With Time-Series-Cross-Section Data in Comparative Politics." *American Political Science Review* 89 (3): 634.

—— 2004. "Time Series-Cross Section Issues: Dynamics." *Unpublished manuscript.*

Beck, Thorsten, Asli Demirgüç-Kunt, and Ross Levine. 2000. "A New Database on Financial Development and Structure." *World Bank Economic Review* (14): 597–605.

—— —— —— 2003. "Law and Finance: Why Does Legal Origin Matter?" *Journal of Comparative Economics* 31 (4): 653–75.

—— George Clarke, Alberto Groff, Philip Keefer, and Patrick Walsh. 2001. "New Tools in Comparative Political Economy: The Database of Political Institutions." *World Bank Economic Review* 15 (1): 165–76.

Beffa, Jean-Louis, and Xavier Ragot. 2008. "The Fall of the Financial Model of Capitalism." *Financial Times*, February 22.

Bell, Daniel. 1960. *The End of Ideology: On the Exhaustion of Political Ideas in the Fifties.* Glencoe, IL: Free Press.

Belloc, Marianna, and Ugo Pagano. 2005. "Co-evolution Paths of Politics, Technology and Corporate Governance." *ECGI Working Paper in Law* (36).

Bellucci, Paolo. 1999. Economic Issues and Economic Voting in a Democratic Transition: The 1994 and 1996 Italian National Elections. Paper read at *ECPR Conference: Political Institutions. Intermediaries Between Economics and Politics*, March 26–31, at MZES, Germany: University of Mannheim.

Belsley, David A., Edwin Kuh, and Roy E. Welsch. 1980. *Regression Diagnostics: Identifying Influential Data and Sources of Collinearity.* New York: John Wiley & Sons.

Beramendi, Pablo, and David Rueda. 2007. "Social Democracy Constrained: Indirect Taxation in Industrialized Democracies." *British Journal of Political Science* 37: 619–41.

Berger, Suzanne, and Ronald Philip Dore. 1996. *National Diversity and Global Capitalism.* Ithaca, NY/London: Cornell University Press.

Berglöf, Erik, and Ernst-Ludwig von Thadden. 1999. "The Changing Corporate Governance Paradigm: Implications for Transition and Developing Countries." *William Davidson Institute Working Papers Series* (263).

Bergstrand, Jeffrey H. 1991. "Structural Determinants of Real Exchange Rates and National Price Levels: Some Empirical Evidence." *American Economic Review* (81): 325–34.

Berle, Adolf Augustus, Gardiner Coit Means, and Columbia University. Council for Research in the Social Sciences. 1932. *The Modern Corporation and Private Property.* New York: Macmillan.

Berry, S., J. Levinsohn, and A. Pakes. 1995. "Automobile Prices in Market Equilibrium." *Econometrica* 63 (4): 841.

Betts, Paul, and James Blitz. 1997. "At the Head of Italy's Table: The Financial Times Interview: Massimo D'Alema." *Financial Times*, December 22.

Beyer, Jürgen 1998. *Managerherrschaft in Deutschland? "Corporate Governance" unter Verflechtungsbedingungen*. Opladen: Westdeutscher Verlag.

—— 2002. "Deutschland AG a. D.: Deutsche Bank, Allianz und das Verflechtungszentrum großer deutscher Unternehmen. Wer beherrscht das Unternehmen." *Max-Planck-Institute for the Study of Societies Working Paper* (02/4).

—— and Martin Höpner. 2003. "Corporate Governance and the Disintegration of Organised Capitalism in the 1990s." *West European Politics* 26 (4): 179–98.

Bhagwati, Jagdish N. 1988. *Protectionism*. Cambridge, MA/London: MIT Press.

—— and Council on Foreign Relations. 2004. *In Defense of Globalization*. New York: Oxford University Press.

Bianchi, Marcello, and Magda Bianco. 2006. "Italian Corporate Governance in the Last 15 Years: From Pyramids to Coalitions?" *ECGI Finance Working Paper* (144/2006).

—— —— and Luca Enriques. 2001. "Ownership, Pyramidal Groups and Separation Between Ownership and Control in Italy." In *The Control of Corporate Europe*, eds. F. Barca and M. Becht. New York: Oxford University Press.

Bideleux, Robert, and Ian Jeffries. 2007. *A History of Eastern Europe: Crisis and Change*. 2nd edn. London: Routledge.

Bishop, Simon, and Mike Walker. 2002. *The Economics of EC Competition Law: Concepts, Application and Measurement*. 2nd edn. London: Sweet & Maxwell.

Black, John. 2002. *A Dictionary of Economics*. 2nd edn. Oxford: Oxford University Press.

Blair, Margaret M. 2003. "Reforming Corporate Governance: What History Can Teach Us." *Georgetown Law aAnd Economics Research Paper* (485663).

—— and Brookings Institution. 1995. *Ownership and Control: Rethinking Corporate Governance for the Twenty-First Century*. Washington, DC: Brookings Institution.

Blais, Andre, Donald Blake, and Stephane Dion. 1993. "Do Parties Make a Difference: Parties and the Size of Government in Liberal Democracies." *American Journal of Political Science* 37: 40–62.

Blais, A., D. Blake, and S. Dion. 1996. "Do Parties Make a Difference? A Reappraisal." *American Journal of Political Science* 40 (2): 514–20.

Blanchard, Olivier and Francesco Giavazzi. 2003. "Macroeconomic Effects of Regulation and Deregulation in Goods and Labor Markets." *Quarterly Journal of Economics* 118 (3): 879–908.

Blanchflower, D. G., A. J. Oswold, and P. Sanfey. 1996. "Wages, Profits, and Rent-Sharing." *Quarterly Journal of Economics* 111(1): 227–251.

Blaug, Mark. 1997. Economic Theory in Retrospect. 5th edn. Cambridge: Cambridge University Press.

Blim, Michael. 2000. "What is Still Left for the Left in Italy? Piecing Together a Post-Communist Position on Labor and Employment." *Journal of Modern Italian Studies* 5 (2): 169–85.

Blitz, James. 1997. "The Driving Force behind Privatization." *Financial Times*, December 10.

Blom-Hansen, J., L. C. Monkerud, and R. Sorensen. 2006. "Do Parties Matter for Local Revenue Policies? A Comparison of Denmark and Norway." *European Journal of Political Research* 45 (3): 445–65.
Bloom, Nick and John Van Reenen. 2006. "Measuring and Explaining Management Practices across Firms and Countries." *NBER Working Paper Series*.
Bobbio, Norberto (Translator: Allan Cameron). 1997. *Left and Right: The Significance of a Political Distinction*. Chicago: University of Chicago Press.
Bolt, Marie. 2000. "Stellungnahme des DGB zum Fragenkatalog der Regierungskommission: Corporate Governance – Unternehmensführung – Unternehmens kontrolle – Modernisierung des Aktienrechts." Berlin: Deutscher Gewerkschaftsbund.
Bonoli, Giuliano. 2003. "Two Worlds of Pension Reform in Western Europe." *Comparative Politics* 35 (4): 399–415.
Boone, Jan 2000. "Competition." *Discussion Paper Series: Centre for Economic Policy Research, London* (No. 2636).
——— J. C. van Ours, and H. van der Wiel. 2007. "How (Not) to Measure Competition." *Discussion Paper Series: Centre for Economic Policy Research, London*.
Botero, J. C., S. Djankov, R. La Porta, F. Lopez-de-Silanes, and A. Shleifer. 2004. "The Regulation of Labor." *Quarterly Journal of Economics* 119 (4): 1339–82.
Boulhol, Herve 2004. "The Convergence of Price-Cost Margins." *Cahiers de la MSE, Maison des Sciences Economiques, University of Paris Pantheon-Sorbonne*.
Bounds, Andrew, and Kate Burgess. 2007. "EU Scraps Plan for 'One-Share, One-Vote' Reform." *Financial Times*, October 4.
Braendle, Udo C. 2006. "Shareholder Protection in the USA and Germany – On the Fallacy of LLSV." *German Working Papers in Law and Economics* (18).
——— and Juergen Noll. 2004. "The Power of Monitoring." *SSRN Working Paper Series* (530482).
Brooks, Sarah M. 2005. "Interdependent and Domestic Foundations of Policy Change: The Diffusion of Pension Privatization Around the World." *International Studies Quarterly* 49 (2): 273–94.
Brown, Donald M., and Frederick R. Warren-Boulton. 1988. "Testing the Structure-Competition Relationship on Cross-Sectional Firm Data." *Discussion Paper, Economic Analysis Group, U.S. Department of Justice* (No. 88–6).
Budge, Ian. 2000. "Expert Judgements of Party Policy Positions: Uses and Limitations in Political Research." *European Journal of Political Research* 37 (1): 103–13.
——— Hans-Dieter Klingemann, Andrea Volkens, Judith Bara, and Eric Tanenbaum, eds. 2001. *Mapping Policy Preferences: Estimates for Parties, Electors, and Governments, 1945–1998*. Oxford: Oxford University Press.
Bull, Martin and Joerg Baudner. 2004. "Europeanization and Italian Policy for the Mezzogiorno." *Journal of European Public Policy* 11 (6): 1058–76.
——— and Martin Rhodes. 2007. "Introduction – Italy: A contested polity." *West European Politics* 30 (4): 657–69.
Bündnis 90/Die Grünen. 2002. *Die Zukunft ist Grün. Grundsatzprogramm von Bündnis 90/Die Grünen. Beschlossen auf der Bundesdelegiertenkonferenz am 15–17. März 2002 im Berliner Tempodrom*. Berlin: Bündnis 90/Die Grünen.
Burkart, M., D. Gromb, and F. Panunzi. 1997. "Large Shareholders, Monitoring, and the Value of the Firm." *Quarterly Journal oOf Economics* (112): 693–728.

Büschgen, Hans E. 1995. "Deutsche Bank from 1957 to the Present: The Emergence of an International Financial Conglomerate." In *The Deutsche Bank, 1870–1995*, edn. L. Gall. London: Weidenfeld & Nicolson.

Callaghan, Helen. 2007. "Insiders, Outsiders and the Politics of Corporate Governance: How Ownership Shapes Party Positions in Britain, Germany and France." *Max-Planck Institute for the Study of Societies Working Paper* (07/9).

Cameron, David R. 1984. "Social Democracy, Corporatism, Labor Quiescence, and the Representation of Economic Interest in Advanced Capitalist Society." In *Order and Conflict in Contemporary Capitalism*, edn J. H. Goldthorpe, Social Science Research Council (U.S.) and Joint Committee on Western Europe. Oxford: Clarendon Press.

Campus, Donatella. 2001. "Party System Change and Electoral Platforms: A Study of the 1996 Italian Election." *Modern Italy* 6 (1): 5–20.

Capelli, P., L. Bassi, H. Katz, D. Knoke, P. Osterman, and M. Useem. 1997. *Change at Work: How American Industry and Workers Are Coping With Corporate Restructuring and What Workers Must Do to Take Charge of Their Own Careers*. New York: Oxford University Press.

Carli, Guido 1993. *Cinquant'anni di vita Italiana*. Rome: Editori Laterza.

Carlin, Wendy, and Colin Mayer. 2003. "Finance, Investment and Growth." *Journal of Financial Economics* 69 (1): 191–226.

Carlton, Dennis W., and Jeffrey M. Perloff. 2005. *Modern Industrial Organization*. 4th edn. Boston, MA/London: Pearson Addison Wesley.

Carr, Chris, and Cyril Tomkins. 1998. "Context, Culture and the Role of the Finance Function in Strategic Decisions. A Comparative Analysis of Britain, Germany, the USA and Japan." *Management Accounting Research* 9 (23).

Castles, Francis, and Peter Mair. 1984. "Left-Right Political Scales: Some Expert Judgments." *European Journal of Political Research* (12): 73–88.

Cavelaars, Paul A. D. 2003. "Does Competition Enhancement have Permanent Inflation Effects?" *Kyklos* 56 (1): 69–94.

Chandler, Alfred Dupont. 1977. *The Visible Hand: The Managerial Revolution in American Business*. Cambridge, MA/London: Harvard University Press.

—— and Takashi Hikino. 1990. *Scale and Scope: The Dynamics of Industrial Capitalism*. Cambridge, MA/London: Belknap Press of Harvard University Press.

Chang, Eric C. C., Mark Andreas Kayser, and Ronald Rogowski. 2008. "Electoral Systems and Real Prices: Panel Evidence for the OECD Countries 1970–2000." *British Journal of Political Science* 38 (4): 739–751.

Cheffins, Brian. 2001. "Does Law Matter? The Separation of Ownership and Control in the United Kingdom." *Journal of Legal Studies* 30 (2): 459–84.

—— 2007. "The New Reality of 'Offensive' Share Ownership." *Financial Times*, June 13.

Chen, Nai-Fu, Richard Roll, and Stephen A. Ross. 1986. "Economic Forces and the Stock Market." *Journal of Business* 59 (3): 383–403.

Chhaochharia, Vidhi, and Luc A. Laeven. 2007. "Corporate Governance, Norms and Practices." *ECGI — Finance Working Paper* (165/2007).

Cioffi, John W. 2002. "Restructuring "Germany Inc.": The Politics of Company and Takeover Law Reform in Germany and the European Union." *Law and Policy* 24 (4): 355–402.

—— 2006. "Corporate Governance Reform, Regulatory Politics, and the Foundations of Finance Capitalism in the United States and Germany." *German Law Journal* 7 (6): 533–62.

—— and Martin Höpner. 2006. "The Political Paradox of Finance Capitalism: Interests, Preferences, and Center-Left Party Politics in Corporate Governance Reform." *Politics & Society* 34 (4): 463–502.

Claessens, S., S. Djankov, and L.H.P. Lang. 2000. "The Separation of Ownership and Control in East Asian Corporations." *Journal of Financial Economics* (58): 81–112.

Clark, Gordon L., and T. Hebb. 2004. "Pension Fund Corporate Engagement: The Fifth Stage of Capitalism." *Industrial Relations* 59 (1): 142–71.

—— 2003. *European Pensions and Global Finance*. Oxford: Oxford University Press.

Clark, Robert Charles. 1986. *Corporate Law*. Boston: Little Brown.

Coase, Ronald H. 1937. "The Nature of the Firm." *Economica* (4): 386–405.

Cobham, D., S. Cosci, and F. Mattesini. 1999. "The Italian Financial System: Neither Bank Based Nor Market Basedn" *Manchester School* 67 (3): 325–45.

Coffee, John. C. 2001. "The Rise of Dispersed Ownership: The Roles of Law and the State in the Separation of Ownership and Control." *Yale Law Journal* 111 (1): 1–82.

Coggan, Philip. 2004. "The Short View: US Profits Hit Record Share of GDP." *Financial Times*, July 6.

Contarino, Michael. 2000. "Italy's December 1998 'Social Pact for Development and Employment': Towards a New Political Economy for a 'Normal Country'?" In *Italian Politics: The Faltering Transition*, eds. M. Gilbert, G. Pasquino, and Istituto Carlo Cattaneo. New York/Oxford: Berghahn.

Conway, Paul, Véronique Janod, and Giuseppe Nicoletti. 2005. "Product Market Regulation in OECD Countries: 1998 to 2003." *OECD Economics Department Working Paper* (419).

—— and Giuseppe Nicoletti. 2006. "Product Market Regulation in the Non-Manufacturing Sectors of OECD Countries: Measurement and Highlights." *OECD Economics Department Working Paper* (530).

Cook, R. Dennis, and Sanford Weisberg. 1982. *Residuals and Influence in Regression*. London/New York: Chapman and Hall.

Corrado, Raffaele and Maurizio Zollo. 2006. "Small Worlds Evolving: Governance Reforms, Privatizations, and Ownership Networks in Italy." *Industrial and Corporate Change* 15 (2): 319–52.

Cova, Bruno. 2005. "The Parmalat Fraud Has Generated Too Little Reform." *Financial Times*, November 7.

Crafts, Nicholas F. R. 1992. "Institutions and Economic Growth: Recent British Experience in an International Context." *West European Politics* 15 (4): 16.

Culpepper, Pepper D. 2007. "Eppure, non si muove: Legal Change, Institutional Stability and Italian Corporate Governance." *West European Politics* 30 (4): 784–802.

—— 2005. "Institutional Change in Contemporary Capitalism: Coordinated Financial Systems since 1990." *World Politics* 57: 173–99.

Cusack, Thomas R., and Lutz Engelhardt. 2002. "Parties, Governments and Legislatures Data Set."

Cusack, Thomas R., and Susanne Fuchs. 2002. "Documentation Notes for Parties, Governments, and Legislatures Data Set." *Wissenschaftszentrum Berlin für Sozialforschung*.
—— and Pablo Beramendi. 2006. "Taxing work." *European Journal of Political Research* 45 (1): 43–73.
Dahl, Robert A. 1958. "A Critique of the Ruling Elite Model." *American Political Science Review* 52 (2): 463–9.
David, Paul. A. 1985. "Clio and the Economics of QWERTY." *American Economic Review* (75): 332–7.
Davis, E. P., and Benn Steil. 2001. *Institutional Investors*. Cambridge, Mass London: MIT.
De Cecco, Marcello. 2007. "Italy's Dysfunctional Political Economy." *West European Politics* 30 (4): 763–83.
De Cecco, Marcello and Giovanni Ferri. 2001. "Italy's Financial System: Banks and Industrial Investment." In *Comparing Economic Systems: Italy and Japan*, eds. A. Boltho, A. Vercelli and H. Yoshikawa. London: Palgrave.
Deeg, Richard. 1999. *Finance Capitalism Unveiled: Banks and the German Political Economy*. Ann Arbor: University of Michigan Press.
—— 2001. "Contemporary Challenges to German Federalism: from the European Union to the Global Economy." *Law and Policy in International Business* 33 (1): 51–76.
—— 2005. "Remaking Italian Capitalism? The Politics of Corporate Governance Reform." *West European Politics* 28 (3): 521–48.
—— and Sofia Perez. 2000. "International Capital Mobility and Domestic Institutions: Corporate Finance and Governance in Four European Cases." *Governance* 13 (2): 119–54.
Delaney, Sarah. 2004. "Parmalat Spurs Call for Reform in Business." *Washington Post*, January 20.
Della Sala, Vincent. 2004. "The Italian Model of Capitalism: On the Road Between Globalization and Europeanization?" *Journal of European Public Policy* 11 (6): 1041–57.
Demsetz, Harold. 1983. "The Structure of Ownership and the Theory of the Firm." *Journal of Law and Economics* 26 (2): 375–90.
—— and Kenneth Lehn. 1985. "The Structure of Corporate Ownership: Causes and Consequences." *Journal of Political Economy* 93 (6):1155–77.
Denis, David J., and Atulya Sarin. 1999. "Ownership and Board Structures in Publicly Traded Corporations: Evidence from Private Equity Financings." *Journal of Financial Economics* 52 (2): 187–223.
Detomasi, David A. 2006. "International Regimes: The Case of Western Corporate Governance." *International Studies Review* 8 (2): 225–51.
Deutscher Bundestag. 1998. "Plenarprotokoll 13/222."
DGB (Deutsche Gewerkschaftsbund). 2003. "Stellungnahme des DGB zum, Aktionsplan der EU-Kommission über die Modernisierung des Gesellschafts-rechts und Verbesserung der Corporate Governance."
Diamanti, Ilvo 2007. "The Italian Centre-Right and Centre-Left: Between Parties and 'The Party.'" *West European Politics* 30 (4): 733–62.

DIW (Deutsches Institut für Wirtschaftsforschung). 1996. "Employment and Social Policies Under International Constraints." In *Study for the Ministerie van Sociale Zaken en Werkgeledenheid of the Netherlands*. Berlin.
Djankov, Simeon, Rafael La Porta, Florencio Lopez-de-Silanes, and Andrei Shleifer. 2008. "The Law and Economics of Self-Dealing." *Journal of Financial Economics* 88 (3): 430–465.
Dobbin, Frank. 2004. "The Sociological View of The Economy." In *The New Economic Sociology: A Reader*, edn F. Dobbin: Princeton University Press.
—— and Dirk Zorn. 2005. "Corporate Malfeasance and the Myth of Shareholder Value." *Political Power and Social Theory* 17: 179–98.
Doidge, C., G. A. Karolyi, K. V. Lins, D. P. Miller, and R. M. Stulz. 2005. "Private Benefits of Control, Ownership, and the Cross-Listing Decision." *NBER Working Paper Series*.
—— G. A. Karolyi, K. V. Lins, D. P. Miller, and R. M. Stulz. 2004. "Why Do Countries Matter So Much For Corporate Governance?" *NBER Working Paper Series* (10726).
—— —— —— 2007. "Why Do Countries Matter So Much For Corporate Governance?" *Journal of Financial Economics*, 86 (1): 1–39.
Donaldson, John. 1989. *Key Issues in Business Ethics*. London: Academic Press.
Downs, Anthony. 1957. *An Economic Theory of Democracy*. New York: Harper & Row.
Draghi, Mario 2000. "Economic Policy Administration." *International Journal of Public Administration* 23 (2/3): 253–74.
Drucker, Peter F. 1976. *The Unseen Revolution: How Pension Fund Socialism Came to America*. London: Heinemann.
Duval, Romain, and Jørgen Elmeskov. 2006. "The Effects of EMU on Structural Reforms in Labour and Product Markets." *European Central Bank, Working Paper Series* (596).
Dyck, Alexander and Luigi Zingales. 2004a. "Control Premiums and the Effectiveness of Corporate Governance Systems." *Journal of Applied Corporate Finance* 16 (Spr/Sum): 51–72.
—— —— 2004b. "Private Benefits of Control: An International Comparison." *Journal of Finance* 59 (2): 537–600.
Dyson, Kenneth. 1986. "The State, Banks and Industry: The West German Case." In *State, Finance and Industry: A Comparative Analysis of Post-War Trends in Six Advanced Industrial Economies*, edn. A. Cox. Brighton: Wheatsheaf.
—— 2002. "Europeanisation of German Economic Policies: Testing the Limits of Model Germany." *Public Policy and Administration* 17 (2): 87–109.
—— and Kevin Featherstone. 1996. "Italy and EMU as a 'Vincolo Esterno': Empowering the Technocrats, Transforming the State." *South European Society and Politics* 1 (2): 272–99.
—— —— 1999. *The Road to Maastricht: Negotiating Economic and Monetary Union*. Oxford: Oxford University Press.
Dziobek, C., and J. R. Garrett. 1998. "Convergence of Financial Systems and Regulatory Policy Challenges in Europe and in the United States." *Advances in Finance, Investment and Banking* 5: 195–215.
Eckbo, B. Espen 2005. "Mastering Corporate Governance." *Financial Times*, May 20.
Edmondson, Gail. 2004. "Parmalat: A Corporate Version of 'Clean Hands'?" *Business Week*, March 1.

Edwards, Sebastian 1992. "Trade Orientation, Distortions, and Growth in Developing Countries." *Journal of Development Economics* (39): 31–57.

Edwards, Tony 2004. "Corporate Governance, Industrial Relations and Trends in Company-Level Restructuring in Europe: Convergence Towards the Anglo-American Model?" *Industrial Relations Journal* 35 (6): 518–35.

Efron, Bradley, and R. J. Tibshirani. 1993. *An Introduction to the Bootstrap*. New York/London: Chapman & Hall.

Eglau, Hans Otto 1989. *Wie Gott in Frankfurt. Die Deutsche Bank und die deutsche Industrie*. Düsseldorf: Econ.

Ehrlich, I., and Z. Liu. 1999. "Sensitivity Analyses of the Deterrence Hypothesis: Let's Keep the Econ in Econometrics." *Journal of Law and Economics* 15 (2): 455–87.

Elsas, Ralf and Jan Pieter Krahnen. 2004. "Universal Banks and Relationships with Firms." In *The German Financial System*, eds. J. P. Krahnen and R. H. Schmidt. Oxford: Oxford University Press.

Enriques, Luca. 2002. "Do Corporate Law Judges Matter? Some Evidence from Milan." *European Business Organization Law Review* (3): 765–821.

—— 2003. "Off the Books, but on the Record: Evidence from Italy on the Relevance of Judges to the Quality of Corporate Law." In *Global Markets, Domestic Institutions: Corporate Law and Governance in the New Era of Cross-Border Deals*, edn C. J. Milhaupt. New York: Columbia University Press.

—— 2004. "R. Kraakman et al.: The Anatomy of Corporate Law: A Comparative and Functional Approach." *American Journal of Comparative Law* 52: 1011–36.

—— 2006. "EC Company Law Directives and Regulations: How Trivial Are They?" *University of Pennsylvania Journal of International Economic Law* 27: 1–78.

—— and P. Volpin. 2007. "Corporate Governance Reforms in Continental Europe." *Journal of Economic Perspectives* 21: 117–40.

Esser, Josef. 1998. "Monopolkapitalismus, Stamokap." In *Lexikon der Politik. Band 7: Politische Begriffe*, eds. D. Nohlen, R. O. Schultze, and S. S. Schüttemeyer. München: C.H. Beck.

Faccio, Mara and Larry H. Lang. 2002. "The Ultimate Ownership of Western European Corporations." *Journal of Financial Economics* 65 (3): 365–95.

Faini, R., J. Haskel, G. Barba Navaretti, C. Scarpa, and C. Wey. 2006. "Contrasting Europe's Decline: Do Product Market Reforms Help?" In *Structural Reforms Without Prejudices*, eds. T. Boeri, M. Castanheira, R. Faini and V. Galasso. Oxford: Oxford University Press.

Fama, Eugene. 1980. "Agency Problems and the Theory of the Firm." *Journal of Political Economy* 88 (2): 288–307.

—— and Michael C. Jensen. 1985. "Organizational Forms and Investment Decisions." *Journal of Financial Economics* (14): 101–19.

Faure, Andrew M. 1994. "Some Methodological Problems in Comparative Politics." *Journal of Theoretical Politics* 6 (3): 307.

Ferrarini, Guido. 2004. "Corporate Governance Changes in the 20th Century: A View from Italy." *ECGI Working Paper* (29): 31–52.

—— and Paolo Giudici. 2005. "Financial Scandals and the Role of Private Enforcement: The Parmalat Case." *ECGI Law Working Paper* (40/2005).

―――― 2006. "Financial Scandals and the Role of Private Enforcement: The Parmalat Case." In *After Enron: Improving Corporate Law and Modernising Securities Regulation in Europe and the US*, eds. J. Armour and J. McCahery. Oxford: Hart.

―――― and M. S. Richter. 2005. "Company Law Reform in Italy: Real Progress?" *Rabels Zeitschrift Für Auslandisches und Internationales Privatrecht*: 69(4): 658–697.

Ferrera, Maurizio, and Elisabetta Gualmini. 2004. *Rescued by Europe?: Social and Labour Market Reforms in Italy from Maastricht to Berlusconi*. Amsterdam: Amsterdam University Press.

Financial Times. December 8, 2004. "Special Report on Germany."

Fischer, Karl-Hermann and Christian Pfeil. 2004. "Regulation and Competition in German Banking: An Assessment." In *The German Financial System*, eds. J. P. Krahnen and R. H. Schmidt. Oxford: Oxford University Press.

Fleissig, Adrian R. and Jack Strauss. 2001. "Panel Unit-Root Tests of OECD Stochastic Convergence." *Review of International Economics* 9 (1): 153–62.

Fligstein, Neil. 1990. *The Transformation of Corporate Control*. Cambridge, MA/London: Harvard University Press.

―――― 2001. *The Architecture of Markets: An Economic Sociology of Twenty-First-Century Capitalist Societies*. Princeton, NJ/Oxford: Princeton University Press.

―――― 2005. "The End of (Shareholder Value) Ideology?" *Political Power and Social Theory* 17: 223–38.

―――― and Jennifer Choo. 2005. "Law and Corporate Governance." *Annual Review of Law and Social Science* 1: 61–84.

Fohlin, Caroline 2005. "The History of Corporate Ownership and Control in Germany." In *The History of Corporate Governance Around the World: Family Business Groups to Professional Managers*, edn. R. K. Morck. Chicago: University of Chicago Press.

Franks, Julian, and Colin Mayer. 1990. "Capital Markets and Corporate Control: A Study of France, Germany and the UK." *Economic Policy* (5): 191–231.

―――― 1994. "Corporate Control: A Comparison of Insider and Outsider Systems." *Mimeo, London Business School, Working Paper*.

―――― 1995. "Ownership and Control." In *Business Organisation: Do Participation and Cooperation increase Competitiveness?*, edn H. Siebert. Kiel: Mohr.

―――― 1997. "Corporate Ownership and Control in the UK, Germany and France." *Bank of America Journal of Applied Corporate Finance* (9): 30–45.

―――― and S. Rossi. 2004. "Ownership: Evolution and Regulation." *Institute of Finance and Accounting Working Paper, London Business School*.

Franzese, Robert. J. 2002. "Electoral and Partisan Cycles in Economic Policies and Outcomes." *Annual Review of Political Science* 5: 369–422.

Freeden, Michael. 1999. "The Ideology of New Labour." *Political Quarterly* 70 (1): 42–51.

Freeman, R. Edward. 1984. *Strategic Management: A Stakeholder Approach*. Boston: Pitman.

Freeman, Richard B., and James L. Medoff. 1984. *What Do Unions Do?* New York: Basic Books.

Frentrop, Paul Marie Louis. 2002. Corporate Governance 1602–2002. Doctoral thesis – Universiteit van Tilburg 2002, Prometheus, Amsterdam.

Frey, Bruno S., and Friedrich Schneider. 1982. "Politico-economic Models in Competition with Alternative Models: Which Predict Better?" *European Journal of Political Research* 10 (3): 241–54.

Frick, Bernd. 1997. *Mitbestimmung und Personalfluktuation: Zur Wirtschaftlichkeit der bundesdeutschen Betriebsverfassung im internationalen Vergleich.* München and Mering: Hampp.

Friedman, Andrew L., and Samantha Miles. 2002. "Developing Stakeholder Theory." *Journal of Management Studies* 39 (1): 1–22.

Friedman, Alan. 1998. "Prime Minister Aims to Make Italy Competitive: Prodi Rolls Out Reforms." *International Herald Tribune*, February 19.

Friedman, Milton. 1970. "The Social Responsibility of Business is to Increase Its Profits." *New York Times Magazine.* September 13, 32–3.

Froud, Julie and Karel Williams. 2007. "Private Equity and the Culture of Value Extraction." *Centre for Research on Socio-Cultural Change, University of Manchester, Working Papers Series* (No. 31).

Fulghieri, Paolo and Matti J. Suominen. 2005. "Does Bad Corporate Governance Lead to Too Little Competition? Corporate Governance, Capital Structure and Industry Concentration." *ECGI Working Paper Series in Finance* (74/2005).

Galbraith, John Kenneth. 1952. *American Capitalism: The Concept of Countervailing Power.* Transaction Publishers.

Gallagher, Michael. 1991. "Proportionality, Disproportionality, and Electoral Systems." *Electoral Studies* (10): 33–51.

—— Michael Laver, and Peter Mair. 2006. *Representative Government in Modern Europe.* 4th edn. Boston: McGraw-Hill.

Garrett, Geoffrey 2001. "Globalization and Government Spending around the World." *Studies in Comparative International Development* 35 (4): 3–29.

—— and P. Lange. 1995. "Internationalization, Institutions, and Political Change." *International Organization* 49 (4): 627.

Gerring, John. 2004. "What Is a Case Study and What Is It Good for?" *American Political Science Review* 98 (2): 341–54.

Gianfrate, Gianfranco. 2007. "What Do Shareholders' Coalitions Really Want? Evidence from Italian Voting Trusts." *Corporate Governance* 15 (2): 122–32.

Giannetti, Daniela and Rosa Mulé. 2006. "The Democratici di Sinistra: In Search of a New Identity." *South European Society and Politics* 11: 457–75.

Gilson, Ronald J. 2001. "Globalizing Corporate Governance: Convergence of Form or Function." *The American Journal of Comparative Law* 49 (2): 329–57

Giuliani, Marco 2000. "Europeanisation and Italy: A Bottom-up Process?" *Southern European Society and Politics* 5: 47–72.

Gjersem, Carl. 2004. "Policies Bearing on Product Market Competition and Growth in Europe." *OECD Economics Department Working Paper* (No. 378).

Glaeser, E., S. Johnson, and A. Shleifer. 2001. "Coase versus the Coasians." *Quarterly Journal of Economics* 116 (3): 853–900.

Goergen, Marc. 2007. "What Do We Know about Different Systems of Corporate Governance?" *Journal of Corporate Law Studies* 7(1): 1–15.

Goldthorpe, John H., edn 1984. *Order and Conflict in Contemporary Capitalism.* Oxford: Oxford University Press.

Golub, Stephen. 2003. "Measures of Restrictions on Inward Foreign Direct Investment for OECD Countries." *OECD Economics Studies* (No. 36/1).
Gompers, Paul and Andrew Metrick. 2001. "Institutional Investors and Equity Prices." *Quarterly Journal of Economics* 116 (1): 229–60.
Gordon, Jeffrey N. 2007. "The Rise of Independent Directors in the United States, 1950–2005: of Shareholder Value and Stock Market Prices." *Stanford Law Review* 59 (6): 1465–568.
Gospel, Howard and Andrew Pendleton. 2003. "Finance, Corporate Governance and the Management of Labour: A Conceptual and Comparative Analysis." *British Journal of Industrial Relations* 41 (3): 557–82.
Gourevitch, Peter Alexis. 2003. "Corporate Governance – Global Markets, National Politics." In *Governance in a Global Economy: Political Authority in Transition*, eds. Kahler, Miles and David A. Lake. Princeton, NJ; Oxford: Princeton University Press.
—— and James Shinn. 2005. *Political Power and Corporate Control: The New Global Politics of Corporate Governance*. Princeton, NJ/Oxford: Princeton University Press.
—— Richard Carney, and Michael Hawes. 2003. Testing Political Explanations of Corporate Governance Patterns. Paper read at *Conference on Economics, Political Institutions, and Financial Markets*, February, at Social Science History Institute, Stanford University.
Grahl, John and Paul Teague. 2004. "The German Model in Danger." *Industrial Relations Journal* 35 (6): 557–73.
Granovetter, Mark. 1985. "Economic Action and Social Structure: The Problem of Embeddedness." *The American Journal of Sociology* 91 (3): 481–510.
Grant, Wyn. 2003. "Corporatism." In *The Concise Oxford Dictionary of Politics*, 2nd edn., eds. I. McLean and A. McMillan. Oxford: Oxford University Press.
Gray, Cheryl W. 1996. "In Search of Owners: Privatization and Corporate Governance in Transition Economies." *The World Bank Research Observer* 11 (2): 179–97.
Greene, William H. 2003. *Econometric Analysis*. 5th edn. London: Prentice Hall International.
Griffith, R., R. Harrison, and G. Macartney. 2007. "Product Market Reforms, Labour Market Institutions and Unemployment." *Economic Journal* 117 (519): C142–66.
Grossman, Sanford J., and Oliver D. Hart. 1980. "Takeover Bids, The Free-Rider Problem, and the Theory of the Corporation." *The Bell Journal of Economics* 11 (1): 42–64.
—— —— 1988. "One Share-One Vote and the Market for Corporate Control." *Journal of Financial Economics* (20): 175–202.
Guiso, Luigi, and Tullio Jappelli. 2000. "Household Portfolios in Italy." *Centro Studi in Economia e Finanza, Salerno* (*Working Paper* No. 43.).
Gwartney, James and Robert Lawson. 2006. "Economic Freedom of the World – 2006 Annual Report." Canada: Fraser Institute.
Hackethal, Andreas. 2004. "German Banks and Banking Structure." In *The German Financial System*, edn. J. P. Krahnen and R. H. Schmidt. Oxford: Oxford University Press.
—— Reinhard H. Schmidt, and Marcel Tyrell. 2005. "Banks and German Corporate Governance: On the Way to a Capital Market-Based System?" *Corporate Governance* 13 (3): 397–407.

Haferkamp, Wilhelm. 1966. "Der Deutsche Gewerkschaftsbund und die wirtschaftspolitischen Grundsätze seines Programms." In *Wirtschaftsordnung und Wirtschaftsverfassung im DGB-Grundsatzprogramm. Referate einer öffentlichen Tagung der DGB-Bundesschule Bad Kreuznach am 4. und 5. April 1966*, edn. Deutscher Gewerkschaftsbund. Düsseldorf: Deutscher Gewerkschaftsbund.

Hall, Peter A., and Daniel W. Gingerich. 2004. "Varieties of Capitalism and Institutional Complementarities in the Macroeconomy: An Empirical Analysis." *Max-Planck Institute for the Study of Societies Working Paper* (04/5).

—— and David W. Soskice. 2001. *Varieties of Capitalism: The Institutional Foundations of Comparative Advantage*. Oxford: Oxford University Press.

—— and R. C. R. Taylor. 1996. "Political Science and the Three New Institutionalisms." *Political Studies* 44 (5): 936–57.

Hansmann, Henry and Reinier Kraakman. 2001. "The End of History for Corporate Law." *Georgetown Law Journal* 89 (2): 439–68.

Hart, Oliver. 1989. "An Economist's Perspective on the Theory of the Firm." *Columbia Law Review* 89 (7): 1757–74.

Hassel, Anke. 1999. "The Erosion of the German System of Industrial Relations." *British Journal of Industrial Relations* 37 (3): 483–506.

Hassel, Anke, and Hugh Williamson. 2004. *The Evolution of the German Model: How to Judge Reforms in Europe's Largest Economy*. London: Anglo-German Foundation.

—— and Wolfgang Streeck. 2004. "The Crumbling Pillars of Social Partnership." In *Beyond the Stable State: A House United Cannot Stand*, eds. H. Kitschelt and W. Streeck. London: Frank Cass.

Hausman, Jerry A. 1978. "Specification Tests in Econometrics." *Econometrica* 46 (6): 1251–71.

—— G. Leonard, and J.D. Zona. 1994. "Competitive Analysis with Differentiated Products." *Annales D'Economie et de Statistique* (34): 159–80.

Hawley, James P., and Andrew T. Williams. 2000. *The Rise of Fiduciary Capitalism: How Institutional Investors Can Make Corporate America More Democratic*. Philadelphia: University of Pennsylvania Press.

Hayek, Friedrich A. von. 1960. *The Constitution of Liberty*. London: Routledge & Kegan Paul.

—— 1967. "Notes on the Evolution of Systems of Rules of Conduct." In *Studies in Philosophy, Politics and Economics*, edn F. A. Hayek. London: Routledge and Kegan Paul.

—— and Erich W. Streissler. 1969. *Roads to Freedom: Essays in Honour of Friedrich A. von Hayek*. London: Routledge & Kegan Paul.

Hedstrom, Peter, and Richard Swedberg. 1998. *Social Mechanisms: An Analytical Approach to Social Theory*. Cambridge: Cambridge University Press.

Helbling, Thomas, Dalia Hakura, and Xavier Debrun. 2004. "Fostering Structural Reforms in Industrial Countries." In *IMF World Economic Outlook (Chapter III)*. Washington: International Monetary Fund.

Hellmann, Stephen. 1997. "The Italian Left After the 1996 Elections." In *Italian Politics: The Center-Left in Power*, ed. R. D'Alimonte, D. Nelken and I. C. Cattaneo. Boulder, Colo. Oxford: Westview Press.

Hellwig, Martin. 2000. "On the Economics and Politics of Corporate Finance and Corporate Control." In *Corporate Governance: Theoretical and Empirical Perspectives*, edn X. Vives. Cambridge: Cambridge University Press.

Hering, Martin. 2004. "Turning Ideas into Policies: Implementing Modern Social Democratic Thinking in Germany's Pension Policy." In *Social Democratic Party Policies in Contemporary Europe*, eds. G. Bonoli and M. A. Powell. London: Routledge.

Hermalin, Benjamin 1992. "The Effects of Competition on Executive Behavior." *RAND Journal of Economics* (23): 350–65.

Hibbs, Douglas A. 1977. "Political Parties and Macroeconomic Policy." *American Political Science Review* (71): 1467–87.

—— 1987. *The American Political Economy: Macroeconomics and Electoral Politics*. Cambridge, MA/London: Harvard University Press.

—— 1992. "Partisan Theory after Fifteen Years." *European Journal of Political Economy* 8: 361–73.

Hibbs, Douglas A., and Christopher Dennis. 1988. "Income Distribution in the United States." *American Political Science Review* 82 (2): 467–90.

Hicks, Alexander M., and Duane H. Swank. 1992. "Politics, Institutions, and Welfare Spending in Industrialized Democracies, 1960–82." *American Political Science Review* 86 (3): 658–74.

Hicks, John R. 1935. "Annual Survey of Economic Theory: The Theory of Monopoly." *Econometrica* 3 (1): 1–20.

Hilferding, Rudolf. 1910. *Das Finanzkapital*. Wien: Verlag der Wiener Volksbuchhandlung.

Hine, David, and Salvatore Vassallo. 2000. "Introduction: One Step Towards Europe; Two Steps Back From Institutional Reform." In *Italian Politics: The Return Of Politics*, eds. D. Hine and S. Vassallo. New York/Oxford: Berghahn.

Hirschman, Albert O. 1970. *Exit, Voice, and Loyalty: Responses to Decline in Firms, Organizations, and States*. Cambridge, MA: Harvard University Press.

Hiscox, Michael J. and Scott L. Kastner. 2002. "A General Measure of Trade Policy Orientations: Gravity-Model-Based Estimates for 82 Nations, 1960 to 1992." *Harvard University Mimeograph*.

Høj, Jens, V. Galasso, G. Nicoletti, and T. Dang. 2006. "The Political Economy of Structural Reform: Empirical Evidence from OECD Countries." *OECD Economics Department Working Papers* (501).

—— Miguel Jimenez, Maria Maher, Guiseppe Nicoletti, and Mikael Wise. 2007. "Product Market Competition in the OECD Countries: Taking Stock and Moving Forward." *OECD Economics Department Working Paper* (575).

Hollingsworth, J. Rogers, and Robert Boyer. 1997. *Contemporary Capitalism: The Embeddedness of Institutions*. Cambridge: Cambridge University Press.

Hopkin, Jonathan and Piero Ignazi. 2008. "Newly Governing Parties in Italy: Comparing the PDS, Lega Nord and Forza Italia." In *New Parties in Government*, edn K. Deschouwer. London: Routledge.

Höpner, Martin. 2001. "Corporate Governance in Transition: Ten Empirical Findings on Shareholder Value and Industrial Relations in Germany." *Max-Planck-Institute for the Study of Societies Working Paper* (01/5).

Höpner, Martin. 2002. *Wer beherrscht die Unternehmen? Shareholder Value, Managerherrschaft und Mitbestimmung in Deutschland*. Frankfurt/New York: Campus Verlag.

―― 2003. "European Corporate Governance Reform and the German Party Paradox." *Max-Planck Institute for the Study of Societies Working Paper* (03/4).

―― and Gregory Jackson. 2001. "An Emerging Market for Corporate Control? The Mannesmann Takeover and German Corporate Governance." *MPIfG Discussion Paper* (01/4).

―― and Lothar Krempel. 2004. "The Politics of the German Company Network." *Competition and Change* 8 (4): 339–56.

Hopt, Klaus J. 2006. "Comparative Company Law." *ECGI—Law Working Paper* (77/2006).

Huang, H., and C. Xu. 1999. "Financial Institutions and the Financial Crisis in East Asia—Growth, Repression, and Liberalization." *European Economic Review* 43 (4–6): 903–14.

Huber, Evelyne, and John D. Stephens. 2001. *Development and Crisis of the Welfare State: Parties and Policies in Global Markets*. Chicago: London: University of Chicago Press.

―― Charles Ragin, John D. Stephens, David Brady, and Jason Beckfield. 2004. "Comparative Welfare Reform Dataset." *Northwestern University, University of North Carolina, Duke University and Indiana University*.

Huber, John D. and Mathew J. Gabel. 2000. "Putting Parties in Their Place: Inferring Party Left-Right Ideological Positions from Party Manifestos Data." *American Journal of Political Science* 44 (1): 94–103.

―― and Ronald Inglehart. 1995. "Expert Interpretations of Party Space and Party Locations in 42 Societies." *Party Politics* 1 (1): 73.

Huffschmid, Jörg. 1995. "Weder toter Hund noch schlafender Löwe: Die Theorie des Staatsmonopolistischen Kapitalismus." *Zeitschrift für sozialistische Politik und Wirtschaft*, 34–48.

Hutton, Will. 1995. *The State We're In*. London: Cape.

Ibison, David. 2006. "Swedish PM Raps Private Equity." *Financial Times*, September 7.

Im, K. S., M. H. Pesaran, and Y. Shin. 2003. "Testing For Unit Roots in Heterogeneous Panels." *Journal of Econometrics* 115 (1): 53–74.

Imbeau, L. M., F. Petry, and M. Lamari. 2001. "Left-Right Party Ideology and Government Policies: A Meta-Analysis." *European Journal of Political Research* 40 (1): 1–29.

Israely, Jeff. 2004. "The Italian Exception." *Time*, May 3.

Iversen, Torben, and David W. Soskice. 2006. "Electoral Institutions and the Politics of Coalitions: Why Some Democracies Redistribute More Than Others." *American Political Science Review* 100: 165–82.

IW (Institut der deutschen Wirtschaft). 1999. "Argumente zu Unternehmensfragen."

Jackson, Gregory. 2001. "The Origins of Nonliberal Corporate Governance in Germany and Japan." In *The Origins of Nonliberal Capitalism: Germany and Japan in Comparison*, ed. W. Streeck and K. Yamamura. Ithaca, NY/London: Cornell University Press.

―― 2003. "Corporate Governance in Germany and Japan: Liberalization Pressures and Responses." In *The End of Diversity?: Prospects for German and Japanese Capitalism*, eds. K. Yamamura and W. Streeck. Ithaca, NY: Cornell University Press.

—— 2005. "Stakeholders under Pressure: Corporate Governance and Labour Management in Germany and Japan." *Corporate Governance* 13 (3): 419–28.
—— Martin Höpner, and Antje Kurdelbusch. 2005. "Corporate Governance and Employees in Germany: Changing Linkages, Complementarities, and Tensions." In *Corporate Governance and Labour Management: An International Comparison*, eds. H. F. Gospel and A. Pendleton. Oxford: Oxford University Press.
Jagannathan, Ravi and Shaker B. Srinivasan. 2000. "Does Product Market Competition Reduce Agency Costs?" *NBER Working Paper* (7480).
Jean, Sebastien and Giuseppe Nicoletti. 2002. "Product Market Regulation and Wage Premia in Europe and North America: An Empirical Investigation," *OECD Economics Department Working Paper* (318).
Jensen, Michael C., and William H. Meckling. 1976. "Theory of the Firm: Managerial Behavior, Agency Costs and Ownership Structure." *Journal of Financial Economics* (3): 305–60.
Johnson, Simon. 2007. "The Rise of Sovereign Wealth Funds." In *Finance & Development: A Quarterly Magazine of the IMF.* Washington DC: International Monetary Fund.
Judson, Ruth A., and Ann L. Owen. 1997. "Estimating Dynamic Panel Data Models: A Practical Guide for Macroeconomists." *Finance and Economics Discussion Series*.
Jürgens, Ulrich, Katrin Naumann, and Joachim Rupp. 2000. "Shareholder Value in an Adverse Environment: The German Case." *Economics and Society* (29): 54–79.
Kakabadse, Andrew, and Nada Kakabadse. 2001. *The Geopolitics of Governance: The Impact of Contrasting Philosophies*. Basingstoke: Palgrave.
Kam, Cindy D., and Robert J. Franzese. 2007. *Modeling and Interpreting Interactive Hypotheses in Regression Analysis*. Ann Arbor: University of Michigan.
Kapner, Fredn 2002. "Investors Aghast at Fondiaria Imbroglio." *Financial Times*, March 22.
—— 2003. "All Roads Lead to Reform." *Financial Times*, April 3.
Karier, Thomas. 1985. "Unions and Monopoly Profits." *Review of Economics and Statistics* 67 (February): 34–42.
Katz, Lawrence F. and Lawrence H. Summers. 1989. "Industry Rents: Evidence and Implications," *Brookings Papers on Economic Activity: Microeconomics*: 209–75.
Katzenstein, Peter J. 1984. *Corporatism and Change: Austria, Switzerland, and the Politics of Industry*. Ithaca, NY/London: Cornell University Press.
—— 1985. *Small States in World Markets: Industrial Policy in Europe*. Ithaca, NY: Cornell University Press.
—— 1987. *Policy and Politics in West Germany: The Growth of a Semisovereign State*. Philadelphia: Temple University Press.
Kay, John A. 2003. *The Truth About Markets: Their Genius, Their Limits, Their Follies*. London: Allen Lane.
—— 2005. "Why Many Mergers Are a Triumph of Hope Over Experience." *Financial Times*, November 15.
Keasey, Kevin, Steve Thompson, and Mike Wright. 1997. *Corporate Governance: Economic and Financial Issues*. New York: Oxford University Press.
Keele, Luke and Nathan J. Kelly. 2006. "Dynamic Models for Dynamic Theories: The Ins and Outs of Lagged Dependent Variables." *Political Analysis* 14 (2): 186–205.
Kenen, Peter B. 1995. *Economic and Monetary Union in Europe: Moving Beyond Maastricht*. Cambridge: Cambridge University Press.

Keohane, Robert O., and Helen V. Milner. 1996. *Internationalization and Domestic Politics*. Cambridge: Cambridge University Press.
Kersbergen, Kees van. 1995. *Social Capitalism: A Study of Christian Democracy and the Welfare State*. London: Routledge.
Khanna, T., J. Kogan, and K. Palepu. 2006. "Globalization and Similarities in Corporate Governance: A Cross-Country Analysis." *Review of Economics and Statistics* 88: 69–90.
Kho, Bong-Chan, René M Stulz, and Francis E Warnock. 2006. "Financial Globalisation, Governance and the Evolution of the Home Bias." *Bank for International Settlements Working Papers* (220).
Kim, Heemin and Richard C. Fording. 1998. "Voter Ideology in Western Democracies, 1946–1989." *European Journal of Political Research* 33 (1): 73–97.
—— 2002. "Government Partisanship in Western democracies, 1945–1998." *European Journal of Political Research* 41 (2): 187–206.
Kimmitt, Robert M. 2008. "Public Footprints in Private Markets: Sovereign Wealth Funds and the World Economy." *Foreign Affairs*, 87 (January/February): 119–30.
Kindleberger, Charles Poor, and Robert Z. Aliber. 2005. *Manias, Panics, and Crashes: A History of Financial Crises*. 5th edn. Basingstoke: Palgrave Macmillan.
King, Gary, Robert O. Keohane, and Sidney Verba. 1994. *Designing Social Inquiry: Scientific Inference in Qualitative Research*. Princeton, NJ/Chichester: Princeton University Press.
Kirchheimer, Otto. 1966. "Germany: The Vanishing Opposition." In *Political Oppositions in Western Democracies*, edn R. A. Dahl. New Haven, CT/London: Yale University Press.
Kitschelt, Herbert, P. Lange, G. Marks, and J. D. Stephens, eds. 1999. *Continuity and Change in Contemporary Capitalism*. Cambridge: Cambridge University Press.
Kittel, Bernhard, and Hannes Winner. 2005. "How Reliable is Pooled Analysis in Political Economy? The Globalization-Welfare State Nexus Revisitedn" *European Journal of Political Research* 44 (2): 269–93.
Klein, B., R. G. Crawford, and A. A. Alchian. 1978. "Vertical Integration, Appropriable Rents, and the Competitive Contracting Process." *Journal of Law and Economics* 21 (2): 297–326.
Klingemann, Hans-Dieter, Richard I. Hofferbert, and Ian Budge. 1994. *Parties, Policies, and Democracy*. Boulder, CO/Oxford: Westview.
—— Andrea Volkens, Judith Bara, and Ian Budge. 2006. *Mapping Policy Preferences II: Estimates for Parties, Electors, and Governments in Central and Eastern Europe, European Union and OECD 1990–2003*. Oxford: Oxford University Press.
Knetter, Michael M. 1989. "Price Discrimination by U.S. and German Exporters." *American Economic Review* 79 (1): 198–210.
Knight, Frank H. 1921. *Risk, Uncertainty and Profit*. Boston: Houghton Mifflin.
Knight, Jack. 1992. *Institutions and Social Conflict*. Cambridge: Cambridge University Press.
Kolla, Peter. 2004. "The Mannesmann Trial and the Role of the Courts." *German Law Journal* 5 (7): 829–47.
Kommission Mitbestimmung. 1998. "Mitbestimmung und neue Unternehmenskulturen." In *Bericht der Kommission Mitbestimmung der Bertelsmann Stiftung und der Hans Bockler-Stiftung*. Guttersloh: Verlag der Bertelsmann Stiftung.

Köstler, Roland. 2000. "Anforderungen der Arbeitnehmer an eine effektive Unternehmensüberwachung." In *Institutioneller Wandel in den industriellen Beziehungen*. Köln, 8–9 (Dezember): Max-Planck-Institut für Gesellschaftsforschung.

Kox, Henk and Arjan Lejour. 2006. "The Effects of the Services Directive on Intra-EU Trade and FDI." *Revue Economique* 57: 747–70.

Kruse, Timothy A. 2007. "Minority Expropriation and Shareholder Activism Following Olivetti's Hostile Takeover of Telecom Italia." *Corporate Governance* 15 (2): 133–43.

Kugler, Adriana D., and Giovanni Pica. 2006. "The Effects of Employment Protection and Product Market Regulations on the Italian Labour market." In *Labour Market Adjustments in Europe*, eds. J. Messina, C. Michelacci, J. Turunen and G. Zoega. Cheltenham: Edward Elgar Publishing.

Küller, Hans-Detlev. 1997. "Das Shareholder-Value-Konzept aus Gewerkschaftssicht." *Betriebswirtschaftliche Forschung und Praxis* (49): 517–31.

Kurzer, Paulette. 1993. *Business and Banking: Political Change and Economic Integration in Western Europe*. Ithaca, NY/London: Cornell University Press.

Kwoka, John E. 1983. "Monopoly, Plant, and Union Effects on Worker Wages." *Industrial and Labor Relations Review* 36 (2):251–7.

La Porta, Rafael, Florencio Lopez-de-Silanes, and Andrei Shleifer. 1999. "Corporate Ownership Around the World." *Journal of Finance* 54 (2): 471–518.

—————— and Robert W. Vishny. 1998. "Law and Finance." *Journal of Political Economy* 106 (4): 1113–55.

———————— 1997. "Legal Determinants of External Finance." *Journal of Finance* 52 (3): 1131–50.

———————— 2000. "Investor Protection and Corporate Governance." *Journal of Financial Economics* 58 (1–2): 3–27.

Lambsdorff, Otto Graf. 1989. "Aktienrecht ist Anlegerschutz – Ist unser Aktienrecht noch zeitgemäß?" In *Institutionelle Rahmenbedingungen effizienter Kapitalmärkte*, edn W. Engels. Frankfurt a.M.

Lamoreaux, Naomi R., and Jean-Laurent Rosenthal. 2004. "Legal Regime and Business's Organizational Choice: A Comparison of France and the United States During the Mid-Nineteenth Century." *NBER Working Paper Series* (10288).

Landman, Todd. 2003. *Issues and Methods in Comparative Politics: An Introduction*. 2nd edn. London: Routledge.

Lane, Christel. 2003. "Changes in Corporate Governance of German Corporations: Convergence to the Anglo-American Model?" *ESRC Centre for Business Research, University of Cambridge, Working Paper* (259): 1–29.

Lane, Philip R. 1997. "Inflation in Open Economies." *Journal of International Economics* 42 (3/4): 327–48.

Lange, Peter, and Geoffrey Garrett. 1985. "The Politics of Growth: Strategic Interaction and Economic Performance in the Advanced Industrial Democracies, 1974–1980." *Journal of Politics* 47 (3): 792–827.

Laponce, J. A. 1981. *Left and Right: The Topography of Political Perceptions*. Toronto; London: University of Toronto Press.

Laver, Michael, and W. Ben Hunt. 1992. *Policy and Party Competition*. New York/London: Routledge.

Lazonick, William. 2007. "The US Stock Market and the Governance of Innovative Enterprise."*Industrial and Corporate Change* (6): 983–1035.

Lazonick, William and M. O'Sullivan. 2000. "Maximizing Shareholder Value: A New Ideology for Corporate Governance." *Economy and Society* 29 (1): 13–35.

Leachman Lori, Vinay Kumar and Scott Orleck. 2002. "Explaining Variations in Private Equity: A Panel Approach." *Working Paper in Economics, Duke University* (02–14).

Leamer, Edward E. 1983. "Let's Take the Con out of Econometrics." *American Economic Review* 73 (3): 31–43.

—— 1985. "Sensitivity Analysis Would Help." *American Economic Review* 75: 308–13.

Lehmbruch, Gerhard 2001. "The Institutional Embedding of Market Economies: The German 'Model' and its Impact on Japan." In *The Origins of Nonliberal Capitalism: Germany and Japan in Comparison*, eds. W. Streeck and K. Yamamura. Ithaca, NY/London: Cornell University Press.

—— and Philippe C. Schmitter. 1979. *Trends Towards Corporatist Intermediation.* Beverly Hills, CA/London: Sage.

Lele, Priya P., and Mathias M. Siems. 2007. "Shareholder Protection – A Leximetric Approach." *Journal of Corporate Law Studies* 7: 17–50.

Leminsky, Gerhard, and Bernd Otto. 1974. *Politik und Programmatik des Deutschen Gewerkschaftsbundes.* Köln: Bund-Verlag.

Lenin, Wladimir I. [1917]1985. *Der Imperialismus als höchstes Stadium des Kapitalismus.* Berlin: Dietz.

Letza, S., X. Sun, and J. Kirkbride. 2004. "Shareholding Versus Stakeholding: A Critical Review of Corporate Governance." *Corporate Governance* 12 (3): 242–62.

Levin, A., C. F. Lin, and C. S. James Chu. 2002. "Unit Root Tests in Panel Data: Asymptotic and Finite-Sample Properties." *Journal of Econometrics* 108 (1): 1–24.

Licht, A. N., C. Goldschmidt, and S. H. Schwartz. 2005. "Culture, Law, and Corporate Governance." *International Review of Law and Economics* 25 (2): 229–55.

Lijphart, Arend. 1971. "Comparative Politics and the Comparative Method." *American Political Science Review* 65 (3): 682–93.

—— 1999. *Patterns of Democracy: Government Forms and Performance in Thirty-Six Countries.* New Haven, CT/London: Yale University Press.

Linneman, Hans. 1966. *An Econometric Study of International Trade Flows.* Amsterdam: North Holland.

Lipset, Seymour Martin. 1962. "Introduction." In *Political Parties: A Sociological Study of the Oligarchical Tendencies of Modern Democracy*, eds. R. Michels, E. Paul, and C. Paul. New York: Collier Books.

—— and Stein Rokkan. 1967. "Cleavage Structures, Party Systems and Voter Alignments." In *Party Systems and Voter Alignments: Cross-National Perspectives*, eds. S. M. Lipset and S. Rokkan. New York: Free Press.

Locke, R. M., and L. Baccaro. 1996. "Learning From Past Mistakes? Recent Reforms in Italian Industrial Relations." *Industrial Relations Journal* 27 (4): 289–303.

Loriaux, Michael Maurice. 1997. *Capital Ungoverned: Liberalizing Finance in Interventionist States.* Ithaca, N.Y., London: Cornell University Press.

Lütz, Susanne. 1998. "The Revival of the Nation-State? Stock Exchange Regulation in an Era of Globalized Financial Markets." *Journal of European Public Policy* 5 (1): 153–68.

—— 2005. "The Finance Sector in Transition: A Motor for Economic Reform?" *German Politics* 14: 140–56.

Maggiorani, Mauro. 1998. *L'Europa degli altri: Comunisti italiani e integrazione europea 1957/1969*. Rome: Carocci.
Mahoney, Paul G. 2001. "The Common Law and Economic Growth: Hayek Might Be Right." *Journal of Legal Studies* 30 (2): 503–25.
Maier, Charles S. 1984. "The Preconditions for Corporatism." In *Order and Conflict in Contemporary Capitalism*, edn J. H. Goldthorpe, Social Science Research Council (U.S.) and Joint Committee on Western Europe. Oxford: Clarendon Press.
Mair, Peter. 2001. "The Freezing Hypothesis: An Evaluation." In *Party Systems and Voter Alignments Revisited*, eds. L. Karvonen and S. Kuhnle. London: Routledge.
Malkiel, Burton Gordon. 2003. *A Random Walk Down Wall Street: The Time-Tested Strategy for Successful Investing*. rev. and upd. edn New York/London: Norton.
Mallin, Chris A. 2004. *Corporate Governance*. Oxford: Oxford University Press.
Manne, Henry G. 1965. "Mergers and the Market for Corporate Control." *Journal of Political Economy* (73): 110–20.
March, James G., and Johan P. Olsen. 1984. "The New Institutionalism: Organizational Factors in Political Life." *American Political Science Review* 78 (3): 734–49.
Markowitz, Harry. M. 1952. "Portfolio Selection." *Journal of Finance* 7 (1): 77–91.
Marks, G., C. J. Wilson, and L. Ray. 2002. "National Political Parties and European Integration." *American Journal of Political Science* 46 (3): 585–94.
Martin, Cathie Jo. 2000. *Stuck In Neutral: Business and the Politics of Human Capital Investment Policy*. Princeton, NJ: Princeton University Press.
Mayer, Colin. 1997. "Corporate Governance, Competition, and Performance." *Journal of Law and Society* 24 (1): 152–176.
McAleer, Michael, Adrian R. Pagan, and Paul A. Volker. 1985. "What Will Take the Con Out of Econometrics?" *American Economic Review*, 75 (3): 293–307.
McCann, Dermot. 2000. "The "Anglo-American" Model, Privatization and the Transformation of Private Capitalism in Italy." *Modern Italy* 5 (1): 47–61.
McCann, Dermot. 2007. "Globalization, European Integration and Regulatory Reform in Italy: Liberalism, Protectionism or Reconstruction?" *Journal of Modern Italian Studies* 12 (1): 101–17.
McCreevy, Charlie. 2007. "Speech by Commissioner McCreevy." *European Parliament Legal Affairs Committee*, October 3.
McHugh, David. 2004. "Parmalat Case raises Questions about Corporate Regulation in Italy's 'Family Capitalism.'" *Associated Press*, January 1.
McLean, Iain. 1987. *Public Choice: An Introduction*. Oxford: Basil Blackwell.
McMillan, John. 2002. *Reinventing the Bazaar: A Natural History of Markets*. New York/London: W. Norton.
Melis, Andrea. 2006. "Corporate Governance Developments in Italy." In *Handbook on International Corporate Governance: Country Analyses*, edn C. A. Mallin. Cheltenham: Edward Elgar Publishing.
Mendoza, Enrique G., and Marco E. Terrones. 2008. "An Anatomy of Credit Booms: Evidence from Macro Aggregates and Micro Data." *NBER Working Paper No. 14049*.
Mengoli, Stefano, Federica Pazzaglia, and Elena Sapienza. 2007. "Is It Still Pizza, Spaghetti and Mandolino? Effect of Governance Reforms on Corporate Ownership in Italy." *SSRN Working Paper* (966085).

Michaels, Adrian. 2007. "How Investor Pacts Hold Back Italy's Prosperity." *Financial Times*, March 27.
—— and Tony Barber. 2006. "Banking on Change: How Italy Hopes to Salvage Good from Its Corporate Wreckage." *Financial Times*, January 18.
Micklethwait, John, and Adrian Wooldridge. 2003. *The Company: A Short History of a Revolutionary Idea*. London: Weidenfeld & Nicolson.
Micossi, Stefano. 2006. "L'impresa tra dirigismo e mercato." *Rivista di politica economica* 96 (7–8): 13–48.
Milgrom, P., and J. Roberts. 1990. "Rationalizability, Learning, and Equilibrium in Games with Strategic Complementarities." *Econometrica* 58 (6): 1255–77.
Milne, Richard, and Hugh Williamson. 2006. "Selective Bargaining: German Companies Are Driving a Hidden Revolution in Labour Flexibility." *Financial Times*, January 6, 2006, 13.
Milner, Helen V., and Benjamin Judkins. 2004. "Partisanship, Trade Policy, and Globalization: Is There a Left-Right Divide on Trade Policy?" *International Studies Quarterly* 48 (1): 95–120.
Mizruchi, Mark S. 1981. *The American Corporate Network, 1904–1974*. Beverly Hills, CA/London: Sage.
—— and Deborah M. Bey. 2005. "Corporate Control, Interfirm Relations, and Corporate Power." In *The Handbook of Political Sociology: States, Civil Societies, and Globalization*, eds. T. Janoski, R. Alford, A. Hicks and M. A. Schwartz. Cambridge: Cambridge University Press.
Modigliani, Franco, and Enrico Perotti. 2000. "Security Markets versus Bank Finance: Legal Enforcement and Investor Protection." *International Review of Finance* 1 (2): 81–96.
Molina, Oscar. 2006. "Trade Union Strategies and Change in Neo-Corporatist Concertation: A New Century of Political Exchange?" *West European Politics* 29: 640–64.
—— and M. Rhodes. 2007a. "Industrial Relations and the Welfare State in Italy: Assessing the Potential of Negotiated Change." *West European Politics* 30 (4): 803–29.
—— —— 2007b. "The Political Economy of Adjustment in Mixed Market Economies: A Study of Spain and Italy." In *Beyond Varieties of Capitalism: Conflict, Contradictions, and Complementarities in the European Economy*, eds. B. Hancke, M. Rhodes, and M. Thatcher. Oxford: Oxford University Press.
Moravcsik, Andrew. 1998. *The Choice for Europe: Social Purpose and State Power from Messina to Maastricht*. London: UCL Press.
Morck, Randall and Lloyd Steier. 2005. "The Global History of Corporate Governance – An Introduction." *NBER Working Paper* (11062).
Moretti, John. 2003. "After the Death of Agnelli, Family Business as Usual." *Italy Weekly*, January 31.
Morin, François. 2000. "A Transformation in the French Model of Shareholding and Management." *Economy and Society* 29(1).
Motta, Massimo. 2004. *Competition Policy: Theory and Practice*. Cambridge: Cambridge University Press.
Mueller, Dennis C. 2003. "The Finance Literature on Mergers: A Critical Survey." In *Competition, Monopoly, and Corporate Governance: Essays in Honour of Keith Cowling*, eds. K. Cowling and M. Waterson. Cheltenham: Edward Elgar.

—— 2005. "The Economics and Politics of Corporate Governance." *ECGI Law Working Paper* (37).

Müller, Wolfgang C., and Kaare Strøm. 2000. *Coalition Governments in Western Europe*. Oxford: Oxford University Press.

Myers, Stewart C. 1977. "Determinants of Corporate Borrowing." *Journal of Financial Economics* 5 (November): 147–75.

Nenova, Tatiana. 2003. "The Value of Corporate Voting Rights and Control: A Cross-Country Analysis." *Journal of Financial Economics* 68 (3): 325–51.

Nevo, Aviv. 2001. "Measuring Market Power in the Ready-to-Eat Cereal Industry." *Econometrica* 69 (2): 307–42.

Neyman Jerzy and Elizabeth L. Scott. 1948. "Consistent Estimates Based on Partially Consistent Observations". *Econometrica* (16): 1–32.

Nickell, Stephen. 1981. "Biases in Dynamic Models with Fixed Effects." *Econometrica*, 49 (6): 417–1426.

—— 1999. "Product Markets and Labour Markets." *Labour Economics* 6: 1–20.

—— 1996. "Competition and Corporate Performance." *Journal of Political Economy* 104 (4): 724–46.

—— J. Vainiomaki, S. Wadhwani. 1994. "Wages and Product Market Power." *Economica* (61): 457–473.

Nicoletti, Giuseppe, and Stefano Scarpetta. 2003. "Regulation, Productivity and Growth: OECD evidence." *OECD Economics Department Working Papers* (347).

—— —— and Olivier Boylaud. 1999. "Summary Indicators of Product Market Regulation with an Extension to Employment Protection Legislation." *OECD Economics Department Working Papers* (No. 226).

Norris, Pippa. 2004. *Electoral Engineering: Voting Rules and Political Behavior*. Cambridge: Cambridge University Press.

North, Douglass Cecil. 1981. *Structure and Change in Economic History*. New York/London: Norton.

—— 1990. *Institutions, Institutional Change and Economic Performance*. Cambridge: Cambridge University Press.

Nowak, Eric. 2004. "Investor Protection and Capital Market Regulation in Germany" In *The German Financial System*, ed. J. P. Krahnen and R. H. Schmidt. Oxford: Oxford University Press.

O'Rourke, Kevin H. 1997. "Measuring Protection: A Cautionary Tale." *Journal of Development Economics* 53 (1): 169–84.

O'Sullivan, Noel. 2000. "Managers as Monitors: An Analysis of the Non-Executive Role of Senior Executives in UK Companies." *British Journal of Management* 11 (1): 17–30.

—— 2001. "Change and Continuity in the French System of Corporate Governance." *INSEAD Working Paper*, May 2001.

—— 2003. "The Political Economy of Comparative Corporate Governance." *Review of International Political Economy* 10 (1): 23–72.

OECD. 1993. "Employment Outlook." Paris: Organisation for Economic Co-operation and Development.

OECD. 1998. "Implementing Structural Reform: A Review of Progress." In *OECD Economic Surveys: Germany*. Paris: Organisation for Economic Co-operation and Development.
OECD. 1999a. "Employment Protection and Labor Market Performance." In *Employment Outlook*. Paris: Organisation for Economic Co-operation and Development.
—— 1999b. "Germany: Competition Law and Policy in 1999–2000." Paris: Organisation for Economic Co-operation and Development.
—— 2000a. "Italy: The Role of Competition Policy in Regulatory Reform." Paris: Organisation for Economic Co-operation and Development.
—— 2000b. "OECD Economic Surveys: Italy." Paris: Organisation for Economic Co-operation and Development.
—— 2002. "Product Market Competition and Economic Performance: A Framework for EDRC Reviews." In *OECD Economics Department, Economic Policy Committee, Working Party No. 1 on Macroeconomic and Structural Policy Analysis, Paris*.
—— 2003. "Privatising State-Owned Enterprises. An Overview of Policies and Practices in OECD Countries." Paris: Organisation for Economic Co-operation and Development.
—— 2005. "Pension Markets in Focus." Paris: Organisation for Economic Co-operation and Development, Financial Affairs Division of the Directorate of Financial and Enterprise Affairs (June 2005, Issue 1).
Oliveira Martins, Joaquim, Stefano Scarpetta, and Dirk Pilat. 1996. "Mark-Up Ratios in Manufacturing Industries – Estimates for 14 OECD Countries." *OECD Economics Department Working Papers* (No. 162).
Olson, Mancur. 1982. *The Rise and Decline of Nations: Economic Growth, Stagflation, and Social Rigidities*. New Haven, CT/London: Yale University Press.
Onado, Marco. 1996. "The Italian Financial System and the Challenges of the Investment Services Directive." *Review of Economic Conditions in Italy* 50: 89–103.
Pagano, Marco and Paolo F. Volpin. 2005. "The Political Economy of Corporate Governance." *American Economic Review* 95: 1005–30.
Pagano, Marco, and Paolo F. Volpin. 2001. "The Political Economy of Finance." *Oxford Review of Economic Policy* 17 (4): 502–19.
Pagano, Ugo, and Sandro Trento. 2002. "Continuity and Change in Italian Corporate Governance: The Institutional Stability of One Variety of Capitalism." *University of Siena Department of Economics Working Paper* (366).
Parker, Simon. 1997. "The Government of the Ulivo." In *Italian Politics: The Center-Left in Power*, eds. R. D'Alimonte and D. Nelken. Boulder, CO/Oxford: Westview Press.
Parsons, Talcott. 1959. "Voting and the Equilibrium of the American Political System." In *American Voting Behavior* eds. E. Burdick and A. J. Brodbeck. Glencoe, IL: Free Press.
—— 1969. *Politics and Social Structure*. New York/London: The Free Press/Collier Macmillan.
Paterson, Tony, and Victor Smart. 1997. "Has Germany Kissed the Strong Euro Goodbye?" *The European*, May 22.
Pilizzo, Riccardo. 2003. "Party Positions or Party Direction? An Analysis of Party Manifesto Data." *West European Politics* 26 (2): 67–89.
Peltzman, Sam. 1976. "Toward a More General Theory of Regulation." *Journal of Law and Economics* 19(2): 211–240.

Perotti, Enrico C., and Ernst- Ludwig von Thadden. 2003. "The Political Economy of Bank and Equity Dominance." *Discussion Paper Series—Centre for Economic Policy Research, London* (3914).
—— and Paolo F. Volpin. 2007. "Politics, Investor Protection and Competition." *ECGI—Finance Working Paper* (162/2007).
Plender, John. 2007. "Private Equity Cannot Escape The Public Eye." *Financial Times*, April 24.
Plümper, Thomas, Vera Troeger, and Philip Manow. 2005. "Panel Data Analysis in Comparative Politics: Linking Method to Theory." *European Journal of Political Research* 44 (2): 327–54.
Pontusson, Jonas, David Rueda, and Christopher R. Way. 2002. "Comparative Political Economy of Wage Distribution: The Role of Partisanship and Labour Market Institutions." *British Journal of Political Science* 32 (2): 281–308.
Porter, Michael. E. 1992. "Capital Disadvantage: America's Failing Capital Investment System." *Harvard Business Review* (72): 65–83.
Portolano, Alessandro. 2000. "The Decision to Adopt Defensive Tactics in Italy." *International Review of Law and Economics* 20 (4): 425–52.
Posner, R. A. 1975. "The Social Costs of Monopoly and Regulation." *Journal of Political Economy* (83): 807–27.
Prasad, E. S., K. Rogoff, S. J. Wei, and M. A. Kose. 2003. "Effects of Financial Globalization on Developing Countries: Some Empirical Evidence." *Occasional Paper—International Monetary Fund* (220).
Prigge, Stefan. 1998. "A Survey of German Corporate Governance." In *Comparative Corporate Governance: The State of the Art and Emerging Research*, edn K. J. Hopt. Oxford: Clarendon.
Pritchett, Lant. 1996. "Measuring Outward Orientation in LDCs: Can it be done?" *Journal of Development Economics* 49 (2): 307–36.
Prowse, Stephen. 1994. *Corporate Governance in an International Perspective: A Survey of Corporate Control Mechanisms Among Large Firms in the United States, the United Kingdom, Japan and Germany*: BIS economic papers, no. 41.
Przeworski, Adam, and Henry Teune. 1970. *The Logic of Comparative Social Inquiry*. New York: Wiley Interscience.
Przybyla, Marcin, and Moreno Roma. 2005. "Does Product Market Competition Reduce Inflation? Evidence from EU Countries and Sectors." *European Central Bank, Working Paper Series* (No. 453).
Quaglia, Lucia and Claudio M. Radaelli. 2007. "Italian Politics and the European Union: A Tale of Two Research Designs." *West European Politics* 30 (4): 924–43.
Quinn, Dennis P. 1997. "The Correlates of Change in International Financial Regulation." *American Journal of Political Science* (91): 531–51.
Radaelli, Claudio M. 2003. "The Europeanization of Public Policy." In *The Politics of Europeanization*, eds. K. Featherstone and C. M. Radaelli. Oxford: Oxford University Press.
Rajan, Raghuram R. and Luigi Zingales. 1999. "The Politics of Financial Development." *Unpublished Working Paper, University of Chicago, Chicago*.
—— —— 2003. "The Great Reversals: The Politics of Financial Development in the Twentieth Century." *Journal of Financial Economics* 69 (1): 5–50.

Reberioux, Antoine. 2007. "Does Shareholder Primacy Lead to a Decline in Managerial Accountability?" *Cambridge Journal of Economics* 31: 507–24.

Rey, Patrick, and Jean Tirole. 1986. "The Logic of Vertical Restraints." *American Economic Review* 76 (5): 921–39.

Rhodes, R. A. W. 1997. *Understanding Governance: Policy Networks, Governance, Reflexivity and Accountability.* Buckingham: Open University Press.

Rhodes, R. A. W. and Patrick Dunleavy. 1995. *Prime Minister, Cabinet and Core Executive.* New York/Basingstoke: St Martin's Press/Macmillan.

Rieckers, Oliver, and Gerald Spindler. 2004. "Corporate Governance: Legal Aspects." In *The German Financial System*, eds. J. P. Krahnen and R. H. Schmidt. Oxford: Oxford University Press.

Rigby, Mike, and Mari Luz Marco Aledo. 2001. "The Worst Record in Europe?: A Comparative Analysis of Industrial Conflict in Spain" *European Journal of Industrial Relations* 7 (3): 287–305.

—— and Rafael Serrano. 2001. *Estrategias Sindicales en Europa: Convergencias o Divergencias.* Madrid: Comité Económico y Social.

Roberts, John. 2004. *The Modern Firm: Organizational Design for Performance and Growth.* Oxford: Oxford University Press.

Rodrik, Dani. 1998. "Why Do More Open Economies Have Bigger Governments?" *Journal of Political Economy* 106 (5): 997–1032.

Roe, Mark J. 1994. *Strong Managers, Weak Owners: The Political Roots of American Corporate Finance.* Princeton, NJ: Princeton University Press.

—— 2001. "Rents and Their Corporate Consequences." *Stanford Law Review* 53 (6): 1463–94.

—— 2003. *Political Determinants of Corporate Governance: Political Context, Corporate Impact.* Oxford: Oxford University Press.

—— 2006. "Legal Origins, Politics, and Modern Stock Markets." *Harvard Law Review* 120: 460–527.

—— and Jordan I. Siegel. 2007. "Political Instability and Financial Development." *Unpublished Manuscript, Harvard Law School.*

Rogowski, Ronald and Mark Andreas Kayser. 2002. "Majoritarian Electoral Systems and Consumer Power: Price-Level Evidence from the OECD Countries." *American Journal of Political Science* 46 (3): 526–39.

Ross, Stephen A. 1977. "The Determination of Financial Structure: The Incentive-Signalling Approach." *The Bell Journal of Economics* 8 (1 [Spring]): 23–40.

Rueda, David. 2005. "Insider-Outsider Politics in Industrialized Democracies: The Challenge to Social Democratic Parties." *American Political Science Review* 99 (1): 1–14.

—— 2006. "Social Democracy and Active Labour-Market Policies: Insiders, Outsiders and the Politics of Employment Promotion." *British Journal of Political Science* 36 (3): 385–406.

—— 2007. *Social Democracy Inside Out: Partisanship and Labor Market Policy in Industrialized Democracies.* Oxford: Oxford University Press.

Sala-I-Martin, Xavier X. 1997. "I Just Ran Two Million Regressions." *American Economic Review* 87 (2): 178–83.

Sartori, Giovanni. 1976. *Parties and Party Systems: A Framework for Analysis*. Cambridge: Cambridge University Press.
Savage, James D. 2001. "Budgetary Collective Action Problems: Convergence and Compliance under the Maastrict Treaty on European Union." *Public Administration Review* 61 (1): 43–53.
Sbragia, Alberta. 2001. "Italy Pays for Europe: Political Leadership, Political Choice, and Institutional Adaptation." In *Transforming Europe: Europeanization and Domestic Change*, eds. M. G. Cowles, J. A. Caporaso, and T. Risse-Kappen. Ithaca, NY/London: Cornell University Press.
Schäfer, Harald J. 2000. "Bilanzrechtliche Aspekte." In *Die Praxis der Investor Relations. Effiziente Kommunikation zwischen Unternehmen und Kapitalmarkt*, eds. K. R. Kirchhoff and M. Piwinger. Neuwied: Luchterhand.
Scharfstein, David. 1988. "Product Market Competition and Managerial Slack." *RAND Journal of Economics* (19): 147–55.
Scharpf, Fritz Wilhelm. 1991. *Crisis and Choice in European Social Democracy*. Ithaca, NY/London: Cornell University Press.
Scheibe-Lange, Ingrid, and Arno Prangenberg. 1997. "Mehr Mitbestimmung via US-Börsenaufsicht." *Die Mitbestimmung* 43 (11): 45–9.
Scherer, F. M., and David Ross. 1990. *Industrial Market Structure and Economic Performance*. 3rd edn. Boston: Houghton Mifflin.
Schmidbauer, Robert. 2006. "On the Fallacy of LLSV Revisited – Further Evidence About Shareholder Protection in Austria and the United Kingdom." *University of Manchester Working Papers in Law*.
Schmidt, Manfred G. 1996. "When Parties Matter: A Review of the Possibilities and Limits of Partisan Influence on Public Policy." *European Journal of Political Research* (30): 155–83.
Schmidt, Reinhard H. 2004. "Corporate Governance in Germany: An Economic Perspective." In *The German Financial System*, eds. J. P. Krahnen and R. H. Schmidt. Oxford: Oxford University Press.
Schmidt, Vivien. 1996. *From State to Market? The Transformation of French Business and Government*. New York: Cambridge University Press.
Schmitter, Philippe C. 1974. "Still the Century of Corporatism?" *Review of Politics* 36 (1): 85–131.
Schreyer, Paul, and Francette Koechlin. 2002. "Purchasing Power Parities – Measurement and Uses." *OECD Statistics Brief* (No. 3).
Schüler, Martin. 2004. "Integrated Financial Supervision in Germany." *Centre for European Economic Research (ZEW), Mannheim. Discussion Paper* (04–35).
Schumpeter, Joseph Alois. 1943. *Capitalism, Socialism, and Democracy*. London: G. Allen & Unwin Ltd.
Schurr, Stephen. 2006. "Fruitless? Activist Shareholders Could Be Losing Their Ability to Shake Managements." *Financial Times*, January 11, 2006, 17.
Segreto, Luciano. 1997. "Models of Control in Italian Capitalism from the Mixed Bank to Mediobanca, 1894–1993." *Business and Economic History* 26 (2): 649–61.
Shleifer, Andrei and Daniel Wolfenzon. 2002. "Investor Protection and Equity Markets." *Journal of Financial Economics* 66: 3–27.

Shleifer, Andrei, and Lawrence H. Summers. 1988. "Breach of Trust in Hostile Takeovers." In *Corporate Takeovers: Causes and Consequences*, ed. A. J. Auerbach. Chicago and London: University of Chicago Press.

―― and Robert W. Vishny. 1986. "Large Shareholders and Corporate Control." *Journal of Political Economy* 94 (3): 461–88.

―― 1997. "A Survey of Corporate Governance." *Journal of Finance* 52 (2): 737–83.

Shonfield, Andrew, and Royal Institute of International Affairs. 1965. *Modern Capitalism: The Changing Balance of Public and Private Power*. London: Oxford University Press.

Siems, Mathias M. 2005. "What Does Not Work in Comparing Securities Laws: A Critique on La Porta et al.'s Methodology." *International Company and Commercial Law Review*: 300–5.

Simmons, Beth A., Frank Dobbin, and Geoffrey Garrett, eds. 2008. *The Global Diffusion of Markets and Democracy*. Cambridge: Cambridge University Press.

Soskice, David. 1991. "The Institutional Infrastructure for International Competitiveness: A Comparative Analysis of the UK and Germany." In *The Economics of the New Europe*, eds. A. B. Atkinson and R. Brunetta. London: MacMillan & Co.

―― and Torben Iversen. 1998. "Multiple Wage-Bargaining Systems in the Single European Currency Area." *Oxford Review of Economic Policy* 14 (3): 110–24.

Sozialdemokratische Partei Deutschlands. 1998. *Grundsatzprogramm der Sozialdemokratischen Partei Deutschlands. Beschlossen vom Programm-Parteitag der Sozialdemokratischen Partei Deutschlands am 20. Dezember 1989 in Berlin, geändert auf dem Parteitag in Leipzig am 17. April 1998*. Berlin: SPD.

Spamann, Holger. 2006. "On the Insignificance and/or Endogeneity of La Porta et al.'s 'Anti-Director Rights Index' under Consistent Coding." *ECGI Law Working Paper* (No. 67/2006).

Spilimbergo, A., J. L. Londono, and M. Szekely. 1999. "Income Distribution, Factor Endowments, and Trade Openness." *Journal of Development Economics* 59 (1): 77–101.

Stigler, George J. 1958. "The Economies of Scale." *Journal of Law and Economics* (1): 54–71.

―― 1971. "The Theory of Economic Regulation." *The Bell Journal of Economics and Management Science* 2 (1): 3–21.

Stiglitz, Joseph. 1985. "Credit Markets and the Control of Capital." *Journal of Money, Credit and Banking* (17): 133–52.

Streeck, Wolfgang. 1992. *Social Institutions and Economic Performance: Studies of Industrial Relations in Advanced Capitalist Economies*. London: Sage.

―― 1996. *Mitbestimmung, Offene Fragen*. Guetersloh: Bertelsmann Stiftung.

―― 1997. "German Capitalism: Does It Exist? Can It Survive?" *New Political Economy* 2 (2): 237–56.

―― 2001. "The Transformation of Corporate Organization in Europe: An Overview." *Max-Planck-Institute for the Study of Societies Working Paper* (01/8).

―― and Anke Hassel. 2003. "The Crumbling Pillars of Social Partnership." *West European Politics* 26 (4): 101–24.

―― and Martin Höpner. 2003. "Einleitung: Alle Macht dem Markt?" In *Alle macht dem Markt?: Fallstudien zur Abwicklung der Deutschland AG*, eds. W. Streeck and M. Höpner. Frankfurt a.M.: Campus.

Streeck, Wolfgang, and Kaozao Yamamura. 2003. *The End of Diversity?: Prospects for German and Japanese Capitalism.* Ithaca: Cornell University Press.

Strøm, Kaare. 1990. "A Behavioral Theory of Competitive Political Parties." *American Political Science Review* 34 (2): 565–98.

Studienkommission Grundsatzfragen der Kreditwirtschaft. 1979. *Bericht der Studienkommission Grundsatzfragen der Kreditwirtschaft.* Bonn: Wilhelm Stollfuss Verlag.

Stulz, René. M. 2005. "The Limits of Financial Globalization." *Journal of Finance* 60 (4): 1595–638.

Sturm, Jakob and Jan-Egbert Sturm. 2005. "Determinants of Long-Term Growth: New Results Applying Robust Estimation and Extreme Bounds Analysis." *Empirical Economics* 30 (3): 597–617.

Summers, Lawrence. 2007. "Sovereign Funds Shake the Logic of Capitalism." *Financial Times*, July 30.

Swank, Duane. 2002. *Global Capital, Political Institutions, and Policy Change in Developed Welfare States.* Cambridge: Cambridge University Press.

Swedberg, Richard. 2005. "Markets in Society." In *The Handbook of Economic Sociology*, edn N. J. Smelser, R. Swedberg and Russell Sage Foundation. Princeton, NJ/Oxford: Princeton University Press.

Swenson, Peter. 1989. *Fair Shares: Unions, Pay, and Politics in Sweden and West Germany.* Ithaca, NY: Cornell University Press.

—— 2002. *Capitalists Against Markets: The Making of Labor Markets and Welfare States in the United States and Sweden.* Oxford: Oxford University Press.

Taylor, Charles. 1970. "The Explanation of Purposive Behavior." In *Explanation in the Behavioral Sciences*, eds. R. Borger and F. Cioffi. Cambridge: Cambridge University Press.

The Economist. 2007. "In the Money: A Special Report on Executive Pay." *The Economist*, January 20.

Theisen, Manuel R. 1998. "Empirical Evidence and Economic Comments on Board Structure in Germany." In *Comparative Corporate Governance: The State of the Art and Emerging Research*, edn K. J. Hopt. Oxford: Clarendon.

Thelen, Kathleen. 2001. "Varieties of Labor Politics in the Developed Democracies." In *Varieties of Capitalism: The Institutional Foundations of Comparative Advantage*, eds. P. A. Hall and D. W. Soskice. Oxford: Oxford University Press.

—— and I. Kume. 2003. "The Future of Nationally Embedded Capitalism: Industrial Relations in Germany and Japan." In *The End of Diversity? Prospects for German and Japanese Capitalism*, eds. K. Yamamura and W. Streeck. Ithaca, NY: Cornell University Press.

The World Bank. 1987. "World Bank Development Report." Washington DC: The World Bank.

Thimm, Alfred L. 1980. *The False Promise of Codetermination: The Changing Nature of European Workers' Participation.* Lexington, Mass.: Lexington Books, D.C. Heath.

Thomas, John Clayton. 1976. *The Decline of Ideology in Western Parties.* Beverly Hills, CA/London: Sage Publications.

Tirole, Jean. 1988. *The Theory of Industrial Organization.* Cambridge, MA London: MIT Press.

Tirole, Jean. 2006. *The Theory of Corporate Finance*. Princeton, NJ; Oxford: Princeton University Press.
Tocci, Nathalie. 2000. "Power or Policy: A Comparative Study of the Cohesion of Italian Coalition Governments in the First and Second Republics." *Journal of Modern Italian Studies* 5 (1): 61–79.
Trentini, Marco, and Ires Lombardia. 1999. "Splits Open Up Between Trade Unions." *European Industrial Relations Observatory (EIRO)*, September 28.
Trento, Sandra. 2005. "Corporate Governance and Industrial Relations in Italy." In *Corporate Governance and Labour Management: An International Comparison*, eds. H. F. Gospel and A. Pendleton. Oxford: Oxford University Press.
Tröger, Tobias H. 2005. "Choice of Jurisdiction in European Corporate Law – Perspectives of European Corporate Governance." *European Business Organization Law Review* (6): 3–64.
Tsebelis, George. 2002. *Veto Players: How Political Institutions Work*. New York/Princeton, NJ: Russell Sage Foundation/Princeton University Press.
Tucker, Sundeep. 2004. "Investors Benefit from New Indices." *Financial Times: Special Report on Corporate Governance*, December 15.
Turnbull, Shann. 1997. "Corporate Governance: Its Scope, Concerns and Theories." *Corporate Governance* 5 (4): 180–205.
Tüselmann, Heinz-Josef and Arne Heise. 2000. "The German Model of Industrial Relations at the Crossroads: Past, Present and Future." *Industrial Relations Journal* 31 (3): 162–76.
Ulman, Lloyd and Knut Gerlach. 2003. "An Essay on Collective Bargaining and Unemployment in Germany." In *Institute of Industrial Relations, Working Papers Series*. Berkeley, CA: Institute of Industrial Relations, University of California.
Useem, Michael. 1984. *The Inner Circle: Large Corporations and the Rise of Business Political Activity in the US and UK*. New York/Oxford: Oxford University Press.
—— 1996. *Investor Capitalism: How Money Managers Are Changing the Face of Corporate America*. New York: Basic Books.
Van Apeldoorn, Bastiaan and Laura Horn. 2007. "The Marketisation of European Corporate Control: A Critical Political Economy Perspective." *New Political Economy* 12 (2): 211–35.
Ventoruzzo, Marco. 2005. "Experiments in Comparative Corporate Law: The Recent Italian Reform and the Dubious Virtues of a Market for Rules in the Absence of Effective Regulatory Competition." *European Company and Financial Law Review* 2 (2): 207–69.
Vincent, Gregory. 2004. Beyond 'Crony Capitalism': Financial Change and Elite Coordination in France. D.Phil. Thesis, University of Oxford.
Vitols, Sigurt. 2001. "Varieties of Corporate Governance: Comparing Germany and the UK." In *Varieties of Capitalism: The Institutional Foundations of Comparative Advantage*, eds. P. A. Hall and D. W. Soskice. Oxford: Oxford University Press.
—— 2003. "Negotiated Shareholder Value: The German Version of an Anglo-American Practice." *Discussion Paper, Wissenschaftszentrum Berlin* (SP II 2003–25).
—— Steven Casper, David Soskice, and Stephen Woolcock. 1997. "Corporate Governance in Large British and German Companies: Comparative Institutional Advantage or Competing for Best Practice." London: Anglo-German Foundation.

Vogel, Sandra. 2007. "Social Partners Divided Over Issue of Co-determination at Company Level." Köln: Cologne Institute for Economic Research, IW Köln.

Vogel, Steven Kent. 1996. *Freer Markets, More Rules: Regulatory Reform in Advanced Industrial Countries*. Ithaca, NY/London: Cornell University Press.

Way, Christopher R. 2000. "Central Banks, Partisan Politics, and Macroeconomic Outcomes." *Comparative Political Studies* 33 (2): 196–224.

Webb, Paul, David M. Farrell, and Ian Holliday. 2002. *Political Parties in Advanced Industrial Democracies*. Oxford: Oxford University Press.

Weber, Manfredn. 2002. "The German Banking Market: I. Structural Change." *Die Bank: Zeitschrift für Bankpolitik und Praxis*, June 2003.

Welch, Jack, and Suzy Welch. 2006. "A Dangerous Division of Labor." *Business Week*, 6 November 6.

Welsch, Roy E. 1982. "Influence Functions and Regression Diagnostics." In *Modern Data Analysis*, eds. R. L. Launer and A. F. Siegel. New York: Academic Press.

Westrup, Jonathan. 2007. "The Politics of Financial Regulatory Reform in Britain and Germany." *West European Politics* 30 (5): 1096–119.

Wiedemann, Herbert. 1980. "Codetermination by Workers in German Enterprises." *The American Journal of Comparative Law* 28 (1): 79–92.

Williams, Karel 2000. "From Shareholder Value to Present-Day Capitalism." *Economy and Society* 29 (1): 1–12.

Williamson, Oliver E. 1975. *Markets and Hierarchies: Analysis and Antitrust implications: A Study in the Economics of Internal Organization*. New York: Collier Macmillan.

—— 1985. *The Economic Institutions of Capitalism: Firms, Markets, Relational Contracting*. New York; London: Free Press; Collier Macmillan.

Windolf, Paul and Jürgen Beyer. 1996. "Co-operative Capitalism: Corporate Networks in Germany and Britain." *British Journal of Sociology* 47 (2): 205–31.

—— and Michael Nollert. 2001. "Institutionen, Interessen, Netzwerke. Unternehmensverflechtung im Internationalen Vergleich." *Politische Vierteljahresschrift* 42 (1): 51–78.

Wójcik, Dariusz. 2006. "Convergence in Corporate Governance: Evidence from Europe and the Challenge for Economic Geography." *Journal of Economic Geography* 6: 639–60.

Woods, Dwayne. 2000. "Transformation in Italian Capitalism: An Analysis of Olivetti's Takeover of Telecom Italia." In *Italian Politics: The Faltering Transition*, eds. M. Gilbert, G. Pasquino, and I. C. Cattaneo. New York/Oxford: Berghahn.

Wooldridge, Jeffrey M. 2002. *Econometric Analysis of Cross Section and Panel Data*. Cambridge, MA/London: MIT Press.

—— 2006. *Introductory Econometrics: A Modern Approach*. 3rd edn. Mason, OH/ United Kingdom: Thomson/South-Western.

Yin, Robert K. 2003. *Case Study Research: Design and Methods*. 3rd edn. Thousand Oaks, CA; London: Sage.

Ziegler, J. Nicholas. 2000. "Corporate Governance and the Politics of Property Rights in Germany." *Politics and Society* 28 (2): 195–222.

Ziliak, James P. 1997. "Efficient Estimation with Panel Data When Instruments Are Predetermined: An Empirical Comparison of Moment-Condition Estimators." *Journal of Business & Economic Statistics* 15 (4): 419–31.

Zohlnhöfer, Reimut, Herbert Obinger, and Frieder Wolf. 2008. "Partisan Politics, Globalization, and the Determinants of Privatization Proceeds in Advanced Democracies (1990–2000)." *Governance: An International Journal of Policy, Administration, and Institutions* 21 (1): 95–121.

Zumbansen, Peer. 2007. "After Enron: Improving Corporate Law and Modernising Securities Regulation in Europe and the US." *Banking and Finance Law Review* 23: 215–22.

Zysman, John. 1983. *Governments, Markets and Growth: Financial Systems and the Politics of Industrial Change*. Oxford: Robertson.

Index

Anglo-American business model 4
agency costs 22, 34, 38, 45–6, 77
   see also principal-agent problem
Arrellano-Bond estimator 208

Berle and Means 71
blockholders 35–7, 39, 52–3
blockholder model 34–42

case studies 214–22, 287
Chandler, Alfred 36–7, 70
Cioffi and Höpner 1, 24–5, 58, 64–5, 155–60, 286
civil law 75–6
Coase, Ronald 69
codetermination 7, 82, 227–8, 233
competition, *see* product market competition
common law 75–6
concentration indices 121–3
conditional effects 171–84
consumer surplus 43
control variables 140–2, 160–5
controlling shareholders, *see* blockholders
coordinated market economy 3, 22
   see also non-liberal market economy
corporate governance 2
   definition 34, 77, 78
   convergence 15–19
   firm level corporate governance 10–15
   measurement 91–115
   and capital controls 165
   and economics 67–72
   and economic growth 165
   and economic rents 1, 45–51, 53, 229–39
   and economic sociology 84–6
   and electoral systems 83–4, 148
   and income inequality 19–21
   and labor markets 20
   and law 72–6
   and legal origin 75–6
   and partisanship 19–25, 154–60, 253–4
   and patient capital 22, 260
   and politics 39–40, 77–84
   and product market competition 45–51, 166–89
   and the European Union 9, 14–5, 89–90
   and EMU 89–90, 269–73
   and regulation 5–10, 27–30, 105–15
   in Europe 5–19
   in France 6–7, 11
   in Germany 7–8, 16, 223–55
   in Italy 8–9, 256–82
corporate governance ratings 11–13, 92–5
   see also GOV score
corporate social responsibility 42

de-equitization 97
Downs, Anthony 57
Draghi, Mario 262, 274–5
Drucker, Peter 81
dynamic modeling 206–13

economic openness 62–3, 126–9
economic rents 1, 33, 229
   definition 42–5
   and labor markets 48–51, 54
   and partisanship 61
   see also product market competition
economic and monetary union (EMU) 269–273, 280
equity share 95–100, 105, 139
extreme bound analysis 190–6
executive pay 20–1
expropriation 38

fixed effects 152

German banks 7, 225–6, 234–9
Global Competitiveness Report 130–1
GOV score 16–18, 94–5
    See also corporate governance ratings
Gourevitch and Shinn 35, 74, 78
gravity models 128–9

Hansmann and Kraakman 16
Hall and Soskice 22, 81–2
Hart, Oliver 67
Hirschman-Herfindahl index 121–3

influential observations 201–6
insider capital, *see* blockholders
insider labor 50–1, 56, 228, 276
interactive modeling 65–6, 148–9, 166–79
international equity issuance 102–5, 139

jackknife analysis 196–201
Jensen and Meckling 70

Katzenstein, Peter 63
Knight, Frank 68
KonTraG 245, 247

lagged dependent variables 153–4, 207
legal origin 75–6
LLSV 71, 72–6
    antidirector rights index 92, 106–112, 112–5

market for corporate control,
    see takeovers
minority shareholders 5, 36–7, 40, 228

NMR index 60, 132–6, 217–18
non-liberal market economy 3, 36

Olson, Mancur 39
openness, *see* economic openness
outsiders 52–3, 55

outsider capital 52
ownership concentration 23, 92–4, 265
OECD Principles 8, 12
markup 123–4

Pagano and Volpin 51, 83–4
panel data analysis 137–189
Parmalat 266, 267
partisanship 19, 141–6
    left partisanship 22–5, 52, 57, 143–6, 220–1, 240–2
    conservative partisanship 24, 52, 57, 58, 143–6
    see also corporate governance and partisanship
pension funds 79–81
pension systems 96–7, 165
perfect competition 45
PMR index 62, 131–3, 222
political parties 31–2, 145–6, 240
political agency 77–81
price-cost margins, *see* profit margins
principal-agent problem 70
private benefits of control 39, 53, 55
private equity 97–8, 288
Prodi, Romano 269, 273–4
producer surplus 43
product market competition 59–61, 63, 217
    measurement 116–136
    surveys 130–1
    and economic openness 62–3
    and labor markets 48–51
    and partisanship 61
    see also economic rents
profit margins 123–6
purchasing power parity 117–18
pyramidal business groups 38, 265, 266

qualitative analysis, *see* case studies

random effects 153
Rajan and Zingales 46, 87–8, 126
real price levels 117–21

rents, *see* economic rents
robustness 190–206
Roe, Mark J. 21–2, 46–7, 64, 75, 77, 154–60

Schröder, Gerhard 248
self-dealing, *see* expropriation
shareholder model 34–42, 85
shareholder value 1, 4, 85
shareholder rights 6
   see also antidirector rights index
Smith, Adam 34
sovereign wealth funds 289

stakeholder model 41
stationarity 149–50
substantive effects 179–89

takeovers 14–15, 231, 267
transaction cost economics 69

value traded 100–2, 105, 139
variables 138–48

Williamson, Oliver 69
Wolf, Martin 1

Lightning Source UK Ltd.
Milton Keynes UK
UKOW041439240412

191378UK00004B/20/P

9 780199 576814